RELIGION
AND
PEACEBUILDING

SUNY series in Religious Studies

Harold Coward, editor

RELIGION
AND
PEACEBUILDING

∽∼∾

edited by

Harold Coward
and
Gordon S. Smith

STATE UNIVERSITY OF NEW YORK PRESS

Published by
State University of New York Press, Albany

© 2004 State University of New York

For information, contact State University of New York Press, Albany, NY
www.sunypress.edu

Production by Kelli M. Williams
Marketing by Michael Campochiaro

Library of Congress Cataloging-in-Publication Data

Religion and peacebuilding / edited by Harold Coward and Gordon S. Smith.
    p. cm. — (SUNY series in religious studies)
Includes bibliographical references and index.
    ISBN 0-7914-5933-0 (HC : alk. paper) — ISBN 0-7914-5934-9 (PB : alk paper)
    1. Nonviolence—Religious aspects. 2. Peace-building—Religious aspects. 3. Conflict
management—Religious aspects. I. Coward, Harold G. II. Smith, Gordon S. III. Series.

BL65.V55R455 2004
201'.7273—dc22
                                                                                    2003061059

10   9   8   7   6   5   4   3   2   1

CONTENTS

ACKNOWLEDGMENTS

This book is a joint project of the Centre for Studies in Religion and Society and the Centre for Global Studies at the University of Victoria. Authors were recruited and then met to present first drafts of their chapters at a seminar hosted by the Centre for Studies in Religion and Society at the University of Victoria in October 2000. Faculty and graduate students attended and helped with the critique of draft chapters. Authors then revised their chapters for presentation in this volume.

Funding for this book project was provided by the Carnegie Corporation of New York. Special thanks are due to Connie Carter (administrator) and Moira Hill (secretary) of the Centre for Studies in Religion and Society for organizing the project meeting and preparing the manuscript for publication.

Harold Coward   Gordon S. Smith

1

A Moment of Opportunity?

The Promise of Religious Peacebuilding in an Era of Religious and Ethnic Conflict

DAVID LITTLE AND SCOTT APPLEBY

During our lifetime, religion has been anything but invisible. Predictions that it would become privatized, removed from the sphere of politics, economic development, warfare, and education, have proven false. In the 1960s, millions of Catholics joined their fellow U.S. citizens gawking in disbelief at the sight of priests and nuns marching with the civil rights movement in the streets of Selma and Chicago. Buddhist monks immolated themselves in protest of the war in Southeast Asia, while yeshiva-trained Jewish messianists brazenly moved their families into the Palestinian-populated territories occupied by Israel after the Six-Day War. During the 1970s and 1980s, religion manifested itself repeatedly in the public realm, often to the surprise, delight, or consternation of onlookers. The Shi'ite-led revolution in Iran was the most prominent example of the resurgence of political Islam; Sunni-based movements also swept across the Middle East, North Africa, and South Asia. Sudan and Afghanistan joined the ranks of Islamist-governed nations, while powerful Islamist parties fomented revolution or threatened political stability in Algeria, Pakistan, Nigeria, Egypt, and Indonesia. In the United States a majority-claiming minority of Protestant evangelicals and fundamentalists laid the groundwork for the emergence of "the

Christian Right," a coterie of congregation-based sociopolitical movements, public action committees, think tanks, and lobbyists led by
preachers who pledged to take back Congress and the Supreme Court
from the secular humanists. The Indian subcontinent during these
decades saw the rise of Sikh extremism, Hindu nationalism, and Muslim
communalism. Sinhala Buddhists fought Tamil Hindus in Sri Lanka,
Israeli Jews squared off against Palestinian Muslims in the Holy Land,
Catholic nationalists attacked and were attacked by Protestant unionists
in Belfast.

These and countless other expressions of "public religion" tended to
put religion in bad odor among many educators, students, journalists,
policy makers, and public officials. Others, however, looked beyond the
headlines to appreciate the multiple constructive dimensions of religion
in its publicness; some of these observers even recognized that the genius
of religiously inspired social welfare and peacemaking activism is rooted
in the same zeal for holiness powering the holy wars and religiopolitical
crusades. Indeed, one of our central themes in what follows is "the
ambivalence of the sacred"—the ability of religion to promote what
might be called militancy on behalf of the other, as well as militancy
aimed against the other. Religion promotes both intolerance and hatred,
that is, as well as tolerance of the strongest type—the willingness to live
with, explore, and honor difference. Whether upholding universal
human rights or denying them to "heretics" or "infidels," religious
actors, of course, always believe that they are doing God's will and thus
serving the common good of humanity, properly understood. It is, however, the obligation of scholars and educators to discriminate between
the zeal that compels true believers to violate the rights of others, and
the zeal that compels them to defend those rights at any cost.

Recognition that religion also promotes the latter kind of activism
has led in recent years to some striking reversals for religion's public
image. In August 1996, President Clinton signed into law a bill over-
hauling the U.S. welfare system that contained a provision allowing
states to contract with houses of worship "without impairing the religious character of such organizations." This "charitable choice" provision permits tax funds to be directed to religious organizations on the
condition that the funds not be used to subsidize acts of worship or
evangelizing. In 2001, newly elected president George W. Bush sought to
expand this program by channeling funds to faith-based organizations
that were permitted to use religious identity as a criterion for employment by the organization.[1]

Internationally, the celebration of the millennium provided opportunities for religious leaders to present their credentials as proponents of

nonviolent social change and reconciliation. One of the world's largest, truly "global" religious bodies, the Roman Catholic Church, celebrated a biblical "year of jubilee" by asking forgiveness for a host of "sins"— evils occasioned not by individual Catholics but, as Pope John Paul II confessed, by the body called "the Catholic Church." Theological terms—repentance, forgiveness, contrition, and reconciliation—found their way into international headlines when the pope carried this message to the Holy Land. There, it must be acknowledged, few Jewish, Christian, or Muslim leaders echoed John Paul's message by adopting a similar stance toward their own community's "sins." Yet the papal apology was but one among several, unprecedented acts of public repentance performed by Christian communities at the turn of the century.[2]

In August 2000, more than 1,000 representatives of transnational as well as indigenous religious traditions gathered at the United Nations for a Millennium Summit of World Religious Leaders. Notwithstanding the prospect that the summit might lead to the creation of a U.N. advisory council of religious leaders, the importance of the event was largely symbolic. It heralded the world community's unprecedented recognition of religious peacebuilding as a viable option, as well as a new willingness among religious leaders and organizations to play a defined role in an integrated, multilayered approach to peacebuilding.

The summit also betokened a greater critical appreciation of the relationship between religion's contributions to public life and the building or sustaining of a robust civil society. Having established a reputation for integrity and service through constant and direct contact with the masses, a long record of charitable work among people in need, and the moral example of its core members, a religious community commands a privileged status among segments of the population. It has also been the case, in settings where religion enjoys a measure of independence from the state, and where government institutions are widely viewed as illegitimate, that civic organizations and government officials have turned to religious leaders to mediate conflicts, reconcile opponents, and assume a larger share of responsibility for social welfare and the common good. Religious actors, after all, are long-term players who live among and often belong to the peoples and groups involved in conflict. In some failed states, where centralized authority has broken down altogether, organized religion has remained intact as "the only institution possessing a measure of credibility, trust, and moral authority among the population at large."[3]

The picture is hardly rosy, however. Not least among the problems facing advocates of religious peacebuilding is the uncertainty and even confusion religious actors experience when confronted with the opportunity to play an unfamiliar role in the transformation of deeply rooted ethnic or religious conflicts. Often religious leaders, especially officials with an institution or tradition they are ordained or commissioned to "protect," are unwilling and psychologically unprepared for the personal conversion that is necessary if they are to embrace genuine dialogue, healing, and reconciliation.

The authors of chapters on specific religious traditions discuss the often formidable obstacles to nonviolent conflict transformation found within sacred texts and living traditions. Assessing Hindu resources for peacebuilding, for example, Rajmohan Gandhi laments Hinduism's promotion of religious nationalism, caste conflict, and the revenge motifs lionized in epics such as the *Mahabharata*. While peacebuilding is an important duty in the Islamic tradition, Frederick Denny notes that it has been focused principally on intra-Muslim relations rather than on Muslim attitudes and behaviors toward non-Muslims. In the same vein, Marc Gopin acknowledges that the Orthodox Jewish community, which includes those rabbis most capable of retrieving and developing legal and spiritual warrants for peacebuilding within the halakhic texts, has turned its attention, instead, to "those rituals and laws of Judaism that would buttress cultural and physical survival."

Nor do the authors fail to acknowledge the unsettling presence of ethnoreligious or "fundamentalist" extremists within contemporary religious communities. We define extremism as a hostile and often violent reaction to pluralism, that most modern of social conditions. Under conditions of duress, religious actors fall into this pattern when they legitimate violence as a religious obligation or sacred duty. Religious extremists expand the cast of threatening outsiders, the targets of the violence, to include lukewarm, compromising, or liberal co-religionists, as well as people or institutions of another or no religious faith. Foreign troops stationed on sacred ground, missionaries, Western business executives, their own government officials, sectarian preachers, educational and social service volunteers, relief workers, and professional peacekeepers—any or all of these might qualify at one time or another. Fundamentalists perceive these "interlopers" as intentional or inadvertent agents of secularization, which they understand to be a ruthless, but by no means inevitable process by which traditional religions and religious concerns are gradually relegated to the remote margins of society where they can die a harmless death—eliminated by what the Iranian intellectual Jalal Al-e Ahmad called the "sweet, lethal poison" of "Westoxication." "True believers" acting in this extremist mode are seldom willing to devote energies and resources to peacebuilding that would involve recognition and even empowerment of the other.

Accordingly, those non-extremist believers who *are* willing, who see peacemaking and dialogue as central to their religious identity, face daunting challenges. To gain a hearing, they may be required to confront combatants and legitimators of violence who propose to speak in the name of, and with the authority of, the religious tradition. This requires not only courage, but cunning. It is always more difficult to evoke forgiveness or tolerance from people who have been oppressed or otherwise injured by the religious or ethnic enemy. The extremist has the psychological edge in such instances. Tolerance and a deeply rooted respect for pluralism must be recovered and restored to the top of the religious community's agenda, if the peacemaker is to stand a chance of building consensus for nonviolent conflict transformation and indiscriminate respect for human rights.

In addition to the need for personal conversion to peacemaking, and the need to build the social and religious capital necessary to counter the appeal of the religious extremist, the religious peacemaker must become a *peacebuilder.* Even the prophet of peace, the religious leader accomplished in the art of moral persuasion, may be ill-prepared to take leadership in the complex process of nonviolent social change. Peacebuilding, as the chapters in this volume indicate, requires something more than a charismatic religious leader who inspires followers and/or sets a moral example of nonviolent resistance to evil.

RELIGIOUS PEACEBUILDING: TRANSFORMING CONFLICT AND RESTRUCTURING SOCIETY

In this book we use the term *religious peacebuilding* to describe the range of activities performed by religious actors and institutions for the purpose of *resolving and transforming deadly conflict,* with the goal of *building social relations and political institutions characterized by an ethos of tolerance and nonviolence.* Thus religious peacebuilding includes not only conflict management and resolution efforts on the ground, but also the efforts of people working at a distance from actual sites of deadly conflict, such as legal advocates of religious human rights, scholars conducting research relevant to crosscultural and interreligious dialogue, and theologians and ethicists within the religious communities who are probing and strengthening their traditions of nonviolence.

According to our definition, peacebuilding entails conflict transformation, the replacement of violent with nonviolent means of settling disputes. This occurs through overlapping processes of conflict management and conflict resolution. Conflict management entails the *prevention* of conflict from becoming violent or expanding to other arenas. Accordingly, it includes the *enforcement* of existing treaties and peace accords. Within these categories religious actors have played several major roles in recent decades, serving as *heralds, observers,* and *peacekeepers. Conflict resolution,* or peacemaking, entails removing, to the extent possible, the inequalities between the disputants, by means of mediation, negotiation, and/or advocacy and testimony on behalf of one or more parties to a conflict. Religious actors have served as *advocates, observers,* and *mediators,* among other roles, in this phase of conflict transformation.

These processes of conflict transformation, when successful, result in ceasefires and peace accords designed to contain the conflict in lieu of (and, ideally, in anticipation of) an essential element of peacebuilding, namely *structural reform*—efforts to build institutions and foster civic leadership that will address the root causes of the conflict and develop long-term practices and institutions conducive to peaceful, nonviolent relations in the society. In this post-deadly-conflict phase of the process, religious actors have served, among other roles, as *educators* and *institution builders.*[4]

Conflict Management (Prevention, Enforcement, Peacekeeping)

At the heart of conflict prevention is diagnosis. As *heralds* religious actors have been harbingers of widening rifts in the social fabric. The prophetic dimension of religion nurtures a heightened sensitivity to subtle as well as open forms of social discrimination, political oppression, and other forms of injustice. Indeed, consciousness-raising among their co-religionists and fellow citizens is the raison d'etre of such "prophets."

Marc Gopin, for example, writes of the "empathic listening" required of the Jewish peacemaker and commanded in the Hebrew bible and in the rabbinical literature. Catherine Morris, writing of Cambodia, underscores the capacity of the sangha to anticipate and prevent violent conflict within Khmer society. Striking illustrations of this point were the annual Buddhist "peace marches" across Cambodia. In the spring of 1993, the sixty-eight-year-old Buddhist patriarch Maha Ghosananda led hundreds of Buddhist monks, nuns, and laity on a dramatic month-long march from Siam Reap in the northwest section of Cambodia throughout the central regions to the capital, Phnom Penh. Held on the eve of the United Nations–sponsored elections of a new national assembly and government, the Peace March, known as Dhammayietra ("Pilgrimage of Truth") II, traversed dangerous territory marked by land mines and firefights. The marchers hoped to build popular confidence in the elections and overcome the fear that had been aroused by Khmer Rouge threats of violence and disruption. By the time Ghosananda and his supporters reached Phnom Penh, hundreds of thousands of Cambodians had encouraged the marchers along their path, and more than 10,000 people had joined their ranks. Ninety percent of the Cambodian electorate voted in the ensuing free and fair elections, the first in the country's history. While the United Nations Transitional Authority in Cambodia [UNTAC] had created the conditions necessary for the holding of the elections, many Cambodians and NGO workers attributed the extraordinary level of popular participation in part to the success of the Dhammayietra.[5]

When they act as heralds, religious actors keep their ear to the ground, recording and interpreting the shifts in religious practice, religious opinion, government policy, public sentiment, and racial, ethnic, and/or religious relations. Often they are positioned as guardians of orthodoxy or prophets pointing to erosions of community identity and boundaries. Yet these local religious and cultural players are often the first to notice the signs of incipient conflict and so their reports may and should figure in the early stages of a conflict resolution process as a kind of early warning system. In the Philippines, for example, religious leaders in Zamboanga City, Jolo, and other sites on the southern islands provided an early warning of the religious tensions developing between Muslims and Christians following the arrival in the 1980s of the Tablighi Jamaat, the worldwide Islamic revival group, and the subsequent formation of the Abu Sayyaf, the fundamentalist Islamic movement, which made kidnapping and ransom a staple of their fundraising and recruiting operations in the late 1990s. Through religious periodicals such as *Silsilah (Chain),* a newsletter of a Catholic-Muslim dialogue group in Mindinao, and through the massive propaganda campaign for and against Christian evangelists conducted across the radio airwaves, the national and foreign press were made aware of the ethnic and religious hostilities brewing in the region.[6]

When conflict erupts between an aggrieved minority and an ethnoreligious majority, or between religious or ethnic forces and the state itself, religiously motivated *advocates* may play a pivotal role. Agitating for the reform of government and the strengthening of civil society, religious advocates have pressed for higher standards of education, improved labor conditions and race relations, and the implementation of constitutional or legal protections of religious freedoms. Moral leadership, up to and including sacrificing resources and possibly lives in a protest action against a military-backed government, was a striking dimension of religious advocacy in East Timor, for example, during the Roman Catholic-led movement for independence from Indonesia, culminating in the bloody attempted genocide of 1998.

In preventing or containing conflict, religious actors may combine the roles of herald and advocate. During the administration of Hosni Mubarak, various levels of the Islamist movement, most notably the moderate wing of the Muslim Brotherhood, have played this role in Egypt. Adil Hussein, editor of *al-Sha'b (The People)* and an outspoken critic of the regime, has seen his newspaper shut down on several occasions and his political party manipulated by a shifting policy of so-called liberalization. When the IMF and the United States conduct reviews of their international aid policies, Hussein complains, the Labor Party and other expressions of political "pluralism" are allowed to flourish—temporarily. In "ordinary time," however, repression and restrictions are the norm. The radical wings of the Islamist movement will not die Hussein warns, "until and unless there exists an atmosphere of democracy that allows freedom and debate." *Al-Sha'b* is one of dozens of underground Egyptian newspapers that have kept alive a steady pulse of dissent and social criticism in an otherwise closed society.[7]

The Society of Engaged Buddhists, to take a different example, numbers among its members several courageous advocates of nonviolent social change. Buddhist liberationists include figures like Sulak Sivaraksa, the Thai monk who was jailed in 1984 after he criticized what he termed the monarchy's cultural abdication to the West. After a group of military leaders took power in Thailand as the National Peace Keeping Council in 1991, Sivaraksa attacked the coup leaders in interviews published in the international press, and delivered a widely publicized pro-democracy lecture at Bangkok's Thammasat University. "Since the first coup in 1947, the military in Siam has not had one new idea," he declared, "and it used every means possible—including the schools, universities and mass media—to undermine pro-democracy movements. Those who resisted, such as leaders of the farmers' movements and labor unions, were arrested and sometimes killed."[8] As a result of the Thammasat University speech, which was embraced by pro-democracy dissidents across the region, Sivaraksa was forced into exile on charges of lèse majesté—insulting royalty, in the person of King Bhumiphol—and defaming the coup's leader, General Suchinda Kraprayoon.

In acting as advocates for an oppressed group, it is also true that religious actors may seek primarily to protect their own privileges. (They may also honestly believe that their religion offers the best cultural conditions for social and economic progress.) In addition, the social disruptions associated with various forms of strife, from low-intensity conflict to outright civil war, provide an opening for religious entrepreneurs intent on increasing their "market share" within a society. These religious actors may take advantage of a conflict situation, as did the hordes of invading fundamentalist and Pentecostal evangelists who established a significant missionary presence in the Philippines during the Marcos era. In such cases conflict leads to a new realignment of social and religious forces, with political implications for the post-conflict period.[9]

Conflict management also involves enforcement and peacekeeping operations. Religious actors are underutilized in these roles, to the detriment of peace processes. Several authors in this volume lament the "missed opportunities" of this kind. In the Middle East, Gopin and Denny might agree, well-chosen religious actors must be included in any potentially successful implementation of a peace plan calling for joint administration of sacred sites located in and around Jerusalem. And in Northern Ireland, which boasts more self-identified "peacemakers" per capita than any other place on Earth, the Good Friday Agreement of 1998, most experts agree, will not be effective on the structural-political level until and unless grassroots, cross-community peace practitioners are involved. A significant percentage of the latter are drawn from the churches or are otherwise religiously motivated to build new local Catholic-Protestant institutions and networks and to strengthen the ones put in place since the most recent Troubles began in the 1960s.

Recent studies of U.N. peacekeeping operations point to the necessity of cultural and religious sensitivity on the part of the peacekeeping forces.[10] *Observers* offer themselves as a physical and moral presence, intended to discourage violence, corruption, human rights violations, or other behavior deemed threatening and undesirable. Far from a passive role, religiously based observers have actively monitored, verified, and in some cases even ensured the legitimacy of elections. Civilian peacekeeping individuals or teams have risked their lives by placing themselves in active conflict situations. In situations where violence is primarily perpetrated by one party against another, these actors have accompanied individuals or groups believed to be in danger, and have maintained a presence in threatened communities. Witness for Peace, an international ecumenical organization founded in the early 1980s, is known for its work documenting human rights violations and providing nonviolence training in Nicaragua between 1983 and 1991. Likewise, the Christian Peacemaker Teams sponsored by the Mennonites and the Church of the Brethren have been active in documenting human rights abuses and providing a protective presence for besieged communities in Haiti (primarily) and in Iraq, Palestine, Israel, the United States, and Canada. Religious volunteers acted as observers of the election of members of the Palestinian National Assembly in 1996, for example, and the Christian churches of Zambia recruited, trained, and deployed monitors for three thousand polling sites in the 1991 election in Zambia.[11]

Finally, religious *educators* lay the groundwork for conflict transformation through long-term service in the classroom, the training seminar, or the institute. They blend experiential as well as theoretical knowledge in imparting to their students and disciples the skills of conflict transformation and peacebuilding. "Educators and training have a role to play during each of the stages of conflict transformation, whether it be to sensitize a society to inequities in the system; to foster the understanding and build the skills of advocacy, conflict resolution, democracy, or living with diversity; or to promote healing and reconciliation," Cynthia Sampson writes, "The key to activity in this category is the dimension of preparation—of teaching or in some way providing a learning experience for others from a position one step removed from direct involvement in conflict intervention."[12]

Religious groups have been particularly active in the area of nonviolence training. In India the Gandhi Peace Foundation, from its headquarters in Delhi and in thirty-three field centers across the nation, conducted research and training programs in nonviolent conflict resolution; in Israel and Palestine, the International Fellowship of Reconciliation, Nonviolence International, and other NGOs provided legal supports to activists; and in South Africa, Bosnia, Sri Lanka, and numerous other sites of deadly violence, religious actors conducted seminars in conflict resolution techniques and in the theory and methods of peacemaking. In Cambodia, Guatemala, El Salvador, and Bolivia, religious actors joined other humanitarian educators in raising popular awareness of citizens' legal rights and democratic procedures.

In developing strategies for opposing social and political injustice nonviolently, religious peacemakers are able to draw upon and refine the religious tradition's ethical warrants for resistance against unjust conditions, using explicit constraints on the use of violence in preventing, ameliorating, or resolving conflicts. Indeed, an important aspect of religious education for peace is the research and writing, conferences, and dialogues dedicated to clarifying religious attitudes toward human rights, in particular the extent and kind of *religious* human rights deserving protection in pluralist societies. Who participates in the rights-defining process? Whose criteria govern the interpretation and practice of human rights? The most intense and conflict-ridden debates—and perhaps, ultimately, the most consequential—are currently being conducted within the religious traditions themselves, as they interact more and more frequently and rapidly with secular actors, with other religions—and with their own diverse and ideologically plural membership. Islam's internal struggle regarding human rights, democracy, the ethics of war and peace, and religious identity is likely the most consequential debate unfolding at present.[13]

Conflict Resolution (Peacemaking)

There are several decisive moments in conflict transformation, but few would doubt that negotiations between the warring parties is one of them. In this crucial phase of the process, religious communities and individuals, as well as religious officialdom (hierarchies, bureaucracies, religiously sponsored relief agencies, and other multinational religious institutions), have intervened with a frequency and level of success that is not widely recognized. Whether or not the conflict involves religious elements, the evidence provided in this book and in other literature strongly suggests that "unofficial" religious communities and individuals have been more successful in bringing disputants together and mediating productive negotiations.

Andrea Bartoli, whose chapter in this volume broadly surveys the peacemaking resources within Christianity, is the vice-president of a religious community that has enjoyed considerable success in mediating and transforming violent conflict. Sant'Egidio, the Roman Catholic lay movement headquartered in Rome, is known internationally for its key role in mediating the negotiations that led to the end of the civil war in Mozambique, for hosting the talks between Muslim and secular parties that led to a yet-to-be-implemented platform for peace in Algeria; and for more modest but nonetheless constructive interventions in Kosovo, Burundi, and Guatemala. What Bartoli says of Christian peacemakers in general may be said resoundingly of his own community: Religious mediators are successful because (and to the extent that) they: (1) exhibit an intimate knowledge of the language and culture of the peoples in conflict; (2) enjoy access to firsthand information about the conflict as it evolves; (3) possess or draw upon political expertise; and, (4) help to develop and embrace a long-term vision of peace for the conflicted society.

These four characteristics of effective religious peacebuilders, Bartoli writes, "may help religious leaders to bridge the gap that is frequently the most relevant obstacle to a peace process: the hermeneutical gap." Conflicts, Bartoli continues, must be "seen" and "read" accurately. Religious actors from within the society who excel in this interpretive task can be especially effective in conflicts that have major cultural, ethnic, and religious components. "Because they are closer to the scene of events, at ease with many actors, and familiar with the language and the issues at stake," Bartoli writes, "religious leaders may offer important interpretative frameworks. This was certainly the case in Mozambique where Christians such as the Community of Sant'Egidio and Archbishop Jaime Goncalves played a significant role. Religious actors were consistently able to contribute to the peace process through their interpretation of events, issues, and possibilities and to orient the debate towards a positive solution."

Religious *mediators* such as Sant'Egidio succeed, in other words, because they build trustworthy relationships, as far as possible, with people on every side of the conflict. Building trust requires, in turn, a willingness to suspend judgment or at least to maintain a principled neutrality. It requires, in short, a certain kind of religious or philosophical sensibility that puts people, their suffering, and their struggles above principle, if and when necessary.

In his chapter "Northern Ireland: Religion and the Peace Process," for example, Patrick Grant alludes briefly to the constructive peace-making efforts of individuals within the churches. More could and should be said, however, in acknowledgment of individual religious actors such as Friar Alec Reid and Reverend Roy Magee, each of whom made the difficult and fateful decision to continue to minister to, respectively, members of the Irish Republican Army and the Ulster Volunteer Force, even after higher-ranking officials of their churches had banned Reid (Roman Catholic) and Magee (Presbyterian) from associating with the extremists. Reid and Magee, each in his own way, decided to remain present to the people and the congregation standing defiantly at the center of the conflict. As Magee later recalled: "I never condoned the violence, and they knew it. I continued to preach the Ten Commandments, including 'Thou Shalt Not Kill.' They wanted me there with them, even on those terms. And when an opening for dialogue came, they also trusted me to be their go-between."

This kind of good-faith mediation, warranted by the proven integrity and trustworthiness of certain kinds of religious actors, can be critical to the success of the delicate approach-and-avoidance dance that often precedes formal negotiations. Thus, Father Reid was instrumental in bringing together Sinn Fein leader Gerry Adams and the moderate John Hume, who eventually collaborated in bringing the nationalists to the peace talks that led to the Good Friday Agreement.[14]

In contrast to religious communities and individuals, official religious establishments seem to fare better as peacebuilders in the post-conflict phase of the process, when structural reform gets under way and the society at large has to come to terms (through truth commissions and the like) with the role of institutions (including the churches) in the conflict. Thus, for example, Roman Catholic bishops were instrumental in investigating human rights atrocities and calling perpetrators to account in Chile, Brazil, Paraguay, Bolivia, and Argentina; and the Anglican Church, other churches, and religious communities participated centrally in the social reconstruction of post-apartheid South Africa.

There are notable exceptions. In 1972, representatives of a transnational religious organization, the World Council of Churches (WCC), mediated the peace talks that brought a decade-long respite in the Sudanese civil war between the Islamic government in the north and the Christian and animist Southern Sudan Liberation Movement. The WCC mediators were able to draw upon the religious sensibilities of the two sides, producing statements of remorse by Muslims and Christians alike, which led to a negotiated settlement. "Religious leaders who come from outside the combat zone provide space to discuss problems and a voice for those who do not have one," one WCC diplomat said. "Furthermore, religious people can hear people of all social levels. They have credibility; they can talk to all sides. They not only listen to leadership, but to the people." Some religious leaders "may hesitate to speak out because they fear it will jeopardize their good works," he noted. "They might be imprisoned or expelled and not be able to continue their ministry." But there are always courageous religious leaders who resist the temptation to assume political power in times of social change, or to unfairly advance the interests of their particular religious body. Thus, they retain the distance that permits them to be critical of all political leaders and serve as honest mediators.[15]

Structural Reform (Institution Building, Civic Leadership)

As we mentioned, structural reform addresses the institutional causes of conflict, including both religious institutions and political and civic institutions insofar as they bear on or are affected by religion. The general objective, of course, is to replace institutions that engender ethnoreligious hostility and violence with those that encourage nonviolence and peace, and, to that end, to cultivate leadership in the religious as well as in the political and civic sectors. In this regard, religious actors can serve as social critics, educators, and institution builders, among other roles. It is clear that the constructive potential of religion in circumstances of severe hostility or violent conflict typically involves the need to reverse or reform intolerant or discriminatory institutional patterns that religious leaders and groups have, with harmful consequences, confirmed and reinforced.

When, for example, the military seized power in most major Latin American countries in the 1960s and 1970s, the Roman Catholic Church, as the dominant religious body on the continent, radically reversed a traditional pattern of complicity with the political-military oligarchy and stepped up their public denunciations of the abuses of power. The bishops of Brazil, Chile, and Argentina issued pastoral letters condemning state-sponsored murder, torture, and the denial of habeas corpus and fair trial; the letters traced the root causes of these violations to the patterns of economic and social exploitation of the poor and dispossessed, often including the indigenous populations, and to an ideology of national security that subordinated the rights of individuals and groups to state expediency. In the 1970s, the churches of Chile, Brazil, Paraguay, Bolivia, and Argentina sponsored human rights commissions designed to bring the atrocities to light and advance reform of political structures.

In such cases, religious communities were often prepared to assume the leadership of social reconstruction after violence ended both as an act of repentance for their own earlier cooperation with injustice and oppression, and because they had eventually taken a stand in favor of ending the conflict and overturning the patterns of economic inequality and political domination that fueled the violence in the first place.

Several of the chapters in this volume make the same point. For example, Russel Botman, in his chapter on the South African Truth and Reconciliation Commission (SATRC), shows how the SATRC, established to supplement the institutions of justice in bringing to account those who committed acts of abuse and oppression under the apartheid regime, was in part a means whereby the South African church might express contrition for its own extensive culpability. "Although violators," he says, "must indeed be held politically and individually responsible for their dastardly acts, the faith communities that formed the perpetrators' mind must also come to terms with the reality of their part in the offences." Botman goes on to argue that the contribution of religious leadership and religious sensibility to the formation and implementation of the SATRC is both central and defensible. It is futile, he says, to try to divorce such an institution from the Judeo-Christian theology of reconciliation that has so profoundly shaped it. Moreover, he considers efforts like the SATRC to be indispensable in post-conflict settings. Despite criticisms, institutions of this sort are "a necessary element of modern peacebuilding" because they offer an effective way of confronting and mitigating the poisonous effects of gross and systematic human rights violations such as those that took place in South Africa during the apartheid era.

It may be added that TRCs, even where they are culturally appropriate, are hardly the only way in which religions and religious actors promote reconciliation and healing in the aftermath of deadly conflict. Religious ethics, rituals, and disciplines can promote humility, compassion, and discernment in their practitioners, and these nonviolent religious militants often display the patience, timing, and judgment required of diplomats and agents of reconciliation alike. Agents of reconciliation, to be effective, must demonstrate empathy for victims on all sides, a profound commitment to the nonviolent management of differences, political insight, and extraordinary quantities of "grace"—forbearance, patience, dedication, and the sacrifice of ego. In addition, they must be able to speak a second-order language that transcends religious and ethnic boundaries and fosters collaboration with secular and governmental agencies and representatives. Discernment—a spiritual discipline as well as a political skill—is perhaps the most crucial quality in this arena of conflict transformation, for it is not difficult to miscalculate the situation and to seek or promise the wrong things at the wrong time. The tactical decisions are exceedingly delicate: Under what conditions should repentance be required or forgiveness sought? How and when should the perpetrator of violence and the victim be brought together?

A process leading to genuine reconciliation also demands leaders whose moral authority commands the respect of both sides. The process can be derailed at the outset if led by those who stand outside the cycle of violence and suffering or, worse, those who have been the oppressors and the perpetrators of violence. Depending on the situation, official religious leaders may or may not possess such authority. Yet other religious actors identify with or even stand among those who have suffered victimization, and this experience itself adds to their legitimacy as guides to reconciliation.[16] Religious actors formed in a religious culture of peacemaking are among those least vulnerable to the error of treating reconciliation as a "efficient," "managed," and expeditious means to a predetermined end. They are also among those least likely to trivialize or ignore the community's history of suffering, the memory of individual victims, or the complex causes of the suffering.

Johnston and Eastvold provide a second example in their chapter on the Bosnian conflict regarding the ambivalent effect of religion on leaders and institutions. While arguing that religion was anything but a "root cause" of the Balkan war, Johnston and Eastvold leave no doubt that religion served in various ways and in varying degrees to reinforce the nationalist fervor that divided the warring parties, Serbian, Croatian, and Bosnian. Against that background, the authors welcome postwar efforts to overcome ethnoreligious hostility by developing new multifaith institutions like the Inter-Religious Council of Bosnia-Herzegovina, and cooperative projects, like the multifaith workshops throughout the Former Yugoslavia that are supported by the Center for Strategic and International Studies in Washington, D.C.

The Inter-Religious Council brings together the four major religious communities in the Balkans, the Serbian Orthodox, the Croatian Catholics, the Bosnian Muslims, and the Jews, and provides a forum for confronting a range of institutional issues crucial to creating a multiethnic society in Bosnia. These include the reconstruction of religious monuments in ethnically cleansed areas and the restitution of expropriated property; the return of minorities and their clerical leaders to places from which they were displaced during the war; and the development of new laws protecting religious freedom and equality throughout the country. Though the authors do not mention it, the Inter-Religious Council has also strongly supported the creation of a Truth and Reconciliation Commission for Bosnia-Herzegovina.

The interfaith workshops, supported by CSIS, and directed by David Steele, are designed to help overcome resentment and political impotence, develop interethnic contacts, and inculcate peacemaking skills. Efforts are now being made to establish a new indigenous, faith-based peacemaking NGO in each of the three republics.

Rajmohan Gandhi writes along the same lines in his chapter on Hinduism. He offers a forthright discussion of the chauvinist tendencies in the contemporary Hindutva movement, and its political analogue, the Bharatiya Janata Party. Gandhi singles out, in particular, two tendencies in the movement that make for division and friction within Indian society, Hindu nationalism and calls for revenge in response to resentment for past injustice. The fusion of religion and country that lies at the heart of the Hindutva movement "defines good Indians as those to whom India is both their homeland and their holy land, a criterion that makes Muslims and Christians unpatriotic by definition." He points out that even those Hindus who are skeptical of such talk "nonetheless think of Hinduism (and Buddhism, Jainism, and Sikhism) as Indian religions, and of Islam, Christianity, Zoroastrianism, and Judaism as foreign." Such attitudes are premised, according to Gandhi, on deep feelings of resentment for past mistreatment—destruction of temples, forcible conversions, mass killings—believed to have been perpetrated by these "foreign" elements. Sacred texts, from the Gita and elsewhere, are invoked in favor of retaliatory violence. Gandhi cites a 1999 study that speaks of Hindutva, as a movement "based on a toxic, belligerent, paranoid, and sectarian nationalism" that sees Hindus as "victims of invasion and conquest." It calls for the creation of an "awe-inspiring Hindu state," capable of settling scores by violence if necessary.

Gandhi points to his grandfather, Mohandas K. Gandhi, as a leader who resolutely opposed such themes and sought to move Indian society away from violence and chauvinism toward multireligious inclusiveness, equality, and tolerance. He drew on alternative sacred sources in his effort to reverse and reform Indian institutions, including, in particular, the caste system. Whether he went far enough, "India's constitutional commitment to equality irrespective of religion or caste would probably not have come about but for Gandhi's political leadership[.]" Moreover, on this account, Gandhi succeeded in "winning much of Hindu society to his version of Hinduism," which included repudiating untouchability and embracing Hindu-Muslim coexistence. The fundamental challenge, implicit throughout Rajmohan Gandhi's chapter, is which of these competing social visions will prevail in contemporary India.

The chapter by Eva Neumaier on Buddhism and ethnic strife in Sri Lanka and Tibet provides yet another description of the ambivalent contribution of religion to building institutions that make for peace. Though she is careful to distinguish the two cases, Neumaier's argument in favor of important similarities between them is surprising and no doubt controversial. Sri Lanka and Tibet are usually depicted in sharply contrasting terms. Nevertheless, there is no doubt that her analysis of "missed opportunities" as regards the social and political influence of Buddhism in both cases is provocative and arresting.

The central claim is that "Buddhist ethics and the practice of mindfulness, if made into a guideline for interacting with the world, could provide effective ways of building peace between individuals, social groups, and nations." However, as demonstrated by the cases of Sri Lanka and Tibet, "[m]uch of Buddhist history is a history of missed opportunities to build peace. Buddhists are like people who hold in their hands the tools to their liberation from imprisonment but who have forgotten how to use them."

Neumaier singles out two obstacles of special importance. One is a consistent disposition to interpret the concepts of peace, harmony, and tranquility, which are undoubtedly basic to classical Buddhism, in an individualistic, inward way, rather than in relation to social and political experience. The second is a frequent tendency in Buddhist cultures "to adopt a mytho-historic narrative as the script of national identity" that encourages ethnic exclusivism and religious nationalism. The implication is that the two obstacles work together. By inwardizing the idea of peace, Buddhist teaching is prevented from helping to shape social and political policies and institutions, and is available instead for manipulation in the name of social division and enmity rather than peace and nonviolence.

The analysis in Patrick Grant's chapter on Northern Ireland further expands understanding of the connections among religion, leadership, and institutional peacebuilding. Although Grant admits that those who minimize the connection of religion to the conflict in Northern Ireland are not altogether mistaken, he provides strong evidence in favor of the salience of "religious sectarianism" in fueling the conflict and in retarding the prospects and arrangements for peace. In this account, sectarianism denotes a strong sense at the grassroots level of ethnic identity, an identity that is distinctly shaped and colored by a religious narrative, both for the Protestants and the Catholics. Questions of faith, church attendance, and spirituality are interwoven with allegiance to the community of one's birth. This creates attitudes and an outlook that are "deeply resistant to the kinds of freedom in and through which the Spirit by which Christians hope to find themselves liberated from the impersonal demands and mechanisms of a tribal or herd morality."

Specifically, such an embedded form of ethnoreligious identity stands in the way of and often works to undermine the much lauded and much publicized efforts of both Protestant and Catholic leaders to advocate and support peace and the building of multireligious and multiethnic political and civic institutions in Northern Ireland. Grant offers interesting evidence to the effect that militant and exclusivist views are much more widespread and fervently held within both the Protestant and Catholic communities than is usually publicly admitted. It would appear that both religious institutions are as internally divided as the top leadership and the rest of the community. The implication is that unified, tolerant religious institutions are a significant part of building unified, tolerant, civic, and political institutions.

Beyond these and other suggestive insights regarding religion and structural reform that are contained within the chapters of this book, there is new, relevant, if somewhat indirect, evidence of broader significance that bears mentioning here. The evidence is contained in Ted Robert Gurr's recent book, *Peoples versus States: Minorities at Risk in the New Century*. Though Gurr pays insufficient attention to the role of religion or says some inconsistent things about it, his study, properly adjusted, has important implications for the place of religion in peace-related institution building.

On the basis of a careful statistical survey of the status of ethnic minorities—275 of them—and the kind of treatment they receive at the hands of states around the world, Gurr contends, rather unexpectedly, that since 1995, ethnopolitical conflict, globally considered, is sharply on the wane. "The breakup of the international system into warring ethnic statelets, which many feared in the early 1990s, has been checked by more effective international and domestic strategies for managing ethnopolitical conflict." "Relations between [ethnic groups] and states in heterogeneous societies changed in the 1990s in ways that suggest that a new regime governing minority-majority relations is under construction."[17]

Gurr documents a global shift from ethnic warfare to the politics of accommodation. In the late 1990s, the most common political strategy was not rebellion, but political participation, and the number of groups using armed violence has now declined after years of steady growth. "By mid-decade a worldwide shift in strategies of ethnopolitical action was taking place." An examination of fifty-nine armed ethnic conflicts under way in 1998 shows that de-escalating conflicts outnumbered escalating ones by 23 to 7, and the remaining twenty-nine have no short-term trend; moreover, two-thirds of all new campaigns of protest and new armed rebellions began in the five years from 1989 to 1993. "Few new ethnopolitical conflicts began after 1994," whether protest movements or rebellions.[18] Moreover, secessionist wars are in especially steep decline. Between 1991 and 1999, sixteen were settled and eleven others were checked by cease-fires and negotiations. It is not only ethnic conflict that spreads by example, but, as Gurr argues, "the successes of conflict management also are contagious."

Perhaps most encouraging of all, Gurr shows that the implementation of international human rights standards has lowered the potential for conflict by reducing cultural and political discrimination, a key reason, apparently, for minority protest and rebellion. Such discrimination eased for more than one-third of the 275 groups reviewed between 1990 and 1998, mainly because of shifts in public policies and practices that lifted restrictions on their political and cultural rights. Groups gained most in the new democracies of Europe, Asia, and Latin America.

Gurr identifies three principles of what he calls "the emerging regime of managed heterogeneity." The "first and most basic" principle is the recognition and active protection of the rights of minority peoples: freedom from discrimination based on race, national origin, language, or religion, complemented by institutional means to protect and promote collective interests. This principle implies the right of national peoples to exercise some degree of autonomy and self-governance within existing states. Armed rebellion in a large number of cases has been mitigated or pacified by autonomy agreements, mainly concluded in the nineties (as, e.g., in Northern Ireland, Moldova, Nicaragua, Burma, Bosnia, Ethiopia, and Bangladesh).

The second principle is that, among political systems, democracy is the most reliable guarantee of minority rights, and, consequently, of ethnic coexistence.[19] Autocracies manifest severe discrimination toward minorities, especially in cultural and political terms.[20] The use of "repression without accommodation," typical of autocracies like Burma, China, Indonesia (before the recent change of government there), and the Sudan, "leads with some regularity to renewed resistance and rebellion." Gurr is also clear that the established democracies have a comparatively good record in dealing peacefully and constructively with minorities.

The third principle holds that disputes between [ethnic] groups and states are best settled by negotiation and mutual accommodation. Since 1990, settlements have ended or led to deescalation of sixteen wars. This remarkable post-Cold War shift toward reliance on negotiations to settle separatist conflicts is consistent with other researchers' findings that ever-larger numbers of civil wars of all kinds are being terminated at the negotiating table.[21] By a ratio of 20 to 7, democratic governments have been particularly successful in working out negotiated settlements.

One of the most interesting features of the growing attraction of negotiated settlements is, according to Gurr, the international connection. The findings indicate that major powers, as well as international and regional organizations, by employing various combinations of diplomacy, mediation, inducements, and threats, have contributed significantly to the resolution or management of ethnic conflict. International actors also make an important contribution to strengthening the other two principles, the protection of collective rights and the promotion of political democracy.[22]

Though Gurr himself overlooks or confuses the role of religion in this process, the overall decrease in the incidence of ethnopolitical conflict, and the general explanations Gurr gives for that decrease, are of the greatest importance in regard to the subject of religion and structural reform.

Observers, such as those represented in this book, face an empirical and interpretive challenge. With this volume they bring readers to the point of plunging deeper into particular cases in order to determine how religious leaders and groups stand in regard to the trends Gurr reports. Is he correct in identifying these trends and are his explanations valid? If so, are religious actors helping or hindering the cause? Are they serving the spread of the norms of tolerance, nondiscrimination, and minority protection? Are they helping to improve the emergence of democratic institutions, and working with international agencies to mitigate conflict and build just and stable settlements? Or, on the contrary, are they standing in the way?

Though some of the authors in this book have begun to advance understanding on religion and structural reform, there remains much further work to be done. The present volume provides an important foundation for that long-term project.

NOTES

1. For background on the debate over the Bush administration's faith-based initiative, see Laurie Goodstein, "Church-Based Projects Lack Data on Results," *New York Times,* Tuesday, April 24, 2001, p. A-12. Mainline and African-American church groups took the early lead in developing the faith-based approach. See also Rob Boston, "The 'Charitable Choice' Charade," *Church & State* 51, no. 2 (Feb. 1998), pp. 7–12.

2. In the year 2000 alone, the Evangelical Lutheran Church of America issued a formal apology for its role in promoting anti-Semitism; the Southern Baptist Convention formally apologized for racist attitudes among its members and for failing to fight racism in society; and mainstream Protestant denominations sought forgiveness from African Americans and Native Americans for their part in justifying slavery.

3. Cynthia Sampson, "Religion and Peacebuilding," in I. William Zartman and J. Lewis Rasmussen, eds., *Peacemaking in International Conflict: Methods and Techniques* (Washington, D. C.: United States Institute of Peace Press, 1997), p. 275.

4. Compare the definitions provided in I. William Zartman, "Toward the Resolution of International Conflicts," in Zartman and Rasmussen, eds., *Peacemaking in International Conflict,* p. 11. Zartman uses other peace-related terms as they are defined by their UN usage; hence, *peacemaking* refers to diplomatic efforts to resolve conflict according to Chapter VI of the U.N. Charter, and *peacekeeping,* to forces positioned to monitor a peace agreement. I have used these terms throughout the text in a more general sense. By the U.N. usage, *peacebuilding* refers to what I am calling *structural transformation,* namely, the provision of structural measures to preclude a relapse into conflict. As mentioned, we use the term *religious peacebuilding* to comprehend all the elements of religious work for peace. See the similar definition in John Paul Lederach, *Building Peace: Sustainable Reconciliation in Divided Societies* (Washington, D.C.: United States Institute of Peace Press, 1997), p. 20.

5. Bob Maat, "Dhammayietra, Walk of Peace," *The Catholic Worker* (May 1995), p. 22. The first Dhammayietra, in 1992, involved a group of Cambodians who had been living in Thai refugee camps. Accompanied by Maha Ghosananda and other Buddhist leaders, these refugees marched across the battlefields of northwest Cambodia to areas where they could settle among their own people within the boundaries of their own native country.

6. Steve Brouwer, Paul Gifford, and Susan D. Rose, *Exporting the American Gospel: Global Christian Fundamentalism* (New York: Routledge, 1996).

7. Martin E. Marty and R. Scott Appleby, *The Glory and the Power: The Fundamentalist Challenge to the Modern World* (Boston: Beacon Press, 1992), p. 136.

8. Sulak Sivaraksa, *Loyalty Demands Dissent: Autobiography of an Engaged Buddhist* (Berkeley: Parallax Press, 1998), p. 213.

9. Yet religious actors are also capable of acting as disinterested advocates. Christian peacemaker teams sponsored by the Mennonites intervene on both sides of the conflict between Israel and Palestine; they have called attention to by attempting to block the destruction of Palestinian homes in Gaza and the West Bank in retaliation for terrorist attacks on Israelis; and they have ridden the Israeli buses targeted for bombing by Hamas. In 1987, to take a second example, Acharya Sushil Kumar, a Jain monk, played a central role in Sikh-Hindu talks over contested sites in the Punjab. Sampson, "Religion and Peace-building," p. 287.

10. William Shawcross, *Deliver Us From Evil: Peacekeepers, Warlords and a World of Endless Conflict* (New York: Simon and Schuster, 2000).

11. Sampson, *Religion and Peacebuilding*, p. 12; Lisa Schirch, *Conflict Intervention by Civilian Peace Teams* (Uppsala, Sweden, Life and Peace Institute, 1995), p. 2.

12. Sampson, "Religion and Peacebuilding," p. 286.

13. Abdullahi A. An Na'im, "Toward an Islamic Hermeneutics for Human Rights." In *Human Rights and Religious Values*, edited by Abdullahi A. An-Na'im, Jerald D. Gort, Henry Jansen, and Hendrik M. Vroom (Grand Rapids, MI: William B. Eerdmans, 1995), pp. 229–242; idem, "Saudi Arabia, Pakistan, and the Universal Declaration of Human Rights," in David Little, John Kelsay, and Abdulaziz Sachedina, eds., *Human Rights and the Conflicts of Culture: Western and Islamic Perspectives on Religious Liberty* (Columbia: University of South Carolina Press, 1988), pp. 33–52.

14. R. Scott Appleby, *The Ambivalence of the Sacred: Religion, Violence and Reconciliation* (Lanham, MD: Rowman & Littlefield, 2000), chapter 5; also see Michael Hurley, S.J., "Reconciliation and the Churches in Northern Ireland," in Gregory Baum and Harold Wells, eds., *The Reconciliation of Peoples: Challenge to the Church* (Maryknoll, NY: Orbis Books, 1997), pp. 118–128.

15. Burgess Carr, "Proceedings of the Tantur conference," unpublished manuscript, August 19, 1995.

16. Robert Schreiter, *Reconciliation, Reconciliation: Mission & Ministry in a Changing Social Order* (The Boston Theological Institute Series. Vol. 3. Maryknoll, NY: Orbis Books, 1992), pp. 15–26.

17. Ted Robert Gurr, *Peoples versus States: Minorities at Risk in the New Century* (Washington, DC: United States Institute of Peace Press, 2000).

18. Ibid. Where Gurr's account becomes obscure, however, and where more investigation and clarification is required, is in regard to the utility of democracy specifically in transitional settings, where societies undertake to move away from extreme forms of autocratic repression and their potential for ethnic divisiveness. In such circumstances, Gurr prescribes a blend of democracy and

autocracy. Unfortunately, Gurr fails at this point to provide much analysis or many details or examples, and he does not explain how this prescription squares with his support, elsewhere, for an unqualified form of democracy as the most reliable guarantee of minority rights.

19. Ibid., p. 167.

20. Ibid., p. 204; see Table 6.1, pp. 198–202, for examples.

21. Ibid., p. 204.

22. Ibid., pp. 176–177, 280, 287.

Part I

Spiritual Resources within Religions for Peacebuilding

2

In Search of the White Path

American Indian Peacebuilding

MICHELENE E. PESANTUBBEE

In this chapter I will survey a number of religious ideas from selected American Indian nations to demonstrate the ways in which peace or peacebuilding is fostered among indigenous people. I will also explain how those same ideas can work to inhibit efforts toward peacebuilding. My decision to draw upon the religious ideas of several American Indian nations, however, requires explanation. First, American Indian religious systems involve complex, interdependent practices and worldviews. To isolate ideas from these systems is artificial. Second, in any study of American Indian religious traditions, the tendency to develop an essentialist or reductionist comparative model is a concern. Do I try to cover the traditions of more than 500 nations, or do I select one nation as representative of all the others?

Since the advent of Indian–white relations, Europeans and later Americans have drawn from their own cultural and religious understandings to formulate theories about American Indian beliefs and practices. Part of this colonial discourse is a homogenizing effect that creates supposed applicable generic terms such as "shamanism," "Great Spirit," or "Mother Earth." Such terms, however, fail to recognize partially or wholly the distinct cultural meanings and effects of the multiple religious ideas that are subsumed under homogenizing labels.

Moreover, the effects of religious change as a result of contact with other indigenous groups or with Europeans and Americans and their religious ideas are lost in this interactive process. Thus, it is with trepidation and awareness of my contribution to continuing colonial discourse that I undertake this chapter.

Before proceeding, however, the limitations of appropriating culturally informed religious ideas to facilitate peacebuilding on a scale larger than Indian nation to Indian nation require some disclaimers. The principles discussed in this chapter derive from particular kinds of communities existing within particular environments. Historically, these ideas developed within relatively small communities whose members were often related by family or clan. Families lived in close proximity to each other, and extended family members often composed a single household. This kinship relationship coupled with a less mobile and technological society than we have today required a more cooperative living tradition. In fact, community was more important than the individual, and the individual gained status through acts that benefited the community's welfare. Such close, interdependent living conditions demanded an emphasis on peaceful, harmonious relations within the community. The individual or the community could not exist without the cooperative social mores informing the actions of both.

The cultural alienation that indigenous peoples have experienced since the advent of European and later American colonization must also be recognized. As various governments and missionary groups worked to assimilate and Christianize American Indians, they also disrupted or destroyed many of the structures that supported communal lifestyles. The allotment of communal lands to individuals, the actions of boarding schools run by non-Indians, and Christian missionization inhibited or prevented participation in ceremonial life and thus the transference of religious ideas between generations. The forced removal of Indian nations from their ancestral homelands in the nineteenth century and urban relocation policies in the 1950s[1] created diasporic, fragmented communities that threatened the survival of Indian nations and communal values. Those ideas that survived colonization pressures were difficult to maintain in the Western world. Separation meant loss of language, ties to the land, and kinship responsibilities that informed and were informed by religious systems. Relocated individuals or families found it difficult to return home to their communities to participate in ceremonies. In addition to dispersal of population and assimilation, Indian communities suffered from the debilitating effects of alcoholism, crime, and orphanage. Today those problems are compounded by gangs and drugs, social concerns that were almost nonexistent prior to European contact. This is not to say that religious ideas have not survived the assimilationist pressures on Indian societies, but that such pressures have had far-reaching effects on the lives of Indian people. American Indian people, whether raised in a rural or reservation community or in an urban area, recognize and experience the difficulties inherent in living according to religious ideas that developed within small, community-oriented societies. To take these traditions even further out of their context by incorporating them into a global context makes the likelihood of their effectiveness or applicability uncertain.

These disclaimers in place, I would also like to address the significance of including American Indian religious ideas in a study of the role religion can play in fostering peace. Many of the stereotypes associated with Indians are of a violent nature. Words such as "savage" or "raider" come to mind. American westerns (movies and books) have fostered the image of barbaric Indians who treat their enemies cruelly and with unparalled revengefulness. These images are continually reinforced today in the well-known tomahawk chop, tom-tom beat, or the war whoop. Caricatures of bloodthirsty warriors proliferate in various media formats from cartoons watched by impressionable young children to adult computer games with abusive themes. By repudiating these negative stereotypes I am not suggesting that violence did not or does not exist in Indian communities. However, I do argue that concerns with peacebuilding predominated in the lives of Indian people more so than ideas of conflict.

A paradox that arises in this study, however, is that the very ideas that can be used by Indian people to foster peace and peacemaking are also used to inform violent actions such as warfare or acts of revenge. However, even as these ideas justify violent acts under certain conditions, they also operate to temper the initiation of conflict among Indian societies. The determination of whether to use violent or peaceful means is dependent on the leadership at the time and the situations that call for a decision such as an enemy attack or economic need. Indian people recognize that both good and malevolence exist in the world and that choice plays a role in the decision made by individuals and communities. Thus, one can choose to take the peaceful path or one can choose to take the path of war. Either way, both decisions look to the same set of religious ideas for affirmation. The dual applicability of such ideas, ideally, will become clear as those ideas are later discussed in this chapter.

As a final consideration before proceeding with the subject at hand, I want to address the issue of colonization as an obstacle to peacebuilding. Inherent in the colonial process of acculturation and appropriation is the unquestioned assumption that the ideas (or practices) of the colonized can be taken for the benefit of the colonizer irrespective of whether the colonizer is working on behalf of the colonized or colonizer. This privileging of the colonizer's goals under the auspices of a greater good has the potential to impede peacemaking because indigenous people continue to experience such appropriation as continuing violence against them. Their resistance to continued colonization, to the colonizer, draws upon religious ideas to support their efforts to maintain sovereignty, religious freedom, and religious and cultural property rights. Thus, the religious ideas that will be discussed in this chapter with respect to peacebuilding are the same ideas that inform resistance to continued appropriation of indigenous religious ideas. American Indians feel strongly that their contributions to a global society must include their involvement in the decision about what religious ideas should be shared and how they should be shared. Simply appropriating those ideas without the input of the religious leaders of the relevant Indian nations is tantamount to violence and will evoke a vehement response.

These concerns aside, I will now examine a few religious ideas that arguably reflect themes common to the various Indian nations in North America. Those themes are the generative power of thought and speech, the unity of creation, and the existence of good and malevolence in the world. Since dialogue is an important tool for peacebuilding, particularly in oral-based societies, it is appropriate to begin with speech and its precursor, thought. Indian people commonly recognize that thought and speech have creative abilities and thus must be carefully considered. Among the Navajo in the Southwest[2] the creation of the world and everything in it began with thought *(Sa'ah Naaghaii)* and was realized through speech *(Bik'eh Hozho)*. Before creation, however, all knowledge already existed. Spirit beings thought the world into existence by manifesting existing knowledge. By commanding knowledge, thought can transform conditions and regenerate life. For example, through thought vegetation can be increased. However, thought, which is associated with form, is actualized by speech. Speech is a kind of action that imposes thought on the external world. In other words, speech, which is an extension of thought, consummates and reinforces the power of thought through ritual action. Therefore, although the world was thought into existence, its consummation or realization occurred when the spirit beings expressed thought through spoken prayer or sung song. Thus, for the Navajo, language does not describe the world, language determines how the world will be.[3]

The way in which the power of thought and speech can be used to transform things is evident in Cherokee medicinal practice.[4] According to Cherokee tradition, generative power resides in thought, and to cure someone or alter a condition or influence elements, one directs that thought through singing or speaking an appropriate prayer four or seven times or by blowing one's breath on a medicine object such as "remade" tobacco (which itself was thought or sung over in the process of remaking it). The reciter may also pause during the process of a ritual to think intently on the purpose of the ritual.[5] For the Cherokee the breath or saliva of a person embodies the power of that individual that enables them to transform thought into speech. The breath (air) that makes speech possible is imbued with power of the individual. It is the agent that transforms things whether through speech or directed exhalation. Thus, the medicine person blows on the tobacco to invest it with the strength of his or her life and being.[6]

Both the Navajo and the Cherokee recognize that the creative power of thought and speech can be used for peaceful or malevolent purposes. In the case of the Navajo, they "emphasize that if one thinks of good things and good fortune, good things will happen. If one thinks of bad things, bad fortune will be one's lot."[7] In a similar way, the Cherokee recognize that malignant emotions can be projected by individuals intent on harm by "thinking" malevolent or malicious thoughts.[8] Both societies view malignant acts as antisocial and harmful. For the Navajo the goal of fostering the positive or good can be achieved through ritual, and the primary purpose of Navajo ritual is to maintain or restore *hozho*, that which is good, harmonious, orderly, happy, and beautiful. Through ritual language that commands, compels, organizes, transforms, and restores, Navajo maintain or restore *hozho*. The idea of *hozho*, however, is not limited to ritual song or prayer; Navajo refer to it frequently in everyday speech.[9] Attention to *hozho* reminds people to be careful and deliberate in choosing their words in order to maintain harmony with the world around them and others.

Among the Cherokee an ethic of harmony forms the core of their values. The idea is to try to maintain harmonious interpersonal relationships with other Cherokee by avoiding giving offense and giving of oneself in terms of time and material goods.[10] However, not everyone behaves in a manner that is beneficial or harmonious with others. To compel a group of people to act kindly toward each other and negate any animosity already existent in any individual affiliated with the group, Cherokee may recite certain prayers along with the use of white tobacco to produce amity and peace. They can also use prayers to negate existing hostile or adverse thinking or defamatory speech. To protect themselves, people who are traveling from group to group may also recite a relevant prayer in order to make friends in each group. Medicine people or powerful people are not the only ones who can use prayers to affect behavior. Any individual can also deal with overbearing or arrogant individuals by thinking or saying a particular prayer before meeting them.[11]

American Indians work toward harmony by thinking in terms of relationships. Indian people recognize that everything in the world is alive and connected through time and space. Joseph Epes Brown, a specialist on plains cultures, describes this relationship as a series of relationships that extend outward from "the immediate family reaching out to the extended family, to the band, outward again to the clan, to the tribal groups; and . . . out to embrace and relate to the environment; to the land, to the animals, to the plants, and to the clouds, the elements, the heavens, the stars; and ultimately . . . the entire universe."[12] Among the Lakota, oneness or unity characterizes this series of relationships.[13] According to their creation story, in the beginning there was only *Inyan* or rock. *Inyan* wished to exercise his power, but could only do so by creating another from part of himself and by giving the other spirit. In that way *Inyan* became the source of all creation[14] and all of the creation was related as a result. From this story Lakota understand that "creation begins because the very nature of power requires relationship and sharing."[15] Through *wakan,* that which is hard to understand or the great mysterious, all of creation is united.[16] Every being or object in the world is believed to have a spirit *(tunwan)* and everything is *wakan.* The Lakota express the unity of *wakan* beings in terms of family relationship or kinship. Thus, they think of *wakan* beings "as they think of their fathers and their mothers" or grandmothers and grandfathers. And the proper way to behave toward relatives is with kindness and generosity.[17]

The relationship between human beings and spirit and human beings and other living beings[18] is maintained through reciprocity. *Inyan*'s initial experience of power shows that "power's mode of functioning is through reciprocity."[19] Reciprocity is the act of giving in response to receiving or in order to receive. In this way balance and harmony are maintained between human beings and spirit and between human beings and other persons including human beings. The way in which reciprocity maintains community and relationships is exemplified by the Lakota *hanbleceya* "into the night he or she goes crying," popularly known as "seeking a vision."[20] In the *hanbleceya* the seeker offers the pipe and prayers to the *wakan* beings in exchange for knowledge. When the seeker returns from the *hanbleceya,* his or her experience is related to others so that the entire community may benefit. Through sharing of the experience, the community enables the seeker to actualize his or her powers received during the *hanbleceya,* and, in return, the community benefits from the power of the seeker who uses the knowledge for the good of the community.

Now that some basic American Indian religious ideas have been laid out I will turn to some ways in which these ideas can inhibit or facilitate peacemaking. Although the goal of Indian people, according to their religious ideologies, is to behave in a positive or good way, in a manner that reinforces positive relationships, they recognize that good and malignant forces exist in the world. That which is good promotes harmony and that which is malignant is anything that prevents or interferes with the good or is antisocial. However, good and malignant are not entirely distinct or in opposition as the means to achieve both rely on similar rituals or prayers. To clarify this point we can turn to Cherokee ideas of medicine and witchcraft. The Cherokee make a distinction between witches and human beings who cause adverse or undesirable changes in persons or things. Witches are "irredeemable beings whose true existence falls outside the realm of humanity."[21] Witches only engage in malevolent activities, they misuse power, and they are not part of humanity.

Human beings, however, have the capacity to behave in positive or negative ways. Among the Cherokee, a person who behaves in a kind way is referred to as having "soul," "heart," or "feeling." An individual who behaves malevolently is considered "evil" and is viewed in the same way as witches.[22] Once a community has determined that a person is kind or evil, that classification can never change. However, a person who is classified as kind can commit negative acts, but as the person is recognized as essentially good, his or her acts can be forgiven.[23] Although the intent of good and evil persons differ, their process in achieving their goals may be similar. For example, a person intent on doing harm to someone may metamorphose into something else like an owl or a cat. The "evil" person alters his or her appearance in order to move among unsuspecting victims. A medicine person who is essentially good, however, may also change him or herself into something else to counter the act of the witch. To protect the intended victim, the "good" medicine person may turn the actions of the witch back on itself and thus cause harm to the witch. By turning back the witch's action, the medicine person is engaging in a negative act in order to protect others.

As we saw in the case of Cherokee conceptions of good and malignance, dualities exist in the world and they can be both complementary and oppositional.[24] This dual applicability allow Cherokee to draw on religious ideas to facilitate peacemaking as well as activities antithetical to harmonious relations. Another duality present in Cherokee ideology is expressed in terms of white and red. The color white reflects purity and peace and the color red indicates "conflict, war, fear, disunity, and danger." White is also associated with old age, which "denotes wisdom, ritual power, and imposes respect."[25] Thus, Cherokee appropriate kinship terms associated with old age to refer to sacred beings such as fire or sun ("two of the most powerful forces in Cherokee cosmology") which are referred to as Grandfather or Grandmother.[26] Conversely, like fire or sun, elders are seen as powerful and wise.

Many American Indian societies have a system of leadership based on this dual model: one to lead in affairs of peace, and the other to lead in affairs of war.[27] Prior to the twentieth century, the Cherokee had a white organization that officiated over the civil and religious government and a red one that functioned during times of war.[28] Thus, Cherokee society required both white and red leaders and individuals could choose to walk the white path or the red path by following one of those leaders. The leader, at any given time, or the path taken, depended on the conditions faced by society. White leaders tended to be elders whose experiences enabled them to think in terms of conciliation, reciprocity, and balance. The red leaders, however, tended to be younger men who had not yet gained the experiences that might temper their decisions regarding warfare. White leaders, or peacemakers, were expected to consider their words carefully. Indians understood the power of words and therefore white leaders had to be able to exercise extreme control over what and how they said something. According to the Onondaga,[29] the *Tatodaho,* leader or chief, had to "speak with soft words, guiding people through logic and spiritual means." They described the *Tatodaho* as someone who had to have "skin the thickness of seven layers of bark" meaning people could speak sharply to the leaders, but the leader would not be harmed by their words.[30]

The Indians in the Southeast also had white towns or beloved towns or peaceable towns that were towns of refuge, and human blood was never shed in them. The only way to shed blood was to somehow force the offending person or persons from the town. The Seneca, an Iroquoian nation in the Northeast, had a town of refuge where Gekeah-sawsa, a female peacemaker, resided. Gaustrauyea was a place where one could escape the distress of war irrespective of nationality. If representatives of both sides of a battle sought refuge in Gaustrauyea at the same time, they were divided by curtains of deerskin while they were lodged and fed. Once having enjoyed the hospitality of the peacemaker, neither side could continue their hostilities after leaving the town, except by her consent.[31]

This system of separation of peace leaders from those who would fight was deeply ingrained in the thought and actions of many Indian societies. The Cheyenne,[32] for instance, had a Council of the Forty-four who had the responsibility, individually and collectively, to help maintain peace within and without the nation. Each member of the Council of the Forty-four was chosen by the existing members of the council according to the instructions given by Sweet Medicine, a legendary hero of the Cheyenne. Sweet Medicine advised the Cheyenne to appoint chiefs who are peacemakers. He said, "Though your son might be killed in front of your tepee, you should take a peace pipe and smoke." Peace chiefs may have been members of war societies, and they may have earned honors in battle, but once they became part of the Council of the Forty-four they could not retain membership in a war society. A peace chief's responsibility was to be unconditionally a person of peace. So well understood and accepted was this responsibility that one chief, Little Wolf, who killed a man in a drunken argument over the other's attention to his daughter, voluntarily exiled himself from his people for the remainder of his life. The peacemakers took their responsibility unquestionably and often martyred themselves in pursuit of peace by knowingly walking into harm's way to deliver messages of peace.[33]

The idea of the white path as the harmonious or peaceful way and the red path as the discordant or bloody way is integrated into the social and political structures of many Indian societies. For example, in Creek[34] culture peace is a desirable state, and, therefore, cooperative action between white towns was encouraged and they referred to each other as *anhissi,* "my friend." White towns formed alliances and were linked to each other in various ways. The Creek referred to their oldest clans, the Wind, the Beaver, the Bear, and the Bird, as *Hathagalgi,* the whites, and recognized them as the "leaders in the establishment and maintenance of peace in the nation." They were distinguished from all the other clans who were referred to as *Tcilokogalgi,* speakers of a different language.[35] The red towns, in opposition to the white towns, were associated with conflict and war, attributes antagonistic to harmony and community. Thus, they were characterized by their individuality and isolation from each other.[36] Historically, the white organization held precedence over the red organization, although the effects of American colonization resulted in a breakdown of this policy.[37] For example, when French colonial authorities in 1748 demanded that Choctaw allies attack their own people who had ties with the English to demonstrate their continued goodwill, they did so. However, they also told the French that "they had done themselves much more violence in killing their own brothers than in killing strangers."[38] The Choctaw knew that they had sacrificed their own customs for ensuring order in the world by submitting to French demands.

Even within a community, the Creek kept the white and red clans, or the followers of each way, separated. The Creek *miko,* or chief of the council of a town, could come from either a white clan or a red clan, but the representatives of the white clans usually chose the leader. At the time of installation of office, the *miko* was specifically told to "always be devoted to the white path of peace" and to "never shed human blood."[39] In the ceremonial square of each town the *miko* occupied a center arbor while the warriors occupied the red arbor and the "second men," the white arbor. The *mikos* governed the white towns, and it is they who met with "ambassadors, deputies, and strangers who came to the town" and represented their town in foreign negotiations. The second men were chosen primarily from white clans and were responsible for the internal affairs of the town such as public works, preparation of sacred medicine for ceremonies, or working of communal fields. They also acted as advisors to the *miko.*[40] Thus, the very structure of society oriented a person toward the positive goals of society.

Being a white leader or peacemaker meant more than speaking with soft words or thinking only in terms of peace; it also meant leading by consensus. In a reciprocal manner, one must give up power to exercise power (to gain the allegiance of followers). A peace leader must not unilaterally make decisions, but must listen to the words of everyone concerned. Leaders do not impose their decisions on the populace, but rather make their case in speeches and wait to see who chooses to follow them. One can choose to follow whichever leader. This can increase chances for conflict intra and intertribally as the goals of a particular community may be achieved in opposing ways at the same time. However, rather than diverse approaches leading to factionalism within a community, the nature of popular leadership allowed for individuals to listen to the words of leaders representing both approaches and to change allegiance without repercussion. In other words, because individuals could choose which leader to follow, it was possible for one town to go to war and another one to remain neutral. It also allowed peacemakers to continue to work toward peace, even in the midst of conflict.

The system of white leaders following the peaceful path while red leaders led others into battle proved disastrous for Indian people when they interacted with Europeans who had a different understanding of political leadership and responsibility. For example, during the American Revolution, Beloved Woman, Nancy Ward and her uncle the Beloved Man, Attakullakulla, were leaders of the White Council of Chota. As peacemakers who could not shed blood nor allow bloodshed within the town limits of Chota, they acted as mediators between the

Cherokee and colonial representatives. To prevent bloodshed, Ward went so far as to warn white settlers at Watauga about impending attacks by Cherokee and to accommodate colonial demands for land. A significant number of Cherokee who believed the diplomacy of the white path was ineffectual in stopping colonial intrusions organized under the leadership of Dragging Canoe. He and two other war chiefs, Raven and Abraham, began carrying out campaigns against white settlers in the Cumberland area. Although Dragging Canoe and his followers, who had seceded from the Overhills at Chota to form the Chickamauga, were responsible for attacks against white settlers, the settlers attacked the Cherokee indiscriminately. They held all Cherokee accountable for the actions of the war parties and attacked peaceful towns. The Cherokee system of white and red paths meant that a small war party could attack a frontier settlement that did not distinguish between red and white towns and thus could engage in a massive retaliation against innocent people who chose the white path.[41]

Many Indians recognized the importance of having leaders who did not exercise autocratic or dictatorial power over their people. The danger of such leadership is related in the story of the coming of the Great Law of Peace to the Iroquois Confederacy. At one time the people lived for centuries without strife and everything around them was refreshing and good. Then came a time when leaders began to rule by their power over the people and their actions brought on a period of great strife or darkness among human beings. Everywhere there was suffering and bloodshed. People became distrustful and deceitful and warred with their neighbors. Only when the Peacemaker brought the Great Law of Peace to the Iroquois did the violence end. In order to prevent autocratic control, the Iroquois clan mothers warn leaders when their actions go against the wishes of the people. If those warnings are not heeded, the clan mothers strip the leaders of their power.[42]

There are times when Indian people engaged in war, or followed the red path, the path of conflict and disharmony. To go to war is to die or to cause the death of one's enemies. And the loss of life, for whatever reason, changes the relationships within a community. It creates an imbalance in society and steps must be taken to restore balance. In the case of loss of life, balance is restored through reciprocity and restoration of relationships. Thus, if one loses a sister or brother, mother or father, the family, clan, or nation is compelled to restore balance to the community by replacing that lost relative. The lives of those killed in battle must be replaced so that the family and the community, in the material and spiritual world, can return to a state of balance. That restoration begins with counterattacks against the nation responsible for the death of the relatives in order to obtain captives. Those captives, in turn, replaced the deceased relatives. The person might be adopted by the family who lost a relative and would take the place of that relative with all the responsibilities and obligations of that person. Or, the captive might be sacrificed in order to release the spirits of those relatives who were killed. Adoption or death restored the family and nation back to a state of balance.[43] The emphasis is on the restoration of balance, not the punishing of the person responsible for the loss of life.

The need to restore balance to society, to maintain relationships, has been called restitution or revenge by those who write about Indian warfare. However, the need for balance and the obligations of relationship did not necessarily lead to warfare. The obligation to seek restitution for a life was not one that was easily carried out evenly. One might launch a counterattack for the purpose of gaining captives, and thus opportunity for restitution, but the confusion of warfare could lead to killing more than the number of relatives lost, thus possibly creating an endless cycle of restitution as each side tries to achieve balance. Also, the loss is not attributable solely to the individual or the victim, but is a corporate loss for which the entire clan takes responsibility.[44] The threat of continued warfare forced consideration of the consequences of undertaking warfare. The custom of restitution helped to circumscribe the occasion of warfare because any act of violence resulting in death could lead to prolonged fighting between families, clans, or nations.[45]

Since all people are related and responsibility is corporate as well as individual, decisions must take into consideration the impact on all people. Such a universal approach includes the ancestors as well as those yet to be born. Among many Indian groups any decision takes into account the effects on the seventh generation. Jake Swamp, Wolf Clan Chief of the Mohawk Nation,[46] says, "Our teachings [state] that we must make a place for our children seven generations into the future."[47] Since relationship extends beyond the present time and place into the future and into the past, any action must consider the next seven generations so that they will know how the future unborn generations will benefit or be harmed by such actions.[48] As the Lakota state, the newborn has just come from the spirit world and the elders are about to enter it.[49] Through the cycle of life all are related. Therefore, decisions must take into consideration the effect on ancestors as well as future generations.

All these elements for fostering harmony—leaders who are elders, separation of white and red leaders, consideration of future generations, and consensus leadership—and the religious ideas that inform those elements, facilitated peacemaking among Indian nations. However, as the earlier Cherokee example indicated, those factors can also inhibit peacemaking efforts. Consensus leadership can be a long, drawn-out process as everyone's concerns are considered. Although the white organization in the Southeast held precedence over the red organization, mechanisms, other than persuasion and concerns for community welfare, did not exist to prevent young warriors from initiating acts of war. In fact, if a group of people disagreed with the decisions of a community, they could separate from that community and organize their own community. Separation was considered a viable and appropriate way to settle differences intratribally. However, when cultures that are informed by different political systems and notions of nationhood come into contact, the result can be disastrous as was the case for the Cherokee during the American Revolution. Colonial settlers viewed all Cherokee as responsible for the acts of the seceded Chickamauga. As a result, a number of Cherokee who chose the white path were attacked by settlers seeking revenge, which, in turn, led to further acts of retaliation.

At the beginning of this chapter, I stated that unquestioned appropriation of indigenous religious ideas in order to construct a model of peacebuilding for a global society is problematic. One of my concerns, among others, is that these ideas developed within specific types of communities where they were relevant and accepted as normative by everyone. They might not fit the reality of other societies. However, Indian people are integrating some of these ideas within a Western context in order to assure a healthy, peaceful world for the coming seven generations. The Navajo, for example, have instituted peacemaker courts as part of their justice system. The idea is that western or American justice looks to punishment while the peacemaker approach looks to restore *hozho*. To impose punishment does not restore *hozho* because the sentenced remains in a state of imbalance, and since everyone is related and affected by the thoughts of others, the community is also in a state of imbalance.

The implementation of mediation is, however, a complex undertaking that has the potential to create further community disharmony because Navajo society no longer exists as a fully distinct, autonomous society. Like other colonized peoples, Navajo have internalized many of the values of Western society including those of any number of Christian groups that can undermine or conflict with traditional Navajo values. Some Navajo who undertake the peacemaker process may not speak Navajo or have limited understanding of Navajo values. Thus, in any given mediation the involved parties risk using a traditional process that may apply non-Navajo internalized values in a way that fails to restore everyone to a state of *hozho*. Or they may utilize Navajo values that may not have relevance in a Western context or to an individual who holds Western values that are incongruent with Navajo ideals. Thus, in appropriating American Indian religious ideas for purposes of peacemaking, as shown in the previous case, one must always be cognizant of the differences among cultures that may exacerbate violence rather than facilitate peace.

This concern with incompatible ideas or conditions aside, a composite of the religious ideas that inform peacemakers among American Indian nations can be offered in hopes that some important attributes may be used to inform contemporary peacemaking efforts. American Indians recognize that harmonious or peaceful relations require one to think in terms of reciprocity (balance) and relationships (past, present, and future). Since the red path is disruptive to the welfare of community, one cannot achieve balance if one is involved in both the white and red ways. Thus, those who are chosen to maintain the peaceful way or white path must be dedicated solely to that purpose. They should act in accordance with the corporate nature of their decisions. In other words, any decision should take into consideration the effect not only on contemporary citizens, but also on the next seven generations. Peace leaders should recognize that every word or act has the potential to create balance or cause disharmony. They should understand the power of speech and speak with well-considered "soft" words. Ideally, peace leaders can focus their attention on maintaining peace within their own communities and with other communities, but, perhaps more important, even in the midst of conflict or war, they can continue to advocate peaceful resolutions among their own people and with others.

NOTES

1. In 1953, Congress passed House Concurrent Resolution 108 as part of the federal government's assimilationist termination policy that included relocating Indians off reservations into urban areas.

2. The Navajo Nation currently occupies a reservation in the four-corners region of Arizona, Utah, Colorado, and New Mexico.

3. Gary Witherspoon, *Language and Art in the Navajo Universe* (Ann Arbor: The University of Michigan Press, 1977), pp. 28–34.

4. Before the arrival of the English, the Cherokee occupied the areas now known as Tennessee, Kentucky, North Carolina, South Carolina, and parts of Georgia and Alabama. During the period 1838–1839, the majority of the Cherokee were forcibly removed to what is now the state of Oklahoma.

5. Jack Frederick Kilpatrick and Anna Gritts Kilpatrick, *Run Toward the Nightland* (Dallas, TX: Southern Methodist University Press, 1967), pp. 6–7.

6. Ibid., p. 11.

7. Gary Witherspoon, *Language and Art in the Navajo Universe*, p. 28.

8. Jack Kilpatrick and Anna Kilpatrick, *Run Toward the Nightland*, p. 170.

9. Gary Witherspoon, *Language and Art in the Navajo Universe*, pp. 18, 34.

10. John D. Loftin, "The Harmony Ethic of the Conservative Eastern Cherokees: A Religious Interpretation," *Journal of Cherokee Studies* 8:1 (Spring 1983): p. 40; Robert K. Thomas, "Cherokee Values and World-View," *Typescript* (University of North Carolina), p. 1.

11. Jack Kilpatrick and Anna Kilpatrick, *Run Toward the Nightland*, pp. 149, 151, 153, 167, and 169.

12. Joseph Epes Brown, "Becoming Part of It," in *I Become Part of It*, eds. D. M. Dooling and Paul Jordan-Smith (New York: HarperCollins Publishers, 1992), p. 11.

13. Lakota, popularly referred to as Sioux, have reservations in North and South Dakota and Minnesota.

14. James R. Walker, *Lakota Belief and Ritual* (Lincoln: University of Nebraska Press, 1980, 1991), pp. 35, 50–51.

15. Elaine Jahner, "The Spiritual Landscape," in *I Become Part of It*, eds. D. M. Dooling and Paul Jordan-Smith (New York: HarperCollins Publishers, 1992), p. 202.

16. Raymond J. DeMallie, "Lakota Belief and Ritual in the Nineteenth Century," in *Sioux Indian Religion*, Raymond J. DeMallie and Douglas R. Parks, eds. (Norman: University of Oklahoma Press, 1987, 1988), pp. 27–28; James R. Walker, *Lakota Belief*, p. 70.

17. Raymond J. DeMallie, "Lakota Belief and Ritual," pp. 30–31; James R. Walker, *Lakota Belief and Ritual*, p. 69.

18. In Indian thought, all beings, animate and inanimate (animal, bird, fish, rock, etc.), are persons and have the behavioral characteristics of humans.

19. Elaine Jahner, "The Spiritual Landscape," p. 196.

20. While *hanbleceya* is popularly referred to as a vision quest, the emphasis on vision is misleading. See Jason Gilbreath, "Making More Sense in Lakxota Ritual: A Memoir on the Modification of Embodied Metaphorical Meaning" (Master's thesis, University of Colorado, Boulder, 1998), pp. 66–80.

21. Raymond D. Fogelson, "An Analysis of Cherokee Sorcery and Witchcraft," in *Four Centuries of Southern Indians*, Charles M. Hudson, ed. (Athens: University of Georgia Press, 1975), p. 119.

22. The idea of "evil" is a concept introduced among the Cherokee by missionaries. I believe that malignance or malevolence more clearly indicates the meaning Cherokee attributed to those who engaged in negative thoughts or actions.

23. Raymond D. Fogelson, "An Analysis of Cherokee Sorcery," p. 127.

24. See Mary Churchill, "Walking the 'White Path': Toward a Cherokee-Centric Hermeneutic for Interpreting Cherokee Literature" (Ph.D. dissertation., University of California, Santa Barbara, 1997), p. 178.

25. Cesare Marino, "Honor the Elders: Symbolic Associations with Old Age in Traditional Eastern Cherokee Culture," *Journal of Cherokee Studies*, XIII (1988): pp. 5–6; Charles Hudson, *The Southeastern Indians* (Knoxville: The University of Tennessee Press, 1976, 1994), p. 235.

26. Cesare Marino, "Honor the Elders," p. 6.

27. Charles Hudson, *The Southeastern Indians*, p. 234.

28. Robert K. Thomas, "The Origin and Development of the Redbird Smith Movement" (Master's thesis, University of Arizona, 1953), p. 12.

29. One of the six nations of the Iroquoian Confederacy.

30. Gregory Schaaf, "The American Indian Peace Movement: Past & Present," *Akwesasne Notes* (Fall 1985): p. 7.

31. James Mooney, "Myths of the Cherokee," in *Myths of the Cherokee and Sacred Formulas of the Cherokees* (Nashville: Charles and Randy Elder—Booksellers, 1982, Reprint of *BAE 19th Annual Report, 1897–98*, 1900), p. 208; Sara Gwenyth Parker, "The Transformation of Cherokee Appalachia" (Ph.D. dissertation, University of California, Berkeley, 1991), p. 84.

32. The Cheyenne originally were located in the Central Plains, but eventually were forced southward into what is now Oklahoma.

33. Stan Hoig, *The Peace Chiefs of the Cheyennes* (Norman: University of Oklahoma Press, 1980), pp. 6–11, 67.

34. Originally located in Georgia, the Creek were later forcibly removed to what is now Oklahoma.

35. Charles Hudson, *The Southeastern Indians*, p. 194.

36. Ibid., p. 235.

37. Ibid., p. 24.

38. *Mississippi Provincial Archives French Dominion, 1749–1763*, Vol. 5, eds. Dunbar Rowland and A. G. Sanders, rev. and ed. by Patricia Kay Galloway (Baton Rouge: Louisiana State University Press, 1984), pp. 13, 16, 31.

39. Ibid., pp. 223–224.

40. Charles Hudson, *The Southeastern Indians*, p. 224; John R. Swanton, "Social Organization and Social Usages of the Indians of the Creek Confederacy," *Smithsonian Institution Bureau of American Ethnology Forty-second Annual Report* (Washington: USGPO, 1928), pp. 276–293; 293–296.

41. Sara Gwenyth Parker, "The Transformation of Cherokee Appalachia," pp. 131–134, 141, 153, 159; Theda Perdue, *Cherokee Women Gender and Cul-*

ture Change, 1700–1835 (Lincoln: University of Nebraska Press, 1998), p. 99; Carolyn Thomas Foreman, *Indian Women Chiefs* (Washington, D.C.: Zenger Publishing Co., Inc., 1976), p 73.

42. "Tree of Peace for Harmony," *Akwesasne Notes* (Summer 1985): p. 5; Gregory Schaaf, "The American Indian Peace Movement," p. 7.

43. John Phillip Reid, *A Law of Blood* (New York: New York University Press, 1970), pp. 74–75, 196; John R. Swanton, "Source Material for the Social and Ceremonial Life of the Choctaw Indians," *Smithsonian Institution Bureau of American Ethnology Bulletin 103* (Washington, DC: USGPO, 1931), pp. 104–110.

44. John Phillip Reid, *A Law of Blood*, pp. 75, 85.

45. John R. Swanton, "Source Material for the Social and Ceremonial Life of the Choctaw Indians," pp. 104–105.

46. One of the six nations of the Iroquois Confederacy.

47. Gregory Schaaf, "The American Indian Peace Movement," p. 7.

48. "Tree of Peace for Harmony," p. 5.

49. Joseph Epes Brown, "Becoming Part of It," p. 12.

3

Hinduism and Peacebuilding

RAJMOHAN GANDHI

THE NAME HINDUISM

In historical terms, Hinduism is a relatively new phrase. To begin with, the word Hindu had a territorial rather than a religious connotation. It implied the Indian subcontinent. Before the start of the common era, the ancient Persians and Greeks ran into the great river Sindhu or Indus, which traversed the land mass now bearing the state of Pakistan, and called the people associated with the river Sindhus or Hindus. Centuries later, the Arabs, Central Asian Turks, Mongols, and Afghans intruding into the subcontinent and confronting the Indus also used the words "Hindu" or "Hindi" to mean a resident of India.

It is by no means clear that before the nineteenth century the diverse groups living in different parts of India thought of themselves as belonging to one "religion," as they did not, in any precise sense, see themselves as members of a single Indian polity. Their customs, beliefs, and rituals varied a good deal, and at times there were sharp doctrinal debates. If asked who they were, rather than saying they were "Hindus," they would probably have mentioned a link to their caste, clan, or localized sect.

However, a commonality in the faith of the people was suggested by the fact that pilgrims from different parts of India had been walking for centuries to holy sites in the north, east, west, and south of the subcontinent, as well as by a widespread reverence for the Mahabharata and Ramayana epics, for the Bhagavad Gita, which was seen as a part of the Mahabharata, and for older texts, the Vedas and the Upanishads.

Politically too there seems to have been a vague sense, right from the Mahabharata time (circa 1000 BCE), of something like an Indian nation, later thought of as "Bharat." Hence the phrase "India that is Bharat" in the post-independence Indian constitution.

When Islam and Christianity entered India (in some parts Christianity preceding, and elsewhere following, Islam), there was awareness among residents and newcomers alike of sharp differences in beliefs and customs—sharper, it appeared, than the differences between different Indian sects. The encounter of the beliefs and customs of the residents with the religions of the newcomers produced the name Hinduism[1] and gave form and a measure of standardization to the religious beliefs of the residents. Henceforth "Hindus" came increasingly to mean adherents of the faith (or faiths) of "Hinduism." The two words acquired a religious meaning. But the geographical sense never died out, and our times have witnessed a conscious and politically controversial bid, which we will shortly examine, to marry the religious and territorial meanings.

It has been argued that the very idea of a "religion," with components including uniform belief, a single or chief God, a principal sacred text, and a chief incarnation or prophet, was probably an "explanatory construct" gifted to India by European Orientalists, who could only make sense of India through the classifications and categories they were used to, and also that a Hinduism "standardized" by the Orientalists was "highly welcome" to Indian nationalists in their struggle for an independent nation.[2]

Long before British rule, some of the Muslims who raided or ruled India, and some scholars in their establishments, had also tried to identify the beliefs, texts, and authorities to which India's residents, the Hindus, offered reverence. A few penetrated beyond surface impressions. Thus, the scholar al-Beruni, traveling to India early in the eleventh century with Mahmud of Ghazni's raiding party, which demolished temples and idols, noted that some Hindu philosophers were "entirely free from worshipping anything but God alone."[3] Six centuries later, Prince Dara Shukoh, heir to the Mughal throne but not fated to obtain it,[4] sponsored and possibly authored the translation into Persian of some of the Upanishads, and saw the religion of the Hindus as "a twin brother of Islam."[5]

While it may be a fruit of India's interaction with the world, the name Hinduism connotes ideas, values, and practices born and grown over the centuries in India. As a name for their ancient faith tradition, "Hinduism" is accepted by modern Hindus and by the world. Other names sometimes proposed, for example, Sanatana Dharma (the Eternal Religion) and Vedanta (the End or Acme of the Vedas), while helpful in certain contexts, have failed to supplant "Hinduism" in general usage.

AUTHORITIES AND SOURCES

Hinduism is famously not a religion of a single book or a founder. Its origins are believed by many Hindus to lie in a primordial, unknowable past, and the names of the poets, priests, and contemplatives who composed or intuited the ancient wisdom of the Vedas and the Upanishads are not clearly known. Moreover, Hinduism offers no text of precise commandments and requires no credal statement from an adherent. At times seeming a religion more of birth or race than of belief, it has been called an "ethnic religion . . . which grew along with the nation that gave birth to it."[6]

A popular definition in India, sometimes accepted in courts of law, states that anyone who is not a Muslim or a Christian[7] is a Hindu. In this perspective, Hinduism is India's "natural" religion and all who have not become Christians or Muslims are Hindus.

But Hinduism is also frequently portrayed as "a way of life." Thus *Hindu Dharma: The Universal Way of Life* is the title of a book on Hinduism by one of its respected modern preceptors, Chandrasekharendra Svami of Kanchi.[8] A way of life is more than a question of birth or ethnicity, and makes Hindu values separable from the soil of India. Though there is no accepted short text, ancient or modern, of the Hindu way of life, what the way is may be gleaned from Hindu scriptures, from the lives of good Hindus, and from competent gurus (teachers).

Hindu scriptures are both similar and dissimilar to the Bible and the Qur'an. They evoke a veneration similar to that received by the Christian and Muslim holy books—many Hindus may swear in court on the Gita. Yet Hindus have rejected items in their sacred books without risking a loss of their Hindu status. Moreover, there seems to be no single sacred Hindu text, not even the Gita, that quite occupies the place in Hinduism that the New Testament and the Qur'an enjoy in their religions, or the place that the Guru Granth Sahib enjoys in Sikhism.

Nonetheless the four Vedas—Rig, Sama, Yajur, and Atharva (circa 1500–2000 BCE)—are the earliest source books and sacred books of Hinduism, followed by the numerous Upanishads (circa 500–1000 BCE). The verses of the Upanishads are sometimes referred to as the flowers of the trees of the Vedas, and their contents described as Vedanta, the culmination of the Vedas.

The Upanishads were followed, historically, by the epics, first the Mahabharata and later the Ramayana, even though the events described in the Ramayana are generally though not universally believed to predate the events portrayed in the Mahabharata. Hindu tradition accepts the two epics as itihaasas (histories) as well as dharmashastras or scriptures, and the Mahabharata has been called the fifth Veda. The Bhagavad Gita ("The Song of God"), often simply referred to as the Gita, appears in the course of the Mahabharata. Some scholars, a minority, see it as an independent, interpolated text.

More known than other Hindu scriptures, the Gita has been the subject of numerous scholarly commentaries from the ninth century, if not earlier. In the thirteenth century, a Marathi version and commentary appeared, the first to do so in a language of the people, as distinct from Sanskrit, the language of the learned and privileged elite. Many a celebrated Hindu of modern times has also attempted a personal commentary.

However, the Gita's impact is complex. Its battlefield setting and the exhortation to fight like a warrior that Lord Krishna makes to Arjuna at the start of the poem have enabled some to interpret the Gita as a call to arms, but the bulk of the Hindus appear to see the Gita outside its battlefield context. In their view, the Gita asks them to do their duty without concern for fruits or results, and contains God's assurance to human beings of grace and protection if they but turn to him.[9] Rich as the Vedas, the Upanishads and the Gita are, and in places poetic and touching, their meaning is not always clear or simple. The average Hindu venerates these Sanskrit texts, some Hindus can recite verses from them, and a gifted few in almost all ages have composed commentaries on the texts. Yet most Hindus shy away from attempting to understand them fully.

It is the epics that the average Hindu is familiar with, and it is from them that "almost all Hindus, from the prince to the peasant, derive their early religious ideas."[10] The modern Hindu learns his Hinduism not so much from the Vedas, the Upanishads, or even the Gita but principally from the following sources:

- Message-stories from the Hindu tradition told in the home, some centered on the epics

- Discourses (frequently epic-linked) by gurus or swamis from neighborhood, temple or public platforms, or, increasingly, on television, radio, cassette, or tape

- Popular devotional songs, frequently based on the Bhakti poetry that flowered across India from about the fifteenth century and was often epic-related

- Popular literature linked to all of these

- Festivals that festoon the Hindu calendar, turning up once a month or oftener, and offering opportunities for entering into the meaning of a prescribed ceremony or a mythological tale.

PEACEBUILDING AND HINDUISM

War is prominent in both the epics, and dominates the Mahabharata. That good triumphs over evil, but after fighting it, is sometimes seen as a key message of the Ramayana. The "message" of the Mahabharata is harder to pinpoint, for although it portrays good versus evil sides—the Pandavas against their cousins the Kauravas—and the "good" Pandavas "win" the war, in the end almost every character in the Mahabharata's huge cast is slain. The Mahabharata can be cited to justify war or prove its unmitigated folly.

Krishna, seen in the Mahabharata as an incarnation of God, leads a mission for peace between the cousins but seems to have greater ardor for the defeat and destruction of the Kauravas. Yet ahimsa (nonviolence), kshama (forgiveness), and shanti (peace) are values mentioned with unequivocal favor in the Vedas, the Upanishads, the Gita, and the Mahabharata, and there are episodes in the epics, and verses in the earlier scriptures, that show the error in hate, anger, and violence, and the advantages of consensus, compassion, and justice.

Making, in his 1978 study, *War and Peace in the World's Religions,* the indisputable remark that "Indian history has not been lacking in wars," John Ferguson added, "and there has been little in Hindu religion to inhibit this."[11] The latter phrase may be questioned if it implies that the Hindu religion fails to stress the importance of peace—peace is prayed for numberless times in the Vedas—or is indifferent toward the values conducive to peace, such as justice, tolerance, and consensus.

Yet it must be conceded that peacemaking is an exercise about which the literature of Hinduism has generally been silent. The index pages of studies on Hinduism almost always reveal entries for yoga, meditation, self-control, truth, and ahimsa, to mention some key words, but peacebuilding, peacemaking, reconciliation, or even peace seldom occurs in an index.[12]

We may note, too, that while Hinduism's concern with peace and pluralism was eloquently brought out at the gathering of the world's religious leaders convened by the United Nations in August 2000, Hinduism's eminent representatives at the gathering did not quite spell out the steps that Hindus (and non-Hindus) could take for building peace.

Such omissions constitute facets of a great paradox that Hindus must face: the extent of continuing bloodshed in a land where calls for peace and nonviolence have echoed for more than 3000 years.

OBSTACLES TO PEACEBUILDING IN HINDUISM

The first obstacle is cultural or psychological, a self-image of innate peaceableness that Hindus have long preserved and handed down. This self-image has successfully withstood past and present explosions of violence among Hindus and in their interactions with others. A modest attempt to disturb this self-perception was made by this author in his *Revenge and Reconciliation: Understanding South Asian History* (New Delhi: Penguin, 1999); here we will merely record the difficulty and acknowledge its significance.

I will also examine three other obstacles: (1) the link between religion and nationalism that Hindu tradition has allowed and often fostered; (2), memory and its calls for revenge, often supported by examples from the epics; and (3), the divisive, hierarchical, and conflict-generating feature of caste.

The bid to marry the religious and territorial connotations of "Hindu" is part of the ideology of Hindutva, which translates roughly as Hinduness. The term was first used, it would seem, by the revolutionary and poet, Vinayak Damodar Savarkar (1883–1957), who engaged for some time in violent activities against British rule and spent several years in prison, but later identified the Muslims as the Hindus' chief enemy.

The Rashtriya Swayamsevak Sangh (RSS), or the National Volunteers' Association, a "cultural" body founded in 1925 by K. B. Hedgewar, and steered from 1940 to 1973 by M. S. Golwalkar, adopted the Hindutva ideology, which Golwalkar developed. The Bharatiya Janata Party (BJP), the political party that leads the coalition government ruling India since 1998, has also from time to time espoused Hindutva, though India's BJP Prime Minister, Atal Behari Vajpayee, has frequently asserted a liberal and secular commitment missing in Hindutva.

Following Savarkar's lead, Hindutva literature defines good Indians as those to whom India is both their homeland and their holy land, a criterion that makes India's Muslims and Christians unpatriotic by definition. Many Hindus uneasy about Hindutva and about such a definition nonetheless think of Hinduism (and Buddhism, Jainism, and Sikhism) as Indian religions, and of Islam, Christianity, Zoroastrianism, and Judaism as foreign.

Hindutva's fusion of religion and country is nowhere franker than in Golwalkar's *Bunch of Thoughts*.[13] Of India's Muslims and Christians, he says: "They are born in this land, no doubt. But are they true to its salt? Are they grateful towards this land . . . ? Do they feel . . . that to serve it is their great good fortune? No." India's Hindus, on the other hand, have sacrificed for Bharat and possess "a common memory of the happy and unhappy experiences of their past life."[14] In fact, according to Golwalkar, the "Hindu People . . . is the Almighty manifesting Himself. . . . The Hindu People is our God."[15]

The extent to which Hindutva's champions can go to make "Indian" synonymous with "Hindu" is also demonstrated in a 1994 publication authored by B. N. Jog and entitled *Threat of Islam: Indian Dimensions* (Bombay: Unnati Prakashan, 1994). Complaining that the Indian National Congress, the body that led the struggle for Indian independence and ruled free India for forty-five years, "propagated" from 1885 (the year the Congress was founded) "the new doctrine . . . that Muslims are nationals of this country" the writer claims that "[In Spain], converted Muslims were given option either to return to their original fold of Christianity, or death or expulsion from Spain. This is the way they found most appropriate to deal with Islam."[16] "By contrast," laments Jog, "in India nobody even thought on the lines of Spain. The resultant effect is there for everyone to see . . . Hindus never thought of bringing back converted Muslims to their original Hindu fold. This serious lacuna resulted in keeping alive Islam."[17]

Jog is buoyed, however, by the 1992 demolition by Hindutva enthusiasts of the Babri mosque in Ayodhya in the state of Uttar Pradesh. The demolition had occurred after a long all-India campaign against the existence of a Muslim mosque on the supposed site of the birth of the Hindu god Rama. A landmark in the campaign was the 1990 "rath yatra" ("chariot drive") conducted by Lal Krishna Advani, the BJP President. Advani traversed India in a Toyota truck that had been converted to look like an epic-era rath or chariot. Viewing the demolition as "the beginning of a new glorious phase of India's long and chequered history," Jog cites with approbation, a comment from the writer V. S. Naipaul:

> The people who climbed on top of these domes and broke them were not bearded people wearing saffron robes and with ash on their foreheads. They were young people clad in jeans and T-shirts. One needs to understand the passion that took them on top of these domes. The jeans and T-shirts are superficial. The passion alone is real. You can't dismiss it.[18]

Following the demolition, Jog's hope is that "the majority of Indian Muslims will be prevailed upon to return to their original fold. This is the only sure way to put an effective end to the suffer[ing of Hindus]."[19] That is, Muslims must become Hindus if they want acceptance as Indians.

Christians, followers of another "foreign" religion, must do likewise. Though Jog lauds Spain's presumed success in expelling Islam, Hindutva is not tolerant of the presence of Christian missionaries, and some Hindutva voices have defended the man believed to be responsible for the 1999 torching, in the Indian state of Orissa, of Graham Staines, an Australian missionary and his two boys.

Until the 1980s, studies on Hinduism often ended with Mohandas Karamchand Gandhi's (1869–1948) nonviolent struggles for independence and social change in India, as well as Gandhi's reinvigoration of Hinduism's nonviolent strands and India's pluralism. More recent studies close with the rise of Hindu nationalism. Gandhi's vision for India and version of Hinduism clashed fundamentally with Hindutva and Hindu nationalism. His ideals of nonviolence, forgiveness, and equality, which he located firmly in the Hindu tradition, were at odds with Hindutva's advocacy of retaliation and Hindu primacy. By example, when Hindu-Muslim violence occurred in 1946–1947, Gandhi asked Hindus to fight attackers but to refrain from initiating attacks.

On 12 September 1947, Gandhi told RSS activists invited by him in New Delhi that Hinduism would be destroyed if Muslims in India were treated as slaves; and Islam would be finished if Hindus in Pakistan were enslaved. One of the activists asked Gandhi whether Hinduism did not permit the killing of an evildoer. Answered Gandhi: "How could a sinner claim the right to judge or execute another sinner?" That right belonged only to a properly constituted government, Gandhi explained.[20]

Hindutva's champions made several attempts on Gandhi's life before the final and successful one on 30 January 1948. The penultimate bid was made on 20 January by a group that included the men who were to succeed later. One of the conspirators, Madanlal Pahwa, whose grenade missed Gandhi, was arrested; the others, including Nathuram Godse, who ten days later would fire the fatal bullets, slipped away. Pahwa told the police that God wanted him to destroy Gandhi, who was Hinduism's enemy. Commented Gandhi on 21 January:

You should not have any kind of hate against [Madanlal]. . . . Those who are behind him or whose tool he is should know that this sort of thing will not save Hinduism. If Hinduism is to be saved it will be saved through such work as I am doing. I have been imbibing Hindu dharma right from my childhood. . . . Do you want to annihilate Hindu dharma by killing a devout Hindu like me?[21]

According to Jog, the Hindutva proponent quoted earlier, Gandhi's flaw and offense were that he asked "Hindus to treat Muslims as brothers."[22]

In *Our Religions,* Arvind Sharma writes about "the new Hindu fundamentalism" that places "Gods rather than Gandhi on the pedestal" and adds "If the current pressures continue, Hindus will increasingly view religious tolerance as a right that one Hindu extends to another Hindu within Hinduism, but as a privilege that must be earned by those outside Hinduism on clearly defined terms."[23]

Hindutva's sense of Islam as "foreign" joins a deep sense that wrongs perpetrated on Hindus by Muslims over centuries—destruction of temples, forcible conversions, massacres—have to be undone. As well, opinion in Pakistan holds that India persists in denying freedom to the Muslims of Kashmir and grudges the existence of Pakistan. Along with this is the reality that India and Pakistan both have nuclear capability. The end result is a hazardous situation for South Asia and beyond.

Hindutva votaries at times claim religious authorization for war, revenge, and violence, citing the killings accomplished in the epics and allegedly recommended in the Gita. Their rhetoric is matched and sometimes outmatched by calls for jihad from Pakistan. Verbal pyrotechnics reached their peak during the Kargil conflict in the summer of 1999. What *Panchajanya,* the RSS's Hindi journal, wrote on 20 June 1999, while the war was on, throws light on the place of memory, revenge, and the Other in the Hindutva mind:

> This has been going on for centuries now. Bharat's borders have always been violated by Islamic invaders. . . . These invaders have always been ruthless and devious. They have always attacked us stealthily in the dark of the night. . . . They never change their ways except when the hands of brave soldiers go for their jugular.
>
> This inhuman lot can never forget 1971! *(India defeated Pakistan in the 1971 war, which resulted in the independence of Bangladesh from Pakistan.)* Like bleating goats, 94,000 jihadis had then stood, their hearts bowed in abject surrender before our brave soldiers. Had it been some Islamic country in our place, it would have beheaded the entire lot and dispatched 94,000 skulls to Islamabad. But true to our own civilized values and culture, we even fed milk to these 94,000 snakes. Fed on our generosity, they all returned well fattened to their homeland. . . .
>
> Six of our soldiers on patrol [were] tortured in such inhuman ways that even hearing or reading about it is intolerable. The blood of every

Indian is on the boil today. From Ladakh to Kanyakumari the entire nation is raising only one demand—Revenge! Revenge!

The time has come again for India's Bhima to tear open the breasts of these infidels and purify the soiled tresses of Draupadi with blood. *(A famous episode from the Mahabharata.)* Pakistan will not listen just like that. We have a centuries' old debt to settle with this mindset.

Arise, Atal Behari! Who knows if fate has destined you to be the author of the final chapter of this long story. For what have we manufactured bombs? For what have we exercised the nuclear option?[24]

The journal's English-language counterpart, *Organiser,* carried (on 20 June 1999) a comment by Rajendra Singh, the RSS chief, that recalled the 1675 beheading, ordered by Delhi's Mughal ruler, of the Sikh Guru Tegh Bahadur and the inhuman killing of the guru's associates. Singh claimed that the Pakistani "mindset" and their "civilization" were "barbaric" and "bestial" from the roots. Pakistani statements at the time suggested that Hindus were death-fearing heathens doomed to defeat at jihadist hands. Dismissing the world of 1999, the comments invoked ancient times—mythical as well as historical—when "our" ancestors were noble martyrs and "their" ancestors were uncivilized oppressors.

A year earlier, Baikunth Lal Sharma "Prem," national secretary of the Vishwa Hindu Parishad (VHP), an RSS affiliate that had led the campaign for the removal of the Babri mosque, announced the VHP's plans to build a Rs. 100 crore ($23 million) monument on a five-acre plot near Delhi's Qutub Minar, which would depict the "massacre of Hindus by Muslim and British invaders."[25]

Gandhi had recommended a different, and perhaps more difficult, attitude toward history's wrongs. "I cannot return evil for evil," he said on 25 December 1947. "Hindus must not remember the wrong that Ghaznavi *(the eleventh-century raider and destroyer)* did. Muslims must realize and admit the wrongs perpetrated under the Islamic rule." [26]

In their 1999 study of South Asian security, Praful Bidwai and Achin Vanaik provide this sobering assessment of Hindutva:

This ideology is based on a toxic, belligerent, paranoid, and sectarian nationalism, which sees Hindus as the classical victims of invasion and conquest, who must now settle scores with the "invaders" (principally Muslims) by "uniting" and "militarizing" themselves, and creating an awe-inspiring Hindu state. This framework regards peace, nonviolence and justice as effete, and secular Gandhi as a villain out to emasculate Hindu "manhood"—someone to be eliminated, as indeed he was by a fanatic inspired by the ideology of the Rashtriya Swayamsevak Sangh.[27]

CASTE

No ancient society anywhere, in China, Greece, Iran, or elsewhere, was free of hierarchies and classes, but the rigidities of the Indian caste system have endured to our day because of the religious support given to it. To eat or marry with those outside your *varna* (caste) or *jaati* (subcaste) took you outside the Hindu pale and can still invite ostracism; contact between a "caste" Hindu and a member of an "untouchable" *jaati* was (and often is, even today) deemed polluting to the former and sinful for the latter.

How Hinduism could espouse *advaita* or nonduality, the notion of all life being one, and simultaneously offer religious support to untouchability and caste inequality is another of its formidable paradoxes—and a lasting cause for conflict. Democracy, recurring elections, the fact that "untouchables" (the "Scheduled Castes" as they are constitutionally described, or Dalits—"oppressed"—the phrase preferred by "untouchable" activists) compose at least 15 percent of the Indian population, and the additional fact that Indian voters are often more interested in a candidate's caste or subcaste than in his or her party or ideology mean that caste is as much a political as a social category. Caste is also an economic category: "lower" and "untouchable" groups are poorer than the "higher" *jaatis*. Hindu society's failure in justice and reconciliation is from time to time proclaimed by the suppression and violence invited by Dalit assertion, and by the frequent anti-Dalit bias of the police and the lower judiciary.

Some opponents of Hindutva have sought, in places successfully, to unite Dalits, the "lower" castes, India's religious minorities (Muslims, Christians, Sikhs, and Buddhists), and India's aborigines or tribals, who are roughly 8 percent of the population,[28] against the "higher" *jaatis*, who add up to less than 10 percent of India. The strategy has been countered, sometimes with profit, by the offer of conspicuous positions in Hindutva's political and religious campaigns to Dalit, tribal or "lower" caste individuals, and by calls to "lower" castes and tribals to lead the defense of Hindu honor.

PEACEBUILDING IN HINDU TRADITION

Hinduism's literature may have failed to classify instances, tales, or techniques of peacebuilding, but Hindu tradition offers several examples of it, and Hindu scriptures clearly authorize peacebuilding. To start with the Vedas, the Atharva Veda has these prayer-lines, an indication of sorrow over war and of a desire for reconciliation with strangers:

Let us have concord with our own people,/ and concord with people who are strangers to us./ Asvins *(celestial twins)*, create between us and the strangers a unity of hearts. May we unite in our minds, unite in our purposes, and not fight against the heavenly spirit within us. Let not the battle-cry rise amidst many slain, nor the arrows of the war-god fall with the break of day. (Book VII: 52)[29]

The word "shanti" (peace) occurs twelve times in the short prayer composing the seventeenth verse of Chapter 36 of the Yajur Veda. Peace is sought in the celestial regions, in the intermediate regions, on earth, for herbs, trees, and plants, to all things in the universe, and to the one praying. The verse that follows reads: "Strong one! Make me strong,/ May all beings look on me with the eye of a friend,/ May I look on all beings with the eye of a friend,/ May we look on one another with the eye of a friend" (Yajur Veda, 36:18).[30] The Yajur Veda refers to forgiveness, compassion, and service as key values (40:6), but exhorts some verses later: "O brave warrior,/ Pounce upon your enemy/Like an Eagle/ And annihilate him" (4:34).[31] Enmity and war seemed part of daily life around the Vedas' anonymous writers. Despite, or perhaps because of that, the Vedas offer promises such as these: "The union of hearts and minds/ & freedom from hate I'll bring you./ Love one another as the cow/ loves the calf that she has borne" (Atharva Veda, III:30; i.).[32]

Then there is the oft-recited invocation for unity and peace with which the Katha Upanishad opens, and that occurs in other Upanishads as well. W. B. Yeats's translation, made in the 1930s with help from Purohit Swami, reads as follows: "May He protect us both. May He take pleasure in us both. May we show courage together. May spiritual knowledge shine before us. May we never hate one another. May peace and peace and peace be everywhere."[33]

We can mark, in the foregoing verse, the preference for "we" and "us" over "I" and "me." We may note, too, that one cause of conflict, pride, is memorably tackled in the line from the Kena Upanishad, "The man who claims he knows, knows nothing; but he who claims nothing, knows." While another cause of conflict, greed, is addressed in the Katha Upanishad line, "The good is one, the pleasant another," the Brihadaranyaka Upanishad's celebrated prayer, seeking delivery from "the unreal to the real, from darkness to light, from death to eternal life," could inspire contemporary Hindus to seek a passage from conflict to peace.

PEACEBUILDING IN THE EPICS

Though the Mahabharata is dominated by a chain of revenge and counter-revenge and ends in all-round slaughter, powerful images of peace punctuate the epic. One of the most dramatic appears after the war. Affected by the grief of bereaved women and of surviving, "victorious" princes over the death of loved ones, teachers, heroes, and cousins, the epic's author, Vyasa, who from time to time enters the scenes he has created, says to the mourners, "I shall dispel your grief."

1. That night, after a roar in the waters, the dead emerge from the Bhagirathi river. In P. Lal's rendering,

> Cleansed of hate and jealousy/ Son met father and mother, wife met husband,/ Friend greeted friend./ The Pandavas met Karna *(their heroic but unrecognized half-brother and their enemies' ally, whom they had killed),/* And embraced him./ A scene of reconciliation:/ No grief, no fear, no suspicion, no reproach,/ Nothing but the meeting of loving minds.[34]

By dawn, however, the reunion is over, and those brought back to life have returned to the depths of the Bhagirathi.

2. In another scene, Yudhishthira, whose wife Draupadi had been cruelly humiliated by Yudhishthira's cousins the Kauravas, answers Draupadi's pressure for revenge: "Draupadi, my beautiful wife . . . / How will the world run/ If bitterness rewards bitterness,/ Injury is returned for injury, hate for hate,/ If fathers suspect sons, sons suspect fathers,/ If trust disappears between husband and wife?"

Adding that forgiveness was the only virtue, that it was sacrifice, the Vedas, and "our tradition," that it was holiness and held the world together, Yudhishthira concludes: "Do not argue me away from forgiveness, my wife."[35]

3. From his deathbed, the Mahabharata's old hero, Bhishma, tells Yudhishthira a story where an old lady, whose son had been killed, replies to a remark, "Killing an enemy brings merit," by saying, "Forgiving an enemy brings greater merit."

4. In another interesting Mahabharata dialogue, Vyasa says to Gandhari, who has lost her sons in the war, "This is the time for forgiveness. Cast off anger, Gandhari. *Cultivate the art of peace.*"[36] (Emphasis added.)

5. To demonstrate Pandava hegemony after the war, Arjuna, the Pandava "star" and Yudhishthira's younger brother, rides across India. In the Saindhava territory (Sindh), he is met outside her palace by Duhshala, sister of the defeated and killed Kauravas, and a child. Duhshala had been married to the Kaurava warrior, Jayadratha, whom Arjuna had (not very fairly) killed. Arjuna asks Duhshala about her son Suratha. "He is dead," says Duhshala, adding: "He died of a broken heart, for he knew that you had killed his father. I now bring you his son, and I seek your protection."

Vyasa proceeds:

Arjuna stared at the ground. Great sorrow afflicted him. "I am your sister," Duhshala said. "You will not refuse me. As Parikshit is to your son Abhimanyu *(deceitfully killed in the war),* this boy is to my son Suratha. I have come to plead for the lives of my people." . . . Arjuna embraced Duhshala, and asked her to return to her palace. *Then he made peace with the Saindhavas.*[37] (Emphasis added.)

The Arjuna-Duhshala encounter is a rare peacemaking event in the Mahabharata. Elsewhere in the nearly 100,000 verses of the epic, revenge is a constantly recurring fact while reconciliation is a fancy; forgiveness is preached but vengeance practiced. Nonetheless, the brief yet powerful Arjuna-Duhshala meeting is part of the Hindu tradition. As has been observed: "The great poet, who does not minimize his words on many other occasions, does not dare to say more here."[38]

The Ramayana: Wars in the epics are between the good and the evil side. Destruction of the evil side, rather than reconciliation between two embittered and flawed sides, is the great theme. Yet the honorable treatment of the defeated side is a positive message from the Ramayana.

After killing Ravana, the demonic ruler of Lanka who had abducted Rama's beautiful and virtuous wife, Sita, the victorious prince Rama gives due honour and autonomy to Ravana's brother Vibhishana, who is installed as Lanka's new ruler. (Failing to bring Ravana to reason, Vibhishana had crossed over to Rama's side.) War and defeat are followed by the institution of a stable, lawful, and indigenous government on the island of Lanka, as well as by decent funeral rites for the enemy deceased. This may be seen as a form of peacemaking, of a positive transition to peace.

Of the several Ramayana texts read and recited in India, the three principal ones are Valmiki's in Sanskrit, the "original" version, perhaps composed around 200 CE; Kamban's Tamil Ramayana prepared in possibly the twelfth century; and Tulsidas's sixteenth-century text, written in the Hindi dialect of the Awadh region of modern UP but understood in most of northern, central and western India. In the main, but with a few detours, Kamban and Tulsidas follow Valmiki.

One of the first English translations of Valmiki's Sanskrit Ramayana was by Manmath Nath Dutt, *The Ramayana.* The following conversation, after Ravana's death, between Rama and Vibhishana, is taken from Dutt.[39]

Rama to Vibhishana: Do thou perform the funeral ceremonies of thy brother and console his wives. *V.:* I do not think it proper to do so for he who was wicked, cruel, [a] liar and who had ravished others' wives. [Ravana] is my enemy and not worthy of my adoration.

Rama: Although [he] perpetrated many vicious and impious deeds still he was powerful, heroic and strong in warfare. . . . Enmity extends [only] up to death—so it hath ended. . . . Do thou perform the ceremony. He is unto me as he is unto thee. It behoveth thee to perform [the ceremony]—thou shalt be praised.

We should mark that Rama's words include a call for objectivity, a plea for wisdom, and an assurance of support—"Don't think I will mind your doing this," he seems to tell Vibhishana. "As he is your brother, he becomes mine too." Finally, Rama speaks of what Vibhishana may gain: "Thou shalt be praised." The components add up to a peacebuilding strategy. Struck by Rama's attitude toward Ravana's funeral rites, Monier Williams wrote in his *Indian Wisdom* in 1875, "Contrast this with Achilles' treatment of Hector."[40]

Another episode of forgiveness included in Valmiki's Ramayana and "treasured by generations of pious [Hindus]"[41] relates to the visit that Hanuman, the monkey-god who is Rama's faithful and resourceful servant, makes to Sita after Ravana's death, who is still in detention in Ravana's garden. Pointing to the demonesses ringing Sita, Hanuman says to Sita that he would like to slay her tormentors. Sita replies:

I wish in compassion to protect the slaves of Ravana. It was under the orders of the titan that these women ill-treated me. He being slain, they will no longer oppress me. There is an ancient saying full of wisdom which a bear uttered in the presence of a tiger; hear it:

"A superior being does not render evil for evil. This is a maxim one should observe. . . . One should never harm the wicked or the good or even animals meriting death. A noble soul will exercise compassion even towards those who enjoy injuring others or [commit] cruel deeds. . . . Who is without fault?"[42]

These words, "Who is without fault?" uttered by the much-loved figure of Sita, innocent object of Ravana's lust and cruelty, constitute a rich reconciling weapon bequeathed by Hindu tradition.

The meaning of a chariot: In the Valmiki and Kamban Ramayanas, when, just before the climax of the war, a Rama who is on foot faces a Ravana ensconced in a strong chariot, celestial voices exclaim, "This

contest is unequal, Rama is on foot, whilst the titan is in a chariot,"
whereupon a celestial chariot descends for Rama. But Tulsidas takes
another path. He puts the lament about the unequal character of the
contest in Vibhishana's mouth, not in "celestial voices."

"Ravana is in a chariot and you on your feet. How will you fight?"
asks Vibhishana. Rama replies in Tulsidas's Ramayana, "Do you know,
Vibhishana, the real meaning of a chariot?"

> Listen friend *(continued Rama)*, the chariot that leads to victory is of
> another kind. Valour and fortitude are its wheels; truthfulness and vir-
> tuous conduct are its banner; strength, discretion, self-restraint and
> benevolence are its four horses, harnessed with the cords of forgive-
> ness, compassion and equanimity. . . . Whoever has this righteous char-
> iot, has no enemy to conquer anywhere.[43]

Hindus have every right to point out to Hindutva champions that
this chariot that Rama describes, with self-restraint as one of its horses,
and cords of forgiveness and compassion to harness it, was mocked by
the Toyota chariot that in Rama's name stirred up dust, passion, and
fear in the autumn of 1990.

In this passage, Tulsidas appears to draw out what is hidden in
Valmiki. Stating, through Rama's lips, that the chariot is only figurative,
Tulsidas almost hints that the Rama-Ravana war too is allegorical, that
the Ramayana is a tale not so much of a war between "good" and "evil"
groups as of the battle between good and evil in every heart.

The distinction is of course supremely significant for peacemaking, and
relevant also to the meaning of the Gita. In the Gita, Krishna, God's incar-
nation, is presented on the battlefield of Kurukshetra ("the field of the
Kurus") as charioteer to Arjuna, the outstanding warrior on the ("good")
Pandava side. Arjuna quails at the thought of killing the elders and teach-
ers ranged with his Kaurava cousins, but after listening in his chariot to
Krishna's discourse on life, death, and self-control, he decides to do
Krishna's bidding, which is to fight.

So is the Gita's teaching to take up arms and fight "the enemy"? Hindutva ideologues have always said, "Yes." But many scholars have disagreed. As stated earlier, some see the Gita as an interpolation into, and
apart from, the Mahabharata. Others take both the Gita and the Mahabharata as allegories. V. S. Sukthankar, one of the epic's most respected
scholars,[44] wrote that the Mahabharata and the Gita both hint at the
"psychological conflict within man of the good and evil propensities."

Pointing out that the Gita calls the body "kshetra" or field (13:1),
Sukthankar sees Arjuna as the human soul, Krishna the charioteer as the
divine guide, and Kurukshetra as "the battlefield of the different emo-

tions and passions in the heart of man."[45] For his interpretation Suk-thankar does not need to draw on his imagination alone. The Yajur Veda and the Katha Upanishad both speak of the soul as riding in a chariot, and of the body as the chariot.

Perhaps the best-known summary of the Gita's message in Hindi-speaking India (roughly a third of the country) is the one-page Gita-Saar, or the Gita-Essence, often stuck on the sides of three-wheeler taxi-cabs or on a wall in offices, schools, tea-shops and barber shops. It makes no reference to war. Part of its text says: "Wipe out mine-thine, high-low, ours-theirs from your mind. . . . Keep offering whatever you do to God."[46]

If Tulsidas, Sukthankar, and the Gita-Saar are right; if the chariots steered by Rama or Krishna are available for carrying humans on the journey of life and not meant for fighting the other side with arrows and guns; if the body is the chariot, Arjuna stands for any individual, and Krishna and Rama are names for the Indwelling Guide exhorting us to fight the battle of life, against despair, against depression and fatalism, against evil, including hatred and fanaticism—if these things are true, then the epics, whose wide influence we noted at the start of this chapter, become the peacemaker's greatest allies.

STORIES FROM THE PURANAS

Put together several centuries after the epics but claiming to chronicle the lives of the Hindu trinity—Brahma, Vishnu, and Shiva (one of whom, Vishnu, is said to have visited the earth as Rama and Krishna)—and of other meritorious beings, the Puranas also command Hindu respect and curiosity. Some Purana stories may help the reconciler and peacemaker. We can look at one of them, taken from the Vishnu Purana.

Two cousins, Kesidhwaja and Khandikya, were mutually hostile. Kesidhwaja, a king endowed with spiritual knowledge, had driven off his cousin Khandikya, an expert in efficacious religious rites, from the latter's small kingdom in the neighborhood to the forests, but found he needed Khandikya's help: a cow in Kesidhwaja's care had been killed, and only Khandikya could teach him the rite for canceling the serious offense.

Rejecting the advice of his counselors, Kesidhwaja sought out his cousin, who, suspicious to begin with, drew his sword. But when Kesidhwaja explained his purpose, the cousin rejected the advice of *his* counselors, who wanted Kesidhwaja killed. Khandikya told them: "True, by such an act (killing) I should become the monarch of the whole earth; he would however conquer the world to come. . . . It seems to me that this world is not of more value than the next, for the next world endureth for ever; the conquest over this is but for a brief season. I will therefore not kill him but tell him what he asks to know."

Khandikya did as he said, and Kesidhwaja was able to perform an adequate rite of penance. When, in due course, Kesidhwaja went, once more against the advice of counselors, to thank Khandikya and offered him, as a pupil must to a guru, "the *dakshina* (gift) of your choosing," Khandikya could have remembered the old ejection and asked, as his advisors urged him, for the cousin's kingdom. Instead Khandikya sought spiritual wisdom, which Kesidhwaja freely offered.

In this story, mutually inimical cousins (who in the Mahabharata and elsewhere in Hindu mythology usually destroy one another) turn to each other for necessary help—for an exchange of technology, one might almost say—and thereby avoid fratricide. We learn from the story that enemies whom we fear and would rather kill may have what we need and want what we have, a basis for a peace deal. Also, kings, chiefs, and leaders can follow what their inner heart desires rather than their advisors. Finally, the argument that "the next world is longer-lasting than this world" may without injury to the story's spirit be taken to mean, "The future is longer-lasting than the present. Let's do what is wise for the future."[47]

RECONCILIATION IN HISTORY

The sorrow and contrition in Asoka, ruler of much of India in the third century BCE, after the carnage of his Kalinga war, and Asoka's subsequent commitment to the paths of peace are cherished items in the Hindu tradition. Buddhism may have been promoted by Asoka, yet Hindus see him as part of their past. Asoka remains one of the most popular names for a Hindu child, and, engraved on rock and pillar, his thoughts have entered the Hindu discourse:

> On conquering Kalinga [the king] felt remorse, for when an independent country is conquered, the slaughter, death, and deportation of people is extremely grievous to [him]. . . . What is even more deplorable to [him] is that those who dwell there . . . all suffer violence, murder and separation from their loved ones. . . . The participation of all men in suffering weighs heavily on the mind of [the king] (13th Major rock Edict),
>
> Whoever honors his own sect and disparages that of another man, harms his own even more seriously. . . . Concord is to be commended, so that one may hear one another's principles (12th Major Rock Edict).
>
> Thus speaks the Beloved of the Gods, the king: One only notices one's good deeds, thinking, "I have done good," but on the other hand

one does not notice one's wicked deeds [or admit], "I have done evil." . . . Now to be aware of this is something really difficult (3rd Pillar Edict). [48]

Ages later, the Bhakti poets, who sprang up from about the fifteenth century in different parts of India and wrote songs in popular languages for the common people, buttressed Hinduism's reconciling, egalitarian, and practical strands. Announcing that Hindus and Muslims worshipped the same God, who valued character more than caste and conduct more than ritual, this poetry fostered Hindu-Muslim accommodation at the grass roots. Loved to this day, and sung by professionals, amateurs, and in the home, Bhakti poetry continues to describe the Other as a soul of equal value. Activists for pluralism and peace tap regularly into it and attempt contemporary versions. A recent figure who employed Bhakti songs for popularizing a reconciling Hinduism was Gandhi.

Looking, in a 1994 study, at conflict resolution in the Hindu context, Harvey Cox and Arvind Sharma speak of "the familiar profile of the man in loincloth, sandals, and spectacles who was perhaps the twentieth century's greatest exemplar of religiously inspired conflict resolution."[49] A colonized India's struggle with Britain, the age-old Hindu-Muslim divide, and the even older divide between caste Hindus and untouchables—these were the conflicts that Gandhi strove to resolve through nonviolence, which to him was principle and strategy both.

Gandhi sought to differentiate his nonviolence from that of the mouse who is afraid of the cat, hates it, and would kill it if it could. The mouse flees from the cat out of fear, not out of ahimsa. Gandhi wanted Hindus (and other Indians) to be strong and unafraid and yet nonviolent. It was an exceedingly difficult goal, yet Gandhi was able, in his lifetime, to persuade large numbers of Hindus toward ahimsa, even if not lastingly.

Insisting that the God of the Hindus was the same as the God of the Muslims and of the Christians, and that morality and humanity were more important than ancestry, Gandhi may also be said to have helped liberate Hinduism from the Indian earth. Offering the exact opposite of the "homeland-holy land" thesis, he helped make Hinduism a matter of the soul rather than of soil, something from India but not chained to India.

Though many Hindus regarded him as a Mahatma ("great soul"), a section saw Gandhi as a violator, on the untouchability question, of scriptural injunctions, and as one who weakened Hindus in their equation with Muslims. On the first criticism, holding that verses from scripture that his orthodox opponents were citing "cannot be above reason or morality," Gandhi added: "It is no good quoting verses from Manusmriti and other scriptures in defence of this orthodoxy. A number of verses in these scriptures are apocryphal, a number of them are quite meaningless."[50]

Inviting Hindus to view untouchability from the angles of humanity and morality, Gandhi, an incorrigible reconciler, also asked the untouchables not to regard caste Hindus as permanent enemies. In recent decades several untouchable leaders have said that Gandhi was not radical enough, but in August 1947, when India became independent, Bhimrao Ramji Ambedkar, a brilliant lawyer leading India's untouchables, agreed, on Gandhi's suggestion, to join the cabinet and chair the committee drafting free India's constitution. The exercise in constitution making was also an exercise in peacemaking between caste Hindus and the untouchables, for which credit is due to Ambedkar and Gandhi both.

India's constitutional commitment to equality irrespective of religion or caste would probably not have come about but for Gandhi's political leadership, but a role was also played by Gandhi's success in winning much of Hindu society to his version of Hinduism. Thanks significantly to his efforts, India seemed to acknowledge the sin of untouchability and also to adopt a phrase that was constantly on his lips, *Ishwar Allah Tere Naam* ("Ishwar and Allah are Your names").

Hindutva loyalists were never happy with the phrase, and the recent growth in their ranks has been accompanied by mounting criticism of Gandhi's supposed appeasement of Muslims. The critics have also alleged that Hindu society was weakened by Gandhi's stress on nonviolence. However, if the rhetoric from India's nationalist or Hindutva establishments or the movies turned out by Mumbai and Chennai offer any indication, the danger of India's being converted to nonviolence is remote.

Enabling tens of thousands of the landless to own land donated by those who had a surplus of it, the Bhoodan or land gift movement of the 1950s and 1960s, led by the Hindu scholar and ascetic, Vinoba Bhave, a younger colleague admired by Gandhi, was a noteworthy demonstration of Hinduism's peacebuilding potential. Currently active Hindu groups that stress ethics, benevolence, and surrender to God and seem to attach importance to peace include, in alphabetical order, the Brahma Kumaris, the Chinmaya Mission, the International Society for Krishna Consciousness, the Ramakrishna Mission, and the Swaminarayan community; this author, however, has not been able to make an adequate study of their roles.

His frank heterodoxy notwithstanding, Gandhi was described in a 1995 book by Chandrasekharendra Sarasvatisvami, the late Paramacharya ("supreme teacher") of Kanchi and a revered orthodox voice of Hinduism, as "one of the greatest redeemers of Hinduism."[51] Earlier, D. S. Sarma had called Gandhi "one of the greatest creative personalities in [Hinduism's] history."[52] Such reactions from orthodox quarters to Gandhi's dissenting initiatives suggest that attempts for a new Hindu theology that stresses peacebuilding are not condemned to failure.

Since the epics have been recognized in this chapter as a major teacher of their faith to members of the Hindu community, the potential in the epics for sanctioning a theology of reconciliation becomes a significant question. This chapter has disclosed veins in both epics that can be tapped for peacemaking.

Our discussion suggests, too, that a new theology of peacebuilding could focus on one of Hinduism's most enduring symbols, the chariot, and attempt to restore to that symbol the meaning that the Vedas and the Upanishads seemed to offer, which was also the meaning that, among others, Tulsidas, Sukthankar, and Gandhi drew from it. If, accordingly, the epics may aid the reconciler more than has been conceded, the Bhakti poets and their modern counterparts are allies already.

Our survey has confirmed the existence of a stream of the Hindu tradition that can assist peacebuilding. From it verses, tales and modern examples have been picked for this chapter. It may be affirmed, in conclusion, that, drawing inspiration and legitimacy from this stream, exponents of a new Hindu theology can foster peacebuilding in our times, in, near, and outside India. One hopes that they can do so in cooperation and dialogue with peacemaking initiatives from other faith traditions. "The Eternal pervades the earth and heaven and all that lies between. On His adorable and divine radiance we meditate. May He prompt our minds!"[53]

NOTES

1. Dermot Killingley suggests that (in 1816) "Rammohun [Roy] was probably the first Hindu to use the word 'Hinduism'." See Killingley, "Rammohun Roy in Hindu and Christian Tradition," The Teape Lectures 1990 (Newcastle Upon Tyne: Grevatt & Grevatt, 1993), p. 60, cited in Richard King, *Orientalism and Religion: Postcolonial Theory, India and 'The Mystic East'* (Delhi: Oxford, 1999), p. 100. According to Lesslie Newbigin, the expression Hinduism, "a common name for the maddening diversity of faiths in India," was used for the first time in the sixteenth century by Catholic missionaries in India. See Newbigin's foreword to Chaturvedi Badrinath, *Dharma, India and the World Order* (St. Andrews: St. Andrew Press, 1993), p. 21.

2. See Richard King, *Orientalism and Religion,* pp. 100–103.

3. Quoted in R. S. Pandit (tr.), *Rajatarangini* (New Delhi: Sahitya Akademi, 1968), p. 751 fn.

4. He was executed in 1659 by his younger brother, Aurangzeb, who became emperor.

5. T. N. Madan, *Modern Myths, Locked Minds* (New Delhi: Oxford, 1997), pp. 126–127.

6. D. S. Sarma, *Renascsent Hinduism* (Bombay: Bhavan, 1966), p. 130.

7. "Or a Jew or a Zoroastrian" is at times added, but India's Jews and Zoroastrians are statistically negligible.

8. Bombay: Bhavan, 1995.

9. For a discussion by this author of how contemporary Indians view the Gita, see R. Gandhi, *Revenge & Reconciliation: Understanding South Asian History* (New Dehli: Penguin, 1999), pp. 1–2 and 17–23.

10. Sarma, *Renascent Hinduism,* p. 133.

11. New York: Oxford, p. 34.

12. Thus the following works contain no index references to peace, peace-making, reconciliation, or forgiveness: K. R. Sundararajan, *Hinduism* (Patiala: Punjabi University, 1969); P. L. Bhargava, *Fundamentals of Hinduism* (Delhi: Munshiram Manoharlal, 1982); Glyn Richards, *A Source Book of Modern Hinduism* (London: Curzon Press, 1985); Robert Minor, *Modern Indian Interpreters of the Bhagavad Gita* (Albany: SUNY, 1986).

13. M. S. Golwalkar, *Bunch of Thoughts* (Bangalore: Vikram Prakashan, 1966).

14. Golwalkar, *Bunch of Thoughts,* p. 127 and p. 123, cited in Chaturvedi Badrinath, *Dharma, India and the World Order,* p. 281.

15. Golwalkar, *Bunch of Thoughts,* p. 25, cited in Badrinath, *Dharma, India and the World Order,* p. 291.

16. B. N. Jog. *Threat of Islam: Indian Dimensions* (Bombay; Unnati Prakashan, 1994), p. viiii.

17. Ibid., p. 466.

18. Ibid, pp. 475–478.

19. Ibid., p. 481.

20. See M. K. Gandhi, *Collected Works* (New Delhi: Publications Division), vol. 89, pp. 177–195; and Brij Krishna, *Gandhiji-ki-Dilli-Diary* ('Gandhiji's Delhi Diary') (New Delhi: 1970), vol. 3, pp. 294–297.

21. M. K. Gandhi, *Collected Works,* vol. 90, pp. 472–473.

22. B. N. Jog, *Threat of Islam,* p. 480.

23. Arvind Sharma, ed., *Our Religions* (New York: Collins, 1993), pp. 55–58.

24. Translation from *Communalism Combat*, Mumbai, July 1999.

25. Statement of 1 April 1998 in *Communalism Combat*, Mumbai, April 1998.

26. M. K. Gandhi, *Collected Works,* vol. 89, p. 375.

27. Praful Bidwai and Achin Vanaik, *South Asia on a Short Fuse: Nuclear Politics and the Future of Global Disarmament* (New Delhi: Oxford, 1999), p. 144.

28. Distributed across India, the tribals, or the Scheduled Tribes as the constitution terms them, can be Hindus, practitioners of tribal faiths, Christians, or a combination. Hindutva supporters have recently stepped up their attacks on alleged attempts to Christianize tribals.

29. Taken from Abinash Chandra Bose, *Hymns from the Vedas* (Bombay: Asia, 1966), p. 14.

30. Bose, *Hymns from the Vedas*, p. 217.

31. Pandit Satyakam Vidyalankar (ed.), *The Holy Vedas* (Delhi: Clarion, 1986), p. 263.

32. Bose, *Hymns from the Vedas*, p. 155.

33. Purohit Swami and W. B.Yeats, *The Ten Principal Upanishads* (New York: Macmillan, 1937 and 1975), p. 25.

34. P. Lal, *The Mahabharata of Vyasa* (Delhi: Vikas, 1980), pp. 343–344.

35. P. Lal, *The Mahabharata of Vyasa*, pp. 144–145.

36. P. Lal, *The Mahabharata of Vyasa*, p. 291.

37. P. Lal, *The Mahabharata of Vyasa*, pp. 353–354.

38. E. R. Sreekrishna Sarma in Bimal Krishna Matilal (ed.), *Moral Dilemmas in the Mahabharata* (Delhi: Motilal Banarsidass, 1989), p. 147.

39. Nath Dutt. *The Ramayana Volume 3* (Calcutta: 1984), pp. 1494–1495.

40. Monier Williams, *Indian Wisdom* (Calcutta: Reprint, 1974) fn 1, p. 360.

41. C. Rajagopalachari, *Ramayana* (Bombay: Bhavan, 1989), pp. 305–306.

42. Hari Prasad Shastri, *The Ramayana of Valmiki* (London: Shanti Sadan, 1970), vol. III, pp. 331–332.

43. Goswami Tulsidas, *Rama-Charita-Manas*, Lanka Kand, Chaupai 80, tr.

44. He died in 1942.

45. See V. S. Sukthankar, *The Meaning of the Mahabharata* (Bombay: Asiatic Society, 1957), pp. 111–120.

46. For a full translation see Rajmohan Gandhi, *Revenge & Reconciliation: Understanding South Asian History* (New Delhi: Penguin, 1999), pp. 22–23.

47. H. W. Wilson (tr.), *The Vishnu Purana*, pp. 505–516.

48. From Romila Thapar, *Asoka and the Decline of the Mauryas* (New Delhi: Oxford, 1990), pp. 255–260.

49. In Douglas Johnston and Cynthia Sampson (ed.), *Religion, the Missing Dimension of Statecraft* (New York: Oxford, 1994), p. 268.

50. Remarks in 1917. See M. K. Gandhi, *Collected Works*, vol. 14, pp. 73–77 and p. 345.

51. Chandrasekharendra Sarasvatisvami, *Hindu Dharma: The Universal Way of Life* (Bombay: Bhavan, 1995), p. ix.

52. D. S. Sarma, *Renascent Hinduism*, p. 187.

53. The Gayatri mantra (morning prayer), as translated in D. S. Sarma, *Renascent Hinduism*, p. 203.

4

Missed Opportunities

Buddhism and the Ethnic Strife
in Sri Lanka and Tibet

EVA K. NEUMAIER

I am the 12-year-old girl, refugee on a small boat, who throws
herself into the ocean after being raped by a sea pirate, and I
am the pirate, my heart not yet capable of seeing and loving.
—Thich Nhat Hanh

This chapter explores the obstacles and potentials the Buddhist traditions harbour vis-à-vis peacemaking and peacebuilding. The introduction talks about the emergence of Buddhism in India, its major religious
and moral concepts and ideals as well as about its diversification and
proliferation. Against this background, a discussion of the innate obstacles toward peacebuilding will be given together with an examination of
the potentials Buddhist teachings provide for building peace. Two case
studies will illustrate the difficulties Buddhist societies encounter when
politics, ethnicity, and religion collide in a field of colonialism and its
aftermath and when different cultures and ideologies clash. The civil
war in Sri Lanka pitches a Buddhist ethnic majority against an ethnic
minority that embraces a different religion, while the tension-loaded dispute over the cultural and political status of Tibet juxtaposes a mainly

Buddhist people with its socialist government. In each case we find Buddhists who eagerly embark on the warpath and other Buddhists who try to build bridges of mutual understanding. A final reflection focuses on those contemporary issues that would benefit if Buddhists would mine the potential of Buddhist ethics for solving them and showcases some Buddhist movements that spearhead such enterprise.

INTRODUCTION

The Buddhist tradition began about 2500 years ago in India. At that time Indian culture had made the transition from a tribal and largely pastoral society to a rich urban culture where arts as well as philosophy blossomed. Villages had turned into cities ruled by groups of noble families (oligarchy). The elite engaged in lengthy philosophical conversations, preserved in the *Upanishads*. It was a period of relative peace as these city-states were more concerned with solidifying their wealth and cultural sophistication than expanding their territory.

The man who became known to the world as Buddha, the Awakened One, belonged to such a noble family ruling over the city-state of Kapilavatthu, located in what now constitutes the border between India and Nepal. After a youth in luxury and comfort, he denied as a thirty year old being heir to his father's position and left his wife together with their newly born son to pursue a state of altered consciousness where neither death nor suffering could afflict him. After years of self-mortification and futile attempts, at the moment of "enlightenment" he gained the insight that his present life was the last in a long series of lives, each shaped by the acts of the preceding ones, that is, the law of *karma*, which informs the Buddhist understanding of ethics. In the past, it often served as an excuse for remaining inactive in the face of social turmoil and injustice, thus, preventing the working toward social peace. The second insight the Buddha had that night is the "four-fold noble truth," which became the very foundation on which the entire lofty edifice of Buddhist thought and soteriology is built. It claims that, first, all experience is marred with being unsatisfactory and thus constitutes a form of "suffering" *(dukkha);* second, this suffering is caused by unrealistic expectations and a clinging or "thirst" *(tinha)* for pleasurable experiences; third, if this "thirst" is brought to an end, freedom from suffering is achieved and that is *nirvana,* a state beyond birth and death and its concomitant sufferings; fourth, there is a path to achieve this lofty goal. This path consists of wisdom, mental cultivation, and a life of restraint *(śila)* whereby all three components are interwoven. Nirvana, an existence in absolute otherness, can only be achieved if and when all attachment to one's social group as well as to oneself is dissolved. Up to the beginning of the Common Era, Indian Buddhism embraced the *arhant* (mendicant recluse who has realized the four-fold noble truth and who will enter nirvana at the moment of death) as the goal of a religious life. Around the beginning of the Common Era a new ideal, that of the *bodhisattva*, arose and replaced in some Buddhist societies the ideal of the *arhant*. The *bodhisattva* epitomizes empathy and compassion. He (only in rare cases do we learn about female *bodhisattvas*) will not only part from all that is dear to him for the sake of others' well-being, including his own life, but also delay his absorption into nirvana for the sake of assisting all sentient beings on their way to nirvana. Unlike the *arhant* who must lead the reclusive life of a monk, the *bodhisattva* is more often a layperson than a monk. Thus, the *bodhisattva* could become a social activist.

A life of restraint as understood by Buddha as well as his followers embraced an ethics based on the principle of nonharming and nonviolating any living creature (gods, humans, and animals). Five precepts articulate this backbone of Buddhist ethics. They incorporate those principles of good citizenry as to refrain from killing (which includes abstaining from causing pain and harm), stealing, harmful sexual activities, lying, and the consumption of intoxicating beverages as well as other rules that pertain to the lifestyle of monks and laypeople who are more serious practitioners. Furthermore, the main emotional rapport with the world should be infused with love, compassion, empathy, and equanimity. The ethics of nonharming rested on the assumptions that a harmful intention, necessary for such an act, has negative karmic repercussions and that all life is interdependent. Therefore, harming an "other" is harming oneself. Thus, we should expect all Buddhists to be vegetarians (not causing animals to be killed) and pacifists (not causing harm to humans and other creatures) and that Buddhist societies are seeking peace and peaceful conflict resolution more than anyone else. The historical reality, as I hope to show, is nevertheless quite different.

After his "awakening" the Buddha criss-crossed the dusty landscape of the eastern Ganges valley for more than forty years answering peoples' queries about life, the meaning of human existence, and, above all, how to understand and cope with the constant presence of suffering in the form of sickness, old age, death, and birth. During these years, a following gathered around him, some adopted his mendicant lifestyle and formed the *sangha*, the Buddhist order of monks and nuns, while some remained laypeople. Initial rules tried to keep monks apart from the political powers. One of the monastic rules states, for instance, that monks are not permitted to enter the palace when the king or a minister is present. Toward the end of Buddha's life, the political landscape of India underwent a significant change. The city-states with their oligarchies were swallowed up by rapidly emerging empires, often locked into enduring warfare over resources in the form of land, people, and access to minerals. Some of the rulers of these new empires saw in the Buddhist movement a useful tool to counteract the dominance of the Vedic priests who had a monopoly on carrying out rituals thought vital for the survival and prosperity of the country and her people. Thus, the rulers patronized the Buddhist *sangha* by building richly decorated monasteries, showering some of them with huge endowments in the form of land and serfs, and, above all, by assigning a role at the court to some monks. Nuns were not part of this process, as the court culture knew of women only as either wives or consorts of the rulers or as courtesans. Neither role was befitting for the nuns. This exclusion by default had far-reaching consequences as it made nuns virtually invisible within Buddhist societies and excluded them from positions of power as well as from any decision-making process within and without the *sangha*. On the other hand, by erecting monasteries that were specifically related and subordinate to the court administration, the moral and intellectual freedom of these monastic groups was severely curtailed, making a critical stance, one of peacebuilding, virtually impossible. Examples of the political system co-opting monasticism can be found, among other Asian Buddhist monarchies, in early Tibet (eighth/ninth centuries) where the court took responsibility for the livelihood of the monks who came from foreign countries, as well as in China where during the Tang dynasty (618–907) Buddhist monks served not only as imperial advisors but also conducted ceremonies to ensure victory over the enemies of the imperial family.[1] By the end of the first millennium (ca. 1500 years after Buddha) one or the other form of Buddhism dominated every Asian country from areas of modern Afghanistan to Korea and Japan and from Tibet to Sri Lanka. In virtually all these countries the Buddhist *sangha* entered an intricate and often tension-loaded relationship with the local rulers and their courts.[2] In many cases Buddhist institutions became accustomed to depending on hand-outs from rulers and governments, hampering their own creativity and jeopardizing their intention to live the teachings of the Buddha. Blinded by a life of prestige and luxury, leaders of the monastic institutions abdicated their potential role as a critical voice that could have called for realizing the socioethical message implied in Buddhist teaching.

The *sangha* is a self-governing body in which seniority by the date of initiation is the only criterion for superiority. When the Buddha was about to pass away, he pointed to his teachings as the only guide for his followers. No successor was appointed. Consequently, Buddhist traditions flourished in diversity and multitude with no central authority to regulate, approve, or disprove any one of them. The teachings of the Buddha, originally handed down as memorized texts, were put to writing some centuries after his passing. As Buddhism blossomed not as a unified movement but as a multitude of local communities, different communities wrote down the teachings of the Buddha in several local languages, preserving different texts. The Buddhist "canon" (theoretically containing the entirety of Buddha's teachings) is not a single authorized body of scripture. Rather it exists as an idea shared by all Buddhist communities that Buddha's words were captured in a number of authoritative texts while virtually not two of these communities agree on the same list of texts nor would they agree on the same meaning of these texts. This does not imply that Buddhist communities cannot agree on anything. In contrast, there is acceptance of a wide range of ideas and narratives among all Buddhists. But, above all, they agree on the multiplicity of Buddha's word and on the diversity of traditions. Thus, Buddhism as a homogenous religion is an academic abstraction while the historical reality knows only of Buddhist thoughts and practices amalgamated with individual cultures. The homogeneity and universalism of Islam or of the Catholic Church (prior to Vatican II) are unthinkable within the Buddhist world. Therefore, the kind of Buddhism that is present in Sri Lanka is radically different from that in Tibet, which restricts comparison between the two case studies to historical and structural similarities and dissimilarities.

The rise and glory of Indian Buddhism coincides with the golden age of classical Indian culture, that is, when India was a vibrant cultural centre that fertilized vast areas of South and Southeast Asia. Often, merchants and artisans were the first to carry notions of these various strands of Buddhism to faraway regions only to be followed by Indian monks who would further spread the Indian-Buddhist culture.

OBSTACLES TO PEACEBUILDING INNATE TO BUDDHISM

Obstacles to peacebuilding, innate to Buddhism, range from the otherworldly ideal of the *arhant* (on the *bodhisattva* ideal I shall reflect in the context of the Tibet/China case study) to philosophical and doctrinal assumptions, such as the concept of karma, as well as to sociohistorical processes, such as the co-optation of monasticism by political systems. The conception of the monk as a recluse and ascetic, who has distanced himself from all concerns of secular society and the world as a whole, although hardly ever enacted in life, nevertheless became the icon of Buddhist spirituality.[3] Embracing this ideal as an approximation prevented the monk from utilizing the power of his highly prestigious and symbolic position to better the situation of the world. Examples of this discrepancy and tension that seem to cripple Buddhist attempts at addressing sociopolitical issues can be found in the Sri Lankan Sarvodaya Shramadana movement as well as in contemporary Tibet. The social aloofness and inwardness of the *sangha* are often justified by pointing out that social as well as individual ills are the result of previous activities (i.e., karma). Thus, the remedy for these ills should be sought in adopting a rigorous Buddhist lifestyle rather than in social and political activism.

The tendency to see social problems only as the result of karma, and, thus, to be addressed exclusively within the realm of individual responsibility, seems to have been one important obstacle for Buddhist societies in recognizing inequality, poverty, social strife, and war as moral obligations awaiting concrete solutions. This trend to individualize and psychologize sociopolitical concerns is evident in the Buddhist understanding of "peace." While the *Oxford English Dictionary* gives three main meanings for peace (freedom from or cessation of war, freedom from civil disorder, and quiet, tranquility), the most widely used Buddhist term for peace is *śanti*, which gravitates on the scale of meanings more toward inner peace and tranquility than toward peace as a state of nonaggression between different political units or between different social groups, a trend Buddhism shares with Hinduism (see chapter 3). Thus, while the modern concept of peacebuilding emphasizes freedom or cessation of war and freedom from civil disorder, conflict, and oppression, the Buddhist concept favors an individualistic interpretation of inner peace and harmony, or tranquility. Consequently, the question arises: Do Buddhists and modern "peacebuilders" speak of the same thing when they say "peace"? This gap in meaning was also noticed by Christopher Queen in his article "The Peace Wheel: Nonviolent Activism in the Buddhist Tradition."[4] The XIVth Dalai Lama's peace initiatives further attest to this situation. In his Nobel Prize lecture he stressed that "[t]rue peace with one self and with the world around us can only be achieved through the development of mental peace."[5] To understand "peace" mainly as mental quality to be cultivated through meditation and not as a social and ethical responsibility is one of the obstacles that prevented traditional Buddhist institutions and their members from recognizing the potential of Buddhist ethics for building harmony and peace between different social groups and nations.

Another major obstacle to peacebuilding is the trend, observed in several Buddhist cultures, to adopt a mytho-historic narrative as the script of national identity that leads to a fundamentalist positioning of this Buddhist culture. Two such narratives will be explored in this chapter. Both texts are not part of the canonical literature, but enjoy authoritative status within a specific Buddhist culture. One of these texts is the *Mahavamsa,* a Pali text that articulates the mission of the Sinhala people as the torchbearers of the *dhamma,* the Buddhist teaching. In the present Sinhala-Tamil dispute the text plays an exemplary role. The other text is the *Mani bka' 'bum,* a Tibetan text dating approximately from the thirteenth or fourteenth century that inscribes a divine status on the Tibetan ruler and his subsequent heirs. Although the text has not reached such a paradigmatic status as the *Mahavamsa* has, its main idea that Tibet is the last country converted to the Buddha's teaching and that her people are appointed as stalwarts of this tradition deeply influences the present Tibetan-Chinese dispute. Both texts, though originating from different and unrelated cultural contexts, share certain features. They construct an interdependency between the continuation of the Buddhist teaching, a certain ethnic group, and the land this group occupies whereby they also erase the existence of other ethnic and religio-cultural communities within the same spatial-historical continuum. Thus, these texts provide a rhetoric that offers itself as a voice of ethnoreligious fundamentalism.

In the following, I will reflect on two situations that both demonstrate, on the one hand, the failure of Buddhists to work toward peace by falling prey to ethnoreligious fundamentalist trends, while, on the other hand, the same situation also harbors possibilities for overcoming these obstacles. The first situation that I will discuss here is the Sinhala-Tamil conflict in Sri Lanka and the second is the Tibetan-Chinese dispute. The Sinhala-Tamil conflict has ravaged the island of Sri Lanka for decades, causing large numbers of casualties on both sides while the Tibetan-Chinese dispute has only occasionally escalated to a level of civil disobedience and sporadic acts of violence. Thus, while one case has already passed beyond the threshold where peacebuilding could have prevented the outbreak of violence, the other case still harbors the potential of a nonviolent solution to settle ethnic and ideological conflicts.

THE SINHALA-TAMIL CONFLICT IN SRI LANKA

Scholars have agreed on the seminal role that a certain view of Buddhism plays in the present Sinhala-Tamil conflict in Sri Lanka. At first

sight, one may react with surprise and ask how a religion that is so set
on nonviolence and that has no concept of a "chosen" ethnic group or
a "sacred land" could be the source of a bitter conflict that is carried out
with immense brutality.[6] Which forces redesigned the Buddhism of Sri
Lanka so that it could provide ideas for a growing ethnoreligious fundamentalism? To answer this question, we need to examine the situation
of Sinhala Buddhism during Sri Lanka's colonial period and afterwards.

When European colonial powers began to conquer the island of
Ceylon, as Sri Lanka was once called, they destroyed not only the
indigenous monarchy together with its social and political institutions
but also affected the Buddhist *sangha* negatively. While the British government initially promised in the Kandyan convention that "the religion of Boodhoo professed by the Chiefs and Inhabitants of these
provinces is declared inviolable, and its rites, Ministers and Places of
Worship are to be maintained and protected," it dissociated itself from
this promise soon after by making conversion to Christianity the prerequisite for Sinhalese to be admitted to the political and economic
elite.[7] In response to this cultural oppression and the perceived dissolution of their traditions, some Sinhalese searched for means to recreate
a cultural identity. Among them Anagarika Dharmapala (1864–1933)
was instrumental in bringing about a remarkable revival of Ceylonese
Buddhism that resulted in what is known as "Protestant Buddhism."[8]
Several factors, all rooted in colonialism, were seminal in the creation
of this form of Buddhism, which then became the seedbed for the rise
of Sinhala Buddhist fundamentalism. First there was the fact that the
canonical and extra-canonical texts of Buddhism were extant only in
the form of palm-leaf manuscripts available to a handful of learned
monks. When Western schooling, offered through British missionary
schools to Sinhalese bent on upward social mobility, woke in them an
appetite for understanding their cultural and ethnic character, they
could only turn to the Western translations of Buddhist texts. Thus, the
printing press and the dissemination of mass literature created not by
Sinhalese, but by Western orientalists who saw in (Theravada) Buddhism the antithesis to a Christianity many of them despised for its perceived ritualism and legends, introduced the emerging Sinhalese middle
class to a Buddhism that had severed its roots and embraced a revivalist vision.[9] Second, adopting the model of missionary schools, middle-
class Sinahalese Buddhists, aided by Westerners, such as Henry Steel
Olcott, one of the founders of the Theosophical movement, created
Buddhist schools in which the English translations of Buddhist texts
became part of the curriculum.[10] These Western-educated economically
well-placed and upward striving Sinhalese, who embraced a form of

Buddhism that was redefined by Anglo-Saxon theosophists and orientalists (thus, "Protestant Buddhism"), soon constituted an urban middle class. They, together with village headmen, civil officers, and schoolmasters (i.e., the village intelligentsia), became avid readers of Dharmapala's pamphlets and books. Although quite well educated in Sinhala-Buddhist secondary schools, these sections of society remained excluded from political power amassed exclusively in the hands of the British and Christian converts. Consequently, "[t]hese groups could identify with Dharmapala and accept his ethic of this-worldly asceticism and the new morality he envisaged. His political message was quickly and eagerly accepted, since these people were self-consciously Buddhist and could easily be swayed by Dharmapala's view of the past."[11] The village elite and a free public educational system disseminated successfully this new Buddhist ethic that provided hope for the poor masses that, one day, their living standards will improve. The politicization of Sinhala Buddhism began with Dharmapala's advocacy for a united Buddhist country and his vilification of all non-Buddhist and non-Sinhala ethnic and cultural groups that have inhabited Sri Lanka for many centuries. "But he directed his fiercest vituperation at Indian merchants (Boras and Parsis), Muslims (whom he contemptuously referred to as *hambayo*), and 'filthy Tamils' *(hädi demalu)*. He considered these groups to be aliens who exploited the Sinhalese economically."[12] Unlike traditional Buddhist societies that adapted the basic rules of Buddhist ethics to suit multiple cultural idiosyncrasies, thus resulting in a large diversity that made Buddhism accessible to many different peasant societies throughout Asia, Dharmapala advocated one set of Buddhist lay ethics that closely emulated Protestant ethics of the Victorian times. In his rhetoric, Dharmapala conflated ideas of religion (Theravada Buddhism), race (Aryan-Sinhalese), country (Sri Lanka), and language (Sinhala) that became a seedbed for a Buddhist revivalism feeding on an ideology of ethnoreligious chauvinism, which continues to fuel the ethnic conflict of today.

Protestant Buddhism renounced the tolerant stance Buddhism usually had taken vis-à-vis other religions, developed a fundamentalist attitude, claimed that Buddhism was not a religion but a philosophy, and relied heavily on English-language concepts.[13] This form of Buddhism that has discarded rituals and legends that were seemingly in conflict with "science" and reason has never acquired a coherent organizational unity or identity, thus, it speaks with a variety of voices. Protestant Buddhism created a romanticized and idealized vision of Sri Lanka's past characterized by the unity of all Sinhala people as Buddhists guided by wise and benign righteous monarchs *(dharmarajas)*. The narrative drew inspiration from various canonical and post-canonical, yet early, Sinhala texts, most noticeable from the *Mahavamsa*, that present a heroic picture of how early Sinhala rulers became patrons of Buddhism.[14] The text creates a crucial linkage between Theravada Buddhism and Buddha's alleged visit to the island resulting in a claim to a Buddhist orthodoxy. The *Mahavamsa*, like similar programmatic texts, draws a starkly simplified picture of the Sinhalese past by obliterating its complexity. A contemporary fundamentalist reading reduces the *Mahavamsa*, which in itself is complex and often contradictory, to a simple and powerful message that fuses the past with the present in an attempt of reestablishing the glory of the ancient yet modern Buddhist Sinhala culture. Because Sri Lanka was ruled in the past by pious Buddhist kings, so the fundamentalist reading argues, in the present there must be cooperation, if not a fusion, between Theravada Buddhism and the state to ensure the spiritual and economic well-being of all (Sinhala) people. In the late nineteenth century, this mytho-historicism enabled Sri Lankan intellectuals to embrace an identity of dignity vis-à-vis the oppressive colonial powers. When Sri Lanka reached independence, this Buddhist mytho-historicism became for many Sinhala the foundational narrative on which their new nationhood was built. "Indeed, while the *Mahavamsa* is not a canonical text, it nonetheless has canonical authority. From a reading of it, Sinhala-Buddhist fundamentalists construe standards for an orthodox ideology about the nature and destiny of the Sinhala people and Sri Lanka. From a reading of it fundamentalists hone a dramatic eschatology about the destiny of the Sinhala people and their enemies that informs action in the present."[15] The simplicity of this message makes it easily available even to the barely literate. The fundamentalist reading culminates in the war cry to turn present Sri Lanka into *dhammadipa,* the "island of righteousness" (embodied in the Buddhist religion) that it had been in the past. A utopian vision of an idealized past becomes the beacon for the future.

When after independence, learned monks became politically active, they argued for a revival of this glorious Buddhist and Sinhala past that often took on a red hue of socialism when they argued for a socialist welfare state based on Buddhist ethics. While this revivalist Buddhism, so heavily influenced by Victorian Protestantism, gained a following among the "village elite," urban merchants and among certain groups of monks,[16] traditional Ceylonese Buddhism continued to exist side by side and often in contraction to the new proselytizers. However, changes in the political and economic structures of independent Sri Lanka privileged the followers of Protestant Buddhism over those Buddhists who adhered to the more traditional style.

While Sinhala nationalists reaffirmed themselves in these mytho-historic narratives as the people who were chosen as the torchbearers of the Buddhist *dhamma,* these foundational myths did not provide a place for non-Sinhala and non-Buddhist people. They became conceived as intruders into a pure (and puritan) Buddhist society that aspired to rejuvenating a Golden Age of Buddhist culture in which Buddhist ethics would fuse with modern democratic values. To achieve this lofty goal, these intruders had to be barred from the decision-making process and confined to an economic and political margin in which their existence was tolerated but not encouraged. Sometimes they were seen as freeloaders on a striving Sinhala economy and culture. The Sinhala-Buddhist fundamentalists rebuilt their shattered cultural pride and identity by conflating belief with ethnicity, language, and land and prescribed this ideological mixture for all people inhabiting the island regardless of their ethnicity, religion, and culture. Those who embraced this ideological and, dare we say, fundamentalist concoction are styled as "us" and "our selves" while those being unable to accept this ideological prescription turned into "other." To the same extent as the revivalist Sinhala Buddhists erased all traces of diversity in their definition of "(Sinhala) nation" so they imposed an artificial (and unrealistic) homogeneity on the "other" (various groups of Tamils, Muslims, Hindus, and Christians). This trend to negate differences within the different ethnic and cultural groups that make up the population of Sri Lanka (and we will see that a similar simplification occurs with regard to Tibet) precludes possibilities for a peacemaking process, a process that would seek out common grounds, small as they might be, that would lead to defusing the explosive situation. From the perspective of Buddhist thought, this position is oblivious of the interdependence of all existing things *(pratityasamutpada)* and of the law of karma. Based on these two concepts, a bridge building could be possible. However, the unmitigated position taken by the advocates of Sinhala tribalism and exclusivity aroused increased opposition from the main target group, the Tamils. When the mainly Sinhala-dominated government responded with oppression and violence to the Tamil opposition to Sinhalas' political, religious, and cultural hegemony, civil war broke out and has since claimed tens of thousands of victims. The escalation of confrontation and violence resulting in civil war has been chronicled with remarkable astuteness by Tambiah, thus, there is no need to repeat it here.[17]

The various Sinhala-Buddhist fundamentalist groups consistently emphasize the unity of the country as a result of the unity of the *sangha.* However, the various Sinhala-Buddhist fundamentalists speak with different voices, and represent a wide range of opinions when it comes to the crucial questions of the supremacy of Buddhism, the hegemony of Sinhala language and culture, the interaction between religion and state, and the situation of the non-Sinhala populations in Sri Lanka. Chandra R. de Silva, relying on the works of Peter Schalk, Donald Swearer, and Gaganath Obeyesekere, concludes that even those monks who are sympathetic to the Tamils' cause nevertheless support the claim to Sinhala hegemony.[18] George D. Bond sees in the Buddhist lay movement of *Sarvodaya Shramadana*, which originated in the late 1950s as a work camp to alleviate the plight of the poorest of the poor and developed into a powerful movement of socially engaged Buddhism, a fruitful attempt to address the militancy and tribalism of Sinhala Buddhist fundamentalism.[19] While Bond affirms the roots of Sarvodaya in revivalist Protestant Buddhism, he highlights the interfaith and cross-ethnic activities of the movement as a significant contribution toward peacebuilding. However, Gombrich/Obeyesekere and Kantowsky disagree with this view.[20] Kantowsky sees Sarvodaya not as an "agency that hopes to improve the so-called 'quality of life' in certain rural areas through technical advice and capital aid,"[21] but as a movement whose ultimate goal is "to awaken man's capacity for a correct understanding of the implications of this Buddhist doctrine of *anatta,* of No-soul or No-self; only then will he be able to free himself from the chains of craving *(tanha),* illusion *(moha),* and aggression *(dosha)* which yoke him to the endless cycle of existence and continuity."[22] Gombrich and Obeyesekere unveil the utopian and revivalist nature of Sarodaya by pointing out that the ideology of its governing body is neither peasant, nor Buddhist based, "but [based] on the class interests and ideological views of the Sinhala Buddhist bourgeoisie, influenced by the reform of Anagarika Dharmapala."[23]

Working toward peace in Sri Lanka will depend on whether the various ethnoreligious communities are prepared to engage in critical self-reflection to demystify their own mytho-historic narratives that gave rise to fundamentalist movements not only among the Sinhala-Buddhists but also among the Tamils and Muslims of the island. At present nothing indicates such moves toward self-reflection have begun. Has Theravada Buddhism failed? Buddhist ethics could provide guidance to cross the only recently erected boundaries between the various ethnoreligious communities if leading Buddhist monks would emphasize the universality of the four-fold noble truth that affects all people while at the same time admit that other communities may have different and even conflicting views. They could point to the interrelatedness of all existence along the teaching of the *pratitya samutpada* and that Tamils, Muslims, and Christians live on the island together with the Sinhala due to a collective karma built up in the past. Thus, living in a multiethnic and multireligious environment could be seen as a challenge that would enhance Buddhist ethics. However, the truth is that Buddhist institutions, particularly the monastic ones, have to a large degree embraced this politicized and fundamentalist view of Buddhism.

THE TIBET-CHINA DISPUTE

The "Tibet question" (i.e., the dispute between the People's Republic of China and exile Tibetans and their supporters about the political status of the China-controlled areas of the Tibetan-speaking world) is frequently presented in the media. Most reports assume that one or the other party is right in its claims while avoiding a discussion of the historical making of this dispute and, more important, disregarding its multilayered complexity. Films like *Seven Years in Tibet* and *Kundun* portrayed Tibet as a realm so unearthly and exotic that attempts to get at the complex reality of the dispute are often discredited.

Comparing the Sinhala/Tamil dispute with the Tibet/China dispute reveals significant differences and some similarities. In the Sinhala/ Tamil dispute, the Sinhala Buddhist fundamentalists find themselves represented and supported by the Sri Lankan government while the governments of the Tibetan Autonomous Region (TAR) and of the Tibetan Autonomous Prefectures in the Provinces of Qinghai, Gansu, Sichuan, and Yunnan are in accord with the central government of the PRC.[24] Thus, rather than speaking of a Tibet/China dispute, it would be more correct to speak of a China/ Exile-Tibetan dispute. Despite the impression created by a number of agencies, such as Free Tibet, the Tibetan Government in Exile (TGE), Tibet Information Network, the vast majority of Tibetans in TAR and in the autonomous prefectures do not share the views and aspirations promoted by the TGE. Unlike the situation in Sri Lanka, the Tibet-China dispute is not one of open violence or civil war, although the situation does harbor the potential for more violent eruptions. And the Tibetan opposition, composed mainly of the TGE, its Western supporters, and small enclaves within TAR, has been unable to unite the majority of Tibetans behind its ideas or to build any organizational coherence or structure. Moreover, in striking contrast to the Sinhalese Buddhist clergy, the Tibetan Buddhist clergy as a whole (still) embraces the traditional monastic ideal of not interfering in sociopolitical issues.[25] Thus, we discuss here a situation that has the potential for violence and even civil war and we will ask the question whether some strands of Buddhism diffuse the explosivity of the situation or contribute to it. Fundamentalist trends based on mytho-historic narratives that wed the Buddhist religion with the land of Tibet, as well as issues of ethnoreligious exclusivity and tribalism rooted in (an often misrepresented) past will again, as in the Sri Lankan case, dominate our analysis and reflections.

The PRC as well as the Tibetan exile community have turned to historical evidence to bolster their own claims, that is, that Tibet was a part of the Chinese empire at least since the Yuan Dynasty if not since Tibet's dynastic period (seventh–ninth centuries), or, respectively, that Tibet has been an independent country since it entered recorded history. Arguments can be found for both sides. On the one hand, Tibetan sources up to the Qing Dynasty render a mixed picture. For instance, a Tibetan inscription of the early ninth century speaks about unifying the two polities *(chab srid)* and about an "uncle-nephew" relationship between the Chinese Emperor and the Tibetan ruler, a phrase that is repeated in later Tibetan historiographic texts. The implication of that phrase is that the "uncle" (i.e., the Chinese Emperor) is the senior and more powerful person in this contract who, however, provides guidance and protection for the "younger" (and that means inferior) "nephew" (i.e., the Tibetan ruler).[26] While most Tibetan sources assert the distinctiveness of Tibetan culture and history, they nevertheless record Tibetan chieftains, religious dignitaries, and even the Tibetan government asking China for help and assistance in the cases of internal fights or foreign invasions.[27] On the other hand, Chinese sources throughout history treat Tibet as a vassal state that has a distinct culture, religion, and political system, but is nevertheless in subordination to China. Modern treaties, signed by Western powers and China, use the word suzerainty to describe this form of subordination. Neither the Republic of China (Taiwan) nor the government of Hong Kong (as long as it was a British colony) have ever endorsed the TGE's claim that Tibet is an independent state nor have any Western powers done so. However, only when the Chinese empire was strong could it enforce its suzerainty while in days of weakness, like during the nineteenth and early twentieth centuries (when China was weakened by the colonial wars and foreign invasions), its claim to oversee the Tibetan affairs was nothing but an empty statement. Thus, many Tibetans of the more recent period had little or no exposure to Chinese presence before the 1950s.[28] Although previous Chinese governments seemed to be content with an often only theoretical suzerainty over Tibet, the newly established PRC felt a need to incorporate Tibet as an integral part of China. The British infiltration of Tibet during the first decades of the twentieth century and, later, the rising American interest in building Tibet up as an anti-Communist base[29] provoked China to assert its position in Tibet, which resulted in its incorporation in the PRC. However, rather than discussing the historical claims any further, I want to analyze the rhetoric of both sides, and reflect on the underlying cultural assumptions, particularly of the Tibetan side.

In the discussion of the Sri Lankan conflict, issues emerged of a people that lay claim to a land of their own, based on a revisionist view of their own history and religion that gave them a privileged position, and we discerned this fusion of ideas and perceptions as the main obstacle toward building peace on the wartorn island. Can we discern similar ideological conflations when we reflect on the Tibet/China dispute?

The rhetoric used by Sinhala Buddhist fundamentalist or revisionists and that of Tibetan separatists (TGE) exhibits striking differences. While the Sinhala Buddhist rhetoric uses terms, phrases, and ideas found in mytho-historical texts of the Sinhala past (e.g., *dhamma dipa* the island of Sri Lanka as a realm of Sinhala Buddhism) to lay a claim to sociopolitical hegemony in the present, the rhetoric of the TGE and the Dalai Lama lacks similar religious terms and phrases. However, in the Dalai Lama's public speeches and statements we find ideas present that can be traced back to mytho-historical texts, such as the *Mani bka' 'bum*. The Sinhala rhetoric is designed to address Sinhala Buddhists and Tamils and other minorities who have been part of the Sri Lankan cultural fabric for many centuries. Thus, the Sinhala Buddhist discourse originates within the same culture whose members it tries to address. The Tibetan discourse originates from within an alien culture (the exile) and targets Western politicians and the public of Western countries who have little, if any, comprehension of Tibetan history and culture. Thus, the Tibetan discourse quickly adopted a Western-style rhetoric that emphasizes human rights issues (a concept unknown in traditional Tibet culture and suspect to most Chinese politicians), lack of freedom (as if the traditional Tibetan government would have ever granted any freedom[30] to commoners), and economic and environmental issues.

Underlying this apparently "modern" and "Western" discourse are visions of Tibet as a country that in its mythic origin was populated by various species of spirits who, after many generations and increasing civilizing activities, became humans—the Tibetan people. The *bKa' thang sde lnga,* a mytho-historic text that Tibetan tradition (in contrast to modern scholarship) dates into the dynastic period (seventh–ninth centuries) and holds in high esteem, gives the attribute "religion protector kings of Tibet" *(bod kyi chos skyong rgyal po)* to the first seven (mythic) kings of Tibet, thus fusing sovereignty over the land Tibet with protecting religion.[31] The same text records as the most important achievements of the first historically documented king of Tibet, Srong-btsan sgam-po (died in 649), the building of Buddhist temples, and the proclamation of the ten precepts as the law of the country, but disregards that he built an empire by conquering vast areas of inner Asia and making Tibet a military power to be reckoned with.[32] The ruler's civilizing activity became apparent in erecting shrines at focal spots marking the limbs and joints of the female demon as whom the Tibetan land presented herself and not by creating an effective bureaucracy and technical innovations. Other Tibetan authoritative, albeit not canonical, texts render a similar picture. Once Buddhist monk scholars became the main historiographers of the country, they interwove ancient myths with Buddhist narratives, resulting in a grand vision that has the ruler of Tibet to be Avalokiteshvara, the *bodhisattva* of ultimate compassion.[33] As recent as 1949, the Tibetan government stated in a formal letter sent to Mao Zedong "Tibet is a peculiar [unique] country where the Buddhist religion is widely flourishing and which is predestined to be ruled by the Living Buddha of Mercy or Chenresig [the Dalai Lama]."[34] While the Dalai Lama himself, without referring explicitly to the ancient narrative that fuses the land of Tibet with the preservation of Buddhism, stated in Washington, New Jersey, in September 1987: "As Buddhist practitioners, you should understand the necessity of preserving Tibetan Buddhism. For this the land, the country of Tibet is crucial . . . there is a real danger that [the Tibetan traditions] will not survive away from the protective nurture of our homeland. So, for the sake of preserving Tibetan Buddhism, which can be seen as a complete form of Buddha Dharma, the sacred land of Tibet is vital. It is unlikely that it can survive as a cultural and spiritual entity if its physical reality is smothered under Chinese occupation. . . . Clearly, in this light, active support for the Tibetan cause is not just a matter of politics. It is the work of Dharma."[35]

This land of Tibet, referred to by the Dalai Lama, comprises not only those areas where Tibetan-speaking people form an overwhelming majority (such as TAR and some of the autonomous prefectures) but also areas where the Tibetan-speaking people form a minority and share the land with Hui, Monguor, Mongol, and Han populations.[36] Amalgamating the concept of an essentialized "Tibet" with the "preservation of Tibetan Buddhism, which is its most complete form" reduces the diversity of religious practices in Tibet that range from local mountain cults, shamanic and exorcistic practices to philosophical studies and from Bon religion to Buddhism, Islam, and a token presence of Christianity, to an idealized form of Tibetan Buddhism, which was purged from what could offend a Western audience whose support in the endeavor of "free Tibet" was sought. This statement also obliterates the multiple and vibrant interactions and cross-fertilizations between Chinese Buddhist groups and teachers and Tibetan Buddhist monastic centers. When I visited the Tibetan monastery Labrang Tashikyil in the southwestern part of Gansu in autumn 1995, I witnessed the visit of the representative of the Chinese Buddhist Association. High-ranking Tibetan monks escorted him while he toured the premises of the monastery. In their interactions it was apparent that Buddhist conversed with Buddhist and that ethnicity was secondary, if it was present at all. By presenting a Western audience of Buddhist practitioners with the view, bathed in the authority of the Dalai Lama, that Tibetan Buddhism in TAR and the autonomous prefectures is in the danger of disappearing, the Dalai Lama erases the efforts and success of his fellow countrymen (I don't have verifiable knowledge of any Tibetan women involved in the revival of Buddhism) to revive Buddhist religious practices. A recent publication by two highly respected scholars documents how a post-Cultural Revolution religious yearning negotiates carefully a path between taking advantage of the possibilities of rebuilding monastic institutions and religious activities, and avoiding conflict with a secular communist state.[37]

During the forty-one years of exile, the Dalai Lama has consistently emphasized that a solution to the "Tibet question" must be brought about in a nonviolent and peaceful manner. He was awarded the Nobel Peace Prize in 1989. In the dual capacity as exiled secular leader of the Tibetans and as their religious leader, embodying ultimate compassion, he opted for Buddhist ethics to guide his political course. However, several Tibetan exile groups, foremost among them the Tibetan Youth Organization, have decried his approach as ineffective. He himself admitted, "I must now recognize that my approach has failed to produce any progress either for substantive negotiations or in contributing to the overall improvement of the situation in Tibet."[38] What are the obstacles to reach a peaceful agreement? Both parties demonize the other side. To the PRC, the Dalai Lama has become the prime "splittist," to the TGE, the PRC has become the sole oppressor as if there were no Tibetans involved in the governance of the TAR and of ethnic Tibet. The essentializing rhetoric of both sides poisons the atmosphere that makes fruitful negotiations difficult. Fundamentalist trends blending concepts of land, ethnicity, and belief make some Tibetans unable to see a reemerging Tibetan religiosity and a revived cultural identity despite the hurdles to overcome. If the Tibetan side would reflect on the "Tibet question" in light of Buddhist concepts such as there are no clearly defined opposites, every appearance is an appearance of the buddha-mind, and the human inclination to essentialize is the root of ignorance and suffering, then, a fruitful discourse could perhaps arise. The *bodhisattva* ideal as a person who is ready to part from all he or she has and who is ready to take on all hardship affecting others could blend with an activist's role. Transforming the *bodhisattva* ideal and the essence of Mahayana teaching into a political will, the Tibetan exile community could perhaps break down the barrier that keeps the PRC and the TGE apart, to the detriment of the Tibetan people.

Similar to the Sinhala-Buddhist fundamentalist, the Tibetan exile is a fundamentalist clinging to an imagined past of Buddhist glory, constructing a "far Other" in the Chinese communist and a "near Other" in those Tibetans who seek cooperation with the Chinese and their government. The Tibetan exile creates an image of his lost homeland as devastated by "Chinese" and "their" habits while ignoring the fact that even in remote villages Tibetans have televisions, that a number of young Tibetans are educated in institutions that are dedicated to teaching Tibetan language, culture, and history, that young Tibetans receive stipends to attend universities and, most important, that Buddhism in Tibet has experienced a significant revival since the end of the Mao era. Thus, if the exiles would approach the situation on the basis of Buddhist ethics and thought by first admitting that a historical situation is the result of *karma,* that all sentient beings, and that includes Communist cadres, should be treated like one's own mother (a popular form of Tibetan Buddhist meditation), that violence should be met with nonviolence, and, above all, that Tibetan religion and culture is as impermanent as all other phenomena, then a chance to reach an agreement seems feasible. The Tibetan exiles have betrayed the very belief for which they have left their native land in the hope to "preserve" it.

MISSED OPPORTUNITIES

Buddhist ethics and the practice of mindfulness, if made into a guideline for interacting with the world, could provide effective ways of building peace between individuals, social groups, and nations. But all too often Buddhist societies became oblivious of the Buddhist message and fell into personal hatred and greed, into prejudice vis-à-vis groups considered "Other," and into political strife. Much of Buddhist history is a history of missed opportunities to build peace. Buddhists are like people who hold in their hands the tools to their liberation from imprisonment but who have forgotten how to use them.

A few issues will highlight this point. Much to the shame of Buddhist societies, they did nothing to improve the fate of women. Buddhist literature, canonical as well as extra-canonical, is rife with gynophobic statements despite a promising beginning. The *Theragatha,* poems attributed to the first Buddhist nuns, speak a bold voice of women's confidence in their abilities and courage. But very soon after Buddha's death the economic and political elite privileged the monks and forgot the nuns. They remained in a fog of invisibility right into our time. Despite other claims, women are not part of the Tibetan political system, nor do they play a role in the monastic hierarchy. They enjoy more sexual and economic freedom than women did in the premodern societies of India and China, but there the "freedom" of Tibetan women ends. Buddhist philosophy that spoke so eloquently to the ephemeral nature of sex failed to influence people's thinking about gender equality.

Neither brought the teaching of *pratitya-samutpada,* "dependent origination," that emphasizes the interdependence of all that exists, an understanding and an empathy of underprivileged groups. Beggars and disabled people are considered as "bad" because bad karma caused them to be born in the present state. If one would truly engage in a meditation that sees every living and breathing creature in the universe as one's mother, how could one not embrace the beggar and the disabled? But the disciplinary code for monks and nuns excludes not only beggars and disabled people from joining the *sangha* but also homosexuals. At the moment of ordination, the male or female candidate is explicitly asked whether he or she is a homosexual. If the answer were "yes," ordination cannot be granted. While the Tibetan monastic system turned a blind eye to male homosexuality, even when the monk policemen were known to abduct and rape young novices, it was unforgiving with regard to female homosexuality. It is rumored that aristocratic ladies were occasionally erotically attracted to their female servants. If they were found out, they faced the death penalty unless their family's connection could spare them the worst. When the Dalai Lama met representatives of gays and lesbians in San Francisco a few years ago, he was clear that homosexuality is understood as "abuse of sexuality."

Buddhist nations are engaged in violence and warfare against other nations or ethnic groups in disregard of the most fundamental rules of Buddhist ethics. Meditation of the "four divine states" encourages, however, the practitioner to expand the feeling of love from oneself to one's kin, friends, acquaintances, and eventually to one's enemies. I found no accounts that Sinhala Buddhists or Tibetans engaged in such meditations by focusing on their ethnic "enemies."

Perhaps one of the most obvious gaps in Buddhist moral behavior is the lack of concern for the environment despite some isolated attempts, such as the "tree-huggers" of Thailand and Nepal. Preparations are under way to build in the vicinity of Bodhgaya, the place where Buddha realized enlightenment, a copper clad statue of the future Buddha Maitreya of the size of a fifty-story high office building surrounded with artificial gardens and water fountains. Protests of the local villagers, who eek out a bare minimum of living in a semi-desert environment where for most of the year the temperature is above 30°C and water is rationed for ten months a year, remained unanswered. No environmental studies were conducted to define the impact of the project on the local water supply or the changes in the local climate due to the sun's reflection off the monumental statue. Above all, the Tibetan Buddhist group spearheading this project that is budgeted for $150 million did not want to entertain the question whether this amount of money would not be better spent on aid to the local peasantry, building schools and hospitals. What about all the animals that will lose their lives and their habitat due to the project? While Buddhists are known to go to the markets to buy animals destined for food, some Buddhist societies are reluctant to address the underlying issue of using animals for food. How can Buddhists remain silent with regard to the loss of habitat, the loss of wildlife, the degradation of the planet?

Some Buddhist groups that originated recently do address these issues that are relegated to oblivion by the majority of Buddhist societies. Soka Gakkai is one of these movements that not only embraces a social agenda based on Buddhist ethics but also raises the environmental awareness across various Asian nations. Individual Buddhist masters took up social and environmental issues, such as Thich Nhat Hanh and Master Cheng Yen. The Taiwanese Fo Kuan Shan movement dedicates much of its human and economic resources to education, health care, and environmental concerns. Unfortunately, the well-established old Buddhist communities seem to be slow in following their younger cousins.

Buddhist societies in Sri Lanka and Tibet would find peace with their perceived enemies if they embraced the wisdom of Thich Nhat Hanh, a Vietnamese Buddhist master, whom I quoted at the beginning of this chapter. If Sinhalese Buddhist fundamentalists could recognize themselves in the Tamil insurgents and if the Tibetans in exile could see what unites them with the Communist cadres, whether Chinese or Tibetan, then peace would be within reach.

NOTES

1. E. K. Dargyay, "Sangha and State in Imperial Tibet," E. Steinkellner, ed., *Tibetan History and Language. Studies Dedicated to Uray Geza on his Seventieth Birthday. Wiener Studien zur Tibetologie und Buddhismuskunde 17* (Vienna: Arbeitskreis für Tibetische und Buddhistische Studien, Universität

Wien, 1991), pp. 111–127; Stanley Weistein, *Buddhism under the T'ang* (Cambridge: Cambridge University Press, 1987), pp. 79ff.

2. Wilhelm Geiger (Heinz Bechert, ed.), *Culture of Ceylon in Medieval Times* (Wiesbaden: Otto Harrassowitz, 1960), p. 203: "The problem of the relation between church and state must be looked at in Ceylon and other Eastern countries from a quite different standpoint as in the medieval and modern Europe. . . . [T]he kingship by which the state was represented was the firmest support of the Buddhist church and the latter that of kingship."

3. Gregory Schopen, *Bones, Stones, and Buddhist Monks* (Honolulu: University of Hawaii Press, 1997).

4. In Daniel L. Smith-Christopher, ed., *Subverting Hatred. The Challenge of Nonviolence in Religious Traditions* (Cambridge, MA: Boston Research Center for the 21st Century, 1998), p. 28.

5. His Holiness the Dalai Lama's nobel (sic) lecture University Aula, Oslo, December 11, 1989 (http:/www.tibet.com/DL/nobellecture.html).

6. "[T]he citizens remained citizens. They shopped, changed jobs, laughed. Yet the darkest Greek tragedies were innocent compared with what was happening here. Heads on stakes. Skeletons dug out of a cocoa pit in Matale." Michael Ondaatje, *Anil's Ghost* (Toronto: McClelland & Stewart, 2000), p. 11.

7. Richard Gombrich and G. Obeyesekere, *Buddhism Transformed. Religious Change in Sri Lanka* (Princeton, 1988, repr. Delhi: Motilal Banarsidass 1990), p. 202.

8. I adopt the term "Protestant Buddhism" by accepting the arguments brought forward by Gombrich/ Obeyesekere, *Buddhism Transformed,* pp. 202–240, while S. J. Tambiah, *Buddhism Betrayed? Religion, Politics and Violence in Sri Lanka* (Chicago and London: University of Chicago Press, 1992), pp. 5–8, prefers the term "Buddhist revivalism." Neither term covers the breadth of the development. On the one hand, "Buddhist revivalism" is deeply influenced by Victorian Protestantism, a fact this term does not acknowledge, while, on the other hand, "Protestant Buddhism" is a revivalist movement, a fact this term does not indicate.

9. A vivid description of how Western publications about Buddhism informed the redefinition of Buddhism in nineteenth-century Sri Lanka is found in Tessa J. Bartholomeusz and Chandra R. de Silva, eds., *Buddhist Fundamentalism and Minority Identities in Sri Lanka* (Albany: State University of New York Press, 1998) p. 19ff., and in Gombrich/ Obeyesekere, *Buddhism,* pp. 207–210.

10. Stephen Prothero, *The White Buddhist. The Asian Odyssey of Henry Steel Olcott* (Delhi: Sri Satguru Publications, 1997); Gombrich/Obeyesekere, *Buddhism,* pp. 204–205. Olcott, supported by Blavatsky, created Buddhist cultural props that echoed those of Anglo-Protestantism: a Buddhist flag, hymns, a "Buddhist catechism," and so on.

11. Grombich/Obeyesekere, *Buddhism,* p. 212.

12. Gombrich/Obeyeseker, *Buddhism,* p. 213. Stephen Prothero, *White Buddhist,* p. 141, quotes a speech given by Dharmapala to the Dravidian Buddhist Society in which he emphasizes Buddhism as an "Aryan" religion "preached . . . to the Aryans."

13. For a full discussion of these traits Protestant Buddhism developed see Gombrich/Obeyesekere, *Buddhism,* pp. 218–224. The authors, for instance, document how the Victorian Protestants' dislike for the ritualism of the Catholic Church affected the revivalist Buddhists who then attributed the same derogatory descriptors to Mahayana Buddhism.

14. Wilhelm Geiger, tr., *Mahavamsa: The Great Chronicle of Ceylon* (London: Pali Text Society, 1912), and K. R. Norman, *Pali Literature. Including the Canonical Literature in Prakrit and Sanskrit of all the Hinayana Schools of Buddhism* (A History of Indian Literature) (Wiesbaden: Otto Harrassowitz, 1983), pp. 117–118.

15. Bartholomeusz/ Silva, *Fundamentalism,* p. 4.

16. Tambiah, *Buddhism Betrayed?,* pp. 15–21, discusses in detail how the radicalization of some groups of mostly young monks happened and how it resulted in authenticating the activist monk, quite in contrast to the monks' traditional roles in society.

17. Tambiah, *Buddhism Betrayed?*

18. de Silva, "The Plurality of Buddhist Fundamentalism," in Bartholomeusz/ Silva, *Fundamentalism,* p. 66f ; Peter Schalk, "Articles 9 and 18 of the Constitution as Obstacles to Peace," *Lanka,* 5 (1990), pp. 280–292; Donald Swearer, "Fundamentalistic Movements in Theravada Buddhism," in Martin E. Marty and R. Scott Appelby, eds., *Fundamentalism Observed* (Chicago: University of Chicago Press, 1991); Gaganath Obeyesekere, "Buddhism, Nationhood and Cultural Identity: A Question of Fundamentals," in Martin E. Marty and R. Scott Appelby, eds., *Fundamentalism Comprehended* (Chicago: University of Chicago Press, 1995).

19. George D. Bond, "Conflict of Identity and Interpretation in Buddhism: The Clash between the Sarvodaya Shramadana Movement and the Government of President Premadasa," in Batholomeusz/Silva, *Fundamentalism,* pp. 36–52; and George D. Bond, "A.T. Ariyaratne and the Sarvodaya Shramadana Movement in Sri Lanka," in Christopher S. Queen and Sallie B. King, eds., *Engaged Buddhism. Buddhist Liberation Movements in Asia* (Albany: State University of New York, 1996), pp. 121–146.

20. Gombrich/Obeyesekere, *Buddhism,* pp. 243–255; Detlef Kantowsky. *Sarvodaya: The Other Development* (Delhi: Vikas, 1980).

21. Kantowsky, *Sarvodaya,* p. 68 (quoted in Gombrich/Obeyesekere, *Buddhism,* p. 246).

22. Ibid., p. 73.

23. Gombrich/ Obeyesekere, *Buddhism,* p. 247.

24. As to what constitutes "Tibet" see Melvyn C. Goldstein, "Change, Conflict and Continuity," Robert Barnett and Shirin Akiner, eds., *Resistance and Reform in Tibet* (Bloomington: Indiana University Press, 1994), pp. 76–90.

25. Melvyn C. Goldstein, "The Revival of Monastic Life in Drepung Monastery," in Melvyn C. Goldstein and Matthew T. Kapstein, eds., *Buddhism in Contemporary Tibet* (Delhi: Motilal Banarsidass, 1999), pp. 15–52.

26. The treaty between the Tang Emperor Mu-tsung and the Tibetan King Khri gTsug-lde-brtsan (821–822), is inscribed on the four sides of a stone pillar near the west entrance to the Jo-khang, the main temple in Lhasa. The inscriptions on the east and west sides of the pillar state several times that the two monarchs agreed to unite their countries *(chab srid gcig tu mol te),* and that they were related as uncle and nephew due to the Tibetan ruler's marriage to Kim-sheng Kong-jo, a Tang princess. The inscriptions on the north and south sides of the pillar record the names and functions of the leading administrators of both countries. The Tibetan text of the inscription, its English translation, as well as a historical discussion of its content are given by Hugh E. Richardson, *Ancient Historical Edicts at Lhasa and the Mu Tsung/ Khri Gtsug Lde Brtsan Treaty of A.D. 821–822 from the Inscription in Lhasa* (London: The Royal Asiatic Society of Great Britain and Ireland, 1952), pp. 35–82.

27. Lack of space prevents me from a further documentation of this statement. I refer to the discussions provided by Melvyn C. Goldstein in *A History of Modern Tibet, 1913–1951. The Demise of the Lamaist State* (Berkeley: University of California Press, 1989); he gives a summary of the events in *The Snow Lion and the Dragon China, Tibet, and the Dalai Lama* (Berkeley: University of California Press,1997); an excellent survey of the crucial events from the Qing Dynasty on into the present is given in M. C. Goldstein, "Change, Conflict and Continuity among a Community of Nomadic Pastoralists: A Case Study from Western Tibet, 1950–1990," in Robert Barnett, ed., *Resistance and Reform in Tibet* (London: Hurst & Company, 1994), pp. 76–111.

28. Lack of communication and education among the Tibetans were responsible for the gap between the historical facts, documented in treaties and edicts, and a subjective view embraced by ordinary Tibetans. This subjective view of the Tibetans that their country was and is distinct and different from China is movingly articulated by Palden Gyatso, *Fire under the Snow. Testimony of a Tibetan Prisoner* (London: Harvill Press, 1997).

29. For a more detailed account of the American interference in Tibet see Tsering Shakya, *The Dragon in the Land of Snows* (London: Penguin, 2000), pp. 71–89, 170–180.

30. Modern Tibetan knows of the term *rang btsan* as "independence" and literary Tibetan uses the term *rang dbang* ("freedom" or "self-power") but exclusively as a religiophilosphical term. As to the social system of premodern Tibet see E. Dargyay, *Tibetan Village Communities* (Warminster, UK: Aris & Phillips, 1982), pp. 16–32.

31. The mythic character of these seven kings "whose tombs were erected in heaven" is discussed by Erik Haarh, *The Yar lu Dynasty* (Copenhagen: Gad's Forlag, 1969), pp. 75, 114, 119, 153.

32. Anon., *bKa' thang sde lnga* (Mi-rigs dpe-skrung khang, 1990), pp. 113–116.

33. Eva K. Dargyay, "Srong-btsan sgam-po's 'Biography' in the *Mani bka' 'bum*," Acta Orientalia Academiae Scientiarum Hungaricae, vol. XLIII (1989), pp. 247–257.

34. Quoted by Tsering Shakya, *The Dragon in the Land of Snow* (New York: Penguin Compass, 1999), p. 27.

35. http://www.freetibet.org/info/file5.htm.

36. The issue of what areas constitute "Tibet" is discussed in detail by Melvyn Goldstein, *Resistance and Reform*, pp. 76–90; see also the map on p. xvii. The claim by TGE to "Greater Tibet" is detailed by M. Goldstein, *Snow Lion*, p. 71.

37. Melvyn C. Goldstein and Matthew T. Kapstein, eds., *Buddhism in Contemporary Tibet. Religious Revival and Cultural Identity* (Berkeley: University of California Press, 1998).

38. http://www.freetibet.org/menu.htm.

5

Confucianism and Peacebuilding

JUDITH A. BERLING

Confucianism is centrally and fundamentally about peace, social order, and harmony at all levels of society. To paraphrase Dr. Seuss, Confucianism is "harmony all the way down." Confucians saw the establishment and sustenance of harmony as a primary goal achieved through the education and self-cultivation of citizens. Although there are certain limits to the Confucian vision in dealing with formidable obstacles to peace, Confucians have much to contribute to an understanding of what is entailed in peacebuilding and peace maintenance. Confucians also challenge and stretch common presuppositions about the process of peacebuilding; they offer approaches to peacebuilding from a moral and educational framework.

BASIC CONFUCIAN TEACHINGS

"Confucianism" represents historically diverse teachings, practices, and social patterns ranging from state-sponsored and enforced orthodoxy to a range of philosophical schools, private school movements, and popular depictions of scholars and officials in literature, painting, and drama. All of these in one way or another look to the teachings of Confucius (551–479 BCE), a teacher, classical scholar, and political commentator. Confucius lived in turbulent times, and although he sought an office to address the issues of his day, his political ambitions were thwarted. Nevertheless his recorded exchanges with his students as well

93

commentaries on the Chinese classics shaped the "Confucian tradition" and traditional Chinese civilization.

Although the imperial Confucian state and examinations to select officials ended in 1911, the importance and influence of Confucian values persist to this day. Confucianism has been so identified with Chinese culture and values that to be Chinese means in some sense to be Confucian. Confucianism is primarily an ethnic or, to be more precise, a cultural marker, and only secondarily a religious marker. In recent years, scholars in China and abroad have articulated a New Confucianism, arguing that a reformed and revitalized Confucianism "is worthy of being considered part of the material and intellectual base for the new ecumenical world order."[1] The New Confucians, such as Wei-ming Tu, would celebrate the inclusion of a chapter on Confucianism in this volume.

Confucius' life and teachings were a response to the distressing political turbulence of his times. Although the Zhou dynasty (1156–256 BCE) was still nominally in power, since 771 BCE various states within the Zhou alliance had become so militarily and politically powerful that the Zhou was forced to recognize their quasi-independence. These states vied for supremacy, annexing their neighbors through conquest, alliance, or dirty tricks, each hoping to supplant the Zhou and establish a new dynasty.[2] The turbulent political climate had violently disrupted lives of people caught up in the warfare or duplicity of the times. It had, however, created an opportunity for educated men who sought positions as advisors to rulers who might conceivably triumph in the fray. Thus flourished "a hundred schools" of political philosophy, most in the Legalist principles of *realpolitik* or statecraft. Ambitious advisors preferred institutional and military strategies that would not only enable rulers to survive in the turbulent struggles of the day, but also to establish a lasting, stable social order, a peace in which the ruler could enjoy the benefits of victory.

Against the dominance of the Legalists' statecraft, Confucius offered an alternative message. He argued that statecraft, strong laws, and military might would ultimately fail to establish a stable, harmonious social order. He warned: "Lead the people by laws and regulate them by penalties, and the people will try to keep out of jail, but will have no sense of shame. Lead the people by virtue and restrain them with rites, and the people will have a sense of shame, and moreover will become good."[3] In other words, although laws, penalties, and military force (a structural approach) might temporarily subdue the populace, they would not establish lasting peace; the people would submit out of fear, but would remain unruly and discontent (have no sense of shame). Rule by virtue and rites, however, would establish "good" citizens who respect the rule of a worthy government.[4] This approach would only work if the ruler himself were good, and recognized as such. Confucius said, "If a ruler himself is upright, all will go well without orders. But if he himself is not upright, even though he gives orders they will not be obeyed."[5] Confucius thus argued that effective sovereignty required personal moral authority to earn the respect of the people. Coercive power was ephemeral and could not establish genuine peace and harmony.

In seeking the basis of stable social harmony, Confucius looked where none of his contemporaries looked—to the practices and institutions of the crumbling Zhou dynasty, and in particular to the court rituals that continued and adapted the practices of Chinese antiquity. In these rituals, Confucius saw not only an emblem of harmony, but its very source and embodiment.[6] The court rituals of Zhou were the antithesis of the plotting, deception, and dirty tricks practiced in the courts of the scheming feudal lords. These rituals were dignified and harmonious; in them every participant had an appropriate role. The harmonious complementarity of these roles created and enacted the order and harmony of the Zhou government.

court

The court rituals had been defined in the classics, storehouses of ancient wisdom. Confucius noted that these classics also defined the complementary roles for everyone in society: parent and child, elder and younger, ruler and subject, husband and wife, friend and friend. He saw these roles as extensions of ritual. Thus, rituals defined or orchestrated the social obligations, conventions, and courtesies that make civilized society (social harmony) possible. Moreover, Confucius argued, they provided a framework for the development of moral virtues that could be expressed or fulfilled through these fundamental human relationships. A humane education based in the classics would foster a virtuous populace aware of its social duties and moral obligations.

Education and learning were a lifetime commitment through which the rough edges of the human mind-and-heart were gradually smoothed away to allow the inner core of refined humanity and wisdom to emerge. Confucius said, "At fifteen, I set my heart on learning. At thirty, I was firmly established. At forty, I had no more doubts. At fifty, I knew the will of Heaven. At sixty, I was ready to listen to it. At seventy, I could follow my heart's desire without transgressing what was right."[7] Followers of Confucius throughout the centuries shared this profound commitment to humane learning as the path of moral self-cultivation and human fulfillment. But how is this commitment to humane learning and self-cultivation linked to the central concern for social harmony and peace? This link is summarized succinctly in "The Great Learning," one of the "Four Books" that were the gateway to a Confucian education:

The ancients who wished clearly to exemplify illustrious virtue throughout the world would first set up good government in their states. Wishing to govern well their states, they would first regulate their families. Wishing to regulate their families, they would first culti-vate their persons. Wishing to cultivate their persons, they would first rectify their minds. Wishing to rectify their minds, they would first seek sincerity in their thoughts. Wishing for sincerity in their thoughts, they would first extend their knowledge. The extension of knowledge lay in the investigation of things. For only when things are investigated is knowledge extended; only when knowledge is extended are thoughts sincere; only when thoughts are sincere are minds rectified; only when minds are rectified are our persons cultivated; only when our persons are cultivated are our families regulated; only when families are regu-lated are states well governed; only when states are well governed is there peace in the world.[8]

Later Confucians built upon and expanded Confucius' vision of a harmonious society to include the entire cosmos, human and beyond. Zhang Zai (1021–1077) wrote a famous inscription on the wall of his study that eloquently expresses the Confucian vision. It says, in part:

Heaven is my father and earth is my mother, and even such a small creature as I finds an intimate place in their midst. Therefore that which extends throughout the universe I regard as my body and that which directs the universe I consider as my nature. All people are my bothers and sisters, and all things are my companions.[9]

This, then, constitutes the Confucian view of peacebuilding.

OBSTACLES AND LIMITATIONS FOR CONFUCIAN PEACEBUILDING

While Confucianism is centrally about social harmony, Confucians throughout Chinese history harbored assumptions that could limit or undermine Confucian contributions to peacebuilding in certain situations.

The Legacy of Opposition to Legalism

As we have seen, the teachings of Confucius were shaped by a response to the dominance of Legalism's "statecraft" thinking. The Legalists were briefly victorious in the political struggles of the late Zhou. The succes-sor to the Zhou was the Qin (221–209 BCE), a short-lived state that enacted Legalist principles with a vengeance. After its demise, Confucianism became the state ideology, and the Legalist approach was thenceforth vigorously maligned as the source of all political ills, hardening Confucian rhetoric against structural and legalistic approaches.

During the Han dynasty (206 BCE–206 CE), the first to adopt Confucian ideology, the government sought monopolies on salt and iron to increase revenues, particularly in support of their military campaigns against "barbarians" on their Western borders. The Confucians argued strongly against this policy on two major counts: (1) "that China should make peace with its neighbors and be content to remain safely within its traditional boundaries"[10] and (2) that the monopolies wrought economic hardships on citizens that made it impossible for them to earn their livelihoods and maintain local harmony. Their argument is entirely consistent with the notion of peace as harmony built from the ground up, family by family, village by village. It also opposes the notion of a strong and expanding state. While the monopolies were established, the policies were modified in accordance with Confucian principles.

The shaping of Confucian political rhetoric in clear opposition to anything resembling Legalist principles sometimes served an obstacle to establishing structural reforms needed to reestablish and maintain peace. In the Song dynasty (960–1279 CE), many believed that significant legal and structural reforms were necessary to redress problems that they blamed for China's susceptibility to external aggression and internal revolt. Wang Anshi (1021–1086) advocated wide-ranging legal and structural reforms. He sought to justify his reforms on the basis of a return to the principles (but not the exact practices) embodied in the Confucian classics. He used clearly Confucian rhetoric to avoid any appearance of Legalist thinking. He wrote, "When moral principles are applied to the affairs of government . . . the form they take and the use they are put to depend upon the laws, but their promotion and execution depend upon individuals. In the worthiness of its individual officials to discharge the duties of office . . . no dynasty has surpassed the early Zhou."[11] While the rhetoric was purely Confucian, the substance of Wang's reforms was thoroughly structural. The sophistication of his fiscal, political, and educational restructuring alarmed more conservative Confucians. Some simply thought he misinterpreted the classics. Others thought he had succumbed to Legalist thinking.

The opposition to Wang's reforms demonstrates how the hardening of Confucian rhetorical opposition to Legalist strategies could become a blind spot for political thinking and reform, and also for peacebuilding, particularly when peace required significant structural reforms.

Confucianism as Norm of State and Culture

Confucians believed that their values and teachings were right and normative for "all under Heaven." Confucius taught that the ancient sages had discerned the moral order ordained by Heaven, expressing this order in their teachings, their conduct, and their government. These values and principles were the normative basis of human civilization.

Starting in the Han dynasty, Confucianism became official "state orthodoxy." In the Han a vast array of local cultures and practices were brought into a synthesis shaped by an understanding of Confucian civilization. The dominance of Confucian orthodoxy was strengthened from the time of the Tang dynasty (618–907), when official candidates were selected by rigorous examinations on the Chinese classics. As officials, they were to impart Confucian moral counsel to the emperor. "Confucianism" normatively defined Chinese state and culture.

Confucian conviction of the normativity or orthodoxy of their values created significant resistance to other understandings of governance, particularly in those periods when China was ruled by foreigners not steeped in centuries of Chinese learning. Thus, the Manchus who conquered China to establish the Ching dynasty (1644–1912) were plagued by the resistance of Confucians who refused to serve an unworthy regime (one that did not honor Confucian values). Lü Liu-liang (1629–1683) was one such resister, refusing any position or salary from a corrupt government.[12] Lü instead devoted himself to revising correct Confucian teaching, believing that the decline of true Confucianism had caused China to fall into the hands of the Manchus. Dissenters like Lü relied on a long and venerated tradition of moral dissent. Unbending commitment to Confucian virtue was deemed heroic, a moral model. Thus Confucians could be quite rigid about not accommodating those who failed to meet their high standards.

Note that Lü's dissent is based on moral grounds. He does not dissent on religious principles per se. This is one implication of Confucianism being more of an ethnic or cultural marker than a religious marker. The unbending moral values on Confucians were bound up with the definition of "being Chinese." As long as others (particularly those of other religions) accepted certain basic moral values, Confucians were not only open to other religions, but often practiced them alongside of their own Confucian rituals and practices. Thus, Confucians also practiced and honored Daoism, Buddhism (a foreign religion that adapted to Chinese ways), and a host of local traditions. Problems arose with foreigners, like the Manchus, who (initially at least) did not accept those basic Confucian (i.e., Chinese) values. The Manchus learned that in order to rule they had to affirm, adopt, and patronize Confucian values and learning; they had, in other words, to "be more Chinese." Problems also arose with monotheistic religions, particularly Islam and Christianity, that strongly rejected the idea of affirming or practicing more than one religion. The notion that one should choose one path and reject all others was foreign to the Chinese religious system, and thus Muslims and Christians appeared to the Chinese to refuse to participate in Chinese culture and community.[13]

Confucianism was also state ideology. The imperial government (like the PRC government) reserved to itself the right to define and enforce orthodox religious practice. The government might become involved in the patronage and bureaucratic oversight of "approved" religious communities, as it does today with the official Protestant and Catholic churches. It might also outlaw and persecute communities or movements it deems dangerous, as it does today with Falun gong. In the imperial period, governmental rhetoric about religion often had a Confucian flavor, although not far beneath the surface were issues about tax policy or social unrest.[14]

Thus, Confucianism functioned as a "norm" in relation to other religions in two very different senses: (1) it represented a set of values and behaviors identified as "Chinese" that all religious movements and communities were expected to affirm, and (2) the state used "Confucian" rhetoric in exercising its power to define and endorse orthodoxy.

Another implication of the normativity of Confucianism was a tendency to excessive establishmentarianism and resistance to social and cultural change. From at least the sixteenth century, Chinese society began to evolve toward the modern world. Cities flourished, uprooting people from the countryside creating new relationships and opportunities; technological advances opened up economic possibilities; and developments in printing expanded literacy further down the social scale. These changes gave rise to new dreams and aspirations.

By the late nineteenth and early twentieth centuries, educated Chinese experienced rising frustration against the strictures of traditional society. Young men chafed at having to wait for their father's demise before assuming their roles as full adults or their share of the family property. Educated women became angry about many forms of oppression: foot-binding, confinement in the home (in the case of elite women), concubinage, divorce available to husbands only, arranged marriages, and intense pressures on young brides. The Chinese were learning about the outside world (Japan, Russia, the West), and they longed for "Science and Democracy," although these were for them little more than romantic slogans. The literary and social uprising known as the May

Fourth Movement (1919) not only espoused the new values, but also virulently denounced Confucianism. Long the pride of Chinese civilization, Confucianism was now its bane, the source of all ills.

Many Confucians were too establishmentarian, too willing to accept the practices of Chinese society (those not expressly forbidden in the classics). In Confucius' time, the teachings of the classics were a trenchant critique of dominant practices, but by late traditional China Confucians had become overly identified with the establishment. There were exceptions, to be sure. As early as the sixteenth century, Li Zhi (1527–1602) argued for a more radical and egalitarian form of Confucianism, including more equality between men and women. He was sharply critical of many other Confucians, and minced no words in offering his critique. The establishment was not amused. In 1602, the government ordered his books burned and threw Li Zhi into prison, where he committed suicide.[15] Such repressive actions by the "Confucian" state convinced the May Fourth protesters that their attacks on Confucianism were justified.

Confucianism was, to a great extent, limited or undermined by its own success. It was in practice, if not in principle, unable to question the justice and integrity of "the system," for it had become overly identified with it. In Chinese culture, it was Daoists who tended to raised issues about the justice of conventional views and to suggest that peace entailed a leveling of unequal relationships based on power, wealth, and gender. Although Daoists suggested an alternative notion of peace and justice, they did not enter the political fray to reform society and establish their ideas; instead, they withdrew from government to seek spiritual peace. They were not active peacebuilders.

Parochialism: The Middle Kingdom Syndrome

Another limitation of Confucianism in regard to peacebuilding is related to the last, and could perhaps be seen as a cultural extension of it. This is the Chinese conviction, based on a long history, of the innate superiority of Chinese culture. This conviction is rooted in part in Confucius' teaching that the classics articulate a normative framework for civilization. In ancient times, this conviction gave form and substance to what it meant to be Chinese. During this early period of Chinese history, scores of local cultures were absorbed into the Chinese cultural orbit; Chinese civilization was "under construction."

By the Tang dynasty (618–907), imperial China dominated the world the Chinese knew; it was indeed the Middle Kingdom (the literal meaning of *Zhongguo*, or "China"), to which princes around the world sent tribute gifts. The Tang had some justification for their sense of cultural superiority; Tang civilization in fact outshone its cultural contemporaries. The glory of the Tang "Middle Kingdom" became the prototype of China's destiny: a Confucian civilization superior to "all under Heaven."

The Chinese sense of cultural superiority far outlived the Tang and even the turbulent events of the twentieth century. The long tradition of Chinese learning, the rich heritage of arts and letters, and the achievements of the imperial system were and are a source of immense pride. Thus, the Chinese are offended when the rest of the world fails to respect their rich cultural heritage. Simply to accuse the Chinese of cultural chauvinism is too facile; Europeans and North Americans have more than their share of cultural chauvinism. The issues are far more complex.

Chinese parochialism and sense of cultural superiority have become issues in international discussions on topics like human rights. Chinese spokespersons often argue that Western criticism of China's human rights record is irrelevant because the West does not understand the values of Chinese culture and the ethics of its political system. Such arguments are often construed as Chinese intransigence about adopting "universal" statements on human rights developed through the U.N. or other international agencies. That is in fact the effect of the Chinese arguments, and it is symptomatic of a limitation of the Chinese (and Confucians) regarding peacebuilding—their reluctance to enter into so-called "universal" international ethical norms and standards.

The Chinese or Confucian counterargument would be: how "universal" are these standards if they have not taken the principles of Chinese culture into account? This is not merely a matter of rhetoric or stiff-necked pride. To lift up just one very complex issue, the Confucian notion of "person" is fundamentally different from the notion of "person" most commonly understood in human rights language. While the West (and most language of human rights) understands the person as an inviolate individual, in Confucianism a "person" is the center of a nexus of particular human relationships that define his or her roles and obligations. There are, to be sure, ethical principles of mutuality and reciprocity that mitigate excessive hierarchy and domination in asymmetrical relationships, but the emphasis remains on the obligation to fulfill one's various roles. It is no easy matter to reconcile Confucian values with Western-dominated notions of individual human rights.

When trade concessions to China (such as Most Favored Nation status) have come before the U.S. Congress, some inevitably oppose them on the grounds of China's poor record on human rights. The U.S. political rhetoric measures China's record on human rights against a U.S. standard, based on a U.S. notion of individual freedoms. The Chinese government dismisses such criticisms as irrelevant because they neither understand nor honor Chinese culture. The cultural misunderstanding here allows the Chinese government to use cultural differences as a screen to deflect any criticisms. The cultural differences are real, but that does not mean that there are not genuine problems with human rights in Chinese society. The challenge is to establish some ground of conversation or dialogue that respects the differences, but does not back off from genuine abuses.

The most serious consequence of this Middle Kingdom syndrome, however, is that the Confucians are unlikely to initiate the sort of horizon stretching that might identify elusive common ground. Confucian peacebuilders historically donned the mantle of benevolent paternalism, expecting parties to defer to them in recognition of their rich heritage and profound values. They were generously willing to offer parental guidance. The contemporary world situation challenges all to recognize many centers of value, and Confucians are challenged to understand how to de-center themselves while sustaining their sense of values and tradition.

Personal Trust versus Institutional Agreements

At least since the middle of the nineteenth century, Westerners have been frustrated in their attempts to make peace or conclude agreements on contentious issues with Chinese institutions. The problem is cultural, and the roots—on the Chinese side—go back to Confucianism. Westerners tend to approach peacebuilding by means of contracts or treaties between responsible institutions (governments, corporations, agencies). That is, they tend to approach such matters through legal, formal, or diplomatic strategies, and to believe that the signing of a contract or treaty is a resolution of differences.

The Chinese, on the other hand, tend to see disagreements as a breakdown of human relationships. Although the contention may affect large groups, Confucians would tend to see the resolution of the matter in the development of an improved relationship between leaders of contending parties. If the leaders can resolve the issue with integrity, they assume, the people will understand and follow.

An excellent historical example of this principle is the role of Zhou Enlai (1989–1976) in the opening of relationships between PRC and the United States. Given the long history of anti-Western and anti-American rhetoric in the PRC, particularly during the years of the Cultural Revolution, the odds were strongly stacked against any possibility of rapprochement with the West in 1972. Many of the Chinese generals and hard-liners were adamantly opposed to any such rapprochement. Zhou

Enlai, however, had enormous respect within the government and within Chinese culture as a wise, shrewd, and loyal statesman. He also had the intelligence and extraordinary personal qualities to earn the respect of and handle the delicate negotiations with representatives of the United States. Although certainly not a Confucian by philosophy, Zhou Enlai represented the qualities of the Chinese gentleman and statesman that allowed him to succeed in this extraordinary act of peacebuilding. The negotiations that "opened" China were not so much a clear shift in the political position of the Chinese government (although there were many significant small steps), as a new relationship made possible by the presence, prestige, and extraordinary personal qualities of Zhou Enlai.

CONFUCIAN CONTRIBUTIONS TO PEACEBUILDING

Confucians have always understood peacebuilding in a moral/ethical framework rather than in a legal framework. Their understanding invites reflection on the causes of the breakdown of peace and harmony, and the bases for lasting or enduring peace.

Peace, the Confucians argue, is a matter of harmonious relationships among people. The loss of peace is the breakdown of such relationships. While specific events and actual or putative injustices are often cited as the destroyers of peace, these are the symptoms of the breakdown of human relationships. Until human beings change their attitudes, their understandings of the facts, their behaviors toward one another, and even their values, the relationships cannot be restored or mended.

Given this understanding, Confucians would argue that a treaty or legal agreement cannot be said to restore peace. Such agreements are fragile and ineffective if not accompanied by a fundamental change in human understandings, behaviors, and values. The Western legal system is understandably a source of great pride, and so are a number of treaties, conventions, agreements, and contracts won through skillful and patient negotiation between contentious parties. But the Confucian might note that all legal resolutions of conflict are based on adversarial assumptions, on the negotiation of difference through adversarial advocacy. In Confucian terms, such agreements at best create a formal suspension of conflict in which well-intentioned persons can work to achieve harmonious relationships and a lasting peace. A treaty might create the conditions in which to work toward peace; it does not create peace. Confucians suggest that the accomplishments of the legal strategies of Western culture are counterbalanced by the litigious nature of those cultures. The adversarial nature of relationships is never quite transcended.

The rebuilding or transformation of human relationships, Confucians argue, is the genuine form of peace. It is immensely challenging and time-consuming; where tensions run deep, relationships cannot be transformed overnight, or even within the space of a generation. Nevertheless, only such transformation will create genuine harmony.

Harmony as the Goal of Peacebuilding

Harmony is the hallmark of the realized Confucian social order. A harmonious society based on Confucian principles is, according to New Confucian Wei-ming Tu, transformed from an adversarial society to a fiduciary community.[16] The ruler facilitates the development of this community through attending to his own moral development and his relations with all aspects of society—respect "the belief that outer kingliness requires inner sageliness."[17] "The Doctrine of the Mean" offers nine principles for Confucian government:

> If the ruler cultivates his personal life, the Way will be established. If he honors the worthy, he will not be perplexed. If he is affectionate to his relatives, there will be no grumbling among his uncles and brothers. If he identifies himself with the welfare of the whole body of officers, then the officers will repay him heavily for his courtesies. If he treats the common people as his own children, then the masses will exhort one another [to do good]. If he attracts various artisans, there will be sufficiency of wealth and resources in the country. If he shows tenderness to strangers from far countries, people from all quarters of the world will flock to him. And if he extends kindly and awesome influence over the feudal lords, then the world will stand in awe of him.[18]

Wei-ming Tu's commentary on this passage notes the specificity with which the various interests and segments of Chinese society are named, particularly those who could potentially undermine or challenge the ruler. The nine principles are not abstract moral principles, but practical advice for transforming an adversarial set of relationships into a fiduciary community of mutual trust and respect, thereby establishing and maintaining social harmony. The attention to potentially contentious relationships demonstrates that the idealism of the Confucian vision is a response to a far from ideal social environment. It is an act of courage and faith, an affirmation that even the most deep-seated human fragmentation can be overcome. The means to overcome such fragmentation will be discussed shortly.

Recognition of potentially contending interests within the human community also shapes the understanding of peace and harmony. Remember that Confucius' teaching was a corrective to positions that sought the submission of the populace through coercion and the threat of punishment. The harmony envisioned by Confucius was not rigid or fearful conformity. As a model for peace, harmony is an image of bringing different voices or notes out of discord and into a pleasing balance. Harmony is neither sameness, nor agreement; it is not unity. Hall and Ames comment, "The accomplished ruler, far from exercising coercive power over his people, grounds his pursuit of order in the richness of diversity and orchestrates his subjects' impulses toward quality in the direction of an aesthetic harmony that maximizes their possibilities for creativity."[19] The orchestration of such harmony requires creative adaptation of models from the past in light of the circumstances of the present, bringing the particular voices at hand into a pleasing composition.

In establishing or orchestrating harmony out of the diverse voices in the human community, a leader is assisted by ritual. Ritual provides, as it were, the aesthetic or musical forms within which harmony and peace can be established. Wei-ming Tu comments,

> It is important to note that the harmonizing function of propriety [i.e., ritual] is valued not because it manages to gloss over substantive conflicts, but because it can assist the ruler to establish real harmony; as a defining characteristic of fiduciary community, it shapes the very nature of human relatedness. If a society is governed by the rules of propriety [ritual], its mode of existence will rest upon a strong sense of mutual trust despite the presence of apparent conflicts among its subgroups.[20]

Thus harmony is orchestrated by a ruler relying on the aesthetic order of ritual.

Confucius had turned to the formal rituals of the Zhou court and the structures of human relations defined in the classics as the model for harmony, but he looked beyond the surface of these formal ritual structures to see in them a model for the development of harmonious human relationships. He philosophically extended the concept or image of "ritual" to encompass the human capacity for civilized patterns of relationship that foster trust, respect, and fiduciary community. For Confucius, "ritual" in this broadest sense creates the very ground and possibility of establishing harmony across the lines of difference.

Peace as understood by the Confucians is an aspiration or ideal that is never finally or perfectly achieved. The transformation of a web of potentially contentious human relationships into a fiduciary community of trust and respect is a never-ending project requiring constant vigilance. This is a utopian ideal to be courageously pursued within imperfect human communities.

The Confucian approach to peacebuilding emphasizes the personal over the legal or structural; it calls for the transformation and harmonization of human relationships through the moral modeling of leaders and the education and moral self-cultivation of persons. It is a balance or counterweight to the legal and structural approaches that have dominated recent history and can seem both inspiring and naive in its idealism. Legal and structural change cannot be neglected, to be sure, but much peacebuilding literature has emphasized them to the exclusion of personal dimensions. The Confucian approach invites further reflection about the human dimensions of peacebuilding and about a long-term commitment to building a solid foundation for peace.

Leaders and Moral Models

Confucian peacebuilding relies on leaders and moral models to guide and inspire, to bring contending voices into accord. Confucius stressed the importance of moral leadership not because it was so readily available in his time, but precisely because it was so rare. He looked to moral models of the past and taught his students how to emulate excellent qualities and avoid faults discerned in others. He said, "When walking in a party of three, I always have teachers. I can select the good qualities of the one for imitation, and the bad ones of the other and correct them in myself."[21] Lacking perfect models, human beings are forced to discern fragments of moral excellence within the behavior of complex human beings and gradually develop their sense of moral perfection.

Confucius and his followers assumed that the good person would attract others, would naturally evoke respect and deference. They saw authority in the integrity of moral character. While this may seem idealistic, it is a conviction shared in part by the modern civil disobedience movement: the moral integrity and courage of Mahatma Gandhi and the Reverend Dr. Martin Luther King, Jr., inspired legions of followers and eventually prevailed against the forces of colonial oppression and legalized racism. Integrity of character was also a significant factor in Zhou Enlai's effectiveness as a peacebuilder.

Confucian peacebuilding was often based on an approach of benevolent paternalism. Traditional China was after all a hierarchical and paternalist society. Contemporary interpreters of Confucius, however, argue that his notion of leadership did not assume that harmony simply emanated from the excellence of the leader. Hall and Ames cite a famous passage about Confucius' character: "When the Master was singing with others and liked their song, he would invariably ask them to repeat it before harmonizing with them."[22] Just as Confucius listened to the song before adding his harmony, the leader must "first listen and only then begin to speak."[23] Thus, harmonizing will fail unless the leader listens for and takes account of all voices. The moral modeling of the leader is in the leader's commitment to the vision and values of the fiduciary community. It is not that others are to blindly imitate the leader's behavior. The moral leader may provide inspiration, but he or she can only motivate and engage people to harmony by listening first and inviting their voices into the harmony. Thus, modeling a commitment to harmony is a high ideal involving patience and perseverance over the long haul.

Education for Peace

Confucians made a philosopher wager that a humane education could help human beings to fulfill their full moral potential. This wager was not based so much on the effectiveness of moral indoctrination as on an understanding of human nature. While Confucius himself said little about human nature, his follower Mencius (372–289 BCE?) addressed the issue in some depth, articulating the Confucian ideal of the goodness of human nature. In one passage Mencius sought to persuade a jaded ruler that even he had the germs of goodness within, using the following example:

> Suppose a man were, all of a sudden, to see a young child on the verge of falling into a well. He would certainly be moved to compassion, not because he wanted to get in the good graces of the parents, nor because he wished to win the praise of his fellow villagers or friends, nor yet because he disliked the cry of the child. From this it can be seen that whoever is devoid of the heart of compassion is not human. . . . The heart of compassion is the germ of benevolence. Man has [this heart] just as he has four limbs. . . . When [it is] fully developed, he can take under his protection the whole realm within the Four Seas, but if he fails to develop [it], he will not be able even to serve his parents.[24]

Mencius does not logically prove that the man in his tale will have the urge to rescue the child; rather, he persuades by inviting the listener/reader to imagine him/herself in the particular situation. If the listener/reader concedes the impulse in him/herself, that "proves" the existence of the germ of benevolence. Second, note that Mencius does not argue that the man will in fact rescue the child; he argues only that he will be "moved to compassion," will feel the urge. The germs of virtue must be developed through practice and education; only then will they result in appropriate moral actions. Third, Mencius points out that if the germs are fully developed, the person can become an effective leader, a moral model for the entire world; if not, that individual will not even be effective within the family.

Confucian education, then, seeks to develop these germs of virtue, the potential for human goodness within each person. It does so by exposing the learners to the humane traditions of the past, to the history and literature of civilization. It encourages critical reflection on past and present to learn how to adapt moral lessons to everyday life, learning from the past and from others while nurturing the seeds within. Finally, it urges practice and reflection on practice; education is self-cultivation in the art of living.

The Confucian wager on the seeds of goodness within people and the positive effects of education was, in their terms, the only possible option. If they gave up on human goodness and educability, they would be left with a vicious cycle of punishment and coercion inflicted on intransigent subjects. The Confucians discerned that human beings in their best moments yearn for goodness and moral models. The Confucian wager evokes the best instincts of human being, and seeks to nurture them for the sake of harmonious civilization.

Confucians believed that education and self-cultivation could change people. Such change would not be magical or sweeping; it would be incremental. It would start close at hand, in personal family lives. Not all people will be the leaders of countries or communities but most will have some leadership role in family, social relations, or the workplace. Confucian education could transform their lives and work on personal relationships. Small beginnings, to be sure, but nonetheless a move toward harmony and not away from it.

This person-by-person approach to peacebuilding may seem remote from solving the large problems of war, conflict, and hatred, but it is surely an approach (sometimes the only approach) to extremely deep-seated conflicts. Passing laws has not eradicated the scourge of racism in the United States; the presence of U.N. peacekeepers has not eliminated conflict in the Balkans; years of attempts to implement negotiated accords have not produced peace in the Middle East. This is not to denigrate the importance of civil rights legislation, peacekeepers, or accords. It simply points out that the creation of lasting peace will require human transformation. Education, personal experience, and conversations can contribute, slowly and incrementally, to such transformation, one person at a time. This general principle is implicitly acknowledged in exchange programs, friendship tours, dialogues, and seminars designed to promote human understanding among races, ethnic groups, religions, and historical enemies. The Confucians would argue that such programs should be seen as integral to peacebuilding.

CONCLUSION

Confucianism offers a distinctive understanding of peace as the harmonization of difference through moral leadership and education. Confucians view peace as first and foremost an issue of human relationship and see education and moral self-cultivation as the means for establishing a genuine, enduring peace. It is a long-term project, requiring patience and perseverance, particularly in the face of deep-seated differences and the history of injustice that so often fuel conflict and discord. Confucians would argue that to neglect the harmonization of human relationships is to miss the foundation of peace.

NOTES

1. John H. Berthrong, *All Under Heaven: Transforming Paradigms in Confucian-Christian Dialogue* (Albany: State University of New York Press, 1994), p. 82.

2. For a discussion of this period, see Benjamin Schwartz, *The World of Thought in Ancient China* (Cambridge, MA: Belknap Press of Harvard University, 1985).

3. *Analects of Confucius* 2:3, translation adapted from Wm. Theodore de Bary, Wing-tsit Chan, and Burton Watson, eds., *Sources of Chinese Tradition* (New York and London: Columbia University Press, 1960), Vol. I, p. 32.

4. While the positive statement (government by rites and virtue will win the respect and assent of the people) is hard for contemporary "realists" to accept, its obverse is more persuasive: corrupt, coercive government undermines the support of the people and tends to create resistance and lawlessness. Confucius goes beyond asserting that good government avoids creating such resentments; he argues that it creates "good" citizens who respect the government.

5. *Analects* 13:6. Cited from deBary, *Sources*, p. 32.

6. On Confucius' understanding of ritual, see Herbert Fingarette, *Confucius—The Secular as Sacred* (New York: Harper and Row, 1972).

7. *Analects* 2:4. Cited from deBary, *Sources*, p. 22.

8. "The Great Learning." Cited from deBary, *Sources*, p. 115.

9. Zhang Zai, *Ximing* (Western Inscription), cited in deBary, *Sources*, p. 469.

10. deBary, *Sources*, p. 220.

11. deBary, *Sources*, p. 412, quoting Wang Anshi from the preface to *Zhouguan xinyi* (New Interpretation of the Institutes of Zhou).

12. See Wm. Theodore de Bary, *The Trouble with Confucianism* (Cambridge, MA: Harvard University Press, 1991), chapter 4.

13. See Judith Berling, *A Pilgrim in Chinese Culture: Negotiating Religious Diversity* (Maryknoll, NY: Orbis Books, 1997), esp. chapters 4 and 8.

14. Ibid., chapter 5.

15. See Wm. Theodore de Bary, "Individualism and Humanitarianism in Late Ming Thought," in *Self and Society in Ming Thought* (New York: Columbia University Press, 1970), esp. pp. 188–225.

16. Wei-ming Tu borrowed this term from Michael Polyani, *Personal Knowledge: Towards a Post-Critical Philosophy* (New York: Harper Torchbooks, 1964), pp. 203–245, and developed it as the Confucian social vision. See his *Centrality and Commonality: An Essay on Chinese Religiousness* (Albany: State University of New York Press, 1989), esp. chapter 3.

17. Ibid.

18. *Chung-yung* 20:13. Cited in Tu, *Centrality and Commonality*, p. 59 [bracket in original].

19. David L. Hall and Roger T. Ames, *Thinking Through Confucius* (Albany: State University of New York Press, 1987), p. 168.

20. Tu, *Centrality and Commonality*, p. 62 [brackets added].

21. *Analects* 7:21. Cited in deBary, Sources, p. 23.

22. *Analects* 7:32. Cited in Hall and Ames, Thinking Through Confucius, p. 283.

23. Ibid.

24. *Mencius* 2A:6. Cited from D. C. Lau, trans., *Mencius* (Middlesex, Eng.: Paragon, 1976), pp. 82–83 [brackets added].

6

Judaism and Peacebuilding

MARC GOPIN

The central axis of Judaism has been rabbinic literature for 2000 years. Classical rabbinic literature has a mix of texts on the subject of conflict.[1] There is an extensive body of literature celebrating peace as a religious value, as a name of God, and as a supreme ethical principle.[2] There is some Talmudic discussion of legitimate and illegitimate wars that Jewish kings may or may not wage.[3] Maimonides (1135–1204 CE) elaborated this and codified it.[4] This, in turn, has given plenty of grist for the mill to Jewish theoreticians of just war, who, in keeping with their Christian counterparts, have tried to develop in recent years some cogent thoughts on just war.

Rabbinic Judaism's discussion of just war has always been theoretical, however. There have never been "rabbinic" kings, that is, kings who were thoroughly steeped in rabbinic Judaism, unless one accepts the traditionalist or fundamentalist position that rabbinic Judaism existed from the beginning of Jewish biblical history. Thus, the present-day discussion rests on tenuous theoretical grounds with no practical experience to draw upon. It seems to be a rather desperate attempt to catch up with the military realities facing a secular state of Israel run almost completely by Jews, which is, in and of itself, a historically unprecedented arrangement.

Most important, the Jewish just war versus Jewish pacifist discussions have not addressed creatively what Judaism has said or could say about how to *prevent* violence, how to keep wars from happening, to deescalate them, or how to heal people once the war has stopped. But Judaism has many things to say about these critical elements of conflict resolution.

The section of the community that would be most comfortable with delving deeply into the *halakhic* (legal/spiritual) sources as the authoritative guide to life, namely the Orthodox community, has been particularly uninterested in confronting Jewish resources on peacebuilding, despite righteous outcries against wanton hatred *(sin'at hinam)* and conflict *(mahloket)*. On the contrary, the prevailing focus of attention has been increasingly on those rituals and laws of Judaism that would buttress cultural and physical survival, which would be specifically aimed against annihilation.

I am referring to rituals that make the Jew different. These include: obligations of protecting Jewish life, education to the uniqueness of Jewish life and practice, inculcating radical levels of defense of any Jew whose life is in danger, and ritual practices that are particularist by definition, such as the dietary and purity laws. Even the laws with universal application, such as the Sabbath, tend to be seen as uniquely Jewish.

This trend especially focuses on minutiae of practice that make a clear boundary between who is in and who is out of the group, who can be trusted and who cannot be trusted, rituals that become, in their modern incarnation, markers of ethnic and national trust, markers of distinction, markers of insulation from a dangerous world. Now this does not do justice to a variety of theologians and rabbis across the religious spectrum, including Orthodox representatives, who have, in fact, addressed issues of universal concern in the post-Holocaust era.[5] But this characterization does explain a definite trend of religious Jewish life that must be understood by conflict analysis theory.

This phenomenon is not dissimilar to trends within the other monotheisms. All of them have significant subcultures today that are selectively winnowing their traditions for what makes their adherents different and alienated from others.

This global fundamentalist and militarist trend expresses itself through a variety of venues in the Jewish context. *Haredi,* ultra-Orthodox life, stands in an oppositional identity to most modern concepts of civil society. The effects on Jewish aggressive responses to the outside world have been varied. For the most part, it has expressed itself in a concerted effort to keep alien and modern influences out of *haredi* realms. But it also expresses itself in aggressive attempts to control, through legislation, personal status issues in Israel.

The kind of violence that this position results in involves rare assaults on property and on persons, non-Jewish or secular Jewish, whose presence in their midst is a threat to the cultural milieu. This is particularly focused on women and the threat that exposure of the woman's body poses to their society. This has obvious parallels in historical Christianity but most especially today in the world of Islam.

The impact of *haredi* separatism on Israel's relationship to Arabs is more complicated. Most *haredi* political influence has had the effect of pitting the pro-peace and anti-peace camps of secular Israeli politics against each other in a fierce competition for who can "buy off" the religious parties with more funds. On the whole, *haredim* clearly have hard, anti-Arab sentiments. Ironically, however, Shas, the most important *haredi* party of all, representing the Oriental Jewish population, has often given a cushion to the pro-peace camp, since its leaders have some pro-peace tendencies. Habad, on the other hand, one of the most aggressive of the *haredi* groups, has been instrumental in several elections in bolstering the anti-peace camp.

The most important and successful obstacle to a Palestinian/Israeli treaty has come from the modern Orthodox community, the religious Zionists, out of whose midst Gush Emunim, the preeminent ideological founders of settler Judaism, and other much more extreme groups have emerged. It is this camp that has populated aggressively the West Bank and Gaza, and who have effectively blocked any prime minister's efforts to slow down or halt the expansion of settlements.

As the results of the uprising of 2000 indicate, it is the inextricability of the Palestinian and settler populations that has made a deal all but impossible. Indeed this was the plan. The settlers are supported globally by modern Orthodox Jewry in other countries, and the latter literally have many of their children living on those settlements. This has made the uprising in 2000 into a very personal life and death struggle for Orthodox Jewish families around the world.

As is the case with Islam, the deadliest combinations in the history of religion are modern and highly politicized ethnonationalist aspirations that merge in new ways with old traditions, rituals, and meaning systems. Just as the complete redefinition of and re-visioning of *jihad* has artfully combined with modern methods of terror, so too old Jewish attachments to the land of Israel, and all the accompanying *mitsvot*, commandments, have been reworked to justify the level of oppression of local populations.

Now I would like to move toward the question of how it is possible to move significant numbers of religious Jews in the direction of peacemaking. Before we can even elicit a theory of conflict resolution from Judaism's pro-social ethics, sacred stories, symbols, and mythologies, conflict theory must creatively respond to the rage that many Jews feel at the world. This is especially true in light of the Holocaust, historically brutal anti-Semitism suffered in the Christian world, and traditionally second-class citizenship endured in the Middle Eastern communities of Islam. If not, peacebuilding as a vocation will be dismissed by the very section of the community that has the longest memory but that needs religiously and culturally rooted conflict resolution the most.

The first stage of a Jewish peacebuilding theory may, for some people, be mourning. Mourning is a close cousin to and healthy evolution out of rage over the past. This is not as unusual as it might seem when it comes to intractable conflicts involving groups that have suffered over many centuries, and it may be relevant to the inner workings of many religious groups across the globe. Peacebuilding theory and practice must develop interventions that address the full spectrum of a particular group's responses to conflict, especially the most violent sections of that group. If an abnormal level of mourning that seems to perpetuate itself over history is a key element of the conflict, an effective religious peacemaking program must directly confront this.[6]

A peacemaking mourning process must speak to the deepest identity needs of a group, and also to the group's sense of threat to its future, its fear of annihilation. Often what is mourned, but mourned in ways that create violence, is a loss of the group's honor, security, or a sense of confidence in its future. There is also a sense of loss of some romanticized time—real, imaginary, or a combination thereof—in which the group had a fulfilled, secure existence.

Aveilus, Jewish religious mourning, is the ritual process of expressing the death of a loved one. That loved one is a part of oneself, one's history, one's very being. It is the ability to acknowledge loss unabashedly, to watch the lost thing[7] or person buried in the ground, especially to be able to engage in burial yourself, and feel the full horror of this. It is to immerse oneself for a very long time in the life and memory of the one who is gone, up to a year for parents. Then, in response to this, it is to be aided by the community and one's relationship to God, to a slow and steady recovery from this loss. The recital of the mourning prayers, *kaddish* and *yizkor,* is critical to this process.[8]

There is no conflict, especially deadly conflict, that does not involve loss. These losses, often unacknowledged, are the fuel of conflict. Many people in conflict hope in vain that by perpetuating the conflict and winning one can somehow make up for what one has lost. But this is illusory, and the sooner that these permanent damages are acknowledged the easier it will be to focus on the concrete moves that need to be made to end the conflict, negotiate and compromise on the concrete differences, and begin rebuilding peoples' lives.

As far as the Israeli-Arab conflict is concerned, to take an example, there is much that *aveilus* can teach. It seems clear to me that a profound transformation of relationship would occur if Arabs and Jews, in addition to negotiating the obvious central issues of land and resource distribution, would engage in a simultaneous process of helping each group to mourn what they have lost. The losses of 100 years, for each group, represent an important time-span that generally includes the memories that people have directly from parents and grandparents. It is this memory that must be addressed. This would involve focusing on all the lost children, husbands, fathers, all the lost time and resources, the lost homes, and of course the lost land.

It would be very powerful indeed if groups of Arabs and Jews, perhaps aided by sympathetic Western Christians—who also have a key role in causing and healing this tragic conflict—would begin, *in detail,* to mourn what was lost. They must begin to visit the dead together, to bury them together in symbolic ways, to memorialize lost lives and lost homes. They need to talk about the losses for as long as it is necessary, to thoroughly indulge the past rather than suppress it, for fear that it would disrupt rational dialogue and conversation. We must do exactly what rational peacemakers have tried to suppress, namely, we must indulge memory. But we must do it, not destructively as it is indulged in the privacy of particular groups, but as a part of peacemaking, as part of an effort to honor each group's memories, at the same time that we struggle constructively over the present.

There are several critical guidelines. One is to utilize religious constructs to (1) heal deep injuries, and (2) reconstitute a cultural and spiritual identity that responds to the need for uniqueness, but that does not need to do this by way of hatred of the outsider. There must be an emphasis on a unique Jewish role and style of engaging this work of conflict resolution and peacebuilding. This responds to the fear of annihilation, but it also channels it into pro-social values.

A culture of peacebuilding that maintains a clearly unique role for Jewish values could then lead at a second stage to tentative statements and agreements about shared values with other groups, be they non-Orthodox Jews, secular Jews, Palestinians, or Muslims. But it must begin from a premise that acknowledges and even values boundaries between cultural entities and respects those boundaries.

I want to move on now to an in-depth analysis of Jewish tradition as it is relevant to peacebuilding. I will divide my analysis into some standard categories in the conflict resolution field that prove useful here: conflict prevention, management and resolution, post-trauma healing, and transformation. Post-trauma healing we have already covered out of order in our discussion of mourning.

Prevention is the most effective tool of all in peacemaking because relationships are easier to mend at very early stages of problems. An example of a conflict prevention value is the mandate to experience self-love, a theme taken up by many moral sense theorists in the nineteenth century as a basis for a moral system.[9] In classical Judaism, the religious psyche is meant to be self-loving in order to be loving in an other-directed sense. The classical basis of this is the Golden Rule, which comes in its earliest monotheistic form from the Torah in Leviticus 19:18, "Do not take vengeance, or a bear a grudge. And you must love your neighbor as yourself, I am the Eternal God." The verse is generally assumed to mean that you must love the Other as you love yourself, which cannot be done without self-love, a practice that for many people takes a lifetime to achieve. This is one of the hardest things for members of a hated minority to truly feel.[10] In my experience, my conflict resolution activists have a hard time with this principle as well, and it negatively impacts their work.

Another key point in the self-oriented values is *imitatio dei*. For the religious human being the fact that one can be like God if one is a peacemaker is a deeply empowering psychological phenomenon. It makes one's experience larger than life, a conquest of mortality, and a unification with eternity, as well as with others past and present who have walked the same path. To the degree to which this experience could be applied to the lonely life of the peacemaker who champions benevolent values, it could have a significant impact on the psychological sustainability of conflict resolution as a vocation.

As we move into values that govern interpersonal relationships, there are a few that are particularly noteworthy. The importance of interpersonal meeting, especially face-to-face encounter cannot be overemphasized. The principal biblical phrase for love is *motseh hen,* to find grace in the eyes of the Other who is encountered. The Talmudic Rabbis (henceforth, the Rabbis) mandated that one should greet everyone with a loving, or literally "beautiful," face, *"sever panim yafot."* They prohibited the kind of language and actions that make the face turn white with embarrassment, making the latter into a sin akin to murder, literally the shedding of the blood of the face. Conversely, they made the honor of the Other into a supreme *mitsvah,* the opposite of humiliation of the face of the Other.[11] Honoring of the Other, in theory, can become an experience of intense religious fulfillment.

Face is a critical category in conflict analysis.[12] Saving face is a key generator of conflict in many situations, for a variety of reasons, including the inability to back down from the action-reaction spiral of aggressive behavior due the fear of losing face. This is especially true of leaders who fear the wrath of their followers who could not cope with the loss of face without turning on the leaders themselves. Collective humiliation is one of the main reasons for the self-perpetuating cycles of numerous international and inter-ethnic conflicts.

Honor, as an intentional peacemaking act, is a rather underutilized strategy of conflict prevention and conflict resolution at the current time. The better diplomats understand this method, but it is rarely made into a conscious process that applies generally to the interaction of large populations. Any Jewish methodology of conflict resolution would have to focus on honor and the necessary engagement with the face of the enemy, on both the elite level and the grassroots level.

I have tried to internalize a discipline and psychology of honor in my own processes of mediation as an insider/partial, as a Jew and a rabbi who is in an adversarial relationship with Arabs, but also a kind of mediator and translator between them and the Israelis. At various junctures I assessed what was wrong with a Jewish/Arab encounter in which I found myself, and I saw it more often than not as principally centered on issues of honor and shame.

I countered this with my enemies by going out of my way to honor, sometimes excessively, as a combination of a moral gesture and an act of repentance or penance. I recall one time when it was clear to me when I met a very high Palestinian military leader that our initial meeting and its context were quite dishonorable to him. I and my partner concluded that, at some personal risk, we had to visit him in his cultural milieu, which we did. He knew how hard it was for us. In turn, he showered us with a lavish vegetarian (kosher) meal, and insisted on sitting with us, even though he himself was engaged in a religious fast! Honor became contagious and the relationship has grown warmer and warmer, each recognizing how hard it is to take this step. The mutual honoring led to substantive talk about the issues and plans for cooperation, which have been put on hold because of the terrible violence as of the end of 2000.

I also recall meeting Mr. Arafat for the first time, six months before the tragedies of 2000, when, for complicated reasons, I was an honored guest at his headquarters. In fact I was seated next to him to facilitate our conversation. I made a decision to bring him gifts. He in turn gave me and another rabbi, and his wife, gifts.

I went one step further. I had known from inside sources that Arafat had felt humiliated by some of his encounters with Barak, and that, in general, various high-level Palestinians had expressed to me that since the end of the Rabin era they would be happy if they were simply treated like human beings. The use of this phrase shocked me, especially because it came from several sources. I decided, therefore, to emphasize to Arafat—despite extremely ambivalent feelings toward him as a Jew and as a target of his past actions as a terrorist and present support of violence—the attitude of Jewish tradition and law to honor the human being. I said these sources repeatedly and emphasized to him that these sources needed to form the foundation of Arab/Israeli negotiations and encounters.

I was sending him a message, and so were my colleagues, that honor and equality were at the core, not the periphery, of our vision of a future between Jews and Palestinians. And I was sending him a message that Jewish religion and monotheism in general, despite the behavior of many extremists, could be the basis of a new relationship, and that, in fact, some religious values and practices could provide a unique bridge between the two sides.

Arafat, in turn, kept emphasizing the honoring of treaties, the Pact of Omar in particular, which were important cultural precedents for him of a Muslim leader in charge of a political realm treating everyone honorably. He said the words "pact of Omar" three times for emphasis.

Now where this kind of exchange could have gone in our relationship with the Palestinian leadership I will never know because we never had the power or the support from the liberal community of diplomats and peacemakers to pursue this avenue of peacemaking. But what I was attempting to do was to create a different and parallel negotiation process, a process that negotiates and builds on fundamental moral/psychological building blocks. The most important one was honor, but there are others such as the acknowledgement of memory, admission of wrongs, visions of the future, and gestures of good will that resonate with religious and cultural institutions of the traditions involved.

The creative extension of some of these rabbinic values to complex conflict is potentially a powerful tool of peacemaking. I would like now to list some others for consideration in Judaism:

1. Involvement in the suffering of others.
2. Taking responsibility to heal that suffering.
3. Social justice, in the form of a reasonable redistribution of resources, as a religious task or *mitsvah*.
4. Constructive social criticism, which usually accompanies the implementation of social justice, perceived as a *mitsvah* as well.
5. A strong sense of responsibility to connect the home and the public sphere by way of the openness of the home to the "street," that is, making one's home and family open to some degree as a refuge from the inevitable harshness of the public sphere.
6. A detailed attention to customs of civility as socially constructive and as, therefore, religious duties.

7. A commitment to voluntarily limit one's physical needs and discourage excessive wealth, in order to make a society in which everyone can live.

8. A *halakhic* commitment to make conflict resolution into a social *mitsvah*, a *mitsvah* of *bakesh shalom ve'radfehu*,[13] "seeking peace and pursuing it," literally a *mitsvah* to go and seek out other peoples' conflicts to solve. This last *mitsvah* is particularly potent as a vehicle through which to advocate conflict resolution training in even the most fundamentalist contexts.

Now let us turn to conflict management, resolution, and reconciliation. Some of the most important constructs of conflict resolution in numerous rabbinic sources are expressed by Midrashic metaphor. The rabbis make the biblical figure Aaron, the High Priest, and brother of Moses, into the paradigmatic peacemaker:[14]

> And thus when two men were in a conflict, Aaron would go and sit with one of them. He would say to him: My son, look at your friend [look at what he is saying], he is tearing at his heart and ripping his clothing. He says, 'Woe is me, how can I lift my eyes and see my friend. I am ashamed before him, for it is I who wronged him. And he [Aaron] would stay with him until he removed all of the jealous rage from his heart. And Aaron would then go to the other man, and say [the same thing]. And when the two would finally meet, they would hug and kiss each other.[15]

The context of this story is a religious universe in which the high priest has the most elevated status in the community. Thus, a key element here is the humility and even self-abnegation of the intermediary. More important, the actions of the third party are a critical role model for the conflicting parties. They demonstrate that the mediator must be prepared to lose a little face in order to do something sublime, something spiritual, a *mitsvah*. In so doing, Aaron prepares the parties for a crucial and difficult stage of conflict resolution or, more specifically, reconciliation, which usually involves swallowing a little pride—in other words, losing a little face. Furthermore, reconciliation generally involves a certain level of remorse, which again entails a psychological loss of pride or face. This, I suggest, is a crucial psychological juncture for conflict resolution that is often overlooked.[16]

Another key element in Aaron's method is empathic listening.[17] The details of the story indicate that he speaks but also stays with each person for an extensive period of time; in fact, he "would stay with him until he removed all of the jealous rage from his heart." This combination of listening, staying with someone who is enraged, and having an open-ended time frame, seems to be crucial to conflict resolution in traditional cultures in general.

The ideal Jewish peacemaker's path, as seen from the Aaron stories, involves: the development of a pious or moral character worthy of respect, the conscious creation of role models of peacemaking, purposeful acts of humility that sometimes involve personal sacrifice or loss of face, active or empathic listening, a method of helping people work through destructive emotions, and, finally, the gift of abundant if not unlimited time.[18]

A critical and unique strategy of Jewish conflict resolution with biblical roots suggests an alternative strategy to the typical focus on dialogue of conflict resolution theory. It does not call into question the importance of communication to conflict resolution, but it does suggest that there are forms of communication other than dialogue. The principal source for this is the biblical *mitsvah* to help your enemy when he is faltering with a burden.[19] There are a variety of rabbinic rationales for this as a conflict resolution device.[20] Essentially, it involves what I have termed the positive uses of cognitive dissonance. The rabbis suggested that enemies have a certain set understanding of each other that plays a vital role in their commitment to hate each other. Conflict resolution theory concurs with this.[21] The purpose of this mandated change in behavior is to create cognitive dissonance, to shatter the conception of the enemy. This leads, in turn, to a moral sense of regret inside the person who is the recipient of the unilateral gesture of physical aid from the enemy. He decides that he really misunderstood his enemy, or that his enemy really is not an enemy, "he could not be if he did this for me." In other words, it is designed to shatter the false *image* of the enemy, and complexify the real person behind the image.

It is also, I would argue, a perfect way to make justice and peace work together as a conflict resolution strategy, rather than be at odds with each other. But it does require great skill and patience. A simplistic belief that such gestures would or should work after one time is foolish, and will cause a backlash. Unilateral gestures of aiding those who are suffering require repeated and surprising innovations. The whole point of cognitive dissonance is that it is undoing something that is deeply entrenched, causing great anxiety, and will only result in a new emotive homeostasis after a great deal of time and struggle.

To take an example, it would take repeated and extensive gestures of Israelis working in Arab and Palestinian villages to build good, permanent homes before it became clear that there were Israelis who understood the Palestinian demand for justice, and were serious about their desire for reconciliation and coexistence. It would take repeated gestures of religious Israelis making donations to the upkeep of mosques before it would sink in that there were many religious Israelis who did not see all Muslims as enemies. It would take repeated offers of condolences, visits, and gestures of comfort, on the part of Palestinians for Israeli victims of bombs for it to sink in that not all Arabs wanted those bombs to go off. It would take many Islamic gestures of hospitality to make religious Jews believe that they are finally welcome back to the Middle East as permanent residents. These bilateral gestures, over time, could create a far greater moderate middle than exists currently in Israel and the West Bank. This, in turn, would shift the population matrix undergirding the rejectionism of various political parties.

Essentially, these gestures move us into the realm of conflict transformation, the transformation of enemy relationships. In Jewish terms, this is best expressed by the statement, "Who is the strongest of the warriors? . . . He who turns one who hates him into one who loves him."[22] What sort of strategies can truly make such a profound transformation of relationship?

There is a process for Jewish personal, interpersonal, and communal transformation, roughly coming under the rubric of *teshuva,* which can mean repentance, but also means literally "returning," or "turning toward." The prophets say in the name of God at one point, "Turn toward me, *shuvu eylay,* and I will turn toward you, *ve'ashuva aleikhem*" (Zakhariah 1:3).[23] There is a covenantal mutuality built into the concept of *teshuva,* and it applies to both the human-Divine form of *teshuva,* and to the interhuman process of *teshuva* for wrongs done and relationships broken.

There are a number of elements to the ideal form of *teshuva.* First and foremost, *teshuva* cannot replace restitution. In other words, restitution must precede or accompany the process of conflict transformation if there have been real damages that require restitution. Beyond financial or physical restitution, however, the restorative aspect of *teshuva* must take place. This is where justice and peace have to work together or not work at all.

The restorative or conciliatory stage of *teshuva* ideally involves a confession of wrongdoing.[24] It is ideal if this confession, if it involves wrongs to other human beings, be done in public.[25] Abraham ben David of Posquières (c. 1125–1198) added that the public confession convinces the wronged party that the change in his adversary is authentic.[26] Other elements of the *teshuva* process involve, according to the Talmudic Rabbis, the giving of charity—always a standard of Jewish penance[27]—a change in one's name or identity, and some argue even a change in one's place, and, last but not least, crying.[28] Maimonides clarified that all these practices and emotional states are elements of authentic change, and he even recommends that a person cognitively dissociate from his own prior self by saying, "I am another person, and I am not the person who did those things." Maimonides continues, "and he changes his deeds completely to the good and to the straight path, and he exiles himself from his current place. For exile atones for sin, because it makes him to be humble and low of spirit."[29]

Thus, there are four basic stages of *teshuva*. There is restitution. There is an expression of deep remorse *(harata)*, a detailed confession, privately or publicly, of what one has done *(vidui)*, and there is finally a commitment to change in the future, to the point of even changing one's identity *(kabbalah le-haba)*.

The outer forms and rituals of *teshuva* are often focused in the Jewish ritual life cycle on fasting and deprivation of the body. The Day of Atonement is the most notable example, although some very pious Jews used to fast every Monday and Thursday, as part of a lifetime process of purification and repentance. Indeed repentance themes are built into many elements of daily prayers.

It is for this reason that in the uprising and tragedies of 2000 I have instigated a series of actions in Jerusalem and elsewhere regarding fasting. The idea is for Jews to fast at the same time as Ramadan, as a Jewish act of solidarity with Muslims who are going through an act of purification. Instead of Ramadan becoming a killing season as it has become in Algeria, the idea is to steal the symbolic thunder from Hamas and make Ramadan a time for sharing of rituals of purification. A colleague in Jerusalem wisely recommended that we make the days of joint fasting to be Mondays and Thursdays in order for it to resonate with Jewish tradition. Also, the focus would be on gestures of feasting together at night, offering gifts of appropriate foods. It was also fortuitous in 2000 that Ramadan, Christmas, and Chanukah all coincided on one day, and thus provided a ritual opportunity associated with one key theme of repentance, which is rebirth, and light in the midst of darkness.

The key with efforts at ritually based and mythically based interreligious peacemaking is the willingness to engage in trial and error and to allow new experiments and gestures time to germinate. For example, for years the religious Zionist peace camp, especially embodied in Oz ve-Shalom, utilized the universalist and peace symbols associated with the holiday of Sukkot, Tabernacles, and the actual booth that every religious Jew constructs outside his or her house, to be a place of Israeli/Arab encounter. This had its counterpart in religious innovations in the United States, especially initiated by Arthur Waskow, I believe, though the history of this should be studied. But suddenly, as a result of the terrible violence unleashed in 2000, the unprecedented riots of thousands of Arab Israelis, and the questions raised by the killing of thirteen Arab Israeli civilians by the police, there was an outpouring of efforts for Jews and Arabs inside Israel to meet. Many met in Sukkot across the country because it was that time of year and because of years of preparation for that ritualistic space to be a place of embrace and reconciliation.

Another ritual form of reconciliation that has been under way is a process of chanting Shalom and Sala'am simultaneously every Friday above the area of the Temple Mount for Jews, the Haram al Sharif for Muslims. This went on right in the middle of the rioting. It has been an effort of Jews and Muslims to engage in a kind of purification and penance right at the site of the birthplace of the conflict.

I want to turn to another major religious institution germane to our topic. There has been much discussion about the value of forgiveness in conflict resolution. From my research it would seem that only when forgiveness is placed in the context of individual cultures can it play a crucial role in conflict resolution. It interacts in complicated ways with competing moral and spiritual responses, such as commitments to truth, justice, apology, repentance, and penance, among others.

Forgiveness plays a role in Jewish forms of reconciliation, but only when embedded in the *teshuva* process, which is either unilateral or bilateral depending on what injuries have been sustained by conflict. The key to a Jewish understanding of forgiveness is the centralization of repentance, and the placing of forgiveness only in that context. To the degree to which, in the enormously varied Christian expressions and articulation of forgiveness, there are parallels to the Jewish formulation, then there can be great cooperation. Indeed, from what I have seen, many Jews, Christians, and Muslims have the same criteria for the practice of forgiveness. But the differences in nuance must be acknowledged. When I hear "forgiveness" in Christian circles my instinct is to assume a diminution of justice or real acts of repentance, and the suppression and burying of history and memory. This may be unfair, but it is real in my Jewish consciousness and my memories of history, and it does have some reality in certain current trends of Christianity. As another example, when injured or minority parties hear talk of "peace" they often hear an effort to bury justice. Thus, as we all engage in these processes it is crucial to be explicit about what we all mean.

As far as the application of this approach to forgiveness and apology, I wonder how powerful such a *teshuva* apology process could be on a much larger scale involving massive injury, murder, and genocide. Surely, it would be a deeper process than simple payment for losses incurred, restitution, or the indictment of selected representatives of the war criminals. The latter is all the international community has been able to orchestrate when it comes to genocide until now, and all that this really even attempts to satisfy is the demands of justice, and it usually fails at that also. Indeed it has to. Who could construct an appropriate restitution for the loss of one's family, one's world? It seems to me that victim communities, and their tormentors, need to do much more to transform the past and present into a redemptive future.

The sites of war, mass graves, and past horrors are critical here. They are places that do not just deserve memorials. They should be places in which confession, apologies, and restitutions are made on an ongoing basis, not in order to inject a sense of self-loathing into former aggressors. On the contrary, it is to free everyone to develop a new sense of self, to mourn the past together with the victims, regularly, to foster a new future.

After all the internal work on a religious tradition and its possible relationship to peacebuilding is done, the most important question facing the interaction of religion and conflict resolution theory is the multicultural, multireligious, and secular nature of most contemporary social settings. Religious traditions, such as Judaism, tend to operate in their theological and moral constructs as if no other system exists. This means that as we think about these traditions in pragmatic terms it must be remembered that we study religious peacemaking, not in order to suggest an imposition of those traditions on society. Rather, we do this to creatively interact with those who *are* religious, to be prepared to creatively integrate pro-social religious traditions with secular, democratic constructs, or constructs from other religions and cultures. Further, we do this in order for the secular community to have the courage to learn from the religious community as well.

NOTES

1. A fuller treatment of this subject is to be found in my *Between Eden and Armageddon: The Future of World Religions, Violence, and Peacemaking* (New York and London: Oxford University Press, 2000), and my *Holy War, Holy Peace: How Religion Can Bring Peace to the Middle East* (New York: Oxford University Press, 2002).

2. There is a large literature on this subject. See the following for selections of rabbinic aphorisms: Avot of Rabbi Nathan 12; T.B. Perek ha-Shalom; Leviticus Rabbah 9; Numbers Rabbah 11. For some contemporary discussion, see Murray Polner and Naomi Goodman, eds., *The Challenge of Shalom* (Philadelphia: New Society Publishers, 1994), and my essay ad loc., "Is there a Jewish God of Peace."

3. On early justifications for war, see the discussion in T. B. Sotah 44b; for a contemporary overview and analysis of the rabbinic discussion, see Reuven Kimelman, "War," in Steven Katz, ed., *Frontiers of Jewish Thought* (Washington, DC: B'nai B'rith Books, 1992), pp. 309–332.

4. Maimonides, *Mishneh Torah,* Laws of Kings 5.

5. See, for example, Menachem Kellner, ed., *Contemporary Jewish Ethics* (New York: Hebrew Publishing Co., 1978); Elliot Dorff and Louis Newman, eds., *Contemporary Jewish Ethics and Morality* (New York: Oxford University Press, 1995).

6. On uncompleted mourning and conflict, see Vamik Volkan, *Bloodlines: From Ethnic Pride to Ethnic Terrorism* (New York: Farrar, Strauss and Giroux, 1997); idem, *The Need to Have Enemies and Allies* (Northvale, NJ: J. Aronson, 1994).

7. *Aveilus* also applies to events in history and objects, such as the Temple in Jerusalem, although this is negotiated in a somewhat different fashion by *halakha,* Jewish law. Nevertheless, its extension to realms beyond the individual/interpersonal suggests its usefulness in dealing with overarching collective experiences of the people.

8. On mourning in Judaism, see Maurice Lamm, *The Jewish Way in Death and Mourning* (New York: Jonathon David Publishers, 1969). *Kaddish* is a formal responsive prayer said by mourners a number of times in the daily prayer service, where there is a quorum present.

9. See, for example, Francis Hutcheson, *An Essay on the Nature and Conduct of the Passions and Affections with Illustrations upon the Moral Sense* (London, 1728). Other key figures included the Third Earl of Shaftesbury, David Hume, and Adam Smith.

10. It is interesting to note that R. Akiva (c. 110–135 CE) considered this the preeminent principle of Judaism. However, his contemporary Ben Azzai stated that the most important principle is the idea that every human being is created in the image of God, and is therefore invaluable. It is superior as a principle to the love principle, lest, "someone say, 'since I have been abused, let my fellow human being be abused, since I have been cursed let my fellow human being be cursed'." *Genesis Rabbah* 24. R. Tanhuma adds, ad loc., "If you do this (abuse others), know who you are abusing . . . in the image of God He made him" [Genesis 5:1]. We have here, in a nutshell, what might be the thought patterns of abused people the world over who, despite a good conscience, feel that, from the point of view of justice, if they have been unloved and abused, why should they treat others any differently? This statement by Ben Azzai is meant to contradict that tendency of feeling within the Jewish people of his time. It means that the only way that a Jewish person could devalue another human being would be to consider him or her not really created in the image of God, not really human, which manifestly contradicts the sacred text.

11. See a fine example of contemporary rabbinic hermeneutics on the relationship of honor for all people as a way of protecting human life, Micha Odenheimer, "Honor or Death," *Jerusalem Report* IX:22 (March 1, 1999), p. 25.

12. B. R. Brown, "Face-Saving and Face-Restoration in Negotiation," in D. Druckman, ed., *Negotiations* (Beverly Hills, CA: Sage, 1977), pp. 275–299.

13. Psalms 34:15.

14. See Marc Gopin, "Is There a Jewish God of Peace?" in Murray Polner and Naomi Goodman, eds., *The Challenge of Shalom* (Philadelphia: New Society Publishers, 1994), pp. 32–39.

15. Avot of Rabbi Nathan 12:3.

16. I leave aside here the inappropriateness of this story as a model for any contemporary solution to a marital crisis. Any husband who throws his wife out of the house can and should be subject to prosecution if he does not come to some more equitable way to separate, if that is what they must do. I urge the reader to see the moral tale in its context, suspend contemporary moral evaluations temporarily, in order to see the pro-social message of the story that is intended to teach mediators how they should behave. We do not use it as a role-model of a husband's behavior or a contemporary solution to that behavior.

17. As a contemporary example, Leah Green, based on the work of Gene Knudsen Hoffman on compassionate listening, has initiated the Middle East Compassionate Listening Project, based in Indianola, WA. It has brought a variety of American Jews to the West Bank and Israel to engage in listening to the full spectrum of Israeli and Palestinian points of view, without engaging in debate, but simply in the discipline of listening. They are one of the only groups, to my knowledge, that listens actively to settlers as well as the more radical Muslims on the West Bank. The Fellowship of Reconciliation also has an extensive program of Compassionate Listening projects.

18. I have raised elsewhere the moral problematics of Aaron's use of subterfuge in his healing process. The question of when and how truth is told or not told has not been honestly dealt with in matters of diplomacy and conflict resolution. There is a great deal of pious commitment to "transparency," but in practice diplomacy is a business of partial truths, and, in particular, the concealment of negotiating positions from 90 percent of populations on both sides of conflicts. I have condemned this on numerous occasions myself but, on the other hand, these are not simple matters. Again, I always return to the family model. Should one repeat *everything* one hears in families? Is there nothing that should be concealed for the purpose of peace? Does not everyone have at least one thing they know about a family member that they wisely choose to not reveal to others in order not to break up the family? What I am interested in is not the justification of lying, or a simplistic application of Aaron's method. Rather I am interested in ways of conflict resolution that struggle with moral categories and the complexity of competing moral claims, such as justice, compassion, forgiveness and truth. They must struggle with each other to create a livable and realistic peace.

19. Exodus 23:5; Deuteronomy 22:4; see also, Proverbs 25:21.

20. See Reuven Kimelman, "Nonviolence in the Talmud," *Judaism* vol. 17 (1968), pp. 318ff. for the rabbinic sources.

21. See Vamik Volkan, *The Need to Have Enemies and Allies*, op. cit.

22. Avot of Rabbi Nathan 23:1.

23. There are potentially fascinating parallels here to other traditions that, if studied jointly, could lead to creative bonds between communities. There is a great deal of Sufi literature on repentance, remorse, and the turning around of oneself. I thank Frederick Denny for pointing this out. This kind of parallelism could lead to joint study between communities, such as are taking place in Jerusalem, but also important rituals of peace that may evolve between the communities over time.

24. T. B. Ta'anit 67a.

25. See T. B. Yoma 86b; Maimonides (1135–1204), *Mishneh Torah*, Book of Knowledge, Laws of Teshuva, ch. 2.

26. See his gloss on Maimonides, ad loc.

27. Cf. to Islam, where generosity in debt disputes that were arbitrated by Muhammad, was seen as a central way to bring about peace between enemies (*Hadith Sahih Bukhari* 3.49.868–870).

28. See T. B. Rosh ha-Shanah 16b and Kesef Mishneh commentary to Maimondes, ad loc., Laws of *teshuva* 2:4.

29. Maimonides, ad loc., Laws of Teshuva 2:4.

7

Islam and Peacebuilding

Continuities and Transitions

FREDERICK M. DENNY

Islam is the youngest of the Abrahamic religions, having much in common with its older siblings Judaism and Christianity. In fact, so close is it to those traditions, that the Qur'an, God's revelation to the Prophet Muhammad (ca. 570–632 CE), declares Islam to be the fulfillment of them, clarifying, purifying, and perfecting their sometimes wayward courses. Although Islam profoundly respects and admires Moses, Jesus, and others of the biblical tradition as authentic prophets, it considers their historical communities to have strayed from the original monotheistic messages and practices that Abraham first introduced as the founder of what it views as true religion on earth.

The Qur'an declares, concerning the older, related faith traditions: "They say: 'Become Jews or Christians if you would be rightly guided.' Say rather: 'On the contrary, the religion of Abraham, the true *(hanifan)*, and he was not of the idolaters.' Say: 'We believe in Allah, and the revelations given to us, and to Abraham, Isma'il, Isaac, Jacob, and the tribes, and that given to Moses and Jesus, and that given to all prophets from their Lord. We make no difference between one and another of them: and we submit to Allah (as Muslims)'" (2:135–136).

Muhammad preached Islam, "submission" to God, as the original religion of the Meccans, established by Abraham in the distant past. The religion suffered progressive decline in Arabia until it became utterly polytheistic and superstitious, retaining only traces of its original purpose and purity. The "Age of Ignorance" *(al-jāhiliyya),* according to Muslim historians, was that long period in Arabia after the decline of monotheism until its restoration by Muhammad's "revitalization" movement, to borrow Anthony F. C. Wallace's model.[1] The old Arabian religiocultural identity was preserved in fundamental ways by means of the reformation of ancient Meccan Ka'aba-centered[2] rites of pilgrimage and by the oral Qur'an as a heaven-sent Arabic text that captured the hearts and imaginations of the poetry-loving tribal Arabs.

Islam is a profoundly ethically based religion. In the Qur'an, we read (from Sura 2:177):

> It is not righteousness that you turn your faces towards East or West; but it is righteousness—to believe in Allah and the Last Day, and the Angels, and the Book, and the Messengers; to spread of your substance, out of love for Him, for your kin, for orphans, for the needy, for the wayfarer, for those who ask, and for the ransom of slaves; to be steadfast in prayer, and practice regular charity, to fulfill the contracts which you have made; and to be firm and patient in pain and adversity, and throughout all periods of severity. Such are the people who bear witness to the Truth, who are God-fearing.

This passage summarizes virtually the whole religion of Islam, emphasizing its ethical nature while not neglecting its ritual obligations and doctrinal principles that sustain the awareness and strength of the believers.

In Sura 5:69 we read: "Those who believe (in the Qur'an), those who follow the Jewish (scriptures), and the Sabians and the Christians— any who believe in God and the Last Day, and work righteousness—on them shall be no fear, nor shall they grieve." There is suggested in this passage an acknowledgment and acceptance of other religious paths than Islam and a conviction that sincere believers beyond the Islamic community have a dignified and secure status in the world. Indeed, Islam upholds an ideal of equality among human beings and between human groups.

Another Qur'anic passage (49:13) is even more universal in its view of the family of humanity: "O humankind! We created you from a male and a female, and made you into nations and tribes, so that you might get to know each other. The noblest of you in God's sight is the most righteous of you." And although, as will be seen, traditional Muslim views and institutions of political sovereignty and relations with non-Muslims were often triumphalist and dominating—as indeed were parallel Christian views and practices—such Qur'anic passages as those just cited have continued to inform Muslims so far as interreligious relations and openness to creative alternatives in mediation and dispute resolution are concerned.

From its inception, Islam championed formation of a new kind of human community, an *umma*,[3] bound together by a common faith rather than kinship relations. This was a fundamental shift in the social paradigm of traditional Arabia, which had before centered on tribal and clan-based affinity systems. Only rarely did the pre-Islamic Arabs reach beyond their tribal social boundaries to make common cause with outsiders, usually for purposes of mutual benefit such as defense. A prominent example is the *hilf al-fudūl*, a mutual assistance agreement of several Qurayshi clans forty years before the rise of Islam (ca. 580 BCE). Generally, the political and social world of pre-Islamic Arabia was a nearly Hobbesian "condition of war of everyone against everyone," as characterized in *Leviathan*. W. Montgomery Watt, a leading modern biographer of Muhammad, compared the new Muslim *umma* to an Arab tribe, indeed a super tribe that transcended kinship and regionalism in favor of an expanding, cooperative brother-sisterhood of Muslims. Never before Muhammad had the Arabs been united in any sense other than having a common language, a rich poetic legacy, and many shared religious, social, and cultural customs. After Muhammad's establishment of the *umma*, based on a common faith and not kinship ties, the ideal of a unified community took root and spread throughout the lands that were to become Muslim in the formative centuries of Islamic civilization.

Muhammad had known privation and marginality as an orphan and poor member of his clan and tribe. He early gained an appreciation of and compassion for the plight of vulnerable persons such as widows, orphans, strangers, sojourners, slaves, and victims of oppression. Muhammad is depicted in the sources as a person who continued, during his career as prophet and leader of the Muslim community in Medina, then all of Arabia, to mend his own sandals and manage his own meager assets, sometimes going without sufficient food rather than demean his office by begging. So influential was his example that his immediate political successors are respected, also, for their self-denial and stewardship of state resources for the good of all and not for their own advantage. The Sufis, Islam's mystics, made a vow of poverty and took the title "mendicant" (Ar. *faqīr*) to signify their renunciation of the material world in favor of peace and following the path to everlasting fellowship with God.

Islam's origins and early development were sustained within a violent world of extreme antagonism between Muhammad and his modest

band of followers, on one side, and the majority Qurayshi tribal oligarchy of Mecca, on the other. Muhammad and his fellow Muslims
would pray at the ancient Ka'aba mosque in Mecca alongside the polytheistic Meccans. Sometimes the Muslims would be abused as they
observed their worship. This was one of the issues that led to his decision to emigrate to the agricultural oasis city of Medina some 300 miles
north of Mecca, in 622.

The Hijra to Medina was not so much a flight, as is often supposed,
as a well-planned emigration to a location with a greatly enhanced
prospect for the security and support of the Muslim community.
Muhammad did not command his fellow Muslims to accompany him;
rather he invited them to be emigrants in the name of God. Medina, for
its part, needed a respected, neutral person of proven mediating and
conflict resolution skills to help resolve the increasingly dangerous situation among the fractious and warring parties of Medina, which
included conflicting Arab tribes with Jews caught in the middle.
Muhammad was called to Medina and he moved only after he had conducted extensive preliminary interviews with Medinan representatives
and gained significant concessions for himself and his Muslim followers,
among which was the acceptance of Islam as the common religion of the
Medinans, except for the Jews who would be expected to occupy a dignified separate status as fellow monotheists.

After the Hijra, Muhammad concluded a pact, known as the "Constitution of Medina." This governance document, preserved in Ibn
Ishāq's (d. ca. 768) *Sīra*, or biography of Muhammad, was a notable
example of peacebuilding among Arab and Jewish factions and set a
precedent for mediation and agreements along peaceful, essentially con-
sensus-centered, mutually beneficial lines. Among the "Constitution's"
significant provisions concerning the several parties, are passages such
as the following:

> The Messenger of God (God bless and preserve him) wrote a writing
> between the Emigrants and the Ansar ["helpers," i.e., the Medinans],
> in which he made a treaty and covenant with the Jews, confirmed them
> in their religion and possessions, and gave them certain duties and
> rights. . . . The security of God is one; the granting of 'neighborly pro-
> tection' by the least of them (the believers) is binding on them; the
> believers are patrons (or clients . . .) of one another to the exclusion of
> (other) people. . . . The peace *(silm)* of the believers is one; no believer
> makes peace apart from another believer, where there is fighting in the
> way of God, except in so far as equality and justice between them (is
> maintained). . . . No one of them (?those belonging to the *ummah*) may
> go out (to war) without the permission of Muhammad (peace be upon

him), but he is not restrained from taking vengeance for wounds. . . . God is the truest (fulfiller) of this document. It is for the Jews to bear their expenses and for the Muslims to bear their expenses. Between them (that is, to one another) there is help *(nasr)* against whoever wars against the people of this document. Between them is sincere friendship and honourable dealing, not treachery.[4]

The "Constitution" is a realistic and pragmatic, yet also idealistic, document for its time and place and depicts Medina as a theocratic society that provided a transcending authority for the unifying purposes of the umma, even in its inclusion of non-Muslims as equally protected beneficiaries of citizenship. And although the document clearly arose within a context in which violence and warfare were frequent and capricious, it spells out clear and consistent principles and regulations for peaceful, civil, and just behavior in a protected setting for the parties involved. The "Constitution" is now perceived by some as a promising model for contemporary Islamic peacebuilding and international and interreligious relations, taking into account vastly different issues of "space and time," in a global context of international relations.[5]

Continuous warfare between Mecca and Medina occurred until 628, when Muhammad and the Meccans concluded a peace treaty allowing him and the Muslims to observe the pilgrimage to Mecca in the following year and henceforth. The polytheistic Meccans would evacuate their city for the duration of the Muslim pilgrimage. The "Peace of Hudaybiyyah," as the compact is known, also stipulated a ten-year truce between the parties, among other things. In 630, the Muslims determined that the treaty had been breached, whereupon they invaded Mecca with vastly superior forces. The Muslims encountered little resistance and Muhammad, victorious, was also magnanimous. After cleansing the Ka'aba of idols, he declared a general amnesty and set about consolidating his Islamic state, which by then included virtually all the Arabian Peninsula now that the Meccans were in the umma as new Muslims.

Although there were some prominent figures in Muhammad's Muslim movement who were sorely disappointed at the loss of an opportunity to visit violent revenge on the Qurayshites of Mecca, most realized that healing and peace were in the best interests of the Muslim community. The making of peace after years of bitter and bloody warfare was an act of forbearance *(hilm)*, a rarely experienced virtue that the pre-Islamic Arabs had always admired and which came to be a major element in Qur'anic ethics, which sees God as the model of clemency. Greater than the domineering powerbroker is the forbearing person who possesses a moral and spiritual power beyond mere force. The uniting of Mecca and Medina in an Islamically ordered manner was concluded through an act of mercy and forgiveness.

SOME BASIC CONCEPTS AND TERMINOLOGY CONCERNING CONFLICT AND PEACE IN CLASSICAL ISLAM

Western stereotypes of Islam as a bellicose ideology and Muslims as intractable aggressors arose largely during the period of the Crusades, although attitudes contributing to this view circulated much earlier in Christian Europe. The fact that many Christians, as well as Jews, lived peacefully and productively under Islamic law, as tributaries, across the Dar al-Islam, the "Abode of Submission," was not a favorite theme of crusaders and their ecclesiastical and royal sponsors in the Christian West.[6]

Medieval Christian critics of Islam and Muslims focused on the Prophet Muhammad as the architect of all that was evil and violent in Islam. The demonization of Muhammad in the Middle Ages colored everything that Christians thought about Muslims. In fact, Western critics appear to have known very little about Muhammad, the Qur'an, Islamic law, and the manner in which war and international relations, including arbitration, were to be conducted from the perspective of a Muslim jurisconsult's rational and prudent religio-legal system. Muslims, who were very effective at extending Islam's influence, also realized that they lived in an extremely dangerous and threatening world, particularly where their borders and Christian ruled territorial boundaries touched.

There are several key terms and concepts that underlie Islamic ideas of conflict, defense, protection, and peacebuilding. The first is the root that produces the name of the religion of Islam, as well as the word "muslim," namely *s-l-m*. This root has much in common with the cognate Hebrew root that gives us *shalom*, "peace, well-being, health." The Islamic greeting *al-salāmu 'alaykum* is exactly parallel, both linguistically and semantically, to the Hebrew *shalom aleichem*, "peace be with you." Islam, "submission," is closely related to *salām* (also *salm, silm*), which means peace, not merely as absence of conflict but, positively, as presence of health and general well-being.

In pre-Islamic Arabia, war was a normal state of affairs in a land without organized governance and the authority to back it up. The major Arabic term for war is *harb*, which may mean either "fighting" or a "state of war" between two or more groups, according to Majid Khadduri, a leading specialist in the subject.[7] Islam prohibited every kind of war to Muslims except holy war, known as *jihād*. This term, meaning "exertion, struggle," may refer to actual armed conflict, but just as often it has a spiritualized and ethical meaning for Muslims, such as one's personal struggle to combat evil, ignorance, and injustice and be a good Muslim. Muhammad characterized the first type as the "lesser" and the second as the "greater" *jihād*. The declaration of *jihād* with intent to engage in armed combat of one Muslim group against another has always been considered a most grave matter and last resort. Actual practice has more often than not been to prohibit the technical status of *jihād* to intra-Muslim fighting. *Jihād* is intended as a remedy against *non*-Muslims, whether for advancing the rule of Islam, spurring conversion, or as self-defense. Muslims, when declaring *jihād* against non-Muslim People of the Book—that is, Jews and Christians—traditionally first offered the option of conversion to Islam, failing which a choice to submit to Muslim rule and payment of a poll tax would spare the military objects the damages of war. Of course, the third option was to engage in combat until one side or the other prevailed.

Jihād has detailed rules, such as not shedding unnecessary blood and respecting the enemy's property. Noncombatants, such as children, women, the blind, aged, monks, and insane persons were to be spared. Combatants who were captured could be killed, enslaved, and their property claimed as spoil. The exact details varied among the several legal schools.[8]

The traditional community of caliphal times viewed its purpose as to be in continual *jihād* until the world submits to God and becomes Muslim. The lands under Islamic authority were known as *Dar al-Islam*, "The Abode of Submission," whereas the non-Islamic world was known as *Dar al-Harb*, the "Abode of Warfare," to be combated, conditions permitting, at every opportunity. The Qur'an declares that "there is to be no compulsion in religion" (2:256), but classical *jihād* doctrine clearly intended compulsion with respect to the spread and consolidation of Islamic political authority and territorial sovereignty. Idolaters, according to late Qur'anic passages (e.g., 9:5), are to embrace Islam or be killed, whereas Christians and Jews could become protected peoples, *dhimmîs*, so long as they submitted to Muslim authority. "When the forbidden months are past [i.e., when Muslims could not engage in warfare], then fight and slay the idolaters wherever you find them. And seize them, beleaguer them, and lie in wait for them in every stratagem; but if they repent, and establish regular prayers, and practice regular charity, then open the way for them: for God is Oft-Forgiving, Most Merciful" (Surah 9:5). This passage, and similar ones, continue to receive considerable exegetical attention by Muslims, particularly concerning whether they are to be understood as applying only to their immediate space and time contexts or generally. Muslim modernist liberals tend toward the former, fundamentalists the latter.

The simple division of the world into Dar al-Islam and Dar al-Harb was eventually augmented by a third realm, called Dar al-Sulh, which may be translated "House of Peacemaking/Truce." That status depended on non-Muslims of such a land paying tribute to the Muslims in exchange for peace and nonaggression. Muhammad himself concluded such an arrangement with the Christians of Najran in Arabia, thus establishing a precedent for the development of the Dar al-Sulh. Sometimes, a contested region was inhabited and controlled by non-Muslims that Muslim forces were essentially unable to subdue. For example, the Nubians were able to defend themselves against Muslim invasion in the early caliphate through their superior archery. The Sultan of Egypt, Abdallah ibn Sa'd (d. 656–658), imposed a tribute in the form of slaves, and distinguished it from the poll-tax *(jizya)* that non-Muslims in the Dar al-Islam were required to pay. It was a good arrangement for the Nubians, for they maintained their independence. Muslim governments sometimes considered an adjoining region, with no Dar al-Harb in between, where Muslims lived but did not rule, as part of the Dar al-Islam, if the non-Muslim rulers were considered to be rebels. Varying legists and schools developed somewhat differing, even conflicting views of the matter, but the arrangements themselves usually exhibit a certain pragmatism and civility. An additional category of a land that is not Muslim nor an enemy of Muslims was sometimes referred to as *dar al-hiyad,* "the world of neutrality," as Khadduri translates it.[9]

Peacebuilding is a most important duty in the Islamic tradition, but it has been focused principally on intra-Muslim matters rather than relations with non-Muslims, when involving fundamental ethical and spiritual principles. And although Islamic standards formally required, from the beginning, Muslims to treat Jews, Christians, and later, other scriptural peoples, with respect and civility, religious minorities were inferior, protected communities with limited privileges. The fortunes of such minorities varied widely over the centuries, depending on the temperaments of Muslim rulers. Religious minorities generally fared much better under Islamic rule than did Jews, for example, under European Christian rule. The expulsion of the "Moors" from Spain in 1492 is an enduring bitter memory for Muslims as well as Jews. On the other hand, Christians and Jews often prospered under Muslim rule in Spain and other regions of classical Islamic civilization, largely because of the Qur'anic and other Islamic sources and customs that fostered tolerance and administrative policies and regulations aimed at maintaining order, justice, harmony, and peace. Christians and Jews sometimes held high government posts.

However, warfare between Muslims and fellow Muslims as well as non-Muslims did continue over the centuries, whether it could be legally justified as *jihād* or simply viewed as *harb,* ordinary "war" or *qitāl,* "combat." Any Muslim was traditionally authorized to grant an *amān,* a certificate of safe conduct, to an individual or small group of *harbīs* ("combatants," citizens of Dar al-Harb), as non-Muslims are technically known in this context.[10] A Muslim leader could grant an *amān* to a whole city, region, or to traders, religious pilgrims (e.g., to Jerusalem), and travelers as a class. When an *amān* had expired, those covered and wishing to remain in the Muslim country could then assume the status of *dhimmīs,* "protected persons" under Islamic law, which means that they would come under the authority of the Dar al-Islam in every respect. There are advantages as well as disadvantages for such persons, obviously. Ideally, they would be treated justly and protected from persecution and violence; but they would also forfeit rights and privileges that they enjoyed in their own domains. A great deal of important as well as detailed and fascinating information on the *amān* is contained in Al-Shaybani's (750–803/805 CE) *Siyar* (conduct of war and peace), translated by Majid Khadduri as "The Islamic Law of Nations."[11] The contents are based on the teachings of the great Iraqi jurisconsults Abu Hanifa (d. 700–767 CE), and Abu Yusuf (d. 795), two founders of the most flexible and liberal of Sunni legal schools, the Hanafiya.

What has been described is obtained from Umayyad and Abbasid times to the thirteenth century CE and related principally to trade and relations between Christians and Muslims in the Mediterranean world. Later, letters of *amān* were largely replaced by state treaties between Christian and Muslim authorities, due to the great increase in trade. The later types of treaties granted more privileges to non-Muslims in Muslim domains.[12]

ISLAM AND PEACEBUILDING IN THE MODERN ERA

So far, the discussion has focused on traditional Islamic attitudes, doctrines, and practices relating to peace. The ongoing *jihād* against the Dar al-Harb was the main condition of existence before all the people of the world surrender to God as Muslims. Even if that were to happen, Muslims themselves presumably would continue to struggle, through the "Greater Jihad," to conquer their own evil tendencies in order be good and obedient servants of God. War and fighting have occupied much of this survey, with peacebuilding a relatively minor yet important dimension of the picture.

The idea of Muslims having become weak and corrupt has informed some influential modernist reformist discourses and not just types that might be considered "fundamentalist" or "Islamist." That is, the Muslim world has been brought low, some have argued, because Muslims strayed from their formative and sustaining ideals and principles. For example, Muslims allegedly became soft through such corrupting, relativistic, and passive spiritual practices as Sufi mysticism, which allegedly devalues law in favor of a private spirituality that tolerates non-Islamic norms and customs. Muslims also let themselves be seduced, according to this discourse, by secularism, social mixing of the sexes, and consumer materialism as they opened themselves uncritically to Western ideas of governance, morality, and economics.

The rise of the West since the sixteenth century, and the colonialist exploitation of Africa and Asia, where the majority of Muslims have traditionally lived, have been viewed in various ways by the victims. For example, Osama bin Laden's rage at the presence of American military forces in the holy land of Mecca and Medina is shared by countless Muslims, most of whom are probably not supportive of al-Qaeda's mission of *jihād* by terrorism. In Islam's worldview, the nonbelievers should never be in positions of superiority over Muslims. The fact that they had been for a very long time produced painful, sometimes conflicting reactions and emotions among deeply humiliated Muslims. Wilfred Cantwell Smith, more than forty years ago, characterized the malaise of modern Muslims as the sense that something had gone wrong with Islamic history. "The fundamental problem of modern Muslims is how to rehabilitate that history; to set it going again in full vigour, so that Islamic society may once again flourish as a divinely guided society should and must." [13]

Muslims who have held this view have not necessarily been passive or fatalistic about it. Some modern Muslim reformist activists have despised any passive or apologetic attitudes and thrown down the gauntlet, both to unbelievers and fellow Muslims, challenging them with a militant Islamic message. Sayyid Qutb (d. 1966), one of the twentieth century's most articulate and influential radical Muslim reformers, viewed the modern world as largely an arena of ungodly ignorance, which he called "Jahiliyya," the "Age of Ignorance," after the traditional Islamic characterization of pre-Islamic pagan Arabia. Qutb held that Jahiliyya applies not only to non-Muslim peoples and their corrupt world, but equally if not more to contemporary Muslims who tolerate and even embrace modern secular values. Qutb called for continued *jihād* against the enemies of Islam, whether they are non-Muslims or Muslims. His words, as contained in his powerful manifesto, *Milestones,*[14] have strongly influenced Muslim opinion all over the world, to the extent of galvanizing radical Islamist movements, such as the Muslim Brotherhood in Egypt (which since those days has become relatively moderate), as well as militant Muslim university student movements in Egypt that were active during the time of President Anwar Sadat, who was assassinated in 1981 by Khalid Islambuli, a member of an underground extremist group known as *Jihad.*

Qutb had contempt for the apologetic manner by which modern Muslims softened the concept of *jihād,* interpreting it as merely a temporary defense posture when Muslims are threatened. Qutb's book was banned, confiscated, and burned by Egyptian authorities. The author, who was embittered by many years of abusive prison confinement, was arrested and secretly hanged in 1966 by the Egyptian government. The location of his grave is unknown in a country famous for elevating its popular Muslim heroes to sainthood.[15]

Since Wilfred Cantwell Smith characterized the global malaise of Muslims, a sea of change in the form of universal Islamic renewal has occurred, taking varied forms. Generally, potentially violent, certainly threatening—to non-Muslims—topics such as *jihād,* have been treated cautiously by most Muslims when representing them to Westerners. In over thirty years of scholarship and travel around the Muslim world, I have until recently only rarely heard the word armed *jihād* mentioned as either a feasible or desirable remedy in dealing with threats or conflicts involving either Muslims or other people. Yet there is a prevailing global stereotype—selectively based on unpleasant facts, as all stereotypes tend to be—that Muslims as a whole are violent and bent on holy war: against Israel, against Christians, against Hindus, and even against some of their co-religionists of liberal, modernist bent. There are many Muslims who forcefully express armed jihadist tendencies, but there are far more who prefer to solve conflicts by means of peaceful arbitration, negotiation, and compromise.

It is true that much Muslim writing on *jihād* in modern times has tended to emphasize its spiritual and not its warlike expressions. This softening of the discourse in comparison to its more traditional forms is based only in part on an apologetic premise that is both conciliatory toward non-Muslims and defensive in the face of still overwhelming Western political, economic, technological, and military power. The overwhelming majority of Muslims in this period of globalization and constant, necessary, and inescapable international relationships sincerely want peaceful international as well as domestic religious and political relations and the institutions and agreements that can make them secure and stable. There are tragic and seemingly intractable exceptions—Sudan, the Arab-Israeli conflict, Kashmir, Indonesia, and Afghanistan come to mind. But Muslims generally want peace as a state of being for all human life and not as an expedient or as a screen for ulterior motives. Peace on earth, for Muslims, is a forerunner of heaven and a practice as well as condition that must be nurtured and celebrated in this world in preparation for the next. The Qur'an is clear on the matter: "The servants of God Most Gracious are those who walk on the earth humbly, and when ignorant people address them, they say 'Peace' *(salām)*" (25:63). The blessed in heaven will experience their highest joy when they hear there the passage from Sura Yā Sīn that is recited at every Muslim's funeral: " 'Peace!'—a Salutation from a Lord Most Merciful" (36:58).

SOME CONTEMPORARY DEVELOPMENTS

There is now an unprecedented, historic global diaspora of Muslims in such places as Europe, Australia, and the western hemisphere. Many Muslims have migrated to the West for better career opportunities, personal freedom, human rights, safety, and education. North America now has the closest thing to a microcosm of the global Muslim umma: an enormously rich and diverse range of Muslims from dozens of countries and cultures. The vast majority of Muslim immigrants, as well as converts, in the United States and Canada, are working hard to be good, law-abiding, religiously and culturally tolerant, and peaceful citizens in a pluralistic setting. Muslims in North America are building strong communities, establishing schools, financial institutions, service organizations, businesses, and reaching out beyond Muslim circles through civic, service, and political activities. Ancient traditions of peace, reconciliation, and negotiation that have marked Muslims' own communal ideals and practices are beginning to be felt in the larger Western societies, particularly in North America, where many Muslims now live and have a place at the table.

Perhaps nowhere is the peacebuilding and mediating ability of Islam and Muslims stronger nor more dramatically visible than in the American corrections system. The Nation of Islam, an African-American millenarian movement with some Islamically inspired aspects, began engaging in prison reform activities many years ago to realize inmates' religious and other rights.[16] Mainstream Muslims have in more recent times also done much to improve the legal environment as well as the routine climate of prisons all over America. The benefits have accrued particularly to inmates of color, such as African Americans, who constitute such a large portion of jail and prison populations. Inmate converts to Islam, people who as one Texas warden put it in a videotaped interview, had "been at war with the system," often have found a new life and a worthwhile purpose in Islam.[17]

One prominent mainstream Muslim prison "chaplain," Imam Warithuddeen Umar, formerly a high official in the New York State Department of Corrections, has argued that many if not most minority inmates from the inner city streets of America cannot be rehabilitated because they had not been "habilitated" in the first place. They often have no clue about living peacefully and productively in society, although they may possess street smarts of various kinds that are essentially antisocial and destructive. Islam has enabled so many inmates from backgrounds of poverty, violence, substance abuse, and crime to "take captivity captive" by habilitating them through personal discipline, dignity, integrity, self-control, hygiene, regular prayer and scriptural study, trusting new relationships with fellow Muslims in a loyal bond, and hope for a future of freedom where honest work and vigorous spirituality prevail. Islam sometimes is, like other creeds, a "jailhouse religion," but it surprises both inmates and officials by its success in bringing so many apparently hopeless criminals to a new life. Islam's record of success in mediating extremely difficult conflicts in prisons is a most promising indicator of the religion's importance in helping Americans face the challenges of diversity, poverty, crime, corrections, and other pressing issues.[18]

Today's Muslims are increasingly engaged in thinking and activities that contribute to or are relevant to peacebuilding in the related areas of international law and human rights. The classical *siyar* (conduct concerning war and peace) discourses, introduced earlier, of Islamic principles for international relations, including treaties, nonaggression pacts, and so forth, are regaining renewed attention and being introduced to curricula in Islamic higher education. A number of prominent Muslim scholars have contributed important discussions to this discourse.[19]

An example of the promise that *siyar* holds for peacebuilding in today's world is in the Islamic international relations thought of Egyptian legal scholar, Muhammad Talaat al-Ghunaimi, who has serious disagreement with the classical doctrines of *jihād*. He favors a return to the fundamental sources of Qur'an and Prophetic Tradition (Sunna/Hadîth), before their contents were captured by the later legal discourses of a Muslim empire. For al-Ghunaimi, the term Shari'a, usually translated as Islamic "law," should be used only with reference to the two primary sources, whereas the secondary, jurisprudential discourses on them, known properly as *fiqh*, should be regarded as provisional standards and procedures, however useful and valid they may be for specific times and places. For example, al-Ghunaimi considers the concepts of Dār al-Islam and Dar al-Harb, treated earlier in this chapter, to have no enduring doctrinal authenticity, because they are neither Qur'anic nor intended for anything other than legally identifying the parties in medieval Islam's continuous conflicts with neighboring non-Muslim countries. "The terms *dar al-Islam* and *dar al-Harb* are an innovation of the *Abbasid* legists. As their idea on the division of the world is dependent on the notion of constant or aggressive *jihad,* and since this notion is not warranted [in the primary sources of Qur'an and Hadith], inevitably the alleged division should collapse too." [20] Al-Ghunaimi considers the basic teachings of Islam to be fully conformable with modern notions of international law, with the added virtue of divine origin.

Similarly, human rights discourses within Islamic contexts are gaining attention, to the point that formal declarations have been issued by Muslim bodies in the past two decades. The Islamic declarations are, in some respects, responses to the Universal Declaration of Human Rights of 1948. They affirm human rights, which are also frequently expressed by the phrase "human dignity." Islamic declarations subsume everything in their contents under the Islamic Shari'a, or law, so that salient aspects of the 1948 UDHR—for example, women's and others' rights, religious freedom, and so on—become irrelevant or moot. Another problem is the cultural relativism that claims the right to define and honor human rights according to individual traditions and cultures.[21]

The September 2000 issue of *The Message International,* published by the New York City–based Islamic Circle of North America, which has strong South Asian Muslim connections as well as activist political and ethical concerns, featured several thoughtful and balanced articles on human rights and Islam. The contributions look at non-Muslims' rights, the rights of parents and children, spouses' rights, minority rights, and the Universal Declaration of Human Rights of 1948 as well as the "Cairo declaration" approved by the 19th Islamic Conference of Foreign Ministers in Cairo in 1990. The two declarations are printed next to each other, without commentary, which I take to be a sincere gesture of openness and an invitation to the development of mediating discussions in this complex, difficult, and often extremely divisive subject.

One may indeed find abundant Islamic scriptural references that provide hope for continuing and significantly extending the peacebuilding ideals and practices of Islam both within and beyond the boundaries of the Muslim community. The renewed interest in Islamic international law—*siyar*—as has been suggested earlier, promises to produce new Islamic discourses on peacebuilding for today's diverse and religiously pluralistic as well as mobile world.

Similarly, Muslim feminists find in the Qur'an, far more than in the Hadith (the teachings and example of Muhammad), ample material from which to argue for women's and human rights (as distinguished from duties) in general. But Muslim jurists, in places where Islamic law continues to prevail (e.g., Saudi Arabia, Pakistan, Iran, Afghanistan) have rarely been Qur'anic scripturalists in a liberal and independent sense, at least. As Ann Elizabeth Mayer reminds us in relation to women's rights, "Typically, it is not the original sources that one consults to find Islamic law. Islamic law has traditionally been a jurist's law. The Shari'a is generally viewed as being stated in the works of authoritative jurists. Depending on their allegiance to various sects and schools of law, Muslims at a given time or place referred to a particular jurist for particular guidance."[22] Mayer is writing with regard to Muslim feminists hopeful of liberation from oppressive laws and traditional male chauvinism based on a new reading of the Qur'an. A similar caution should be exercised when considering the prospects for peacebuilding and general human rights in conservative, particularly fundamentalist Muslim legal thinking. Yet there are also legal and rights scholars and activists who are exploring and testing new avenues to conflict resolution in specific regions and situations, such as Lebanon, Jordan, and Sudan.[23]

Although issues and developments leading up to the tragic events of September 11, 2001, may suggest otherwise, it is nevertheless true that the vast majority of Muslims today are strongly dedicated to peacebuilding with their fellow human beings, as well as the maintenance of universal human rights, without stipulating or imposing Islamic beliefs and behavioral norms beyond affirming their authority for themselves in a pluralistic order. Bassam Tibi, an Arab Muslim political scientist at Germany's University of Göttingen, writes, about human rights, that they should not be equated with Western "values and legal norms." International human rights law standards are, he argues, an achievement of cultural modernity and are not, as such, "Western" if they can be proven to "be based on universal legal norms and ethical values underlying universal morality," in which case they "ought not to be confused with [Western] political power and hegemonic rule."[24] Al-Ghunaimi would appear to agree with Tibi, in essence, as would an increasing number of Muslim thinkers who know and understand both Muslim and Western discourses in depth and with reference to power relationships that might sometimes elude Western human rights and international law scholars.[25] One of the contributors to the *The Message International* issue on Islam and human rights regretfully recalls that,

> Some of us have conveniently divided the modern world into Darul Islam and Darul Harb. Some have lately charted out another territory by the name of Daru-s-Sulh, projecting history into the realm of present realities. I do not know if this is a valid and fair classification; nor am I knowledgeable about its conformity with the basic doctrine; but I am always weary of spinning a web of mythology around the Islamic Aqida [traditional Islamic doctrines], using ancient historical events and archaic semanticism.[26]

NOTES

1. Anthony F. C. Wallace, "Revitalization Movements," *American Anthropologist,* LVIII (1956), pp. 264–281. Wallace considers Islam to have originated in a revitalization movement and there is evidence to support his position.

2. The Ka'aba is the ancient cubical structure in Mecca's sanctuary. It was a pilgrimage destination long before Muhammad preached the Islamic message and transmitted the Qur'anic revelation. In Muhammad's time (ca. 570–632 CE), there had been some 360 idols situated at the Ka'aba, until they were destroyed by the Prophet when he and the Muslims conquered pagan Mecca in 630 and presided over the inhabitants' peaceful conversion to Islam.

3. See Frederick M. Denny, "Umma," in *The Encyclopaedia of Islam*, New Edition, Vol. X, Fascicules 177–178, pp. 859–863, for an overview.

4. W. Montgomery Watt, *Muhammad at Medina* (Oxford: Oxford University Press, 1956), pp. 223–225. Watt's translation.

5. See, for example, the contemporary Turkish intellectual, Ali Bulaç's "The Medina Document," a translation from Turkish of two related articles published in Turkey in 1992 and 1994–1995. Contained in Charles Kurzman, ed., *Liberal Islam* (New York: Oxford University Press, 1998), pp. 169–178.

6. According to Norman Daniel's balanced and absorbing study, *Islam and the West: The Making of an Image* (Edinburgh: Edinburgh University Press, 1960), p. 127.

7. *The Shorter Encyclopaedia of Islam* (Ithaca, NY: Cornell University Press, 1953), "Harb," p. 180. See also, Majid Khadduri's classic study, *War and Peace in the Law of Islam* (Baltimore: The Johns Hopkins Press, 1955), and *The Islamic Law of Nations: Shaybani's Siyar,* translated with an introduction, notes, and appendices by Majid Khadduri (Baltimore: The Johns Hopkins Press, 1966).

8. This paragraph is based on Khadduri's summary in *Shorter Ency-clopaedia of Islam,* p. 180. An excellent, wide-ranging contemporary study is *Just War and Jihad: Historical and Theoretical Perspectives on War and Peace in Western and Islamic Traditions,* edited by John Kelsay and James Turner Johnson (New York: Greenwood Press, 1991). Also recommended is *Cross, Crescent, and Sword: The Justification and Limitation of War in Western and Islamic Tradition,* edited by James Turner Johnson and John Kelsay (Westport, CT: Greenwood Press, 1990).

9. *War and Peace,* p. 258.

10. The material on *amān* in this paragraph is derived principally from Joseph Schacht's article "Amān," in *The Encyclopaedia of Islam,* New Edition (Leiden: E.J. Brill, 1960), vol. 1, pp. 429–430.

11. See n. 7.

12. Examples of such treaties are found in English translation in S. M. Stern, ed., *Documents from Islamic Chanceries,* First Series, Oriental Studies 3 (Columbia: University of South Carolina Press, 1965).

13. Wilfred Cantwell Smith, *Islam in Modern History* (New York: Mentor Books, 1959; first published 1957), p. 47.

14. Sayyid Qutb, *Milestones,* revised translation (Indianapolis: American Trust Publications, 1993). Originally published in Arabic as *Ma'ālim fī-al-tarīq* in 1964 in Cairo.

15. A balanced and well-detailed survey article is "Qutb, Sayyid," by Shahrough Akhavi in *The Oxford Encyclopedia of the Modern Islamic World,* ed. John L. Esposito (New York: Oxford University Press, 1995), vol. 3, pp. 400–404.

16. The Nation of Islam has not been accepted as authentically Islamic by global Islam, although the NOI appears close to embracing the Sunni main-stream as of 2003.

17. *Christian Science Monitor* television series on "Islam in America," seg-ment on Muslims in prison, 1990.

18. For an overview, see Frederick M. Denny and Olga Scarpetta, "'Jail-house Religion': The Challenge of Corrections to the American Muslim Com-munity," in *Studies in Contemporary Islam,* vol. 1, no. 1 (Spring 1999), pp. 62–71.

19. See, for example, Ralph H. Salmi, Cesar Adib Majul, and George K. Tanham, *Islam and Conflict Resolution: Theories and Practices* (Lanham, MD: University Press of America, 1998).

20. Mohammad Talaat Al Ghunaimi, *The Muslim Conception of Interna-tional Law and the Western Approach* (The Hague: Martinus Nijhoff, 1968), p. 184. Al-Ghunaimi's ideas are discussed in some detail in Salmi, Majul, and Tan-ham, *Conflict Resolution,* op. cit., pp. 92–99.

21. The work on this subject of Sudanese legal scholar Abdullahi A. An-Na'im is significant—for example, his "Religious Minorities Under Islamic Law and the Limits of Cultural Relativism," *Human Rights Quarterly* 9 (1987), pp. 1–18. An-Na'im's bold and independent liberal Islamic thinking, along with that of his mentor, Mahmoud Mohamed Taha, who was executed for apostasy in Sudan in 1985, is surveyed in Salmi, Majul, and Tanham, op. cit., pp. 107–114.

22. Ann Elizabeth Mayer, *Islam and Human Rights: Tradition and Politics,* 2nd edition (Boulder: Westview Press, 1995), p. 95. Mayer has expanded on this point, and addressed some of its subtleties, in the 3rd edition of her book, published by Westview Press in 1998, pp. 97–98.

23. See, for example, Paul Salem, ed., *Conflict Resolution in the Arab World: Selected Essays* (Beirut: American University of Beirut, 1997). A valuable and varied anthology of previously published articles and chapters is *Peace and Conflict Resolution in Islam: Precept and Practice,* edited by Abdul Aziz Said, Nathan C. Funk, and Ayse S. Kadayifci (Lanham, MD): University Press of America, 2001).

24. Bassam Tibi, "Islamic Law/*Shari'a,* Human Rights, Universal Morality and International Relations," *Human Rights Quarterly,* 16 (1994), p. 289.

25. For a representative range of modern and contemporary Muslim thinkers and activists in this area, see Kurzman, ed., *Liberal Islam,* op. cit.

26. Waheeduddin Ahmed, "The Question of Human Rights and Minorities," *The Message International,* September 2000, p. 37.

8

Christianity and Peacebuilding

ANDREA BARTOLI

In Nigeria, in the heart of Africa where the long-term expansion of Christianity and Islam meet, tensions are high. Many predict bloodshed. There are several indications that this might actually happen.[1] Yet in the midst of this urgent and uncertain situation a most improbable scenario has occurred: a vibrant Evangelical Christian Pastor decided together with a Muslim Imam to start an interreligious dialogue, a dialogue that could bring peace to the region and the whole country.[2] What might, one wonders, the religious contribution to peace be?

In the Democratic Republic of Congo when many Congolese parties involved in the deadly conflict that ravages the region were exploring the feasibility of a national debate to pave the way to a peaceful resolution, they asked for the facilitation of the Community of Sant'Egidio, an international Catholic organization. After its successful facilitation in Mozambique, members of the Community of Sant'Egidio have been able to encourage, support, and achieve significant results in the area of international peacemaking in countries such as Algeria, Albania, Burundi, Guatemala, and Kosovo.[3]

From the Indian-Pakistani conflict in 1948 (which led to the Nobel Peace Prize to the Quakers) to the Mennonite intervention in the Nicaragua conflict, the list of successful engagements in peacemaking by individuals and groups affiliated with the Anabaptist tradition has been highly significant. Indeed, any scholar interested in conflict resolution, as well as the many practitioners with long-term commitments to the resolution of conflicts around the world, will recognize the contribution of Mennonites and Quakers to both the practice and the theory of conflict resolution today.[4]

Likewise, the profound and peaceful transformation of South Africa owns a great deal to the creative intervention of various Christian churches. In short, across the world today and throughout history, the relationship between Christianity and peacebuilding is dauntingly rich, complex, and yet somehow elusive.[5] Nonetheless, the examples pointed to previously do provide ground for the formulation of a set of highly pertinent, general observations arising out of the contributions to peace made by contemporary Christian organizations as well as from the long history of human inquiry prompted and produced by those who have been seeking to live the Gospel message fully.

Christianity must be understood through the revelatory framework historically inaugurated by the benediction of Noah and affirmed through the experience of Abraham, who was made aware of the special relationship between the human family and the one and only God. In Christian terms, this relationship is revealed, and is not merely discovered or constructed. The Abrahamic heritage, shared in different ways by Jews, Christians, and Muslims, relates to Jesus' message profoundly. Jesus accepts and proclaims the notion of faith in the one and only God and always respectfully refers to the example of Abraham. Jesus did not come to abolish the old revelation, but rather to "fulfill it."[6] This fulfillment was passed on to his followers and the world at large through Jesus' own life and has come to us through the testimonies of others. Jesus, who was crucified after a dubious trial, refused to use violence against adversaries and lived a radical message of forgiveness and reconciliation beyond enmity. Jesus never held office, never commanded armies, and refused to pass judgment. He was peaceful and yet his teaching would divide "brother from brother." In his wake would come a paradoxical revelation of a possibility of love that may be divisive in its capacity to reveal human attitudes. Jesus' silence is as significant as his words, and he refused to be a judge; yet his example allows a self-recognition process by the disciples first and by many followers afterwards. Jesus' Gospel, then, may be better understood in light of the human need for understanding through self-awareness.[7] Humans need distinctions, and the famous "Repay to Caesar what belongs to Caesar and to God what belongs to God"[8] gives us a glimpse of a very fruitful line of interpretation that led eventually to a distinction between religious and secular powers that has proven to be a useful tool in conceiving and developing tolerant practices within institutions. Likewise, Jesus' command "to love your enemies and pray for those who persecute you"[9] and his "Blessed are the peacemakers"[10] had very different resonance throughout history, often prompting fruitful innovations as response to the Word.[11]

After Jesus' death and resurrection, the communities of his disciples had to remember what Jesus taught and find ways to live his teaching. Their answers to these challenges, as reported by the New Testament, were many, diverse, and dynamic.[12] Consequently, after two millennia it is impossible to claim a satisfactory treatment of the relationship between Christianity and peacebuilding based on the assumption of a uniformity shared and agreed on by all members of the Christian community. Christians now number more than 1.5 billion and are present in all countries of the world. The Catholic Church alone has nearly a billion members[13] and the World Council of Churches has a membership of over 330 churches in more than 120 countries.[14] Some of these churches emerged as distinct entities many centuries ago, and some more recently after the Reformation. Yet, despite this Christian diversity, the desire for love, unity, and agreement motivates most Christian traditions, especially among those committed to peacebuilding.[15] Certainly, the core message of Scripture, shared and recognized by the great majority of [16] Christians today, strongly encourages a radical commitment to peace.[17] Christians who avoid using arguments to justify, condone, and wage war and violence, either among themselves or against non-Christians, find that they share a significant spiritual—and at times practical—communion[18] beyond their denominational differences.

Personalities such as Saint Francis of Assisi, a Catholic, Martin Luther King, a Baptist, Dietrich Bonhoeffer, a Lutheran, Patriarch Athenagoras, an Orthodox, or Desmond Tutu, an Anglican, are not only recognized by many in the Christian tradition but also in the world at large. Dorothy Day had an impact well beyond her Catholic Workers circles. Yet it is also clear that the pursuit of peace can cause its own kind of trouble. For instance, a dedicated Christian pacifist such as Lev Tolstoy could be perceived more as a dangerous troublemaker than an honest and radical follower of Jesus' teachings.

At other times, as in the case of wars and oppressive regimes, peace requires the determination of martyrs. In the last century alone thousands gave their lives to keep their faith in times of darkness. They were Christians of all confessions and denominations. Their lives and deaths are the testimony of one of the greatest gifts of Christianity to peacebuilding: keeping the very possibility of hope, life, and peace alive in times of violent persecution.[19]

In responding to the challenges of this contradictory history in which heartening examples are juxtaposed with horrendous crimes, Pope John Paul II invited the Church and all Christians to recognize their wrongdoing and ask forgiveness. The Pope wrote:

As the Successor of Peter, I ask that in this year of mercy the Church, strong in the holiness which she receives from her Lord, should kneel before God and implore forgiveness for the past and present sins of her sons and daughters. All have sinned and none can claim righteousness before God (cf. 1 *Kgs* 8:46). Christians are invited to acknowledge, before God and before those offended by their actions, the faults, which they have committed. Let them do so without seeking anything in return, but strengthened only by the 'love of God which has been poured into our hearts' (*Rom* 5:5).[20]

The Pope called for a purification of memory that many Christians and non-Christians alike have welcomed. It is a courageous effort to distill from more than 2000 years of history a sense of orientation that may open the way to an ever "old and new" understanding of Jesus' gospel.

OBSTACLES TO PEACEBUILDING

Two major tendencies have contributed to the unfortunate transformation of Christianity or aspects of Christianity into an obstacle to peacebuilding. The first is the intolerant and at times violent treatment of differences, both internally (heretics) and externally (nonbelievers). Both tendencies involve the use of political and military power to resolve differences perceived as threats to truth and right by the exclusion, rejection, and elimination of "others" both within and outside the communities of Christians. For the victims, both kinds of Christian hegemony are tragic.

Christianity seems especially to become an obstacle to peacebuilding when it aligns itself too closely with secular power, while at the same time developing an intolerant attitude toward others. This problematic relation has emerged dramatically at times when war was waged "in God's name," as in the Crusades and in the Puritan experience. The temptation to resolve religious differences through a use of force must certainly be included as a main obstacle to peacemaking.[21]

Immediately after its inception, Christianity, while experiencing the trauma of the split from Judaism, emerged as a complex web of communities and beliefs without access to political and military power. Although disputes were deep at times, they did not produce violent confrontations. Only when a strict definition of belief and heresy was combined with the power to enforce decrees by military and political means did the categories of nonbelievers and heretics emerge as the grounds for conducting political battles fought on secular and ecclesial ground, thus substituting a major obstacle to peacebuilding. In short, the evolution of

Christianity into a majority religion created the conditions for an intolerant use of political and military force to obtain uniformity in the realm of belief and to resolve conflicts by force.[22]

The association of religious and political power under Constantine changed the Christian experience forever. Placing religion at the core of the social and political contract ensured that the regulation of heresy and the opposition between Christians and non-Christians became essential to the maintenance of a peaceful Christian life, which in turn was identified with the whole civil society.

Consequently, within the boundaries of a divided Europe, Christianity became a major means of homogenization. The absorption of pagans was pursued relentlessly for centuries and religious leaders, especially the Roman pontiff, emerged as powerful political players. In their political role, religious leaders were involved in provoking conflicts as well as in resolving them, on the one hand calling for the defense of truth, and on the other pragmatically exploiting the realm of political possibilities. Not surprisingly, some of the most violent, protracted, and deadly conflicts were within Christianity itself. Communities and individuals fought one another in the name of religion for centuries, using violence to resolve theological disagreements and defend religious peace. The use of religion by powerful states and military and political actors has also been a consistent feature in the history of Christianity since Constantine, both within its own boundaries and in its relation with the non-Christian world. The Religious Wars in Europe that followed the Reformation were, in this sense, only one chapter in a longer and sorrowful history of religion combining with military power to consolidate political hegemonies.[23] This path of violent confrontation is especially evident in the attitudes of Christianity to the expansion of Islam and to European colonialism.

The prophetic revelation to Muhammad was able to attract many followers in a very brief period of time, first unifying Arab tribes and then a great number of people from India to Spain. The propagation of Islam and its radical message of submission to God were met, politically and militarily, by the Christian Crusades. This confrontation is still deeply embedded in the collective imagination of many Christians.[24] Islam has been a powerful presence in world history since its beginning and in many instances has proven itself able to inspire political structures more tolerant of religious diversity than Christianity. From the experience of medieval Spain to the Ottoman Empire, Islam has an intriguing record of selective tolerance. For Christians, Islam was consistently perceived as the adversary and violent confrontations between the two sides have been frequent.

Analogous violence and antagonism emerged as a consequence of colonial expansion by Christian nations. From the fifteenth century, Christian kingdoms expanded their influence and control from Europe to the world, linking commercial, sovereign, and religious experience with the military conquest of large empires. Spain, Portugal, England, France, and the Netherlands acquired control of extensive territories in the Americas, Africa, and Asia. By the end of the nineteenth century, European powers had engineered a system of almost global colonial control. This disproportionate political and military might, while not wholly or singularly Christian, was deeply connected with Christianity, which contributed to the ideological framework within which conquest rather than concord or conciliation could occur. Christianity also provided the legal framework for the division of global interests. Thus, for instance, the Roman pontiff arbitrated the colonial concession between Spain and Portugal, while other European powers were to rely on their ability to impose claims by less, though still religiously identifiable, military and political means. Moreover, the whole outward experience that the "discoveries" of colonialism brought to Europe enabled a massive missionary movement in all Christian denominations that strengthened the colonial adventure and at times condoned the use of violence in religious terms. The consequences of these movements are still with us and are in many ways intertwined with contemporary conflicts. For instance, tragedies such as the massive transportation of slaves from Africa to the newly discovered Americas would have been unthinkable outside the colonial framework.

The colonial adventure created the conditions for the emergence of the United States, which also has strong links with Christianity. The Pilgrims who sought refuge from religious persecution in Europe were ready to evangelize new lands. Nonetheless, the diversity of religious experience in the emerging United States produced an institutional setting where, thanks to the separation of church and state, no denomination was allowed to exert control over the others or over non-Christians. Although religious bigotry and intolerance also have a long history in the United States, institutional arrangements have allowed many diverse religious groups to flourish.

Currently, it must be noted that the emergence of the United States as the world's only superpower is perceived by many as an obstacle to peacebuilding, especially when the United States asserts itself as a powerful defender of Judeo-Christian traditions. Yet, many Christians by and large recognize that the identification of any political regime with one people, one language, one territory, or one religion is problematic. The large majority of Germans, many of whom were Christians, supported Hitler. Was that support enough to make that regime a "Christian" one? Certainly, Dietrich Bonheffer and the martyrs of the Confessant Church would disagree. The Church also supported Franco's regime in Spain. But was that support enough to make this political arrangement a "Christian" one? Many, including Pope Paul VI, who refused to lend his support to the regime and called for reforms on several occasions, would disagree.

The first years of Christianity were characterized by the experience of a minority without much power or recognition. Christians accepted a pluralistic environment and were recognized by others as people who attempted to live Jesus' dangerously real notion of love: "This is how all will know that you are my disciples, if you have love for one another."[25] The first Christian centuries were a time of growth and martyrdom. The models within the Christian community in this period were nonviolent and based on a Christ-like witnesses of the faith by believers who preferred to die rather than to respond violently, as in the case of Stephen's martyrdom.

Another key obstacle to peacebuilding is forced conversions. First in Europe, and later worldwide—specifically in countries colonized by "Christian" nations—pressures of various kinds were used to convert the colonized peoples to Christianity. Threats to life, punishment, and harsh treatment were routinely utilized by an alliance of sacred and secular powers. Although in many cases conversions were genuine and freely decided, overwhelming proof exists that the use of force was deemed an acceptable tool to obtain assent. The scars that this procedure left in the collective memory are hard to evaluate. Yet it is important for Christians to acknowledge these unpleasant facts. Pope John Paul II included forced conversion in the list of sins for which Christians should repent and ask forgiveness. During the recently concluded Jubilee, individual and collective sins committed by Christians were acknowledged and forgiveness was requested. Clearly, it is of central importance for Christian peacebuilding to continue in the task of acknowledging the disparity between the radical and absolute commandment of the Lord Jesus and the actual historical experience of millions of Christians.

CHRISTIANITY AS A FORCE FOR PEACEBUILDING

The basic Christian injunction to peacemaking derives from the dying Jesus, who is reported to have said about those who were crucifying him: "Father, forgive them, for they know not what they do."[26] Jesus' references to peace are also abundant throughout the New Testament[27] and always reflect the spirit of his dying words. Thus, when he sent his disciples to preach the Gospel, Jesus told them, "When you enter in a house, say 'peace be upon you'." Peace is needed in order to live fully, and Jesus relates peace to health when he says, "Go in peace and be cured of your affliction"[28] in response to the woman who was afflicted by hemorrhaging blood. It is therefore possible to interpret the most widely recognized quotation of Jesus on the issue of peacebuilding— "Blessed are the peacemakers"—as a particular form of communion with the divine that comes as a gift from on high. Peacemakers do not so much "make" peace as reveal and revel in it.[29]

Jesus presented himself and was perceived by his disciples as "the fulfillment" of a relationship between God and humans inaugurated at the creation, revealed through the law and the prophets, and aimed toward a condition of fullness. In Christian terms, peace has been central to the understanding of God's plan for the whole creation and Jesus brought his peace, as Paul later said—"reconcile all things in him." This redemptive action did not take the form of a conquest but of a fragile path, exemplified by a suffering servant of God who was able to explore, present, and reveal the possibilities of a forgiving love.

The followers of Jesus' peaceful way soon found themselves responding to at least three major cultural streams that contributed to the emergence of Christianity as a new religion, these being Jewish, Greek, and Latin. The Christian understanding of peace was enriched by these different traditions that bring to bear the Hebrew notion of *shalom*, the Greek *eirene*, and the Latin *pax*.

The term *shalom* was familiar to Jesus and to his first disciples, who were Jews, and it is central to the Christian understanding of peace. This word occurs often in the Hebrew Scriptures and it is and was widely used in daily conversation. It refers to a condition of wholeness, of complete welfare that encompasses the whole person. *Shalom* pertains to the individual, the community, and the web of relationships in which a person lives. It is a form of salutation that is both a wish and a blessing. It does not describe a political arrangement or an institutional system of power in which the absence of war is guaranteed by force. On the contrary, it is an expression of personal and collective well-being that occurs when justice exists in the relationships and systems of a society.

The Greek term *eirene* describes the absence of war. Thus, in Homer, *eirene* is presented as a cessation of violent action, whether among the gods or among humans. When injustice and violence momentarily stop, *eirene* is granted to the community, which can therefore experience relief from the tragedy, destruction, and devastation of war.

Christianity was born also under *pax Romana,* the political and military attempt to avoid war through domination. In this context, *pax* describes a situation in which the absence of war is created by an overwhelming imbalance of power that renders violent confrontation unreasonable. Because deterrence permits putting a heavy price on anyone attempting to destabilize the *pax,* it becomes its own form of prevention: the reaction to any attempt to alter the power structure is so strong that such attempts are usually subdued before they become a serious threat. The first few Christian centuries were marked by a significant tension between the Christian communities and Roman power. After all, Jesus himself was killed by crucifixion, a specifically Roman way to illustrate dominion of a territory by Roman troops. Christians did not benefit from the *pax Romana* until Constantine used the might of the Roman Empire to their advantage and this chapter argues that the Christian attempt to use military and political power was, to say the least, ambivalent. On one hand, a direct political involvement by Christians helped to effect a transition from one system to another during the dissolution of the Roman Empire, inaugurating a long medieval history in Europe, during which much that we enjoy today in terms of knowledge and culture was either formed or preserved. On the other hand, the availability to institutional Christianity of political and military power made possible such disastrous, violent interventions as the Crusades.

Yet the legacy of the *pax Romana* endures also in the modern world if we consider the many occasions on which prominent Christian leaders have been called to act as caretakers during turbulent transition periods, as in the Philippines, Chile, East Timor, or the Democratic Republic of the Congo. The peaceful transition from communism to liberal democracy in Eastern Europe cannot be explained without reference to the role of Christians (Protestant, Orthodox, and Catholics) who were able to preserve notions of human dignity, solidarity, and civil commitment beyond the all-encompassing control of totalitarian states. This role seems to be still very much a point of reference in the North-South tension, which has planetary and global implications.[30] In short, Christian understanding of sin as both an individual and collective reality has led to efforts to respond creatively and to imagine, design, and preserve ethically sound political responses in a variety of political and historical situations.[31]

A further important Christian contribution to peacebuilding is the diversity of arguments within Christianity about the legitimate use of force. While the first generations of Christians were preoccupied with violence against them, the new arrangement following the dissolution of the empire in the West prompted some prominent thinkers, especially

Augustine of Hippo, to elaborate a theory of Just War.[32] Based on classical antecedents, this was an effort to control, tame, and use violence constructively. The point of departure is that peace needs to be just in order to be legitimate. If unjust conditions exist, under certain conditions peace can be achieved through war. The final aim is always peace, but it is accepted that there are historical constructs that require a violent upheaval to restore peace to its integrity. The Just War position, elaborated by Thomas Aquinas, Martin Luther, and John Calvin, is an attempt to conceive, secure, and defend peace by waging a war that must be justified *(jus ad bellum)* and in which there are limitations to the use of force *(jus in bellum)*. The main idea is that war is a reality that must be used prudently. Arguments in this vein, especially on the proportionality of response, could be heard during the NATO bombing campaign in the Balkans, and attempts to tame war by protecting civilians and victims are also directly related to this line of thinking.[33]

Throughout history Christians have struggled to understand how best to follow Jesus' peaceful message, especially in a world in which violence and injustice are permanent features. Some have created regimes that included and justified the use of force; others have felt that violence is always wrong, and that Christians should be mindful of Jesus' words to Peter at the moment of his arrest in the Gethsemane: "Put your sword back into its sheath, for all who take the sword will perish by the sword."[34] Consequently, some Christians feel that it is inconsistent with their religious principles to kill, or even to bear arms or serve in the military. Christian pacifism has been a significant, even if often persecuted, element in Christian tradition. Even though some Christians have found reassurance that strong military and political power could ensure order by the use of threat or force, others have consistently held to the Gospel message of "non resistance to evil."[35] While some enthusiastically promoted the Crusades, others, like St. Francis of Assisi, peacefully found ways to enter into dialogue with Muslims.[36] While Catholics fought against Protestants, both Catholics and Protestants persecuted the radically pacifist Anabaptists,[37] who have offered a highly significant resistance to the links between religion and politics that result in condoning the legitimate use of force. The Anabaptist assumption that Christians could not participate in any act of violence, not even if requested by a legitimate authority, was certainly destabilizing in an environment in which the identification of religion and power was so strong as to engender the principle of *"Cuius Regio Eius Religio."* The pacifist stand taken by the Anabaptists forced them into a nonviolent defensive mode and the most striking contribution of the Anabaptist peace churches was in the United States, where they found a more tolerant and inclusive political climate.[38]

Besides such organized movements, we must acknowledge also that many women and men across the centuries have attempted a wide variety of ways to embody the injunctions of the Christian scriptures in their own lives by being peacebuilding people. They have individually and collectively responded to Jesus' message as peaceful persons, pacifists, and peacemakers.[39] Here it is important to notice the distinctions between faithfulness to one's belief and tradition and intolerance. Too often terms as "fundamentalist," "traditionalist," "conservative" are incorrectly associated with intolerance. Many pacifists have been highly traditional and very concerned about how to interpret their tradition faithfully; certainly, to be traditional does not necessarily mean being intolerant.

A further relevant distinction along the same lines is between conflict and violence. It is sometimes mistakenly supposed that conflict is necessarily violent, and that violence is merely another name for conflict. Yet conflict is not always (and certainly not necessarily) violent; more often than not, conflicts are conceived, expressed, and resolved without violence. Conflict develops from incompatibility and the response to it does not necessarily entail violence. Moreover, awareness and acknowledgment of a conflict are often the first beginnings of asserting change. Those who seek a just, genuine peace may often provoke conflict in order to address the root causes of an injustice that needs to be addressed.

In this vein, the most striking example of a peaceable troublemaker is Dr. Martin Luther King Jr. Together with his two famous predecessors, Mahatma Gandhi and Lev Tolstoy, King was deeply convinced that real peace could not come by simply accepting the unjust, oppressive, and unequal reality. His work is deeply connected to that of Gandhi and Tolstoy by a shared commitment to the notion of nonviolent resistance to evil and *satyagraha*. Change for these men was not a neutral option; it was a moral duty. However, their nonviolent principles made it clear that conflict could bring about change without violence. Clearly, conflict and violence need to be dissociated, as well as the notion that stability is necessarily good and positive. Stability can be, and has been, violent and it is wise to remind ourselves that, in this very century, more people have been killed by the states that were supposed to represent and defend them than by all other wars combined. Therefore, to be peaceful in a nonviolent way might require the stamina, determination, and courage to provoke change.

With this in mind, we might ask, what can be selectively and specifically identified as the religious dimension in peacemaking? How can we extrapolate the "religious" dimension of this entangled enterprise?

Moreover, what can specifically be identified as Christian in such an enterprise? Although a quick look at Christian history can give us a series of examples of men and women who played a role in peacemaking as an action facilitating agreement among warring factions, such examples will not provide a clear pattern of performed functions that may be easily identified as specifically Christian. Moreover, conflict resolution skills such as the ability to listen, to understand positions, to convey messages, to explore alternatives, and to communicate are highly diverse and the search for a specifically religious dimension can be elusive.[40] On the one hand, religious conclusions to political conflicts are possible; on the other, religious discourse can be reduced to a merely political dimension.[41] A brief look at both factors may offer us a clearer insight into the complexities of religion and peacebuilding than the attempt to define a specifically "Christian" dimension.

What seems to be significant now is that, in fact, religious leaders (especially Christians) frequently play a role in transitional societies at the time in which distribution of power is unclear and stability is far from being established. As in the time of transition from the Roman Empire to the Middle Ages, religious leaders today share basic characteristics, which can be listed as follows:

1. Knowledge of language and culture
2. Access to firsthand information
3. Political expertise
4. Long-term vision

These characteristics can especially help to bridge the hermeneutical gap that is frequently the most serious obstacle to peacebuilders.[42]

Conflicts need to be "seen" and "read" properly, especially those that have major cultural, ethnic, and religious components. External actors may find it difficult to have access to knowledge unique to the situation that enables them to use their analytical framework properly. Religious leaders, because of their training and their role, can be better positioned in interpreting a conflict. Because they are closer to the scene of events, at ease with many actors, and familiar with the language and the issues at stake, religious leaders may offer important interpretative frameworks. This was certainly the case in Mozambique where Christians such as the Community of Sant'Egidio and Archbishop Jaime Goncalves played a significant role. Religious actors were consistently able to contribute to the peace process through their interpretation of events, issues, and possibilities and to orient the debate toward a positive solution.[43]

In today's world, it is impossible to find a single conflict in the world in which there is no Christian serving victims, defending human rights, educating children and adults, and defending the space of civil society from the oppression of violence. Christianity offers a remarkable network of people across the world, which is transnational and constantly moves people, goods, services, information, and ideas, making much of today's peacebuilding possible. Still, Christians now need especially to participate in the conceptualization of a process of peacemaking in a way that allows cultural traditions to be transmitted over time and space (as Augustine did at the end of the Roman empire), in the preservation of the riches of the past (as the Irish monks did for centuries), but also in the dialogue with others (as occurred with Islam in the Middle Age). Today, Christians need to preoccupy themselves with political and institutional arrangements that, while fragile and temporary, ambiguous and imperfect, might contribute significantly to peacebuilding. These constructs will not be Christian per se but should be open to a Christian contribution that may remind all of us of the need to not only limit violence at the moment of outbreak but also to strive for justice as a preventive measure. Moreover, these constructs will incorporate mechanisms to sustain an effective communication among former enemies and adversaries. Reconciliation may be a difficult goal and forgiveness a sensible way to proceed only for some, but it seems indispensable to envisage occasions in which concepts of this sort may be considered as building blocks in a more peaceful and inclusive political order.[44]

In this vein there is one case that still bears particular relevance to the analysis of Christian contributions to peacebuilding today because of its synthesis of religious, spiritual, and institutional dimensions, captured in a political agreement that still maintains its validity and is still largely unexamined by specialists. Nicholas von Flue,[45] whose influence remains significant in his native Switzerland, was born near Sachseln in the Obwalden Canton in 1417. He lived an ordinary life, marrying Dorothea Wissling and fathering ten children. As any other able man in Switzerland, he served in the forces of his canton and was actually involved in the war against Zurich in 1439. He was also a captain in the occupation of Turgau in 1453. When he was fifty years old, with the consent of his wife, he chose an eremitical life in Ranft, near his native village. There he lived for almost twenty years in great asceticism and simplicity. In 1481, after the Swiss Confederation acquired its independence, the tension among the cantons was high and the situation was moving in the direction of civil war. The representatives of the different parties chose Nicholas as the mediator. Without a formal process or a specific intervention, he was able to turn the attitudes of the enemies toward collaboration.[46]

Nicholas's case is significant for several reasons. First, the results of that intervention are still with us today: Switzerland is, institutionally, the best example of internal institutional peacebuilding. It is interesting to note that, in Nicholas's terms, "first comes an attitude of friendliness." For him, issues were less a problem of content and more a problem of perceptions. Second, Nicholas himself had military experience and was certainly not a "pacifist." His experiences as a soldier did not prevent him from playing, at a crucial moment, the role of peacemaker. He was certainly well informed and was able to understand the positions and the interests of the different parties. However, his success was due more to his ability to help the negotiators change their attitudes than to his ability to devise a specific "political solution." Revered in Switzerland, Nicholas remains one of the most striking figures of Christian peacemaking during the time that briefly preceded the religious wars in Europe. Interestingly, although the movements of the Reformation divided Switzerland, its generally prudent political atmosphere helped to keep the confederation united.

Nicholas' experience helps us to identify some elements that seem to be constantly in evidence when Christian leaders play a role in peacebuilding: a deep personal faith, a warm respectful human attitude, a curious attentive mind, a sense of humility and belonging, a dedication to service, an awareness that rationality is useful but has limitations, and an openness to unveiling the mystery of life.

Nicholas was able to live a version of Christian experience that is becoming familiar again in many dimensions of Christian life today. This experience involves witnessing, being present, discerning, vulnerable, nonviolent, not taking charge but ready to address social inequalities, and building relationships in openness while experimenting with opportunities. This path is not very different from the successful Christian peacemaking initiatives of the Community of Sant'Egidio, the Quakers, and the Mennonites. Christianity, after more than 2000 years, seems to be still in the making, especially in its relationship with peacebuilding.

What is intriguing about these emerging forms of Christian peacemaking is their ability to use both traditional and nontraditional elements, and to enter into dialogue without necessarily relying on the formal structures of secular politics. The expression "working from the margins"—so dear to the contemporary Mennonite understanding of peace work—seems to indicate exactly this relationship with people and their problems without necessarily using the channels of formal political representation. For these new actors the central problem is not "how to get the power which is necessary to impose a Christian peace," but rather "how can we relate the needs of the people, especially the poor and the victims to their aspiration to a just peace?"

In its rich and diverse forms, Christianity is basically engaged in a search for a sustainable and just peace for all. Its acceptance of others, its support for human rights, its embrace of religious freedom, its commitment to the poor, together with the realization that the great majority of Christians now live not in the rich and powerful North of the planet but in the poorer South, are indications that Christianity may still contribute significantly to the redefinition of the notions of peacemaking as well as the nonviolent resolution of conflicts arising from an unequal distribution of resources and opportunities.

SUMMARY/CONCLUSION

Christianity has been deeply involved in many wars and yet has offered great insights and practical contributions to peacemaking. Although a minority group with marginal influence at the beginning of its development, Christianity came to constitute a powerful presence in the world through an alliance with political and military powers. Yet many communities within Christianity continued seeking a closer relation with the original message of Jesus. While its intolerant treatment of "others" left many scars, its effort to transmit the nonviolent message of Jesus of Nazareth contributed greatly to the conceptualization of many notions we use today to describe peacebuilding in a coherent and effective way. Deeply divided, and yet longing for communion and unity, Christianity has, through the experience of division itself, produced some understanding of how conflict can be nonviolent and promote peace.

Many Christians who have grasped this difficult truth have, in turn, attempted to follow the Way of the Master who tells us: "You have heard that it was said: 'You shall love your neighbor and hate your enemy'. But I say to you, love your enemies and pray for those who persecute you, that you may be children of your heavenly Father, for he makes his sun rise on the bad and on the good, and causes the rain to fall on the just and the unjust."[47] Many, including Pope John Paul II, have attempted to address this tension between the message and the historical reality by acknowledging sins, asking forgiveness, and repenting. It is a work of memory that tends toward purification. The present time certainly gives us some signs of an always old and always new understanding of the Gospel message as it interacts with historical realities.

Examples such as the Evangelical Pastor in Nigeria, the Anglican bishop in South Africa, and the Community of Sant'Egidio confirm that possibly a new season of Christianity in its relationship with peacemaking is emerging. It will be a season marked by a sense of respect for others, service to the world, especially the poor, and dedicated to peace. Although it requires great imagination and energy to conceptualize and implement a global polity that is respectful of differences and in harmony with the whole, it is indispensable in such a task to count on the best that Christianity can offer: a passionate, engaged, joyful commitment to the words and message of Jesus of Nazareth.

NOTES

I would like to thank Steven Bourke, Anita Matta, Sarah Moses, and Tanya Walter for their priceless research and editorial work. I would also like to thank Terry Anderson and Patrick Grant for their comments and collegial revision of this chapter. However, while the author remains committed to the findings presented here, he deeply believes that the present version must be understood as a work in progress that he will try to improve beyond the publication of the present volume.

1. Peter M. Lewis, "Nigeria: The Challenge of Preventive Action," in Barnett R. Rubin, ed., *Cases and Strategies for Preventive Action* (New York: Council on Foreign Relations, 1998), pp. 93–112.

2. Muhammad Nurayn Ashafa, and James Movel Wuye, *The Pastor and the Imam: Responding to Conflict* (Lagos, Nigeria: Ibrash Press, 1999), pp. 1–5.

3. Roberto Morozzo della Rocca, *Mozambico, dalla guerra alla pace: Storia di una mediazione insolita* (Milano: Edizioni San Paolo, 1994), pp. 1–77.

4. Sally Engle Merry, "Mennonite Peacebuilding and Conflict Transformation: A Cultural Analysis," in Cynthia Sampson and John Paul Lederach, eds., *From the Ground Up: Mennonite Contributions to International Peacebuilding* (New York: Oxford University Press, 2000), pp. 203–217.

5. Philip M. Parker, *Religious Cultures of the World: A Statistical Reference* (Westport, CT: Greenwood Press, 1997).

6. Matthew 5, 17b.

7. Vladimir Solov'ev, *I fondamenti spirituali della vita* (Lipa Edizioni, Roma, 1998), pp. 131–133.

8. Mark 12, 17.

9. Matthew 5, 44.

10. Matthew 5, 9.

11. Matthew 7, 24: "Everyone who listens to these words of mine and acts on them will be like a wise man who built his house on rock."

12. As an example of this diversity, see the controversy over the conversion and circumcision of gentiles in Acts, chapters 10, 11 and 15.

13. For updated information on the Catholic Church see its official website at http://www.vatican.va/.

14. For update information on the World Council of Churches see their official website at http://www.wcc-coe.org/.

15. One of the many signs of this is the ecumenical movement that aims at reconciling differences within Christianity through a patient work of respectful appreciation and dialogue. As an organized trend within Christianity the ecumenical movement emerged in the first half of the twentieth century when churches became concerned with the theological basis of the Church and what its unity may consist of. The World Council of Churches was inaugurated in 1948. The movement, which started as solely Protestant, attracted both Orthodox and Catholics. After the II Vatican Council the Catholic Church became actively involved in the ecumenical dialogue together with many other denominations and traditions. For further information about the ecumenical movement, see Nicholas Sagovsky, Ecumenism, *Christian Origins, and the Practice of Communion* (New York: Cambridge University Press, 2000).

16. At the moment, a few mainstream areas can be identified as reference for millions of individuals within the realm of the so-called contemporary Christianity-Catholicism, Orthodoxy, and Protestantism. Within these groups, position and experiences vis-à-vis peacebuilding has been significantly different. For more information on Christian diversity, the World Council of Churches offers a relevant entry point with its web page at www.wcc-coe.org. As per a Catholic perspective, see http://www.vatican.va/ and especially the Dogmatic Constitution on the Church Lumen Genitium.

17. The Greek word eirene is used 91 times in the New Testament, of which 24 times in the four Gospels, 4 in Matthew, 1 in Mark, 13 in Luke, and 6 in John. Paul uses the term 43 times. However, many more quotations refer to peace and the attitudes that should be fostered among the disciples and with all.

18. One of the most all-encompassing expressions of this is the Focolare Movement. Founded by Chiara Lubich in the aftermath of World War II, the movement strives to seek unity. Among the many publications in English by Chiara Lubich, see Chiara Lubich, *When Our Love Is Charity* (Brooklyn, NY: New City Press, 1991).

19. Andrea Riccardi, *Il secolo del martirio* (Milano: Mondadori, 2000).

20. John Paul II, *Incarnationis Mysterium,* 11; cf. *Tertio Millennio Adveniente,* 33.

21. Ronald H. Bainton, *Christian Attitudes Toward War and Peace: A Historical Survey and Critical Re-evaluation* (New York: Abingdon Press, 1960), pp. 101–121.

22. The first three centuries were of great importance in the self-understanding of Christians. A long process of identification occurred and dogmas were developed to express the Christian understanding of Jesus' life, words, experience, and presence. Starting with the first Council in Jerusalem until the post-Constantine councils of the fifth century, Christians debated issues of great relevance for their own understanding of the divine. Significantly, the councils were also moments of a stronger bond between the secular and the religious. Emperors summoned councils and the enforcement of their decrees was often carried out by military means. A tendency toward control and homogeneity at times fostered intolerance aimed at establishing a more uniform setting.

23. Ronald H. Bainton, *Christian Attitudes Toward War and Peace: A Historical Survey and Critical Re-evaluation* (New York: Abingdon Press, 1960), pp. 136–151.

24. As a reference on the Crusades see Sir Steven Runciman, *A History of the Crusades* (Cambridge, University Press, 1951–1954).

25. John 13, 35.

26. Luke 23, 34.

27. John 14, 27, John 20, 20.

28. Mark 5, 34.

29. Mathew 5, 9. Significantly, the word peacemaker appears only once in this context in the entire Bible.

30. Reinhold Neibuhr, *The Children of Light and the Children of Darkness: A Vindication of Democracy and a Critique of its Traditional Defense* (New York: Scribner, 1944).

31. Reinhold Neibuhr, *Moral Man and Immoral Society* (New York: Scribner, 1932); Gregory Baum, *Religion and Alienation: A Theological Reading of Sociology* (New York: Paulist Press,1975).

32. James T. Johnson, *Just War Tradition and the Restraint of War: A Moral and Historical Inquiry* (Princeton, NJ: Princeton University Press, 1981).

33. Gerald F. Powers, Drew Christians, Robert T. Hennemeyer, eds., *Peacemaking: Moral and Political Challenges for a New World* (Washington, DC: Georgetown University, 1995).

34. Matthew 26, 52. Stanley Hauerwas "The Peaceable Kingdom" (University of Notre Dame, 1983); Lisa Sowle Cahill, *Love Your Enemies: Discipleship, Pacifism, and Just War Theory* (Minneapolis: Fortress, 1994); John Howard Yoder, *The Politics of Jesus* (Grand Rapids, MI: Eerdmans, 1972); Glen H. Stassen, ed., *Just Peacemaking: Ten Practices for Abolishing War* (Cleveland, OH: Pilgrim Press, 1998).

35. Matthew 5, 39.

36. Fonti Francescane (Assisi: Editrici Francescane, 1987).

37. Cornelius J. Dyck, *An Introduction to Mennonite History* (Scottdale: Herald Press, 1993), p. 118.

38. Marc Gopin, "The Religious Component of Mennonite Peacemaking and its Global Implications," in Cynthia Sampson and John Paul Lederach, eds., *From the Ground Up: Mennonite Contributions to International Peacebuilding* (New York: Oxford University Press, 2000), pp. 233–255.

39. Peaceful is a person or a group that seeks peace and lives peacefully. It is a quality of the spirit that is reflected in the way one lives. It pertains to the quality of the relationship that individuals and groups can establish within themselves, with others and with their environment.

The word pacifist is much more recent and refers to the intentional decision of individuals and groups to foster peaceful relationships between states and groups in human societies through political arrangements. It must be noted here that pacifism refers specifically to a refusal to cooperate with or participate in the organized use of force by governments to achieve political ends. Very often, pacifists are peaceable or, to be more precise, are aiming toward being peaceful.

As per the word peacemaker, the precise meaning of that expression is still debatable. It is, in fact, unclear whether the blessing refers to a peacemaking effort, to a peacemaking result, or whether it refers to individuals or groups. Certainly it could not be reduced to narrowly identify peacemakers as those who are offering mediation services in interstate conflict. Possibly the word peacemakers refers to those who intervene positively in any human relationship.

40. As in the case of Bernard of Clairvaux, powerful mediator in medieval Europe and violent proponent of the war against Islam and the Tatars.

41. Scott Appleby, op. cit., pp. 281–282.

42. Andrea Bartoli, "Forgiveness and Reconciliation in the Mozambique Peace Process" in *Forgiveness and Reconciliation: Religious Contributions to Conflict Resolution,* Ray Helmick and Rodney Petersen, eds. (Rednor: Templeton Press, forthcoming).

43. Roberto Morozzo della Rocca, op.cit., p. 117.

44. Donald W. Shriver Jr., *An Ethic for Enemies: Forgiveness in Politics* (New York: Oxford University Press, 1995); L. Gregory Jones, *Embodying Forgiveness. A Theological Analysis* (Grand Rapids, MI: Eerdmans, 1995); Robert J. Schreiter, *The Ministry of Reconciliation: Spirituality and Strategies* (Maryknoll, NY: Orbis Books, 1998).

45. Eugene-Th. Rimli, ed., *Histoire de la Confederation* (Zurich: Editions Stauffacher, 1967), pp. 203–206; E. Bonjour, H. S. Offler, and G. R. Potter, *A Short History of Switzerland* (London: Oxford University Press, 1952), pp. 133–137; Marie McSwingan, *Athlete of Christ: St. Nicholas of Flue 1417–1487*

(Westminster, MD: The Newman Press, 1959); Ernst Bohnenblust, *Niklaus von Flue 1417–1487* (Zurich: Atlantis Verlag, 1945).

46. "The agreement of Stans (22 December 1481) is notable rather for the fact that an understanding was reached at all than for the clauses of the document that was sealed on behalf of the eight states" in E. Bonjour, H. S. Offler, and G. R. Potter, *A Short History of Switzerland*, pp. 133.

47. Matthew 5, 43–44.

PART II

Case Studies in Religion and Peacebuilding

9

Creating Spaces

Interreligious Initiatives for Peace

DIANE D'SOUZA

In this chapter I share a few stories of people from different religious and spiritual traditions who are working together for peace. There are many people engaged in such work—which makes it difficult to choose which stories to tell. Some of the most exciting initiatives are seldom chronicled, taking place at grassroots levels, away from the headlines and outside religious structures and hierarchies. High-profile organizations such as the World Conference on Religion and Peace or the International Association of Religious Freedom also work hard at building peace.[1] Many of their initiatives are already widely known or documented sufficiently to be accessible. In contrast, it is much harder to find information about grassroots movements or initiatives led by women.[2] When documentation does exist, it is not always taken seriously. Often it fails to reach policy-making or -debating circles. Consequently, people often assume that nothing important is happening at such levels—or, more correctly, that the crucial steps toward peace are being taken at more "official" levels.

To ammend this view, the present chapter focuses on some of the easily overlooked elements of interreligious peacebuilding especially at the level of personal encounter. I look at spaces that have been carved out and shared by people separated by violence, injustice, and prejudice, and highlight their struggle to form and maintain connections across boundaries. I pay special attention to difficult moments in these initiatives in order to identify obstacles in building and maintaining peace, as well as creative ways in which those obstacles can be overcome.

My argument is that spaces that bring together people on tough issues—including those that divide Palestinians from Israelis, or African from European Americans—are powerful arenas for stimulating personal and societal transformation. To show this, I highlight two such interreligious initiatives: the Jerusalem Link, a part of the women's peace movement in the Middle East, and the Interfaith Pilgrimage of the Middle Passage, which addresses the roots of American racism.[3]

THE ISRAELI-PALESTINIAN STRUGGLE

> At the root of this [the Israeli-Palestinian conflict], the biggest issue is what it means to deal with two separate narratives. How to have room for both, how to make room for both. Because the views on history, the aspirations, the stories are so very different. How can we [in Israel] talk about one country when about twenty percent of the population can't look at the flag without feeling physically sick?
> —Terry Greenblatt, Director, Bat Shalom[4]

In the late nineteenth century, some European Jews decided to renew Jewish settlements in the region known as Palestine and to establish a refuge for Jews fleeing anti-Semitism across the world. This initiative grew into Zionism, a political movement aimed at reestablishing a Jewish state in the historical homeland of the Jews. At the time, Palestine was inhabited mostly by Muslims, but also some Christians. With the arrival of Jewish settlers, intermittent conflicts arose. Some Jews sought to compromise with the Arabs, while others believed that it was their right and destiny to own all the land that had belonged to the Israelites during biblical times. The British government's 1917 Balfour Declaration gave support to the idea of a Jewish homeland, and following World War I this was incorporated into the League of Nations mandate giving Great Britain administrative control over Palestine. Britain's colonial-style presence satisfied neither the majority Arabs—who vigorously opposed Zionism—nor the rapidly growing Jewish population. By 1947, escalating tensions and violence prompted the British to pass the question of Palestine back to the United Nations, which voted to partition the land, creating the nations of Israel and Jordan in 1948.

In the fifty years since then, a series of wars and a tide of aggression and terrorism have left tens of thousands of Israelis and Arabs dead, and even more injured. Many Palestinians have fled their homes to live in refugee camps or become exiles. During the 1967 war, Israel captured the Gaza Strip, the Sinai Peninsula, the Golan Heights, the West Bank of the Jordan River, and East Jerusalem. Today, in the name of security, it continues to hold much of this land,[5] retaining control over more than two million Palestinians. In the years since the Occupation began, the government has implemented a number of policies designed to encourage Palestinian migration and strengthen Israeli control over the "territories." These include building settlements for Israeli Jews on confiscated land, imposing residency restrictions on Palestinians, conducting aggressive house demolition programs, limiting the movement of Palestinians in and through Israel, and establishing discriminatory zoning, building, and taxation policies. Such moves have escalated Palestinian frustrations and resistance and have fed a spiral of violence that shakes Israel and the occupied territories even as negotiations for peace stumble forward.[6]

WOMEN'S INITIATIVES FOR PEACE

> Most Israelis had learned to ignore what was happening in the territories through the first twenty years of occupation, but with the outbreak of rebellion there, terrible stories began to surface. Now, on top of the twenty years of oppression, new episodes were revealed of the brutality of Israeli soldiers in trying to quell the uprising. These were "our sons," eighteen or nineteen years old, clubbing people and opening fire into crowds.
>
> —Gila Svirsky, peace activist[7]

It was in 1982, in response to Israel's invasion of Lebanon, that Israeli women first lobbied for peace as an independent political entity based on gender. An even stronger wave of women's action began after the first Palestinian resistance movement, the *intifada,* broke out in December 1987. Within a year, nearly fifteen Israeli women's groups were demonstrating against the Occupation, the most visible being Women In Black.[8] Over the next decade, a wide array of women's protest and action groups emerged as part of the larger Israeli peace movement. Deputy Speaker of the Knesset, Naomi Chazen, argues that such organizations and movements have been crucial in nurturing a desire for peace on both sides. She points out that persistent, dedicated women's groups were among the first to push a number of risky positions in Israel including calling for negotiations with the then unrecognized Palestinian Liberation Organization, encouraging a two-state solution to the conflict, and suggesting that Jerusalem be a shared capital. Women's groups have offered a "crucial brake against despair," refusing to give up even when the mainstream peace camp is frustrated or silent.[9]

Gila Svirsky, Co-Founder of the coalition Women for a Just Peace, agrees that women's initiatives for peace have brought something unique, although she cautions against absolutizing the differences between men's and women's efforts. She suggests that women's groups have tended to devote more time to dialogue and to building relationships than mixed gender groups have done. "As women we have invited Palestinian women into our homes or have gone to their neighborhoods to listen to what Occupation means."[10] An inclination toward engagement, toward listening and struggling to establish positive relationships seems characteristic of such initiatives. A striking example is a united effort between Israeli women activists and Palestinian women living in Hebron, a place that in many ways epitomizes the Palestinian struggle. Tension and anger run at constant, dangerously high levels in this town where thousands of soldiers protect 400 Jewish settlers while 120,000 Arabs struggle with restrictions on daily life and movement. For a joint pursuit of peace, women from both sides needed courage: Israelis to walk into a site known for explosive hatreds, Palestinians to discuss a common platform with people seen as the enemy. In 1996, women were meeting twice a week to explore possibilities for action. Gila describes part of the process:

> In warm and mutually respectful meetings, using local English teachers to construct a halting common language, we decided on a plan for a grand march through the streets of Hebron. Some tension arose in our efforts to find slogans for the march that would be acceptable to us both. While our side vetoed 'Jerusalem for Muslims Only,' the Palestinians took us aback by vetoing all our slogans that implied legitimacy for the state of Israel—'Two States for Two Peoples,' etc. 'We personally agree with this,' they said, 'but in Hebron we cannot carry such signs.' It was disappointing to us that they could not defy that position, and perhaps even share it. Nevertheless, we were all eager to find that narrow ledge of consensus on which we could cling to each other and balance together.

Struggling for a "narrow ledge of consensus" meant the women had to reconsider their assumptions about common ground. The Israelis, for example, had not considered that the Palestinians could not publicly affirm the legitimacy of two states. Because they were committed to taking action, the women persisted through the process to finally reach a compromise. They then planned a risky demonstration despite warnings of escalating violence. Finally, on an agreed-upon day, more than eighty women and girls gathered to carry banners and signs through the streets affirming in Hebrew, Arabic, and English: "Implement International Agreements," "Settlements Are an Obstacle to Peace," and "Yes to Peace! No to Occupation!" Gila continues the story:

> As we turned the corner into the main street, the whole city of Hebron seemed to wake up to our presence. We blocked cars in both directions, drivers pulled over to watch, storekeepers came out to see what all the fuss was about, market vendors put down their tomatoes and shook our hands, greeting 'Shalom, Salaam, Peace' as we walked by. A huge procession formed behind us, more women, children, shoppers, loiterers, the unemployed, the revolutionaries, the bored. . . . Media people—ever orbiting the Hebron planet in hopes of a camera-worthy tragedy—swooped down on us, filming, snapping pictures, taking notes in tiny orange pads. I found myself talking into lenses in unrehearsed platitudes: "Solidarity of Israelis and Palestinians . . . no more bloodshed . . . no more violence . . . a true and just peace." A Palestinian woman put her arm around me and I put mine around the woman on my other side, and we were all marching with our arms together, *"yad be-yad"* as we say in both Hebrew and Arabic, "hand in hand."
>
> None of us had envisioned that it would be this powerful, this inspiring. We stopped waiting for the sound of an explosion, stopped looking for the disaster. Now we were feeling buoyed by the sense of common purpose, by the great longing in all our hearts for those very platitudes—no more bloodshed . . . a true and just peace. Thus we marched through the streets of that town of despair, feeling hopeful for a whole morning, hearing the sounds of a song that all of us were marching to together, though we walked in silence.
>
> I feel again right now as I felt yesterday, unwilling to let go of that moment. I don't think we ever will let go, not those in Hebron nor those of us in Israel who experienced it. It was not a piece of paper signed between governments, but it was a vision of something that can really be, that can really happen, a vision of a reality that is more profound than paper, and that could light the darkness until we find our way to get there.[11]

Initiatives such as this one in Hebron can be a powerful means of gaining understanding, building relationships, and renewing commitment. The process of meeting, working together, and taking risks helps in building new ties. It also offers a chance for people who are isolated from each other to move beyond stereotypes. Gila speaks of her unwillingness to let go of the moment, of her and others' determination not to abandon a vision of "something that can really be." Their shared experience is energizing, inspiring and sustaining. It is also a crucial part of the dynamics that have given life to and helped sustain the Jerusalem Link.

THE JERUSALEM LINK

As difficult as times have been over these last months [since September 2000], and it has been very, very difficult—and a hundred times more difficult for the Palestinians—as difficult as times have been, this is a group of women who understand that if we leave the table now, if we abandon the process, there are no other options. This is it. If things are going to get better, if they are going to move forward, we're going to have to do it ourselves. . . . You see, the original idea was that the Jerusalem Link could be a model for co-existence. In the very difficult space we've created for ourselves, every stumbling block, every challenge, is just a part of the process.
—Terry Greenblatt, Director, Bat Shalom[12]

Working together is by no means easy. We continually challenge barriers of bitterness, fear and mistrust, and we are constantly developing our capacity to see 'the others' as partners rather than occupiers or enemies. . . . At this time, with the peace process completely paralyzed and a sense of frustration, depression and lack of faith growing rapidly, our work is becoming far more challenging and difficult than ever before. At the same time, precisely because of these problems, it has taken on an unprecedented significance. We, Palestinian and Israeli women, are bound together, wholly engaged in the search for a just and lasting peace between our peoples . . . we cannot afford the luxury of hopelessness.
—Sumaya Farhat Naser, Director,
Jerusalem Center for Women[13]

The Jerusalem Link was founded in 1993 as part of the struggle for dialogue and common action between Israeli and Palestinian women. In May 1989, the European Commission sponsored an international conference in Brussels that brought together prominent Israeli and Palestinian leaders and activists. A second women's conference was held in Belgium in 1992. The exchange at both gatherings was intense and difficult.

The women finally succeeded in working out a joint declaration covering a number of traditionally divisive points. They also framed a structure and mechanism for enhancing communication, cooperation, and mutual respect: the Jerusalem Link, a coordinating body for two new and independent women's centers—Bat Shalom in West Jerusalem, and Markaz al-Quds al-Nisā (the Jerusalem Center for Women) in East Jerusalem. The Link was designed to give scope for joint planning and action while also enabling Palestinians and Israelis to construct and pursue independent agendas to serve the specific needs and interests of their own communities.[14]

Having separate, independent identities and projects has been as important to the Link as running joint programs. A policy that stresses independence as well as unity reflects an understanding of and respect for two very different realities. For Palestinians, the primary struggles are for liberation, state-building, and nation-coalescing. Key challenges include poverty, deficiencies in education, and other social support systems, and limitations on economic and social development arising from restricted movement, the imprisonment of family members, and other consequences of life under Occupation. For the Israelis, the primary struggle is to convince government, military, and a diverse citizenry to change their policies, attitudes, and actions, including bringing an end to the Occupation. A key concern is also the militarization of Israeli society and its repercussions on women and the family.

Both organizations have boards that bring together politicians, activists, and other prominent leaders, enabling women with a wide range of skills and experience to meet and address a common set of problems. Separately, the groups are involved with education and awareness-building in their constituencies, while together they plan and participate in common initiatives including lectures and discussions, the issuing of joint statements, dialogue efforts similar to the Hebron initiative already described, and activities like the 1997 program "Sharing Jerusalem: Two Capitals for Two States." This latter five-day event was typical of the Link's programs in that it tried: to bridge the gap separating Israelis and Palestinians through sharing the culture, history, and vision of "the other"; to bring greater awareness about systematic government policies affecting the Palestinian population; and to create a united forum to support the idea of sharing Jerusalem. The symposia, music and art expositions, "alternative" city tours, demonstrations, and a final concluding march and rally were widely attended by the public and well covered by the press. A report of the event made by the Jerusalem Center for Women (JCW) gives a sense of some of the challenges that the women had to face:

There were political as well as bureaucratic obstacles. Both women's centers were the target of criticism and threats. On the Israeli side, many people object even to voicing the idea that the future of Jerusalem is under question, and many, even on the left of the political spectrum, do not want to publicly challenge the popular consensus that Jerusalem is the 'eternal capital of the state of Israel.' Right wing Jewish extremists went so far as to threaten the life of Sinead O'Connor, who subsequently canceled her scheduled appearance at [the] . . . Gala Concert. . . . Palestinians, on the other hand, criticized the idea of holding joint events with Israelis, on grounds that it signified acceptance of the occupation. Others objected to the idea of 'Sharing Jerusalem' since they felt that it infringed on Jerusalem's as yet unresolved status. Israeli officials from the Jerusalem municipality also worked hard to place obstacles in the project's path: posters about 'Sharing Jerusalem' were banned; ticket outlets refused to sell tickets to the events; and some art galleries were too afraid of risking municipal funding to carry pictures from the joint exhibition.[15]

The risks of this particular project are typical of the obstacles faced by Israeli and Palestinian peace workers. Israeli political parties only stand behind ventures that they believe their constituencies support, and Palestinians are wary of collaboration that in any way signals a normalization of the oppressive status quo. Both sides of the Jerusalem Link also regularly face determined opposition by fringe groups threatening violence. Yet the fruit of pushing risky positions, of identifying alternatives and making support for them visible, can be seen in the peace process today. As JCW Director Sumaya Farhat Naser recalls, "When we first said this [the proposal to share Jerusalem], people actually laughed at us. Others challenged us, some attacked us. . . . Now even [Prime Minister] Barak at the recent negotiations conceded that it is possible. When we look at where people are now compared to ten years ago there is tremendous change."[16]

CAN OBSTACLES BE OVERCOME?

Everything has changed for the worse since 28 September [2000]. There is still an active and cooperative and hopeful peace effort, but it has really taken a blow. I've been in touch with people in Palestine and Israel and we've tried to analyze what's going on. . . . Based on my experience living there last year, I would say that desperation seems to be driving the Palestinians. . . . On the Israeli side, fear seems to be driving the reaction now, with people buying into the notion that the

Arab world is a monolith, and the monolith wants to see them annihilated. But there are still some Israelis standing firm on their belief—and mine—that the Occupation is the heart of the problem. That if the tanks and soldiers and settlers would just leave, the situation would begin to change for the better.

—Karen Hamdon, representative,
Humanserve International[17]

You have to understand our mentality. It was only sixty years ago that we had the Holocaust. Israel was founded by Holocaust survivors and our public institutions—government and so on—were subsequently conceived and established by the first and second generations of families torn apart by the Holocaust. This issue [the Palestinian right to return][18] takes us right to our deepest fears. Our fears of annihilation, of being pushed into the sea.

—Terry Greenblatt[19]

At the time of writing this chapter, more than 350 people have been killed in the four months since controversial Israeli leader Ariel Sharon staged his visit to a disputed sacred site in East Jerusalem. Reportedly more than 15,000 Palestinians have been injured in what is widely considered to be Israel's most brutal response to violent protest. The ongoing conflict has frozen formal communication between the Israeli and Palestinian wings of the Jerusalem Link due to curfew-like restrictions on Palestinian movement, and to pressures on organizations like the JCW to curtail cooperation with groups associated with Israel. The anger on both sides is explosive. Yet informal communication within the Jerusalem Link continues, including work on negotiating a joint statement on the deeply divisive issue of Palestinians' right to return to their former homes or be compensated for their loss of property. This issue caused much strain and tension within the Link. As Terry Greenblatt points out, it raises some of the deepest fears for Israelis, while also going to the heart of the Palestinians' traumatic experience. The current search for a statement which both sides can affirm is a new and risky venture complicated by the brutality and horror of what amounts to undeclared war.

Women associated with the Jerusalem Link are well acquainted with the difficult and painful process of trying to overcome divisions caused by their highly stressful situation. Often tempers fray as anger and grief fuel feelings of futility and hopelessness. Each side sometimes feels that the other does not hear or understand the story or position they are trying to express. There is a pull to retreat, to give up on communication and remain isolated. Yet, despite these challenges, the Jerusalem Link has persevered. Having invested in relationships, having struggled to overcome stereotypes, the women engage in a process calling for personal and collective risks, for listening to uncomfortable truths, and for staying with the process through its bleakest moments. The group is marked by a tenacity grounded in relationship and mutual commitment. And a determined hope that their action will make a difference.

Such a constellation of factors has been instrumental also in a very different initiative to address racism in North America, and to which we now turn.

THE INTERFAITH PILGRIMAGE OF THE MIDDLE PASSAGE

If you drained the Atlantic Ocean, you would find a trail of bones leading from the western shores of Africa to the east coast of the United States. The bones of millions of black men, women and children; the legacy of the Middle Passage. . . .[20] This African holocaust and diaspora has laid the foundation for the trauma and isolation underlining African-American life today. 30 million Africans were kidnapped from their homes and dragged screaming to the New World. One third died on slave ships under conditions horrific beyond imagining.[21] As a white American, I presume to be free of racism. . . . But when I first heard about the Interfaith Pilgrimage of the Middle Passage, I realized that I've lived the past thirty years with little if any contact with African-Americans or their community.

—Daniel A. Brown, participant,
Interfaith Pilgrimage of the Middle Passage[22]

Spiritually, this journey has been trying. At times it is difficult to be on the land where my African ancestors gave their lives in order to feed White capitalism.

—Renay A. Mercer, participant,
Interfaith Pilgrimage of the Middle Passage[23]

The plan in the beginning was that we would take a ship to make the Middle Passage. To cross over the oceans as our ancestors had done. It never worked out [for the majority of us].[24] The ancestors could have made it happen but they didn't. Maybe they knew it wasn't necessary. . . . I've come to realize that we didn't need the boat. We experienced the Middle Passage journey in our minds, our hearts, our guts. It was so turbulent—as turbulent as any sea. . . . We were there. We traveled that route; we traveled the darkness of the Middle Passage in all that we went through.

—Ingrid Askew, organizer,
Interfaith Pilgrimage of the Middle Passage[25]

A VISION FOR HEALING

The "Interfaith Pilgrimage of the Middle Passage" began on 30 May 1998 from the Leverett Peace Pagoda in western Massachusetts. Sister Clare Carter, a nun of the Nipponzan Myohoji Buddhist order first conceived of the event in 1993 while on a peace pilgrimage in Sri Lanka.[26] When Sister Clare returned to the United States, a friend put her in touch with Ingrid Askew, an African-American cultural activist, who later became her co-collaborator. Ingrid liked the idea of retracing the slave route for the purpose of healing. Her main objection concerned the direction of the journey. As she explained, "No one I know of African descent could ever bear to go back to Africa to leave it again." The pain would be too great. Instead she suggested that the pilgrimage reverse the horrific history of slavery by walking backward in time, "reclaiming what we lost, what was taken from us—our motherland." Through such an action, Ingrid felt, "we would be able to give back honor and respect to those stolen Africans, our ancestral parents."[27]

The organizers, along with a carefully selected Board of Advisors,[28] worked for nearly five years. They saw the pilgrimage as "a step in the healing of the wounds [of racism] inflicted even until today, and a purification of the heart of all those connected . . . with this history." The aim of the event was "to nourish seeds of genuine consciousness, so that in the next century, a more humane, compassionate and equitable world can be realized."[29] Anyone who agreed with these basic principles was welcome to join; the main requirements were an ability to cover one's expenses (which many did through sponsorship), and a willingness to take part in a daily pattern of interfaith prayers.[30] People could participate for a few months, a few hours, or a few days. A small band, including Ingrid and Clare, participated for the full thirteen months. The number of pilgrims who walked the daily 15–20 mile route fluctuated from more than a hundred to less than ten, the numbers periodically swelling as locals joined the procession. Pilgrims walked down the eastern U.S. coast to New Orleans, then traveled on to the Caribbean. The group then split, with four pilgrims traveling to Brazil, while others went to West Africa. The group then reunited to continue their journey to South Africa where the closing event was held on 12 June 1999.

The route was charted through sites marked by slavery, racism, and resistance. A key assumption was that the full impact of race-based oppression has not been acknowledged in American society. Consequently, a first step in a process of healing was to make people's stories known, to expose the wounds still festering within a history of injustice and violence. Sister Clare describes this dynamic:

> In witnessing . . . to the stories of the history of enslavement and ongoing racism, we also had to acknowledge that we are still living, still creating this whole thing. We are keeping it alive here and now. For the people of African descent this was especially traumatic. They have lost so much. Their history is one of being cut off and cut off and denied and denied. So the Pilgrimage was something they felt they needed to do, to begin to really address this terrible loss. To begin to gain power to change the present.[31]

Local coordinators elicited help from churches, community centers, and voluntary groups to provide the pilgrims with food and a place to sleep, as well as connections to regional history, personalities, and events. The host communities were key points of interaction. A day might include 2–8 hours of walking, with the remaining time spent visiting auction blocks, slave quarters, ports for slave ships, the grave of someone killed in the civil rights movement, a lynching tree, a stop on the underground railroad, or the counter where an African American first ordered coffee in a whites-only luncheonette. The pilgrims spent evenings attending events or lectures, making presentations to local groups, or having internal meetings. There was little free time. They rose at 5:30, met for an interfaith prayer service at 6:00, and were on the road by 8:00 A.M., a colorful band of men and women of different ages, races, and religions, from different backgrounds and experiences, holding banners and flags and walking to the beat of the Buddhist drum and its floating prayer *"namu myoho renge kyo."*[32]

WEAVING THE THREADS OF SPIRITUALITY

> We in the West spend too much time trying to analyze, dissect and intellectualize. When trying to combat something as evil as racism and slavery you must look to God and Spirit for guidance.
>
> —Ingrid Askew[33]

In visiting sites of terrible acts of inhumanity, of rape and murder and the crushing of a people, the pilgrims touched the rawest wounds of racism. Most who joined the pilgrimage felt the need for a spiritual response. Clare used the metaphor of weaving a cloth: "The threads are the cloth: they are what it is and what holds it together. In the Pilgrimage, spirituality was the thread . . . it was everything. . . . That, and people's pure intentions."[34]

Spirituality took different forms. The Buddhists, as initiators of the pilgrimage, led morning interfaith worship with ten to fifteen minutes of traditional drumming and prayers, to which participants then added their own prayers and religious elements. An altar on which people placed personal symbols was a focal point that evolved and grew rich with meaning as the pilgrimage progressed. African expressions of spirituality—including traditional rituals, prayers for ancestors, dancing, and African-style drumming—also grew deeper and stronger as time went on. Particularly powerful were the cleansing ceremonies at sites of brutality and violence. The offering of libations—the pouring out of water or other liquid as a means of honoring God and invoking the spirits of the ancestors—were a central part of the pilgrimage, especially for those of African descent. Ingrid explains why:

> There had been so much violence, horrific violence. And people [the victims] never had a proper send off, never had proper burials. There was never a chance for others to properly express their grief. Because of this the spirits were unsettled. We needed to go to those lynching tress, to those slave ports, to those slave blocks, to places of death and violence. We wanted the ancestors to know we were there. We wanted a chance for grief and prayers to be expressed. We also wanted the ancestors to have a chance to come with us as we journeyed back to the motherland.[35]

At times, especially as they first started to evolve, the ceremonies were polarizing, leaving some European Americans or Buddhists struggling for points of connection.[36] But, in general, spiritual expressions were a source of strength, contributing to feelings of community in the face of much more explosive divisions.

THE PAIN THAT DIVIDES

> Being born with white skin or black skin is something over which you have no choice. You can't hide it. That's what makes racism different from every other divide. You can't ever hide what you are. It's out there all the time. So that

means you get targeted no matter what. Whether it's by police
brutality or what happens at a high class cocktail party. You
can't escape.
—Elaine Kenseth, home-based liaison person and organizer,
Interfaith Pilgrimage of the Middle Passage[37]

As Elaine, a former Massachusetts refugee resettlement field officer,
points out, racial divisions are inescapable. In America they are complicated by the facts of slavery, oppression, prejudice, and privilege for
those having white skin. It is not surprising that the different experiences
and histories of African and European Americans that have tended to
polarize North American society also affected the pilgrimage. Daniel
Brown, an artist and former elementary school teacher specializing in
diversity training, described how pilgrims of African descent were traumatized by sites of death and despair, while the European Americans
who were present felt only "a jarring curiosity." For him, these differences in perception came to a head in Williamsburg, Virginia.

> Like Sturbridge, Williamsburg is a living history museum of Colonial
> America, with period costuming, prim shops and hordes of tourists.
> In the center of town are the stocks and pillories where families can
> insert themselves for a great photo-op. To me, it's all very quaint. Our
> procession spontaneously sidetracks over to the stocks. I'm about to
> jokingly put myself in them when I hear the sound of anguished cries
> rising from the black women near me. Several of them have fallen to
> the ground, weeping. I stop in my tracks, then slowly back away.
> Other women wordlessly take water and slowly bathe the wooden
> edifice, a ritual cleansing of its pain, blood, and terror. They are
> encircled by their brothers and sisters as the Buddhist monks imme-
> diately form an outer circle of prayer around them. The air becomes
> electric. Several white men in colonial costumes and tricorn hats
> wander by oblivious to this transformation happening in their midst.
> Ramona Peters (Nosapocket), of the Mashpee Indian nation, shocks
> us by naming a reality deleted from the history textbooks. Her eyes
> flash as she speaks, "Is this what you want to see in the middle of
> your town? People brutalized and humiliated. Violence as entertain-
> ment. They did this to their women, their children, their African cap-
> tives, and anyone who dissented. And they are still doing this to us
> today!" She is so upset, she is shaking. Tizita Assefa, an Ethiopian
> woman of immense grace and dignity, quietly places herself in the pil-
> lory. Creating connection with her African ancestors, tears roll down
> her eyes and stain the bleached, grey wood. Bill Ledger, a veteran of
> both the Vietnam War and earlier pilgrimages, puts his camera aside
> and lovingly begins to caress her face. It is a act of compassion and
> bravery, happening at a time when some black participants have

expressed their leeriness about their white counterparts even being present at such an emotional outpouring. But we seem to be carried along by a spirit larger than ourselves here. Prayers are said, libations are poured . . . and the walk is resumed. As our stunned group departs, a visiting family come along and laughingly photographs their children in front of the structures.[38]

Daniel goes on to tell how African-American pilgrims secluded themselves shortly afterwards, their cries of grief and rage rending the air. Hearing their voices, their pain, he wonders whether white Americans will ever fully comprehend what the ordeal of slavery has meant for African-American peoples.

In touching the history of slavery, the ongoing oppression of racism, emotions run deep: shame, rage, pain, grief, fear. The feelings are not easily confined to one side or another. They also touch the deepest parts of one's identity—as a people, a man, a woman—haunting the psyche far below the surface. For the "oppressor" there can be shame; the feeling that one needs to atone for terrible wrongs, to recover from a loss of humanity. There can be fear of rage and indignation from a people oppressed by a system of which one is part. There can also be anger or denial in being associated with a reality so appalling, so shameful. For the "oppressed," especially those who continue to be victims of the violence of a racist society, there can be rage and frustration at blatant injustice, but also self-directed anger and humiliation in knowing that one did not succeed in resisting oppression. There can sometimes be a pull to yield to or claim the negative stereotypes directed against one by society, as well as feelings of shame at a historic failure to save even the weakest, the most dependent from torture and humiliation: children, women, family, elders. Shame often accompanies reflection on the terrible choices one makes when faced with the destruction of body and spirit. This murky and unacknowledged trauma, these subterranean emotions, have seldom found adequate space to be explored, exposed, and ultimately overcome. The pilgrimage, with its months of intensive travel, offered a first step, a tentative beginning.

IS HEALING POSSIBLE?

When you establish your intention, when you incline yourself towards healing, you can only be present. You cannot do something "bigger" because there is no final solution which can be reached. The disease is so big, so complex, it defies an end product. We'll have to see what route healing takes.

> How it moves forward. Because you can legislate a lot of
> stuff, but you can't legislate people's hearts and minds, or
> their good will.
>
> —Elaine Kenseth[39]

In reporting on the pilgrimage, journalist Stephanie Kraft observed that "the battle against racism—whether fought in courts or in politics—doesn't always result in the kind of personal learning that transforms the quality of relationships between people." She contends that it was precisely at the level of relationships that the pilgrimage had its greatest impact. Pilgrims were forced to adjust to each other even as they confronted hard truths that divided their history. She interviews Jennifer Iré, a native of Trinidad and a university lecturer in women's studies, who describes her experience:

> When we would go into a place where there was some hard stuff—places where we saw lynching trees, or one place where we were told, "The Klan is having a meeting Saturday in our town"—sometimes it was like, "White people shouldn't be on this walk. How can white people change anything?" Sometimes we would talk until midnight, working out all this stuff. People would be upset. People get mad, but they say, "What are we doing about food this evening?" or, "There are two showers and forty or so people, and how are we going to organize this?" And they get back to relating. The feeling is, "We're having this dispute, yes. But I still love you."[40]

In having European and African Americans traveling together, revisiting a painful history that binds them, the pilgrimage offered a chance for relationships to build across a gulf of experience. For many, it brought personal transformation, giving rise to a new understanding of oneself and "the other." At times it brought struggle, with pilgrims describing traumatic moments with words like "nightmare" or "living hell." Yet a commitment to relationship, and to a larger vision of the pilgrimage—of a path of healing that lay in walking a road together—galvanized people to press on. Sister Clare describes the commitment that fueled the event:

> The Pilgrimage was really just a microcosm of society, with all its ills. But we were committed to the process of healing. [Advisory Board member] Danny Black said this best. He said we are retracing the Middle Passage, and in doing that, we are all together on the boat. A symbolic boat. You know that when the African peoples were enslaved, two thirds or more of all who traveled . . . died. If we are to reverse the

Middle Passage journey, he said, we need to be about not losing people. We need to struggle to keep everything, everyone, on that boat. To
not lose anyone. To not let a single person go.[41]

Most of those who took part in the Interfaith Pilgrimage of the Middle
Passage, and at least some of the people and communities who interacted with it along the way, found their experience both draining and
energizing. The goal of creating greater awareness about racism and the
institution of slavery was achieved, as well as the opportunity to bring a
spiritual component of healing to sites and communities traumatized by
violence. There were also deep personal ties forged around a new experience, a shared story. Ingrid Askew tells how former pilgrims are today
organizing marches, creating websites, protesting against police brutality, designing educational tools, giving lectures, starting new study programs, making personal changes, and lobbying for societal change.
Looking back on the experience, having herself chosen to move to South
Africa to continue her cultural activism, she sees the pilgrimage as a cat-
alyst that has launched many new beginnings:

> The process has changed everyone who took part into some kind of
> new revolutionary. People have not gone back to their regular life . . .
> [they] are applying the things they learned in their own communities.
> It just keeps going on and on. It's also happening with me . . . I don't
> think the Pilgrimage will ever die. It's just going through a different
> process. It's metamorphasizing into other things. Outstanding things.[42]

A Few Concluding Observations

The two very different groups that I have briefly described in this chapter are examples of movements that create spaces where people separated by conflict work together for common goals. Such spaces are crucial during times of conflict and also during less overt phases of struggle.
They are particularly valuable when joint platforms are few. Part of the
strength of these groups lies in their coming together for a tangible purpose: in the case of the Link, a campaign to end the Occupation, to create awareness, and to build bridges between the two communities; in the
case of the pilgrimage, to raise awareness about and start a process of
healing race-based violence.

Both groups have gone through difficult moments when divides
seem impassable. They have encountered places or issues where trauma
and anger go deep. During such times, it is not uncommon for people to
retreat into separate groups, to grieve or rage among those who share a

common history and experience. In both initiatives, the pull of unfinished joint work again draws people back together. Thus, it seems that
both times of separation and times of joint work or struggle are essential to the journey toward reconciliation. For the pilgrimage, spiritual
expressions were important in dealing with deep-rooted injustice and
conflict; in contrast, the women in the Jerusalem Link generally associated religion with the institutions of oppression and thus gave it little
importance in healing divisions.

The final outcome, the eventual shape of what will be—of how
blacks and whites can be true neighbors, of how Palestinians and Israelis
can break bread together—is still to be realized. Recovering from
oppression, from trauma, hatred, war, and terror is a lengthy process.
Although, for example, we might celebrate the release of Nelson Mandela, the framing of a new constitution for South Africa, and the official
end to apartheid, we are still faced with that land's legacy of racist policies. Long after the papers are signed and the handshakes are over, the
dismantling of generations of separation, prejudice and violence continues. This often uncelebrated work of peacemaking, which starts with
personal relationships and aims at transforming societal patterns and
structures, is challenging. It is also essential in moving toward healing a
traumatized society. As the history of Bosnia shows, if injustice, hatred,
and suspicion are left unattended, they easily become a foundation for
new or continuing acts of terror. Trying to expose and heal the wounds
of violence and oppression, providing spaces for people to walk together
in mutual respect and commitment, helping people struggle to hear
uncomfortable truths, provides a light that challenges the darkness of
racism, division, and hatred. Such initiatives help to illuminate the beck-
oning but still uncharted paths toward a lasting peace—and give us
strength to make the journey.

NOTES

1. Other prominent organizations that see themselves as having a global
impact include: the World Congress of Faiths, the World Council of Churches,
the International Interfaith Centre, the Temple of Understanding, the United
Religions Initiative, the Council of a Parliament of World Religions, and
Thanksgiving Square.

2. Partly this is because the energies and resources of grassroot activists are
already stretched to the limit in carrying out programs and activities. Many
activists also feel that tangible projects are more important than efforts to write
up or intellectualize about them.

3. My effort to convey these stories is possible only with the encouragement of many people. Among them I would like to thank Bruce Gregersen of the United Church of Canada who always succeeds in providing me with challenges; the United Church of Canada, the Mennonite Central Committee, and the Anglican Church of Canada for infrastructure and support; Patrick Grant for much appreciated editorial assistance; my co-author colleagues for their excellent feedback and insights; my family for cheerfully enduring the vagaries of a writer; and, most important, the women and men of the Jerusalem Link, the Interfaith Pilgrimage, and other movements for change for taking time to share their thoughts, feelings, and visions. I dedicate this chapter to the inspiring efforts of those who are working, often with little recognition, on the front lines of peacebuilding.

4. Interview, 7 December 2000. Palestinians are approximately 20 percent of Israel's citizens. This does not count Palestinians living in the occupied territories, or the diaspora community living in neighboring countries and other parts of the world.

5. Israel returned the Sinai Peninsula to Egypt in 1979 in exchange for recognition of the state of Israel as a legitimate part of the Middle East.

6. Three books by Benny Morris offer a good overview of Israeli-Palestinian relations: *The Birth of the Palestinian Refugee Problem, 1947–1949* (Cambridge: Cambridge University Press, 1987), *1948 and After: Israel and the Palestinians* (Oxford: Clarendon Press, 1990), and *Righteous Victims: A History of the Zionist-Arab Conflict 1881–1999* (New York: Knopf, 1999).

7. From her unpublished book, *Standing for Peace: The History of Women in Black in Israel* (1996), p. 12.

8. The Women in Black movement started in January 1988, when ten Israeli women dressed in black stood in nonviolent protest against the Occupation. Despite vocal and sometimes violent resistance, the weekly one-hour vigils spread across Israel. The ups and downs of the movement are best chronicled in Gila Svirsky's unpublished book *Standing for Peace: The History of Women in Black in Israel* (1996). A brief account of early days, the movement's spread outside Israel, and the challenges presented by the Gulf War are found in talks by Debbie Lerman and Louisa Morgantini, the edited contents of which are found in "Fundamentalist Politics in Israel and the Vatican," *Women Against Fundamentalism Journal,* no. 7 (1995): pp. 36–39. Unfortunately, a more detailed discussion of Women in Black is outside the scope of this chapter.

9. Naomi's comments were originally published in *The Jerusalem Post* (March 1998) on the occasion of International Women's Day. They were reproduced by Gila Svirsky in an e-mail message/report entitled "What the Media Do Not Report," dated 31 March 1998; retrieved 7 October 2000 from the world wide web: http://www.ariga. com/svirsky033198.html. All subsequent Internet references in this chapter are taken from the world wide web (http).

10. Interview, 7 December 2000.

11. Gila Svirsky, "Israeli Women Struggle for Peace," November 1996. Retrieved on 5 October 2000 from www.salam.org/palestine/israel1.html.

12. Interview, 7 December 2000.

13. Quoted from "Director's Message" posted on the JCW website; retrieved on 28 September 2000 from www.j-c-w.org.

14. For more details, see the history posted at the websites of Bat Shalom (batshalo@netvision.net.il) and JCW (www.j-c-w.org).

15. Retrieved on 28 September 2000 from www.j-c-w.org.

16. Interview, 19 December 2000.

17. Personal communication, 10 December 2000.

18. The issue is based on UN Resolution 194/111 (adopted on 11 December 1948) that affirms the Palestinian right to return to their former homes or be compensated for the loss or damage of their property.

19. Interview, 7 December 2000.

20. The Middle Passage was part of the slave route by which traders of European descent transported millions of Africans to the Americas.

21. As John Henrik Clarke notes in his Introduction to Tom Feelings' *The Middle Passage* (New York: Dial Books, 1995), there is no way to calculate exactly how many Africans were captured and perished. It is estimated that from 1482 to 1888, 30–60 million Africans were captured, of which perhaps two-thirds died before reaching a new life of slavery.

22. "Walking the talk with the Interfaith Pilgrimage of the Middle Passage," 1998; retrieved 5 October 2000 from www.peacepagoda.org/dab3.htm.

23. Letter dated 24 January 1999; retrieved 5 Oct. 2000 from www.peacepagoda.org/dab3.htm.

24. As a matter of fact, two of the four pilgrims who traveled to South America did make the trans-Atlantic crossing on the *Sortilege,* a ship dedicated to tracing the history of African enslavement as part of an American educational project. Pilgrims eventually came to see these travelers as symbolically taking the journey for the whole pilgrimage. However, setting aside the vision of traveling back together to Africa by sea (with planned prayers and rituals of healing over an ocean that had claimed the bodies of so many ancestors) was initially a deep disappointment for many connected with the journey.

25. Interview, 3 December 2000.

26. In addition to this pilgrimage, which traveled across Sri Lanka and on to South India, the Nipponzan Myohoji Order has organized a number of other international interfaith events, including a 1991–1992 walk from Panama to Washington, D.C., in solidarity with indigenous peoples to mark the five hundredth anniversary of the arrival of Columbus, and a 1995 pilgrimage from Auschwitz to Hiroshima on the fiftieth anniversary of the dropping of the atomic bomb.

27. Interview, 3 December 2000.

28. Consisting of over two dozen leaders and scholars from secular, religious, and political backgrounds. Bishop Desmond Tutu of South Africa functioned as honorary chairman.

29. From the brochure of the pilgrimage. This and other pilgrimage materials can be found at the Leverett Peace Pagoda website: www.peacepagoda.org.

30. Participants were also asked to commit to a policy of no drinking, drugs, or weapons, and to follow the guidelines of local organizers.

31. Interview, 12 December 2000.

32. Some Buddists leaders, including Sister Clare, suggest that this phrase cannot be adequately translated. According to them, it is beyond meaning, coming from the heart of the Buddha and encompassing all the most precious spiritual insights of his compassion and enlightenment.

33. Personal e-mail communication, 29 September 2000.

34. Interview, 12 December 2000.

35. Interview, 3 December 2000.

36. See, for example, the comments of Skip Schiel, "A ritual led by pilgrims and sojourners of African descent," July 1, 1998; retrieved 8 October 2000 from http://www.brightworks.com/quaker/midp-ss18.html.

37. Interview, 7 December 2000.

38. Daniel A. Brown, "Walking the talk with the Interfaith Pilgrimage of the Middle Passage."

39. Interview, 7 December 2000.

40. Stephanie Kraft, "Faith meets the lynching tree: A traveler from the Interfaith Pilgrimage of the Middle Passage talks about life on the road," *The Valley Advocate*, 1 July 1999; reproduced in "New Mass Media Publications," retrieved 10 October 2000 from www.newmassmedia.com/search.phtml.

41. Interview, 12 December 2000.

42. Interview, 3 December 2000.

10

Case Studies in Religion and Peacebuilding

Cambodia

CATHERINE MORRIS

Over the past decade, Cambodia has been the focus of some of the world's most concentrated peacebuilding activities in history. More than $1.8 billion was spent on the work of the United Nations Transitional Authority in Cambodia (UNTAC) alone. The world associates Cambodia's conflicts with the horrifying Khmer Rouge regime and its aftermath, but its troubles have not been isolated to the past three decades. Historically, Cambodia has been caught between expansionist neighbors, European colonial interests, Cold War superpowers, and agendas of "globalization." Religion and religious leaders have been important in Cambodian politics and conflicts,[1] but the record does not conspicuously show determinative roles for religion in peacebuilding. Cambodian Buddhism was nearly annihilated during the Pol Pot period. Nonetheless, a striking religiously inspired Cambodian peace movement has drawn international attention since the early 1990s and provides impetus for this case study.

Cambodia's state motto is "Nation, Religion, King." Cambodians are said to have a distinct sense of identity based on the glories of the

Angkor empire, the ancient Khmer language, and a Buddhist heritage. Angkor's grandeur between the ninth and fifteenth centuries has been used to cultivate nationalism and advance the ambitions of ideologically diverse regimes that have dominated Cambodia over the past century.[2] More than 90 percent of Cambodia's 11.4 million people adhere to Theravada Buddhism, the endemic religion of Khmer people since the fourteenth century. Cambodia's current constitution makes Buddhism the state religion. Popular Khmer-Buddhism, deeply connected with Khmer identity, is inextricably interwoven with Indic Brahmanism and animism that predate Buddhism. Historically, village wats (pagoda-monasteries) were central in schooling, moral education, community decision making, political advice, spiritual counsel, and conflict resolution. Now, knowledge and practice of Buddhist ethics and meditation are shallow, but Cambodians participate widely in religious ceremonies and festivals. Buddhist clergy still evoke popular deference.

This chapter uses illustrations from Cambodian history and current events, emphasizing religious activism in 1993 and 1998 elections,[3] to demonstrate that religion has been unconstructive in conflict resolution or peacebuilding when disengaged from social issues or, alternatively, when politically aligned or manipulated. Religion has contributed to peacebuilding when its leaders have played active nonpartisan roles in teaching, conflict resolution, and advocacy for public ethics and nonviolence at grassroots and national levels.

Resources have been teased from English language materials from several disciplines, including news reports. About fifty unstructured interviews were conducted in Cambodia (in English or through interpreters) in 1998 and 2000 with Buddhist and Christian clergy and lay leaders as well as human rights, legal development, conflict resolution and peacebuilding scholars, and practitioners within civil society and government.[4] The focus is on popular expressions of Khmer-Buddhism. Christianity is also considered because of the high-profile work of foreign Christian development and evangelistic missions. Brief comments are made about nonreligious peacebuilding efforts.

When considering Cambodia, one must remember the world's involvement, complicity, silence, or apathy in the devastation of the country and its people's suffering. A Cambodian monk says, "we must be responsible politically and personally. Everyone was implicated in some way, intentionally or unintentionally." Speaking about foreigners, a Christian priest who has worked with Cambodians for decades cautions: "We must be very humble."

ROOTS OF CAMBODIAN CONFLICTS

External factors have been important in Cambodia's conflicts. Vietnamese and Thai expansionism of the eighteenth and nineteenth centuries was curbed by installation of a French protectorate in 1864. The French legacy included an anticolonial nationalist movement. Buddhist clergy sometimes participated in sporadic protests during the nineteenth and twentieth centuries, and after 1945 were among leaders in the communist movement. Communist leaders also included men and women educated in France and influenced by Marxism, including Saloth Sar (later Pol Pot). National autonomy and preservation of Khmer-Buddhist identity, together with complex dynamics of the Vietnam War, were factors in the ultimate rise of the 1975–1979 Pol Pot regime.[5]

The regime's radical collectivism, nationalist isolation, and internal purges caused deaths of about 1.7 million men, women, and children— up to a quarter of Cambodia's population—from privation, illness, torture, or execution. Historical and religious archives were destroyed. Wats were demolished. Religious practice was abolished. Ethnic and religious minorities were persecuted. Along with doctors, lawyers, teachers, artists, and scholars, most monks and nuns were killed, died, fled, or disappeared. Fewer than 5000 of Cambodia's 65,000 monks survived the 1970s; more than 25,000 were executed.[6]

Vietnam's ouster of the Khmer Rouge in 1979 was followed by a decade of international isolation. Powerful Western countries supported insurgency by the republican Khmer Peoples National Liberation Front (KPNLF), the monarchist Front Uni National pour un Cambodge Indépendant, Neutre, Pacifique et Coopératif (FUNCINPEC) and the Khmer Rouge. The breakdown of Cold War politics created conditions for several years of regional and UN peace efforts resulting in the 1991 Paris Peace Accords.

UNTAC-organized 1993 elections produced a fragile coalition between FUNCINPEC and the incumbent Cambodia People's Party (CPP), successor to the Communist Party of the previous regime. The new government created a liberal democratic constitution, but continued factional power mongering thwarted all progress. Increasing tensions erupted in military violence in July 1997. Hun Sen's CPP secured control. Elections in 1998 resulted in another coalition controlled by Hun Sen. In late 1998, the remnants of Khmer Rouge insurgency forces were given amnesties and integrated into the Cambodian armed forces.[7]

With increased political stability, life has improved for many Cambodians. But the country remains among the poorest in the world. The shift from centrally planned socialist policies to neoliberal free market practices prescribed by international financial institutions is implicated in the growing gap between rich and poor. Cambodia remains fraught with inequality, corruption, violence, ethnic prejudice, and factionalism.

The United Nations and nongovernmental organizations (NGOs) refer to Cambodia's climate of human rights abuse and poor law enforcement as "a culture of impunity." Issues include violence and bullying by authorities, sexual and labor exploitation of children and women, labor conflicts, and widespread land rights disputes. Military, police, and government officials often turn a blind eye or are actively involved. Courts lack independence and resources. There are no trusted government human rights complaint mechanisms. Public frustration with impunity of offenders has led to violent mob "justice." There is much preoccupation with how to come to terms with past atrocities, including plans for a UN-approved tribunal to try selected Khmer Rouge leaders.

Generations of war and conflict have broken down community structures, religious practice, and relationships at the grass roots. Deep divisions, suspicion, violence, and trauma maintain their grip on institutions and morale.

Political discourse remains polarized along factional lines. Factions are based on personal loyalties as much as political values.[8] Obligations to patrons, family, or friends militate against taking differing views or even impartial stances. Concepts and practices of nonpartisanship, neutrality, and impartiality are ill defined and undeveloped. Impartial conflict resolution and decision-making processes are strongly urged for Cambodia, including independent courts, human rights bodies, and other entities. There is frustration about how to implement neutrality in a political culture in which the very idea of independent decision-making bodies is an anathema to power holders who benefit from the status quo. There is no tradition of power sharing. Instead, power holders and power seekers seem to stockpile and garrison their influence as though it were scarce, threatened property essential for zero-sum, life-and-death contests.[9]

One problem with "neutrality" is its diverse connotations. The Cambodian term *apyearkret* (neutrality, impartiality) is defined as "in the middle, representing those in the middle, not entering any group."[10] The definition is capable of several meanings, including the taking of moderate positions, being independent, or being apart from relevant parties.[11] One civil society leader suggests that "neutrality" tends to be disrespected in Cambodian politics because "neutral" stances are interpreted as "neutralized, passive, and non-vocal." Literature from the field of conflict resolution suggests that dominant groups tend to see "neutral" ideas or people as those that implicitly or explicitly conform to the dominant groups' prevailing social norms. "Normal" may be anything but "neutral" in the eyes of nondominant and minority interests.[12] A Cambodian human rights leader spells this out: "If you stand 'neutral' between the bad and the good, the bad will like you . . . this is not [true] neutrality." He used the example of much criticized "neutral" stances of embassies whose policies were believed to advantage the powerfully ensconced CPP after the July 1997 conflicts and during the 1998 elections.[13] In his view, "true" neutrality involves taking ethical stands. This principled approach to "neutrality" is challenging in Cambodia's polarized political culture. The first-mentioned civil society leader puts it this way: "if you express an opinion, you are put either in the government basket or the opposition basket. Independent views are colored one way or the other." Thus, it is difficult to identify Cambodians at the national level who are impartial in the sense of being respected and trusted by all sides.

RELIGION, CONFLICT, AND PEACEBUILDING IN CAMBODIA

For the Khmer-Buddhist majority, Buddhism is the only institution that cuts across political and social divisions. Monks have exceptional power to sway people at the grass roots. Their very presence in public activities has a legitimizing effect. This section discusses the clergy's tradition of political neutrality, and its mediating role between people and rulers.[14]

Traditional and Contemporary Roles of Buddhism in Governance

In traditional Khmer-Buddhist thinking, the nation is held together by the clergy *(sangha)* and the righteous ruler *(dhammaraja)*, the two reciprocally supportive wheels of Buddhist *dhamma* (truth, law, ethical teaching). A *dhammaraja* is a person of merit who has risen to rule through right actions in previous lives *(kamma)*. Historically, the *sangha* maintained royal support by subordinating itself to the king. The ruler maintained *sangha* support, popular legitimacy, and social control by observing the *dhamma*. Righteous rulers (and, by extrapolation, public officials) observe Ten Royal Virtues: liberality or generosity concerning the people's welfare; morality including noncorruption; duty, including self-sacrifice for the people; integrity, including truthful sincerity; kindness, including concern about people's hardships; austerity, including simple living, spiritual discipline, and self-control; non-anger; nonviolence; forbearance; and "non-opposition" to the people. The concept of non-opposition is seen as a "Buddhist endorsement of democracy."[15] Traditional Buddhist ethics and governance principles are seen as resonant with liberal democratic conceptions of public participation, equality, and protection of human rights.[16]

For centuries, Cambodian politics have flown far from the benign and reciprocal traditional Buddhist governance model with ruler, *sangha*, and people all following the *dhamma* with compassionate loving-kindness and dedication to the common good. Historically, powerful religious rhetoric and the *sangha* itself have been involved in politics. Religion has frequently been exploited, manipulated, or inverted for political purposes.

During the colonial period, intermittent political protests by clergy aimed to protect Buddhism. For example, a 1942 French proposal to Romanize the Khmer alphabet was seen as an attack on Buddhism. When Achar Hem Chieu led a monk protest, he was forcibly defrocked and arrested for plotting a coup. The insult and arrest provoked an "umbrella war" of a thousand people in Phnom Penh including hundreds of saffron-robed monks carrying their customary umbrellas. Hem Chieu died in prison. He remains a popular Cambodian hero.[17] Nationalist movements were primarily noncommunist until the French tried to reassert authority after World War II. Some clergy joined the communist movement in 1946 and rose to prominent leadership until Pol Pot (then Saloth Sar) became leader in 1962.

During the 1950s and 1960s, Sihanouk exploited Buddhist rhetoric with policies of "Buddhist Socialism."[18] The Khmer Rouge, while denouncing religion, instituted rules for cadres that imitated precepts for monks, aiming to show their conduct as "more perfect than the practice of monks."[19] In 1979, the Vietnamese-sponsored People's Republic of Kampuchea (PRK) regime bolstered its legitimacy by partially restoring Buddhism, including arrangements for ordination of seven former Cambodian monks including Venerable Tep Vong, who became head monk of a unified Cambodian *sangha* until Sihanouk reestablished the Thommayut order in December 1991 at which time Venerable Tep Vong became (and remains) Supreme Patriarch of the Mohanikay order. Until 1989, PRK constraints on Buddhism included restriction of ordination to men over fifty and a tax on wats.

Although pagoda restoration began in 1979 after the Vietnamese took over, the pace increased dramatically after 1989. Revival over the past decade means approximately 4000 pagodas have been restored, mainly with villagers' lay offerings. There are now more than 50,000 monks. Few have education or experience. Novices often have only primary education. Most monks are young men and teenagers ordained temporarily for education or as part of traditional expectations that males serve some time as monks. Shortage of educated, experienced monks means lack of discipline for young monks. There are anecdotes about monks leering at women, and even standing by giggling while mobs beat suspected thieves.[20] Education is improving. In 1992, the Buddhist Institute reopened and began distributing scriptures to libraries and pagodas. The first Buddhist high school for monks reopened in 1993. The Buddhist University reopened in 1997. Japan's donation of a million copies of Khmer language Buddhist scriptures means young monks can read them. Divisions are appearing as young monks challenge elders concerning monk discipline, tradition, and social engagement.

Cambodia's estimated 20,000 nuns[21] have lower status and prominence than monks, partly because nuns are unordained (as in all Theravada traditions since the sixth century). Nuns are usually disciplined, responsible older women with no family responsibilities. Usually uneducated, nuns traditionally work in pagodas as housekeepers. The Association of Nuns and Lay Women of Cambodia (ANLWC) has been training nuns in Buddhist concepts of human rights, and skills for conflict resolution, leadership, trauma counseling, and social work for street children. Nuns sometimes now serve on pagoda committees that are influential in village decision-making.[22] Nuns and lay Buddhist women have been visible and courageous in sometimes dangerous peace walks. They are driving, organizing, and coordinating forces for much of Cambodia's peacework.

Internal divisions in the *sangha* mean increased ability of political players to manipulate religion. All political parties seek *sangha* legitimization by inviting monks to bless events and by visiting and donating to wats. The *sangha* is divided into two denominations. The tiny Thommayut denomination, restored in 1991 by Prince Sihanouk, is associated with the royal family and FUNCINPEC. The Mohanikay denomination, constituting more than 90 percent of monks, is headed by Venerable Tep Vong, long identified with the CPP. However, many younger Mohanikay monks do not identify with the CPP.

Poor education, institutional weakness, divisions, and political alignments mean the *sangha* currently is not positioned for strong roles in governance, conflict resolution, or teaching of ethics to leaders or populace. Nevertheless, the popular authority of Buddhism is such that Cambodian political players try to co-opt it, manipulate it, or control it. Later discussed is the CPP's use of force and coercion on monks.

Conceptions of Monk "Neutrality" and Social Engagement

Theoretically, traditions of political neutrality mean that monks are in a unique position to hold to the Middle Path, standing on Buddhist precepts, principles of ethical governance and nonviolence. There is consensus that Cambodian monks should stand for righteousness, nonviolence and political neutrality. But practical meanings of "righteousness" and "neutrality" differ along a continuum from disengagement to political alignment.

Conservative Buddhists emphasize individual piety and a disengaged approach to "neutrality." This view of neutrality favors silence about controversial political or social issues. Many monks take this approach.

Engaged Buddhists subscribe to traditional monk roles but add emphasis on active social engagement, nonpartisan and nonviolent approaches to social justice, and the alleviation of oppressive or conflict-producing social structures and situations.[23] Education goes beyond prescribing personal piety and aims to develop a critical mass of peaceful individuals who live out Buddhist ethical precepts. Thus, peace radiates outward from individuals to families, to communities, to society. Engaged Buddhists point to scripture and traditions that support nonviolence, human dignity, ethical governance and economic policy, active peacemaking, consensus-based participatory decision making, and nonpartisan *sangha* advocacy on behalf of people and the environment. Engaged Buddhists are a small minority in Cambodia, but their activism, particularly that of Maha Ghosananda[24] who led annual peace walks in Cambodia between 1992 and 1998, has resulted in his nomination for the Nobel Prize four times between 1994 and 1997.

Another stream of thinking in the continuum seems closer to the style of Cambodia's monk political activists of the past two centuries, represented by the iconic Hem Chieu. This stream does not shun political activism, but claims neutrality by standing for righteous governance regardless of party affiliation. During 1998 post-election conflicts, some young monks representing this thinking leaped into the middle of clearly partisan opposition political demonstrations while asserting a nonpartisan motivation. Concepts and lines between the various approaches to "neutrality" are blurred and confused.

From an engaged Buddhist perspective, Venerable Yos Hut points out that "public activities that challenge injustices are often seen as partisan by Cambodia's leaders,"[25] and therefore monks must follow the Middle Path strictly: "Non-partisan activism in favor of peace walks a fine line between neither endorsing nor opposing any party in a conflict and making clear statements of opposition to policies which lead to violence and suffering." Yos Hut acknowledges that Cambodia's polarized political climate makes this stance controversial and difficult; monks who take public roles are accused of "meddling in politics and over-stepping the bounds of their religious duties."

Conflict resolution practitioners involved in Cambodia's peace movement have outlined the practical mind-set required for neutrality from an engaged Buddhist perspective. The first principle is avoidance of actual or perceived partisan alignment with any individual or group or its interests.[26] Second, silence and social disengagement are not considered neutral; practical results of disengaged silence may be continued dominance of the powerful to the detriment of the weak. By contrast, an engaged Buddhist conception of neutrality contemplates engagement without attachment, "neither joining the fight nor hiding from it."[27] Third, "engaged" neutrality springs from commitment to the *dhamma*'s teaching concerning mindfulness, detachment, and compassion.[28] Engaged neutrality means mindful detachment from interests of self or parties, avoidance of prejudices, *and* compassionate attention to needs of all concerned.[29] Fourth, engaged neutrality involves active commitment to justice. Yos Hut maintains that to justify passive inaction in the face of injustice is to misunderstand Buddhist teaching.[30] Finally, engaged neutrality recalls Maha Ghosananda's emphasis on balancing compassion with protective wisdom:

> retaliation, hatred and revenge only continue the cycle [of violence] and never stop it. . . . Reconciliation does not mean that we surrender rights and conditions, but rather that we use love. Our wisdom and our compassion must walk together. Having one without the other is like walking on one foot; you will fall. Balancing the two you will walk very well, step by step.[31]

Cambodian clergy have become politically active at certain points in history, but there is no long-standing pattern of this kind of nonpartisan social engagement. Conservatism, non-engaged passive neutrality and cooperation with rulers have been more the norms. Currently, even conventional clergy roles in grassroots moral education and community conflict resolution are weak. Some clergy have been involved in development work, including Heng Monychenda,[32] who founded Buddhism for Development. He has also been involved in peacework. However, nonpartisan engaged Buddhist approaches are the exception.

Low clergy involvement in peacework and development is largely due to the near extinction of organized Buddhism during the 1970s. Heavy loads rest on a handful of educated and experienced monks and nuns. Also, the *sangha* has not had much space to develop apart from government control. Activist monks have become more cautious since a crackdown on monk demonstrators after the 1998 election. CPP strength continues to penetrate most of the country down to the village level where local monks are not exempt from political pressures.

Election Conflicts: 1993 and 1998

Buddhist clergy and laity, particularly through the *dhammayietra*[33] movement, played positive roles in surprisingly peaceful 1993 and 1998 elections. In contrast, when monks joined opposition demonstrations against outcomes of the 1998 election, the *sangha* became entangled in public violence and controversy.

The 1993 election was one of UNTAC's successes. Ninety percent of the electorate exercised their secret ballot with remarkably few incidents of violence and fraud despite intimidation from the Khmer Rouge and the CPP and considerable pre-election violence and deaths.[34] Peace walks led by Maha Ghosananda just prior to the election contributed to encouraging and calming the population. An organizer of the 1993 peace walk remembers that "people were afraid before the election— they expected bloodshed . . . Venerable Maha Ghosananda was influential in awakening people with his peace walks. The symbol of thousands of saffron robes and miles of walkers lessened their fears." People had stored food rations for fear of election violence, but they came out and cooked for the walkers, she recalls. Monk encouragement also provided moral authority for public participation in the election. Cambodians thronged to the polls in a massive, peaceful demonstration of popular will.

In July 1998, Cambodia ran its own multiparty elections with international support and observation. There was considerably less pre-election violence than in the 1993 election. Despite reports of considerable pre-election intimidation by the CPP, and lack of equal media access by opposition parties, again people peacefully came out to vote in overwhelming numbers. NGO coalitions played notable roles in voter education and election observation.[35] Civil society organizations, including Buddhist laity, monks, and nuns, organized an impressive coalition to campaign for a peaceful election. With support from many sectors, this campaign is credited with helping to prevent violence through peace education and other activities in sixteen provinces, including peace walks in ten provinces. Venerable Maha Ghosananda participated in pre-election peace activities in Phnom Penh as did Supreme Patriarch Tep Vong.[36]

Election results showed the CPP ahead. FUNCINPEC and the Sam Rainsy Party (SRP) alleged irregularities in vote counting. The National Election Commission, appointed to run the election, was criticized for lack of neutrality and inability to handle hundreds of complaints. Lack of timely, effective complaint resolution is regarded as one cause of escalating conflict, demonstrations, and violence after the election.[37] Opposition parties, notably the SRP, orchestrated nonviolent demonstrations in late August to protest irregularities including poor transparency in vote counting. Students became involved. After violent clashes between authorities and demonstrators in early September, a number of young monks joined the demonstrations.[38] One witness says the monks' unplanned involvement was impulsive, motivated by desire to deescalate conflict. But some monk demonstrators appeared to have political motives, claiming Hem Chieu as inspiration and role model.[39]

Whatever the monks' diverse motives, their "open defiance of traditional Buddhist edicts and orders from their elders not to participate made them targets of a violent government crackdown."[40] Monks were beaten and publicly disrobed. Authorities searched pagodas, fired guns within wat precincts, and restricted monks' movements. Eighteen monks and a nun were among seventy-seven injured during suppression of demonstrations. Among fifty-three missing are four monks.[41] Many monks went into hiding. A senior monk said on television that monks' involvement in the demonstrations was against the rules of Buddhism. Monks' injuries were not caused by beatings, he said, but happened when they "fell down and struck each other" in the confusion.[42] It is believed that this statement was coerced.[43]

Cambodians were shocked and frightened by beatings and disappearances of clergy, but opinion became polarized. Many were outraged at the treatment of monks and nuns. Some lauded the monks for a brave stand for justice. Others criticized their involvement in opposition politics. Some suggested that the monks were manipulated by the opposition. Media statements by senior clergy and others fomented public controversy about "political" or "undisciplined" monks versus cooperative "neutral" monks who stay out of politics.

The 1993 and 1998 elections demonstrate contrasting fruits of monk involvement. Buddhist monks, nuns, and laity made significant contributions to a peaceful voter turnout during both elections. But the aftermath of the 1998 election saw monks embroiled in political conflict. Passive forms of neutrality or complicity by senior monks were viewed as either coerced or partisan on the CPP side. Association with political demonstrations was seen as partisan on the opposition side.

Both these approaches are contrasted with the Buddhist-inspired non-partisan peace activism practiced in carefully planned and disciplined ways, and widely seen as conducive to religious integrity, social justice, and peace.

Given confusion and controversy about monk roles in society, together with still-strong moral authority provided by clergy, a current challenge for the Cambodian monkhood is to grapple with issues of *sangha*-state relations, including practical meanings of "neutrality." Questions include: Should monks be involved in social issues? What kinds of issues and how? Should monks vote? Should they be involved in political discussions and demonstrations? What kinds of demonstrations and how? If monks should be engaged in development and social issues but not partisan politics, how are "politics" defined, and where is the line drawn for involvement?

The Cambodian Peace Movement

Positive, peacebuilding roles of clergy and lay religious leaders in the 1993 and 1998 elections did not "just happen." They were a part of sustained peacework over two decades.

The work inspired by Maha Ghosananda is the most frequently cited example of religiously based peacebuilding in Cambodia. Beginning in 1978, he built nonpartisan relationships by visiting refugee camps of all factions. With other monks, including Yos Hut, he attended international peace talks to encourage the factions toward settlement. Although the Peace Accords were reached only after the UN stepped in, the effect of the monks' presence and their moral authority with the factions should not be dismissed.

Maha Ghosananda is the founder and spiritual leader of the *dhammayietra* movement in Cambodia. Considerably inspired by Gandhi, the movement has taught and exemplified active nonviolence to foster peace and reconciliation. Beginning in 1992, monks, nuns, and laypeople conducted annual *dhammayietra* processions through armed conflict zones.

The increasingly prominent movement has been marked by planning and preparation. Training has included theory and practical disciplines of nonviolence, nonpartisanship, and conflict resolution. Preparation for the 1996 walk included twelve training workshops in eight provinces for 600 people. The 1998 pre-election peace campaign included training workshops, practice sessions, poster and media campaigns, and extensive logistical preparation coordinated largely by Cambodian NGOs. Connected to the *dhammayietra* movement is the work of the Coalition for Peace and Reconciliation[44] which has sponsored grassroots training in conflict resolution and nonviolence for many Buddhist monks, nuns and others. International support has been provided by groups like the International Network of Engaged Buddhists (INEB).

ROLES OF OTHER RELIGIONS

Christian presence in peacebuilding is small but influential and respected at grassroots and national levels.[45] Foreign Christian efforts have been most prominent in social services, health care, and rural development. Quakers, Mennonites, and Catholics have been most prominent in peacework. Christian peaceworkers have labored alongside Cambodian monks and laypeople for the past two decades. Christians have been involved in the *dhammayietra* movement of the 1990s, grassroots conflict resolution work, the 1998 election Campaign to Reduce Violence for Peace, initiatives such as the Cambodia Centre for Conflict Resolution, and weapons reduction work. Christians have been prominent in the Cambodia Campaign to Ban Land Mines which, as part of the International Campaign, is credited with providing moral pressure that contributed to signing of the 1997 Treaty to Ban Land Mines by 122 countries including Cambodia. Cambodians, including Buddhist leaders and NGOs, have seen the work of foreign Christian peaceworkers as complementary and facilitative of their own local initiatives.

Not all foreign Christian presence has been conducive to peacebuilding. Evangelical Protestant Christianity is attracting a number of Cambodians whose suffering over past decades has led to crises of faith.[46] Insensitive proselytization has offended many.[47] Some view Christianity as a potential threat to Cambodia's Khmer-Buddhist identity. Christians and Buddhists see increased interfaith dialogue as important to prevent growth of any seeds of religiously based conflict.

Other religions in Cambodia include Mahayana Buddhism practiced among the Vietnamese minority. Folk religions are practiced by indigenous peoples. Islam is practiced by the Cham people, who have received support for rebuilding mosques from Malaysia, Saudi Arabia, and Pakistan. Roles of these religions in peacebuilding are beyond the scope of this study.

ROLES OF OTHERS IN PEACEBUILDING

Comparatively small religiously based peacebuilding initiatives have been overshadowed by nonreligious activities. UNTAC was the most visible and expensive peace effort. UNTAC was praised for its success in the 1993 election and for creating a safe climate for development of human rights and civil society organizations. UNTAC is criticized for its lack of fit with (or knowledge of) Cambodia's culture or power patterns, and its marginalization of local knowledge and skills.[48]

Currently, diverse perspectives are taken concerning peacebuilding, legal development, and human rights. Some take a Western legal approach toward identification and accountability of individual offenders. The UN focus on trials for key Khmer Rouge leaders is an example.[49] The theory is that trials will set an example by bringing to justice individuals chiefly responsible for the genocide, thereby addressing current impunity problems. Some take a cultural perspective, saying effective peacebuilding lies in enhancement of local knowledge based on Khmer-Buddhist culture and Cambodian conditions. The dominant institutionalist approach of UN and democratic donors concentrates on development of liberal democratic legislative, judicial, executive, and ombuds-type institutions. Sorpong Peou, originally from Cambodia, defends institutionalist approaches, arguing that neither trials nor traditional governance models can transform Cambodia's personalist style of governance, which he sees as a root of power abuse and conflict.[50] However, institutionalist approaches to governance are often the hand-servants of neoliberal economic development that is implicated in Cambodia's grassroots poverty, child labor, and environmental problems. Some Cambodian peacebuilders use eclectic strategies, combining local knowledge approaches with institutional capacity development. For example, Dr. Kao Kim Hourn of the Cambodian Institute for Cooperation and Peace has organized multisectoral think tanks among scholars, NGOs, political leaders, and Cambodian institutions to encourage less polarized dialogue and increase capacity and respect for impartiality. The Cambodia Centre for Conflict Resolution uses Western and Buddhist concepts for training urban and rural government officials and civil society workers.

Dominant foreign efforts for peacebuilding still tend to give lip service to understanding Cambodian political, social, and religious culture. Few resources have been put into sustained research to elicit and enhance Cambodian approaches to conflict resolution and peacebuilding. Some research has been done on local wat-based participatory governance[51] and village conflict resolution.[52] Cambodians repeatedly express interest in learning more about mediation for community conflicts, legal disputes, and human rights conflicts.[53] Recent initiatives for mediation of land disputes illustrate the need for better understanding about what kinds of mediation processes will be effective.[54] Whether traditional, Western-inspired, or combined models are adopted, the development process needs to be driven and informed by Cambodians.

LESSONS TO BE DRAWN

Cambodians have many lessons to teach the world. One is that it is important for peacebuilders to pay attention to the politics and grass-roots power of religion even when conflicts are not centered around religious animosities, and even when the religious establishment is weak. The weakness of Cambodian Buddhism together with popular attachment to religion and religious leaders means that Buddhism is potentially powerful, but easily manipulated by dominant forces.

Second, this study provides insights into concepts and practices of "neutrality" that can prevent cooption of religion, and enhance clergy and lay roles in peacebuilding and conflict resolution. When "neutrality" is defined as silence or passivity, a neutral religious community is malleable to whomever dominates society. At the opposite pole, partisan political actions by religious leaders have been implicated (however inadvertently) in Cambodia's twentieth-century spiral into the Khmer Rouge genocide that ended up turning on religion itself. Monk involvement in the 1998 demonstrations shows that activism, however well intentioned, can be divisive when it becomes politically aligned—or perceived as politically aligned. The lesson to be drawn concerns the power of "engaged neutrality" that includes taking stands on public ethics while remaining actively nonviolent, nonpartisan, fair, and righteous. When "neutrality" is defined this way, a nonpartisan monk-hood could conceivably become a force toward sustainable peace and justice. Several Cambodian monks, nuns, as well as lay women and men are providing dynamic leadership to this end.

Third, further research on Cambodian and Khmer-Buddhist concepts of impartiality could illuminate ways to increase capacity for independent courts and human rights bodies. Fourth, local Cambodian capacity, knowledge and will for effective religiously based peacebuilding is alive among many laity, a number of monks and nuns, and some foreign supporters. These can be strengthened and harnessed to inspire government and religious leaders toward ethical and accountable governance suited to the needs of Cambodians in the twenty-first century.

Fifth, we see the fruits of interfaith Buddhist-Christian collaboration. We have witnessed the impact of locally initiated work led by a nonpartisan and multifaith religious community, such as anti-landmines work and the *dhammayietra* movement. This work has inspired people in Cambodia and elsewhere to see that nonpartisan nonviolence can be an effective third way between violent insurgency and docile acquiescence to injustice. Sixth, from a development perspective, religiously based peacework in Cambodia shows the good fruits of facilitative foreign approaches to peacebuilding and development, compared to advisory, top-down, "we-know-best" approaches. Increased foreign efforts would be well spent on action research to facilitate expansion of local and regional knowledge and strategies. Seventh, we learn about striking synergies that can result when grassroots organizational skills are combined with the dynamism of charismatic leaders like Maha Ghosananda.

Finally, we are reminded of the call of Buddhist and Christian leaders in Cambodia for responsibility and humility, recognizing that "we are all implicated, intentionally or unintentionally." Therefore, I close with a question: There is still a long way to go for people in Cambodia on their *dhammayietra*. Who will walk with Cambodian peacebuilders patiently, on their terms, step by step?

NOTES

Thanks are due to many people in Cambodia and North America who generously gave their time to correspond and speak with me. Several people provided comments on drafts, including former Canadian Ambassadors to Cambodia Gordon Longmuir (1995–1999) and Martin Collacott (1993–1995); Peter Gyallay-Pap, Khmer-Buddhist Educational Assistance Project; William A.W. Neilson, University of Victoria; Sorpong Peou, Sophia University, Tokyo; Judy Saumweber, Director of the American Friends Service Committee in Cambodia, and her colleagues. The diverse perspectives of these and other commentators have improved this chapter. I am responsible for its content, perspective, and remaining errors. Funding came from the University of Victoria Centre for Studies in Religion and Society, the Institute for Dispute Resolution, Emmanuel Baptist Church, and the law firm of Clay & Company.

1. Ian Harris, "Buddhism *in Extremis:* The Case of Cambodia," *Buddhism and Politics in Twentieth-Century Asia,* ed. Ian Harris (London, New York: Pinter, 1999), pp. 54–78; Charles F. Keyes, "Communist Revolution and the Buddhist Past in Cambodia," in Charles F. Keyes, Laurel Kendall, and Helen Hardacre, eds., *Asian Visions of Authority* (Honolulu: University of Hawaii Press, 1994), pp. 43–73; Yang Sam, *Khmer Buddhism and Politics from 1954 to 1984* (Newington, CT: Khmer Studies Institute, 1987), pp. 8–16.

2. David Chandler, *A History of Cambodia* (Chiang Mai, Thailand: Silkworm, 1996).

3. Since this research, commune elections occurred in February 2002, too late to allow for discussion in this chapter.

4. All unattributed quotes are based on notes of confidential interviews with key informants and are not footnoted separately.

5. Ben Kiernan, *How Pol Pot Came to Power: A History of Communism in Kampuchea, 1930–1975* (London: Thetford Press, 1985).

6. Peter Gyallay-Pap, "From Conflict to Reconciliation in Cambodia?" (Battambang, Cambodia: unpublished paper, 1993).

7. See Laura McGrew, *Truth, Justice, Reconciliation and Peace in Cambodia: 20 Years After the Khmer Rouge* (Phnom Penh, unpublished paper funded by the Canadian Embassy, March, 2000).

8. For a description of Cambodia's patronage system, see Kate G. Frieson, "The Cambodian Elections of 1993: A Case of Power to the People?" in R. H. Taylor, ed., *The Politics of Elections in Southeast Asia* (Cambridge, UK, and New York: Cambridge University Press and Woodrow Wilson Center Press, 1996), pp. 224–251, at p. 231.

9. David Chandler, "Might Makes Right, "*Far Eastern Economic Review* 162:36 (1999), pp. 54–56; Ing-Britt Trankell and Jan Ovesen, "Introduction," *Facets of Power and Its Limitations: Political Culture in Southeast Asia,* ed. Ing-Britt Trankell and Laura Summers (Uppsala, Sweden: Department of Cultural Anthropology, Uppsala University, 1998), pp. 9–18.

10. Chuon Nath et al., *Dictionnaire Cambodgien* (Phnom Penh: Institut Bouddhique, 1967), p. 1658. *Apyearkret* derives from Sanskrit.

11. Caroline Hughes, with Real Sopheap, *Nature and Causes of Conflict Escalation in the 1998 National Election* (Phnom Penh: Cambodia Development Resource Institute, 2000), pp. 32–38; SILAKA, *The Political Neutrality of Cambodian NGOs* (Phnom Penh: Cambodian NGO Support Network and SILAKA, 1998).

12. See Catherine Morris, "The Trusted Mediator: Ethics and Interaction in Mediation," *Rethinking Disputes: The Mediation Alternative,* ed. Julie Macfarlane (London and Toronto: Cavendish Publishing, and Emond-Montgomery, 1997), pp. 301–347, at pp. 329–330. Problematics of terminology, concepts, practice, and ethics of "neutrality" and "impartiality" are not confined to Cambodia.

13. See David W. Ashley, "The Failure of Conflict Resolution in Cambodia: Causes and Lessons," *Cambodia and the International Community: The Quest for Peace, Development, and Democracy,* ed. Frederick Z. Brown and David G. Timberman (New York and Singapore: Asia Society and Institute of Southeast Asian Studies, 1998), pp. 49–78.

14. This section draws on William Collins, *Grassroots Civil Society in Cambodia* (Phnom Penh: Center for Advanced Study, November 1998); Peter Gyallay-Pap, "From Conflict to Reconciliation in Cambodia?"; Peter Gyallay-Pap and Hean Sokhom, eds. *Buddhism in Cambodia,* special issue, *Cambodia Report* II (2) (Phnom Penh: Center for Advanced Study, 1996); Charles F. Keyes, "Communist Revolution and the Buddhist Past in Cambodia"; Somboon Suksamran, "Buddhism, Political Authority, and Legitimacy in Thailand and Cambodia," *Buddhist Trends in Southeast Asia,* ed. Trevor Ling (Singapore: Institute of Southeast Asian Studies, 1993); Somboon Suksamran, "The Buddhist Concept of Political Authority and Society as Basis to Rebuild the Khmer Society and

Nation," *Buddhism and the Future of Cambodia,* ed. Khmer Buddhist Research Center (Rithisen: Khmer Buddhist Research Center, 1986).

15. Aung San Suu Kyi, "In Quest of Democracy," *Freedom from Fear,* 2nd edition, ed. Michael Aris (London: Penguin, 1995), p. 173.

16. For example, Yos Hut Khemacaro, "Steering the Middle Path: Buddhism, Non-Violence and Political Change in Cambodia," *Safeguarding Peace: Cambodia's Constitutional Challenge.* Special Issue, *Accord* 5 (1998), p. 73.

17. Bunchan Mul, "The Umbrella War of 1942," trans. Chantou Boua, *Peasants and Politics in Kampuchea, 1942–1981,* ed. Ben Kiernan, and Chanthou Boua (London: M.E. Sharpe, Inc., 1982).

18. Yang Sam, *Khmer Buddhism and Politics from 1954 to 1984,* pp. 8–16; also see Ben Kiernan, *How Pol Pot Came to Power,* pp. 169–248.

19. Yang Sam, *Khmer Buddhism and Politics from 1954 to 1984,* p. 70.

20. Seth Mydans, "Mob Justice Rules over Cambodia's Ailing Courts."

21. Naurin Ahmad-Zaki, "Association of Nuns and Lay Women (ANLWC): Women, Morality and Reconciliation" (Phnom Penh: Heinrich-Böll Foundation, n.d.), retrieved 14 January 2001 from http://www.hbfasia.org/cambodia/adlwc.html.

22. Kassie Neou, "Human Rights in Action—Developing Partnerships Between Government and Civil Society—Our Unique Non-confrontational Approach in Cambodia," Occasional Paper 35—Cambodia Country Study, Human Development Report Office Occasional Papers (Phnom Penh: United Nations Development Program [UNDP], 2000), retrieved 19 November 2000 from http://www.undp.org/hdro/ oc35.html.

23. Soraj Hongladarom, "Buddhism and Human Rights in the Thoughts of Sulak Sivaraksa and Phra Dhammapidok (Prayudh Prayutto)," *Journal of Buddhist Ethics Online Conference on Buddhism and Human Rights, 1–14 October 1995,* retrieved 4 January 2001 from http://jbe.la.psu.edu/1995conf/honglada.txt; Christopher S. Queen and Sallie B. King, eds., *Engaged Buddhism: Buddhist Liberation Movements in Asia* (New York: State University of New York Press, 1996).

24. For a biography, see Maha Ghosananda, *Step by Step: Meditations on Wisdom and Compassion,* ed. Jane Sharada Mahoney and Philip Edmonds (Berkeley, CA: Parallax Press, 1992).

25. Yos Hut Khemacaro, "Steering the Middle Path," pp. 73–74. See Chea Sotheacheath, and James Eckardt, "Activist Monks Dare to Defy Authorities," *Phnom Penh Post,* Special Edition, 7:20 (September 12–17, 1998); Pok Sokundara and Beth Moorthy, "Monks Walk a Tightrope between Peace and Politics," *Phnom Penh Post,* 7(22) (October 2–15, 1998).

26. Yeshua Moser-Puangsuwan, and Marissa Maure, "One Million Kilometres for Peace: Five Years of Peace Action Walks in Cambodia" (Bangkok: Non-

violence International South East Asia Program, undated). Retrieved 13 January 2001 from http://www.igc.apc.org/nonviolence/niseasia/dymwalk/dy1.htm.

27. Yeshua Moser-Puangsuwan, and Marissa Maure, "One Million Kilometres for Peace."

28. For elaboration on doctrinal and scriptural sources please refer to sources cited. Also see Eva Neumaier's chapter in this volume.

29. John A. McConnell, *Mindful Mediation: A Handbook for Buddhist Mediators* (Bangkok: Buddhist Research Institute, Mahachula Buddhist University, and others, 1995), pp. 245–257, which discusses Theravada Buddhist theory as it relates to community conflict and mediation, with extensive references to scriptural sources. A Khmer translation is published by the Cambodia Development Resource Institute in Phnom Penh.

30. Yos Hut Khemacaro, "Steering the Middle Path," p. 73.

31. Maha Ghosananda, Yeshua Moser-Puangsuwan and Marissa Maure, "One Million Kilometres for Peace."

32. Heng Monychenda was a monk for seventeen years until 1997.

33. *Dhammayietra* literally means *dhamma* walk and is translated "pilgrimage of truth."

34. Kate G. Frieson, "The Cambodian Elections of 1993: A Case of Power to the People?" *The Politics of Elections in Southeast Asia,* ed. R. H. Taylor (Cambridge, UK, and New York: Cambridge University Press and Woodrow Wilson Center Press, 1996), pp. 224–251.

35. Chea Vannath, "The 1998 Cambodian Elections: Progress and Challenges," *National Elections: Cambodia's Experiences and Expectations,* ed. Kao Kim Hourn and Norbert von Hofmann (Phnom Penh: Cambodian Institute for Cooperation and Peace, 1998), pp. 30–35.

36. Thida Khus and Ouk Chettra, eds., *The Campaign to Reduce Violence for Peace during the 1998 Election Campaign: Summary Report* (Phnom Penh: Forum for Peace Through Love and Compassion and SILAKA, 1998).

37. Caroline Hughes, *Nature and Causes of Conflict Escalation in the 1998 National Election,* p. 55.

38. There are rumors that many monks involved in the demonstrations were imposters in robes, or were ordained just for the demonstrations. Although I did not investigate this point, I heard only supposition to support the idea, although some informants acknowledged the possibility. I spoke to several witnesses who saw, hid, or helped fleeing people known to be monks.

39. Michael Hayes, "The Legacy of Achar Hem Chieu," *Phnom Penh Post* 7(22) (October 2–15, 1998).

40. Yos Hut Khemacaro, "Steering the Middle Path," p. 76. Also see Chea Sotheacheath and James Eckardt, "Activist Monks Dare to Defy Authorities;" Pok Sokundara and Beth Moorthy, "Monks Walk a Tightrope between Peace

and Politics"; Laura McGrew, "Buddhism and Beatings," *Phnom Penh Post,* 7(22) (October 2–15, 1998); discussions with researchers and civil society leaders (Phnom Penh, May–June, 2000).

41. Special Representative of the United Nations Secretary-General for Human Rights in Cambodia, *Monitoring of Election-Related Intimidation and Violence, August 20–October 28, 1998* (Phnom Penh: Cambodia Office of the High Commission for Human Rights (COHCHR), 28 October 1998); COHCHR, *Killings and Other Instances of Violent Deaths Documented in and around Phnom Penh between 7 and 19 September 1998* (Phnom Penh: COHCHR, September 25, 1998).

42. Chea Sotheacheath and James Eckardt, "Activist Monks Dare to Defy Authorities."

43. Laura McGrew, "Buddhism and Beatings."

44. Yeshua Moser-Puangsuwan and Marissa Maure. "One Million Kilometres for Peace"; Liz Bernstein, "Buddhism and Conflict Resolution Seminar for Cambodians" (Phnom Penh: Unpublished paper, n.d. circa 1992).

45. Cambodian Christians, a tiny minority of about 40,000 including 15,000 Catholics, have few resources for peacebuilding. For history of Catholics and Protestants respectively see François Ponchaud, *Cathedral of the Rice Paddy: 450 Years of History of the Church in Cambodia,* trans. Nancy Pignarre, and Bishop Salas Cambodian Catholic Center (Paris: Le Sarment, Fayard, 1990) and Don Cormack, *Killing Fields Living Fields: An Unfinished Portrait of the Cambodian Church* (Crowborough, UK: Overseas Missionary Fellowship, 1997).

46. Don Cormack, *Killing Fields Living Fields,* p. 440; François Ponchaud, *The Cathedral of the Rice Paddy,* pp. 169–170; Nancy Smith-Hefner, "Ethnicity and the Force of Faith," pp. 24–38.

47. Phelim Kyne and Bou Saroeun, "Cambodians Who Turn from Buddha to Jesus," *Phnom Penh Post* 9:14 (July 7–20, 2000); Nancy Smith-Hefner, "Ethnicity and the Force of Faith: Christian Conversion among Khmer Refugees," *Anthropological Quarterly* 67:1 (1994): pp. 24–38.

48. UNTAC has been discussed extensively elsewhere. For diverse perspectives, see Steve Heder and Judy Ledgerwood, eds., *Propaganda, Politics, and Violence in Cambodia: Democratic Transition under United Nations Peacekeeping* (Armonk, NY, and London, UK: M.E. Sharpe, 1996); Caroline Hughes, *UNTAC in Cambodia: The Impact on Human Rights,* Occasional Paper No. 92 (Singapore: Institute of Southeast Asian Studies, 1996); Ben Kiernan, ed. *Genocide and Democracy in Cambodia : The Khmer Rouge, the United Nations and the International Community* (New Haven, CT: Yale University Southeast Asia Studies, 1993); Pierre P. Lizée, *Peace, Power and Resistance in Cambodia: Global Governance and the Failure of International Conflict Resolution* (Chippenham, UK: MacMillan Press Ltd, and New York: St. Martin's Press, 2000); Sorpong Peou, *Conflict Neutralization in the Cambodia War: From Battlefield*

to Ballot-box (Kuala Lumpur: Oxford University Press, 1997); Alexandra Tennant, AUNTAC's 'Top-Down' Approach: Insensitivity or Pragmatism?" *Safeguarding Peace: Cambodia's Constitutional Challenge*. Special Issue. *Accord 5* (1998), p. 53.

49. In February 2002, the UN pulled out of several years of stop-and-start talks with the Hun Sen government aimed at setting up a UN-approved tribunal to try Khmer Rouge leaders. The government has asked the UN to reconsider. See Puy Kea, "Cambodia Asks U.N. to Return to Talks on Khmer Rouge Trial" *Kyodo News* (July 5, 2002).

50. Conversation with Sorpong Peou, Phnom Penh, 21 May 2000.

51. William Collins, *Grassroots Civil Society in Cambodia*.

52. William Collins, *Dynamics of Dispute Resolution and Administration of Justice for Cambodian Villagers* (Phnom Penh: Center for Advanced Study, 1997).

53. For example, see William Collins, *Evaluation of the Impact of CIHR Training for Seila Participants in Principles of Management and Good Governance: A Report to UNDP/CARERE*. Draft Final Report (Phnom Penh: Center for Advanced Study) 1999, p. 94.

54. Shaun Williams, *Land Ownership Disputes in Cambodia: A Study of the Capacity of Five Provinces to Resolve Conflicts over Land* (Phnom Penh: OXFAM (GB), February, 2000).

11

History Unrequited

Religion as Provocateur and Peacemaker in the Bosnian Conflict

DOUGLAS M. JOHNSTON AND JONATHON EASTVOLD

For eighteen days in February 1984, a divided world set aside its rhetoric and took its differences to the ski slopes. The occasion was the XIV Winter Olympics, held in Sarajevo, Yugoslavia. Despite the death of Soviet president Yuri Andropov and the ongoing violence in Beirut, reporters remarked that "the scene in Sarajevo was a kind of Balkan Oz—sweet and surreal and dreamlike in its detachment from all other places and all other happenings on the rest of the planet."[1] Indeed, more than one observer remarked on the "powerful irony in the fact that Sarajevo, the hotbed of political intrigue that touched off World War I, should be so laid back when it came to the volatile events of 1984."[2] Optimism ran high. Even *U.S. News & World Report* commented that the games signaled "a brighter future for this grimy industrial city in the mountains of Yugoslavia" and forecasted that "when the Olympic torch will be extinguished, Sarajevo will be among the winners."[3] Given its strategic location between East and West, its leadership role in the Non-Aligned Movement,[4] and the way that it had apparently managed to suppress the deep ethnoreligious divisions afflicting the country,[5] Yugoslavia seemed poised for even greater success.

Seven years later, Sarajevo was the scene of the most harrowing European siege since Leningrad's 900–day ordeal during World War II. The comparisons to an Oz-like fairyland were abruptly supplanted by apt descriptions of wartorn Sarajevo as a "hell on earth."

ROOTS OF THE CONFLICT: FOUR INTERPRETATIONS

In the Bosnian conflict, religion was deemed so inconsequential—at least by the intellectual élite—that one commentator could quip that the three sides "are of the same race, speak the same language, and are distinguished only by their religion—in which none of them believe."[6] The ferocity of the conflict belies such a simplistic explanation, however.

Three possible explanations present themselves, each of which provides part of the story.[7] The first is that the outbreak of fighting in the 1990s was merely the latest chapter in a long history of an ethnic conflict that is too complex for outsiders to understand and too intractable to be resolved. Its logical conclusion is perhaps best expressed by a contributor to an Internet newsgroup: "Let them keep on killing each other and the problem will solve itself."[8] A second and related possibility maintains that the conflict is an inevitable fault-line conflict consistent with Samuel Huntington's "clash of civilizations." This notion is popular among belligerents on all sides, who tend to give the conflict a strongly religious dimension by portraying it, in the words of Croatian sociologist Srdjan Vrcan, as "centuries-long conflicts between essentially opposed human types, types of cultures and civilizations . . . [one of which is portrayed] as quasi-immaculate and as the side of the Good as such [and the other] in demonical or satanic terms as the incarnation of evil as such."[9] As Bosnian Serb nationalist Radovan Karadzic stated in a 1993 interview, "[the] West will be grateful to us some day because we decided to defend Christian values and culture."[10] A perhaps more balanced perspective is provided by Mitja Velakonja, a sociologist at the University of Ljubjana:

> In certain parts of the former federal state, the population was so integrated that their nationality was not distinguishable, and in such places former brothers became "eternal" enemies. By way of this Croats became "genocidal *Ustasha*," Bosnians are "Islamic *mujahedin*" fighting a "*jihad*," the Serbs are born *Chetniks,* and the Slovenes, Austria's stable-hands. . . . The principal community needs an enemy against which it can establish itself as the radical opposition and, by way of this, define its complementary imaginative mythical order. For the enemy to play its role effectively, it also has to assume some metaphysical dimensions.[11]

A third alternative emphasizes the long history of coexistence between religious and ethnic groups in cities like Sarajevo, and argues that the conflict was not inevitable but was rather fanned into flame by political opportunists like Slobodan Milosevic who, foreseeing Communism's demise, made a "compact with nationalism" as a means of staying in power.[12] This perspective is summarized well by Richard Holbrooke, architect of the Dayton Peace Accord: "Yugoslavia's tragedy was not foreordained. It was the product of bad, even criminal, political leaders who encouraged ethnic confrontation for personal political and financial gain. Rather than tackle the concrete problems of governance in the post-Tito era, they led their people into a war."[13]

Much of the apparent clash between these schools can be attributed to differences between those Serbs residing in urban centers such as Belgrade and those living in rural communities. As University of Washington political scientist Sabrina Petra Ramet argues in her article "Nationalism and the 'Idiocy' of the Countryside: The Case of Serbia," although the culturally and ethnically heterogeneous city is very often tolerant, cosmopolitan, and sophisticated, the countryside tends to be very loyal to "the way things have always been" and suspicious of "foreigners" (whether they are from the next village or the next continent). Rural dwellers thus tend to view the world in terms of the ongoing struggle to defend their pristine way of life against a hostile world. Indeed, as one observer notes, "the great divide within Yugoslav society was increasingly that between rural and urban communities, not that between peoples."[14] Due to the Communist era's deemphasis of ethnic and religious distinctions, it was much more common (and easier) for mixed marriages to occur in urban centers. As a result of this intermarriage, people's municipal identities became much more important to them than their national identity;[15] a Croat living in Sarajevo had more in common with her Muslim neighbor than her compatriots in rural Herzegovina.

This heterogeneity did not carry over to the rural population, however, notwithstanding ongoing attempts to address rural problems of illiteracy and cultural insularity. In Serbia, at least, much of the resurgent nationalism surfaced first in Kosovo, where Serbs in several rural enclaves still cherished bitterness against what they viewed as the Albanian 'usurpation' of their ancestral homeland. Between 1981 and 1987, political pressure and repeated protests by the Kosovar Serb peasantry provided the impetus for getting the Serbian government to adopt a harder line.[16] The coalition of Serb peasants, political opportunists, and nationalist-minded intellectuals[17] proved irresistible.

Ramet contends that Titoist Yugoslavia attempted to impose "the values of the city" on the primarily rural Serbian population. In the late

1980s, as the 'Yugoslav project' crumbled, Slobodan Milosevic rode the wave of Serbian nationalism to power as the countryside triumphed over the city.[18] In the 1990 Serbian election, for example, support for Milosevic's Socialist Party of Serbia (SPS) derived more of its support from the villages and small towns than the opposition parties, whose support was concentrated in Belgrade and other large cities.[19] Illustrative of the rural-urban cleavage was the refusal of many Serbs to side with their rural compatriots against their non-Serbian neighbors of many years during the early phases of the war in Bosnia-Herzegovina; those Serbs who defended their neighbors were often killed or interned along with them.[20]

To some extent, each of these perspectives has merit. The "primordial hatreds" view is generally espoused by those urban dwellers who focus their analysis on rural dwellers.[21] Travelogues such as Robert Kaplan's *Balkan Ghosts*—in which a Western journalist compiles interviews with rural populations embroiled in ethnoreligious rivalry—are a case in point.[22] Similarly, the "clash of civilizations" view is the generally preferred interpretation by the belligerents—mostly rural dwellers voicing rural concerns—who see the differences as intractable and the choice not one of war or peace but of winning or losing. Finally, there is the "paradise lost" view of the urban dwellers, based on the unique history of inclusiveness of such cities as Sarajevo.[23] Each school of thought accurately describes one aspect of the conflict. Taken together, the short-sightedness of external parties acting from only one of these perspectives becomes clear (see Table 11.1).

Perhaps this analytical complexity is best addressed by adopting a composite approach that takes into account the strengths and weaknesses of each of these perspectives: one can acknowledge the existence and importance of the beliefs and claims made by the rural nationalists without recognizing their legitimacy. To the extent that these beliefs influence the behavior of a major faction, they are a factor. Whether or not they are legitimate or even true has little bearing on whether they need to be taken into account. Although historical arguments can be mustered to refute such a perspective, the fact that people treat it as true precludes its dismissal by a "better informed" elite. Regardless of its validity, adherents to a religious-nationalist vision of history will regard it as factual and behave accordingly. As Serbian author Darko Tanasković argues (specifically with respect to interpretations of a book by Alija Izetbegović, the president of Bosnia-Herzegovina [hereafter BiH]),

> Even if by some chance the Serbs and Croats were mistaken when they understood the *Islamic Declaration* as a threatening manifest of

Islamic fundamentalism, their hermeneutic principles should have been taken into account. Politically and later militarily, they behaved in accordance with their own, rather than Western convictions, and this fact proved to be decisive in determining the course of events and deterioration of circumstances in Bosnia-Herzegovina.[24]

Against this backdrop, the drama unfolded that ultimately destroyed the mosaic known as Yugoslavia. Although it is difficult within the confines of a single chapter to do justice to even one aspect of the Bosnian ordeal in this broader context, an attempt will nevertheless be made to treat the Serbian dimension, with secondary mention of other groups as needed.

HISTORY OF THE CONFLICT

The First Yugoslavia: Kingdom of the Serbs, Croats, and Slovenes

Following World War I, the breakup of the Ottoman and Austro-Hungarian empires led to the creation of the Kingdom of Yugoslavia (also known as the "Kingdom of the Serbs, Croats, and Slovenes"), which lasted until it was conquered by Germany in World War II. In large part, this united kingdom was a marriage of convenience among the different ethnic groups. For Croats, joining in a federation with the previously independent Serbs seemed like an ideal way to avoid being devoured by Italian expansionism along the Adriatic Coast. (As evidenced by the later Italian moves on Albania and Greece during the early years of World War II, this was no frivolous worry.) Serbia, on the other hand, had been an independent country before 1914, and was principally interested in bringing all Serbs together under the political roof of a "Greater Serbia."[25] This desire to incorporate all areas with large numbers of Serbs outside of Serbia into a single country in which Serbs composed a majority of the population was the principal motive both for their initial support of a union of South Slavs and for their opposition to its breakup decades later. The guiding vision of this multiethnic kingdom was that of "a harmonious [and equal] community of fraternal nations: compatriots and relatives"; similarity, not sameness, was the goal.[26]

The Second Yugoslavia: Titoist Communism

After World War II, the Communist guerrillas who formed the backbone of the Yugoslav resistance took power under Josip Broz, better known

TABLE 11.1
Typology of Major Perspectives

Characteristic	Primordialist	Clash of Civilizations	Constructivist	Self-Critical Constructivist
Focus	Rural dwellers: hopelessly locked into a cycle of 'ancient hatreds'	Rural dwellers: defenders of the essential aspects of their civilization	Urban dwellers: 'decent people' whose peaceful coexistence is shattered by external forces	Both rural and urban dwellers are relevant actors. Conflict is fueled by rural dwellers, much to the dismay of mostly tolerant urban dwellers.
Point of view	Urban dwellers	Rural dwellers	Urban dwellers	Both rural and urban. Rural perspective should be taken into account, but not adopted uncritically
View of history	Harmful and unescapable	Beneficial to understanding of real differences	Harmful if focused on, but can be escaped	Beneficial to understanding of real differences, but is not necessarily binding
Nature of tradition	Unchanging	Unchanging	Malleable	Malleable

(continued on next page)

TABLE 11.1 (*continued*)

Characteristic	Primordialist	Clash of Civilizations	Constructivist	Self-Critical Constructivist
Depth of conflict	Deep: rooted in age-long hatreds stemming from major differences	Deep: conflict between fundamentally conflicting civilizations	Shallow: recently provoked by demagogues through media manipulation	Deeply held concerns recently revived and distorted by demagogues.
Possibility of peaceful coexistence?	No: differences are irreconcilable	Yes: "détente" is possible if differences respected	Yes: differences can be transcended (and possibly eliminated)	Yes, provided that differences are respected and not disregarded.
Policy implications for the West	Stay out and let the Balkan peoples fight it out	Respect civilizational differences: use civilizational ties to restrain belligerents (Huntington) or take sides with civilizational partners (belligerents)	Intervene to stop the conflict and foster conditions for democratic and economic reform	Take ethnoreligious concerns seriously, and attempt to expose the current distortions of those concerns; to achieve a lasting peace, the belligerents must perceive that such a settlement is more in line with their heritage than continued war

Source: Adapted from Jonathan C. Eastvold, "'A Heavenly Kingdom and Not an Earthly Kingdom': A Religio-Historical Reinterpretation of the Yugoslav Conflict," Senior Honors Thesis, Wheaton College, May 1999.

as Marshal Tito. Like Marx, Tito viewed religion and culture as vestiges of backward institutions designed to ameliorate the masses. Given the power of the ethnoreligious violence that had been unleashed during the war, the Communists recognized that they could not immediately extirpate these older loyalties. They instead adopted a two-pronged strategy to reduce the political salience of these distinctions. First, they created a federal system that gave weight to each republic's concerns in order to avoid hegemony by any particular group. Second, they built an elite consensus around materialist and Marxist values in hopes that this consensus would trickle down to the upwardly mobile provincial masses.[27] As one historian notes, the religious and nationalist "mythologies" were replaced by the new mythology of the "national liberation struggle" against the Axis powers, which simultaneously united most Yugoslavs (with the possible exception of Croats) and gave the ruling party a modicum of moral legitimacy.[28] To this end, Tito launched a withering attack on the Serbian Orthodox Church (*Srpska Pravoslavna Crkva,* hereafter SPC), imprisoning many of its most dedicated priests. Moreover, the ethnoreligious violence that had been unleashed during the war led a significant number of Yugoslavs to reject religious belief and practice in reaction.[29] These two phenomena left the SPC scrambling for options. Some years later, when Tito judged that his repression of the SPC had run its course, he offered it a modicum of official patronage. Confronted with plummeting church attendance, dramatic shortages of funds, and the depletion of its clergy through retirement and imprisonment, the SPC had little choice but to accept this offer on Tito's terms.

THE FALL OF YUGOSLAVIA

The confederal system created by Tito's 1974 constitution, which required unanimity on the part of all republics in all decisions, enabled the rest of the country to defy the will of the Serbs. In the 1980s, as discrimination against Serbs by Albanians in Kosovo increasingly concerned the Serbian leadership (both ecclesial and political) and no real administrative solution was apparent, the stage was set for a charismatic figure to champion the Serbian nationalists' cause. These measures disturbed the Croats and motivated them to more aggressively pursue the opportunity presented by Communism's fall to reassert a more authentically Croatian identity. Fearing Serbian domination, they began to push for greater autonomy, with an eye toward total independence at some point in the future. This, in turn, caused the Serbian minority in Croatia's *Krajina* region to fear for their rights. The Croatian move to allow only street signs in the Roman alphabet (as contrasted with the rest of Yugoslavia, which used both the Roman and the Cyrillic alphabets)[30] raised fears that Croatia was determined to blot out any Serbian influence. Croatia's later adoption of the checkerboard symbol (the symbol of the hated *ustasha* that massacred innumerable Serbs during World War II) as its national emblem terrified Serbs, for many of whom the memory of the war was still painfully fresh.

In Bosnia, Serb reactions to the stirrings of Kosovar Albanian irredentism led Bosnian Muslims to express solidarity with their co-religionists. This, in turn, was used to corroborate the Serbian nationalist claim that the Serbs were threatened by a pan-Islamic conspiracy.[31] Similarly, the much higher birthrate among Muslims gave the nationalists a pretext to allege that when the Muslims gained a majority of the population they would establish a Muslim state. Bosnian president Alija Izetbegović's reassurances that BiH could not be turned into a Muslim state because there was not a Muslim majority thus gave rise to fears that the prospect of "some kind of Islamic, Muslim state . . . is not rejected but simply postponed."[32] In short, political leaders preyed on the lurking fears of their constituencies to galvanize support for their political aims. Inasmuch as these aims were mutually exclusive (i.e., Croatia could not be both an independent state and part of a Serb-controlled Yugoslavia, and the Bosnian Serbs could not be under Serbian rule if Bosnia retained its integrity as a separate republic), any peaceful resolution was rendered exceedingly difficult. Political leaders like Milosevic attempted to garner support for themselves by provoking their constituencies to action against their enemies. Like the sorcerer's apprentice, however, the power of that provocation was greater than what they had bargained for, and the bluff of forceful action soon metamorphosed into a credible threat that they had to follow up. In addition, unlike the normal instruments of state power that can be applied and removed in a Clausewitzian fashion, public sentiment once aroused is averse to compromise. One does not negotiate with eternal enemies. As Dean Pruitt and Jeffrey Rubin observe in *Social Conflict: Escalation, Stalemate, and Settlement*, "escalated conflict often weakens a community's capacity to deal effectively with further conflict."[33] The gods of war, once summoned, do not depart empty-handed.

WHY THE BREAKUP OCCURRED

Broadly put, Yugoslavia dissolved into ethnoreligious war because the normal give-and-take of the political process was stalemated by a federal system that required unanimity among the republics on major issues. The incompatible political aims of each ethnicity's elites were therefore dealt with outside the established channels; and, in the political equivalent of tipping a pinball machine, each side rallied grassroots support for its agenda by preying on the deepest fears of its constituencies, spreading propaganda and distorted news coverage. The fragile bonds of interethnic trust that had been painstakingly constructed during Tito's regime were easily shattered by the venom of the state-run presses. Once people believed that the other ethnoreligious groups were conspiring to exterminate them, they saw no choice but to resort to violence to protect themselves, their families, and their nation.

RELIGION'S ROLE IN THE CONFLICT

The question at hand is what role religious actors played (positively or negatively) in the development and course of the conflict, as well as what role religious actors might play in resolving it. Even if religion was not a root cause of the conflict, as this chapter argues, its implications for the issues of ultimate reality that influence people's identities and behavior are significant and need to be addressed. By ignoring generally religious issues, the West overlooked one of the major elements of this conflict, not only inhibiting a correct diagnosis but also overlooking (if not spurning) the assistance of possible allies within the religious traditions in question.

Specifically, the West's focus on economic incentives is of only partial utility. Economic incentives may be decisive considerations for policymaking and economic elites, but a populace (once it is successfully mobilized on ethnoreligious grounds) is less likely to be swayed by such calculations. Given the elite appeal of such incentives, therefore, applying them to a country like Milosevic's Serbia is problematic: those to whom the strategy is most specifically targeted are precisely the ones who are using religious nationalism as a tool to stay in power and thus, since they have a vested interest in not discouraging ethnoreligious mobilization, will likely be the most difficult to persuade. The rank and file, on the other hand, have little to gain and much to lose by continued warfare, and are therefore likely to be much more receptive to peaceful solutions. Since their support of the extremists is in large part grounded in ethnoreligious rhetoric, however, they may view backing down from religious imperatives in response to strictly political and economic incentives as "selling out" for material gain.

Faced with such a situation, a Western policy maker has a choice between targeting societal elites (by ensuring, through promises of aid and threats of coercion, that cooperation with the West will be more beneficial to them personally than what they could have by defying the West) or targeting the elites' support base (by providing assurances of their security and working through existing mediating institutions to appeal to their nobler side).

Even when the religiocultural factor is only rhetorical, it becomes an important factor to the extent that it is taken seriously by the "rank and file." An understanding of the *realpolitik* factors motivating a country's elites is important, but it in no way obviates the need to know what is going on at the grassroots level. Although religion's role at the level of the elites was for the most part superficial, at the level of the masses it was taken quite seriously. [34]

CULPABILITY OF RELIGIOUS LEADERS

The recent war in Yugoslavia was not a religious war in the normal sense of the term. Religion was clearly invoked as a rhetorical tool by all sides, but (with the possible exception of Bosnian Muslim leader Alija Izetbegovic and Bosnian Serb leader Radovan Karadzic) its role was strictly a means to a political end, not an end in itself. As Warren Zimmermann, the last U.S. ambassador to Yugoslavia, points out,

> The major proponents of destructive nationalism weren't driven by religious faith. Franjo Tudjman had been a communist most of his life; he converted to Catholicism when he turned to nationalist activities. Milosevic, a lifelong communist, never, as far as I know, entered a Serbian Orthodox church except for blatant political activities. I recall a visit he made for electoral reasons to a Serbian monastery on Mt. Athos in northern Greece. Not even the official photographs could disguise the disconcerted and uncomfortable look on his face. [35]

While it can be conceded that religion was not a central factor in the conflict, the argument that whatever role it did play was solely negative in nature is open to question. The inquiry thus moves from causation to culpability; were religious leaders culpable both in what they did and what they did not do?

Before one can understand the present state of church-state relations in the former Yugoslavia, it is necessary to examine the intimate relationship between religion and the state in the Balkans across the centuries. [36] Especially difficult to understand is the concept of "ethnoreligious" identity in which ethnic and religious traits co-mingle as one. As religion scholar Paul Mojzes defines the issue,

> [The conflicts in Yugoslavia] have distinct ethnoreligious characteristics because ethnicity and religion have become so enmeshed that they cannot be separated. . . . The fusion or overlapping of ethnicity and religion is a well-known phenomenon in much of Eastern Europe, especially in the Balkans. For centuries the church was the people and the people were the church. . . . [In 1989,] the coalescence of ethnic and religious identification returned with such a vengeance that it is mandatory to use the single word "ethnoreligious."[37]

A brief survey of Balkan history will help illuminate this point.

BYZANTIUM AND THE "SYMPHONY" OF CHURCH-STATE RELATIONS

The people of the Balkans (and especially the Serbs) inherited the collaborative relationship between church and state established by the Byzantine empire. The two were essentially intertwined in an almost "symphonic" relationship, working toward the same goal of achieving "a good harmony conferring whatever is useful for the human race."[38] As Justinian, perhaps the most famous Byzantine emperor, noted in his *Corpus Iuris Civilis,*

> The greatest gifts given by God to men from His heavenly clemency are the priesthood and the imperium—the former ministering to divine things, but the latter presiding over and exhibiting diligence for human things. Proceeding from one and the same source, the priesthood and the imperium equip human life. Therefore nothing will be so keen for emperors as priests' dignity, since priests pray to God for emperors themselves.[39]

In practice, however, *raisons d'état* frequently trumped priestly dignity, and it was quite clear who conducted the symphony of church and state. As Justinian noted in a rather detailed piece of ecclesiastical legislation regulating matters such as liturgy and the appointment of bishops,

> God, through His good will towards men, has entrusted Us, how much more reason is there not for Us to compel the observance of the sacred canons, and Divine Laws, which have been promulgated for the safety of Our souls? . . . We notify all ecclesiastics that if they should violate any of these provisions, they must render an account of their conduct on the terrible judgment Day of Our Lord and Saviour Jesus Christ; and that We, when informed of these matters, shall not disregard them, and leave them unpunished.[40]

As the Church increasingly became a subsidiary of the state, the precedent of using religion to "baptize" a ruler's secular political aims was firmly established, and separating religious and political affairs (i.e., disassociating one's religion from one's nation or state) became increasingly difficult.

THE OTTOMAN EMPIRE AND THE *MILLET* SYSTEM

After the sacking of Constantinople by the Ottoman Turks, religion became the senior partner in this partnership. Rather than attempting to homogenize their ethnically and religiously diverse empire, the Ottomans developed an elaborate system for managing religious and cultural diversity. Under this *millet* system, the central functions of the state (security, foreign policy, etc.) were carried out by the Ottoman bureaucracy, while each cultural community was given significant autonomy in governing its own internal affairs. To simplify matters, administrative control of each *millet* was assigned to that community's religious leaders. Throughout the centuries of Turkish occupation, the religious communities thus became the primary vehicle for the preservation and transmission of culture and national identity. Even into the twentieth century, there has been a strong link between nationality and religion (although Titoist Yugoslavia weakened these ties to a considerable degree). In the census of 1953, the last official survey that took religion into account, the correlation between national and religious identity was almost perfect. In Bosnia-Herzegovina, for example, 99.5 percent of Orthodox believers also considered themselves to be Serbs and 98.1 percent of Catholics considered themselves to be Croats. In the distinctly ethnic republics, this pattern also held true. In Serbia 95.2 percent of the Orthodox considered themselves also to be Serbs, and 94.6 of Catholics in Croatia were also Croats.[41]

The experience of Norwegian anthropologist Tone Bringa sheds light on the *millet* system's legacy:

> At the beginning of my stay in rural central Bosnia, when I was not known to people there, I was often asked, "What *nacija* [nation] are you?" . . . The answer which made sense was not Norwegian, but Protestant. It was only when people asked additional questions to clarify [that] . . . related to characteristics of the known Bosnian *nacije* of Muslim, Catholic, or Orthodox. . . . [A] religious identity is also a social and cultural identity and in the Bosnian context has an ethnic context, since a person usually "inherits" his or her religious identity from his or her parents.[42]

ROMANTIC ERA: THE RISE OF SERBIAN NATIONALISM

Within the Balkans, conflict between the Serbs and Slavic Muslims dates from the fourteenth and fifteenth centuries (about the time that the Slavic Muslims converted from Christianity[43] and assumed rulership over the Serbs and Croats). The elaborate mythology associated with the battle of Kosovo (1389)[44] was not actually constructed, however, until the Serb revolt against Ottoman occupation. Indeed, contemporary Serbian nationalism finds its roots in the Romantic period, during which Western Europe's intelligentsia reacted to the rationalist internationalism of the preceding Age of Reason by affirming the legitimacy and primacy of national identity. Interestingly, the Slavic non-Muslims'[45] struggle for independence from the Ottoman Empire during this era was a cause célèbre among Europe's Romantic poets and artists. Once again, the sacred was enlisted in support of the nation's secular aims.

Much of this construction was carried out by Serbian poet (and forefather of Radovan Karadzic) Vuk Karadzic (1787–1864), who compiled Serbian folk literature into four volumes that became "the canonical source and voice of the 'national spirit.'" As the religion scholar Michael Sells recounts,

> As Vuk Karadzic carried out the canonization of the folk epic, selecting those poems that were to be identified with the Serb nation as a whole, Serb revolutionaries were moving Serbia toward independence. . . . The Kosovo legends became part of the Serbian revolutionary movement and those parts of the tradition especially meaningful for such a movement were preserved and emphasized.[46]

In 1847, Montenegrin Prince-Bishop Petar II Petrović, Njegoš, published the still-popular "Mountain Wreath," a verse cycle that commemorates the *Istraga Poturica* ("the extermination of the Turkifiers"), a Christmas-eve massacre of Slavic Muslims by the Serbs in the late eighteenth century. This glorification of religious violence, when it was combined with the contrived parallels between Prince Lazar's death and the crucifixion of Jesus (complete with Slavic Muslims assuming Judas Iscariot's role as betrayer) that were also being formulated in the mid-nineteenth century, laid the foundation for a very significant distortion of truth that Serb nationalists gradually came to accept as truth itself. Significantly, this clearly delineated conflict between "the children of light and the children of darkness" never occurred. After the conquest of the Serbs by the Turks, Serbs (led by Serbian nobility) fought alongside Turks in support of the Turkish incursion into Europe.[47]

ETHNORELIGIOUS FACTORS

Following Tito's rapprochement with the Church, a "clerical-political underground" began to take root among many of the younger Orthodox clergy who sought to increase the Church's influence in the political realm. In the early 1980s, these clergy began calling attention to the plight of Serbs in Kosovo, who were experiencing discrimination at the hands of an increasingly restive Albanian majority, which itself was beginning to clash with the federal authorities over issues of autonomy. The Serbian Orthodox Church, which had a large number of monasteries, churches, and other religious sites throughout Kosovo, was caught between the federal authority and the Albanians. Its appeal to alleviate the Serbian plight did little to sooth these tensions, however: "It is no exaggeration to say that planned GENOCIDE [emphasis in original] is being perpetrated against the Serbian people in Kosovo!"[48] The charge of genocide found its way into the general Serbian discourse on Kosovo, and only encouraged the nationalist Serbs in Kosovo to redouble their efforts to legitimate these concerns.

As nationalist forces began to rise in prominence, these clergy saw an opportunity to advance their goals by aligning with a member of the nomenklatura-turned-nationalist like Slobodan Milosevic, who, in turn, needed a religious sanction to buttress his political nationalism. Although the younger clergy and Milosevic did not completely trust one another, more accommodating and generous state policies toward the SPC easily secured their support for his actions.[49] Furthermore, the nationalist ideology addressed the religious and cultural issues that were explicitly ignored by the Communists, suggesting that even if the nationalists were not perfect they were better than what had gone before. In addition, Milosevic claimed to share the SPC's concern about the plight of the Serbs in non-Serbian areas, thus appealing directly to its traditional pastoral role as preserver of the Serbian nation throughout the long centuries of Turkish and Communist occupation.[50]

"FALL FROM GRACE"

At the same time, this marriage of convenience between the SPC and Milosevic did not alter the fact that many priests were deeply opposed to his socialist orientation and actually felt they had much more in common with the Bosnian Serbs, who, despite their glaring faults, were non-Communist and explicitly pro-Orthodox.[51] As early as May 1992, the SPC leadership called for Milosevic's resignation, attacking his "godless" regime for, among other offenses, "closing their eyes to crimes" committed by Serbian paramilitary groups in Bosnia.[52] The tensions were heightened in 1994 when Milosevic vetoed an SPC-sponsored bill to strengthen restrictions on abortion.[53] When Milosevic began to act in accordance with his own political interests at the expense of his stated loyalty to the Serb diaspora, he dispelled any remaining illusions the SPC may have had that he was a necessary evil in defending the Serbian people. From 1996 to 2000, increasingly large segments of the SPC opposed Milosevic either openly or implicitly.

THE ISLAMIC DIMENSION

If any faction in the war could be said to be "victimized," it was the Muslims of Bosnia-Herzegovina. As the ethnic group that most identified with the appellation of "Yugoslav" and one of its most secular groups, it had perhaps the most at stake in the second Yugoslavia. Further, it was militarily least prepared for a civil war, sandwiched between heavily armed Serbia-Montenegro and separatist Croatia. To suggest that Islamic leaders were culpable in mobilizing the nationalist fervor of their constituencies is to exaggerate the truth. At the same time, the ethnic Muslims unwittingly exacerbated the situation in two significant ways. First, they failed to sidestep the public relations traps set for them by their opponents' propaganda machines, thus playing into the hands of those who were intent on starting a war. Even innocent actions were often portrayed as outright aggression by the nationalist presses. As the weakest party, discretion would have dictated toning down any expressions of national identity that, while innocuous on the face of it, could be read as aggressive when viewed through the existing prisms of suspicion. Their defensive actions against Serbian nationalists were, in turn, used by their enemies to corroborate unfounded accusations of an Islamist conspiracy against the Serbs.

Second, Muslims understandably reacted to their opponents' religious nationalism by assuming a much more aggressive Islamist posture, possibly jeopardizing future peace in the process. The Serbian nationalist tendency to invoke religion in support of its war aims essentially backfired. Rather than curbing whatever Islamist threat was posed by a mostly secularized, nominally Muslim population, the religious rhetoric provoked a reaction from throughout the Muslim world. Fresh from dealing the now-defunct Soviet Union a humiliating defeat in Afghanistan, scores of foreign mujahideen flooded into Bosnia, their noses attuned to the scent of Muslim-Christian bloodshed. Within

Bosnia, moreover, religion-based violence radicalized the nominal Muslims. The reaction of the Muslims at the rank-and-file level is typified by this statement from a young Bosnian Muslim soldier:

> I never thought of myself as a Muslim. I don't know how to pray, I never went to mosque, I'm European, like you. I do not want the Arab world to help us, I want Europe to help us. But now, I do have to think about myself as a Muslim, not in a religious way, but as a member of a people. Now we are faced with obliteration, I have to understand what it is about me and my people they wish to obliterate.[54]

The combination of religious hostility against them and apparent indifference from the West led many Bosnian Muslims to seek refuge among their fellow Muslims and—more significantly—to adopt a more orthodox adherence to Islamic faith and practice. A good example of this phenomenon was the adoption of Islamic law by the elite Bosnian unit known as the Black Swans, involving, among other practices, two hours of daily religious instruction by Islamic chaplains.[55] The efforts by some Muslim clerics in Bosnia to pass laws implementing Islamic cultural prohibitions on issues ranging from mixed marriages to the consumption of pork and alcohol to the playing of traditional "Serbian" music on the radio illustrate the extent to which the war served to radicalize the Muslim population.[56] The multiethnic foundations of the Bosnian Federation (the Muslim and Croatian part of BiH) were profoundly shaken by fears of an increasing tendency toward hard-line Islam. In February 1995, the five non-Muslim members of the seven-member Bosnian presidency publicly decried the "ideologization and the negative instrumentalization of religion" by Bosnian Muslims, as specifically demonstrated by the Islamic trappings and battle cries of the 3000-strong Seventh Muslim Brigade.[57]

RELIGION'S ROLE IN PEACEMAKING

Beyond statements signed by the leaders of the three prominent faith traditions calling for an end to the conflict and a cessation of ethnic cleansing, religion's role in ending the hostilities was negligible at best. In Bosnia, as in so many other wars of communal identity, religion was effectively co-opted by the forces of nationalism and used both as a mobilizing vehicle and a badge of identity.

In a 1999 interview with Radio Free Europe, Hieromonk Sava from Decani Monastery in Kosovo described the efforts that the SPC was taking toward peace. He provided three explanations for these efforts' failure in swaying the Serbian people toward a more peaceful outlook. First, Milosevic's control of the media (and the public sphere as a whole) inhibited the spread of the SPC's message and prolonged the extremists' dominance; in fact, Sava argued, SPC statements expressing critical attitudes toward the Milosevic regime were often misquoted by official media sources so that they sounded like uncritical endorsements. Second, the lack of centralization within the SPC made it difficult for the central leadership to crack down on SPC clergy acting inappropriately. Third, the SPC was so weakened by Communist rule and post-Communist manipulation that it was often unable to mount an effective challenge to Milosevic's agenda.[58] Many nationalists "celebrate the Serbianness of their Church but reject the anti-war posture of the Church hierarchy."[59] As James Cairns, the Sarajevo project director for the World Conference on Religion and Peace notes, the peripheral role of religious leaders in starting the conflict severely limits their influence in stopping it.[60]

This explanation does not square, however, with the commonly cited SPC condemnation of Milosevic's agreement to the Dayton Accords; at Dayton, the agreement that was signed significantly undercut the interests of the Bosnian Serbs, who had (in a deal overseen by the Serbian Orthodox patriarch himself) given Milosevic the authority to negotiate on their behalf. While there is some truth to the assertion that this condemnation means that elements within the SPC were even more nationalistic than what was officially sanctioned from Belgrade, much of this apparent collaboration comes from a genuine and open-eyed pastoral concern. As the Holy Synod of the SPC stated on 5 November 1994, "[We] do not consider ourselves identical with the governments on either side of the Drina River but we cannot separate ourselves from our, although sinful, nevertheless still a People of God in the ecumenical family of peoples, but stay with them on the cross upon which they are crucified."[61] In view of the deep and legitimate Serbian concerns about Islamic rule in Bosnia and Kosovo, the SPC gave conditional support to the Serbian political leadership—not because it wholly agreed with it, but rather out of pastoral concern for the Serbian people. While there can be little doubt that the outcome of this decision played into the nationalists' hands, the fact that SPC support began to fade as the truth became more apparent suggests that their motives were not as inappropriate as has been alleged. Subsequent to the Dayton Accords, a sustained effort was mounted by the World Conference on Religion and Peace to bring Bosnia's religious leaders together in formulating and adhering to a common moral agenda. With valuable assistance from others, including Mercy Corps International, the U.S. Institute of Peace, and the U.S. Ambassador to Austria, a Statement of Shared Moral Commitment was consummated and a secretariat established to assist in implementing its provisions.

The faith-based cooperation that has subsequently taken place between the four religious communities (Catholic, Orthodox, Islamic, and Jewish) has highlighted the important role of interreligious dialogue as an ingredient in post-conflict reconciliation. For its practical, collaborative prospects on a number of fronts (e.g., sponsoring dialogue among local clerics in BiH municipalities and pressing for legal reforms relating to religious property, assembly, and expression) and its symbolic role as one of the country's strongest and most autonomous interethnic institutions, the council has received widespread acclaim.

That said, the council is currently struggling with a broad range of highly complex issues, including (1) the reconstruction of religious monuments in ethnically cleansed cities, (2) the return of clerical leaders of demographic minorities to their homes and places of worship, (3) inadequate revenues to provide needed social services, (4) inadequate protection of basic religious freedoms at the local level, and (5) the restitution of expropriated and nationalized property. The challenges are never-ending, but so too has been the commitment of the council in meeting them.

Another effort, among many, that deserves mention is an initiative of the Washington-based Center for Strategic and International Studies, which for more than four years has been conducting conflict resolution training workshops for religious clergy and laity from the involved faith traditions in Bosnia, Croatia, and Serbia. Although these workshops began while the conflict was still raging, they were undertaken without any expectation that they would have any effect on the then-existing hostilities. Rather, they were initiated to plant the seeds for longer term reconciliation (out of a conviction that no military or diplomatic solution could ever break the cycle of revenge). The underlying premise was that unless a spiritual component can be introduced into international politics that gets to the heart of forgiveness and reconciliation, history will be doomed to an endless repetition of returning violence for violence.

The workshops have been conducted at three levels, with the first level dedicated to helping participants overcome their sense of victimhood (both individually and collectively), the second to conveying the skills of peacemaking, and the third to building community across republic lines and addressing the systemic problems within each republic's social system that contribute to ethnic animosity. By next year—barring the unforeseen—the project will achieve its immediate goal of establishing an indigenous, religious-based peacemaking capability firmly anchored in an NGO in each of the three republics.

In looking ahead even further, it is important to recognize that moves by the West to bring all the religious factions together to smooth over their differences, as a prerequisite to restoring multiethnic harmony, are unlikely to succeed. While there are certainly a number of commonalities between these religions on questions of social ethics, the frequent Western contention that their differences are insignificant ignores reality and will in all probability produce counterproductive results.[62] As is commonly noted, religious and ethnopolitical identity in the Balkans are intimately linked to the extent that religious conversion is viewed as both religious apostasy and political treason. Consequently, any interreligious effort that treats religious differences as insignificant is likely to be regarded as politically suspect and will retain its credibility only among those who are already predisposed to interreligious cooperation. Rather than exhorting religious people to stop fighting because their differences do *not* matter, it will be far more productive to work within each tradition to show that peace is necessary precisely because their beliefs *do* matter. Muslims, Catholics, and Orthodox alike should be counseled to pick up the gauntlet laid down by the Koranic admonition to the "people of the book" that they "compete with each other in good works" (Sura 5:48). By the same token, the validity of the Christian message is not demonstrated by victory on the battlefield but by its expression of supernatural love: "Love your enemies and do good to those who do you harm" (Matthew 5:44).

In practical terms, it is inherently more fruitful to work toward peace within, rather than across, religious traditions. Particularly in a conflict in which religion is a major theme, an embattled religious group seems more likely to be receptive to its own co-religionists than outsiders; this is especially the case if their foreign brethren *tangibly* demonstrate solidarity with them even as they continue to call (and work) for peace. Such a display would help to break the false equation of religion with nationality and remind the belligerents of the need to think in transnational terms.

LESSONS LEARNED

A number of helpful insights can be drawn from the Yugoslav conflict. First, religious considerations were not the only, or even the most important, factors in the conflict. But the fact that former Communist elites, despite their previously observed contempt for all things religious, still bothered to stoke the fires of religious nationalism demonstrates that religion was enough of a motivator at the grassroots level to merit their condescension. In light of this, the international community should not let this issue slip from view.

Second, efforts to bring religious communities together must include a focus at the grassroots level. At the same time that rural nationalism engendered a deep loyalty to traditional religious values, it also created a distrust of religious establishments. As political scientist Sabrina Petra Ramet points out, in Serbia "nationalists celebrate the Serbianness of their Church but reject the anti-war posture of the Church hierarchy."[63] For any religion-based solution to have a lasting impact, it must be convincing to the average layperson.

Third, in societies where no normative consensus transcends ethnoreligious lines, other ethnoreligious groups frequently come to be characterized by their "otherness" rather than their common humanity. In the resulting zero-sum game, a costly victory is often seen to be preferable to a bloodless and mutually beneficial compromise. As two experts on the Balkans have noted, "the breakdown of a community presupposes that for at least some of the members there is no longer any basis for normative consensus or any joint frameworks worth maintaining. Rejection of common goals, procedures, or rules of conduct has been a very part of the process of dissolution in the Yugoslav case."[64] In such a situation, strict adherence to procedural democracy is a mistake, since any inkling of the common good will fade into the ether under the onslaught of a tyrannically disposed (and virtually omnipotent) majority. It is the fear of this eventuality that continually drives ethnoreligious minorities to seek their own states. As Vladimir Gligorov, the son of contemporary Macedonia's first president, sardonically observed, "Why should I be a minority in your state when you can be a minority in mine?"[65] In such a case, equality of representation ("one person, one vote") must frequently be sacrificed to keep the political process from becoming, in the words of Plato's Thrasymachus, merely a legitimation for "the will of the stronger." While significant work has already been done on consociational political arrangements as a means of channeling communal conflict, much more needs to be done to design solutions that are more in keeping with a given group's ethnic and religious sensibilities.[66]

Fourth, with the exception of the nationalist intelligentsia and their political counterparts, who could be said to have a vested interest in conflict and "ethnic cleansing" almost for its own sake, one gets the definite impression that most of the people on each side are driven by fear, not hatred or aggression. This is reflected in the fact that many of the unquestionably aggressive actions took on the quality of preemptive strikes (e.g., if early action was not taken to address a threat, worse things would have happened to oneself).

Fifth, not all religious leaders bought into the religious-nationalist synthesis. Of those who did, moreover, the dominant majority did so because they were forced to choose between two inappropriate options: either standing by as the people they were charged to shepherd were exterminated or becoming an unwitting accessory to genocide. Regardless of their respective miscalculations or moral shortcomings, most religious leaders were on the side of peace and justice—and, while they will quarrel about the precise meaning of those terms, most of them will ground their definitions in a right ordering of one's love for God and for one's neighbor. Given the international community's difficulty in keeping ethnoreligiously motivated "rogue states" under control, it should not compound its problem by driving its natural allies into the arms of the demagogues who find it strategically efficacious to portray themselves as the only defenders of the religious leaders' flocks.[67] Rather than writing religious leaders off as a part of the problem, it is both possible and necessary to empower them to become an integral part of the solution through the following avenues of assistance.

1. Information. In the highly polarized atmosphere created by the breakup of Yugoslavia, each republic's government-controlled media produced its own version of the truth. The accounts varied so radically that it caused one to wonder whether or not they were referring to the same conflict. As U.S. Catholic Conference analyst Gerard Powers notes,

> The ubiquitous war propaganda spewed out by government-controlled media in each country and sometimes unsubstantiated allegations by international organizations and human rights groups led religious leaders, like many others in these countries, to disbelieve accusations of atrocities and to give their own governments the benefit of the doubt.[68]

It should thus come as no surprise that the Serbian Orthodox hierarchy would place more stock in the Serbian government's media than in that of Bosnia or Croatia. As a result, it was easy for the state-controlled media to feed them precisely whatever was needed to keep them docile.

Providing balanced information to religious leaders in such settings could profoundly enhance their resistance to ethnoreligious demagoguery. Given the natural distrust for foreign sources that a highly polarized environment produces, broadcasts from the Voice of America or other official channels are probably of limited utility. Existing relationships of trust between religious leaders in a rogue state and their counterparts in the diaspora can sometimes provide a more trustworthy conduit for accurate reporting.

2. *Confidence-building.* Once religious leaders begin to hear—through channels they trust—about the atrocities committed by their own side, a tension is created between their visceral loyalties to blood and soil and their allegiance to a higher law. In an ideal world, they would take their new information at face value and reject what they have heard from their state-controlled media. In reality, however, it is difficult to wholly accept information (even from a reliable source) that directly contradicts what everyone else in their society believes and is telling them. This is particularly the case if the actions of the international community at the time are insensitive to the religious imperatives of the nationality in question.

A dramatic case in point was the recent NATO decision to bomb Serbia on Orthodox Easter. One could have arguably bombed twice as much the day before and/or the day after, but it was a decision the Serbs will never forget.[69] In immediate terms, it gave added credibility to the Milosevic regime's pretense of waging a religious war against the forces of Islam and its anti-Christian advocates in NATO. As Russian Orthodox Patriarch Alexei II maintained shortly before the Easter bombings, if NATO bombed on Easter it would demonstrate that "they are not Christians; they are barbarians."[70] Further exacerbating the situation was President Clinton's earlier determination not to attack Iraq during Ramadan because such an action would be "profoundly offensive to the Muslim world."[71]

To convince clergy who have a pastoral concern for those of a particular nationality that one means their flock no harm, it is essential that one remain sensitive to their religious and cultural underpinnings. Neglect of these factors can result—as it did in this case—in the international community inadvertently playing into the nationalist propaganda.

To neutralize the demagogues' ability to manipulate religion to inappropriate purposes, the international community must do all it can to address the legitimate concerns voiced by religious leaders. To do otherwise is to force those who would otherwise be natural allies to make the difficult choice between siding with extreme nationalists for the sake of their people or siding with the enemies of their people for the sake of theological purity. By the same token, appeals to religious leaders should never be couched in terms of moral and religious equalizing (i.e., "all religions are just different roads up the same mountain"). As Powers observes, "The best way to counter religious extremism or manipulation of religion is with strengthened, more authentic religion, not weakened religion."[72]

It is also the case that *using* religion instrumentally as a means of achieving peace rather than encouraging people to work for peace as a natural outgrowth of their religious convictions is as problematic in the long run as the religious appeals made by a demagogue. Such a misappropriation causes the advocate of peace to lose the moral high ground by ignoring his or her legitimate claim to be representing a less distorted orthopraxy than that being proclaimed in the streets by political figures. In the absence of such a truth claim, it is highly unlikely that a counter-intuitive foreign interpretation will win out over an indigenous interpretation which speaks to an ethnic population fearing for its safety—nor should it.

CONCLUSION

For a religion-based peace initiative to bear long-term fruit, it must come from the religious leaders (whether clergy or laity) within the religious tradition in question, and it must be genuine. This is a difficult concept for Western policy makers who are accustomed to applying whatever carrots or sticks may be needed to convince other political actors to do what they want. In dealing with religious leaders, however, the needs are different. On the one hand, the carrots in a policy maker's toolbox, which are mostly economic in nature, are not legitimate incentives for religious leaders; on the other, threatening the use of sticks to convince a religious leader to change his or her teaching is simply inappropriate and infringes on religious freedom.

At the same time, it is increasingly apparent that religion and politics cannot be completely isolated from one another. Some interchange between the two is therefore both necessary and appropriate. When, as is inevitable, disagreement arises between Western policy makers and indigenous religious leaders, it is essential to recall that when the state gets involved in religious affairs it should be the junior partner (as the church should be to the state in explicitly political affairs). Such an arrangement only makes sense when one realizes that the state is intervening in areas that are much more familiar and more important to an indigenous religious leader than to a foreign diplomat.[73] In a setting as delicate and as context-laden as the religious aspects of a mobilized ethnoreligious group, apparently minor errors can lead to disaster; such a minefield is better navigated by a shepherd caring for his (or her) flock than by a faceless Weberian bureaucrat.

Among other factors, enlisting the cooperation of religious leaders requires a resort to a higher truth, for example, through appealing to the same behavioral norms called for in their sacred texts. An example of this could involve making available to these leaders credible information about atrocities committed by their "flock" and seeking to stimulate theological reflection about the implications of that information. Such a process should be characterized by deference, not condescension; exhortation, not coercion; and dialogue, not intimidation.

There are undoubtedly other lessons that can be drawn from the Bosnian experience. Determining what they might be, however, could pose a significant challenge in light of the multifaceted nuances and complexities. An even greater challenge, though, is that of assimilating the more apparent lessons previously listed in ways that can help prevent future conflict. Meeting this latter challenge will likely require an effective coupling of astute diplomacy with the transcendental potential of religious reconciliation. Anything less, in all probability, will only lead to an endless continuation of the cycle of revenge.

NOTES

1. William Oscar Johnson, "They're off to a Flying Start," *Sports Illustrated* 60.8 (20 February 1984), p. 16.

2. Ibid.

3. Stewart Powell, "Winter Olympics' Real Winner is Sarajevo," *U.S. News & World Report* (13 February 1984), p. 35.

4. Warren Zimmermann, *Origins of a Catastrophe* (New York: Times Books, 1996), p. 4.

5. Indeed, a 1985 survey conducted found that only 17 percent of Bosnians characterized themselves as religious believers (Zimmermann, p. 210).

6. P. J. O'Rourke as quoted in Peter Berger, "Secularism in Retreat," *National Interest* 46 (Winter 1996–1997), pp. 11–12.

7. For a more developed version of the discussion to follow, see Jonathan C. Eastvold, "'A Heavenly Kingdom and Not an Earthly Kingdom: A Religio-Historical Reinterpretation of the Yugoslav Conflict," unpublished senior thesis, Wheaton College, Spring 1999.

8. Quoted in Michael Sells, *The Bridge Betrayed: Religion and Genocide in Bosnia* (Berkeley: University of California Press, 1996), p. 142.

9. Srdjan Vrcan, "Religion and Churches and the Post-Yugoslav War," *Religion and Nationalism*, ed. J. Coleman and M. Tomka (Maryknoll, NY: Orbis Books, 1995), p. 65. Quoted in Gerard Powers, "Religion, Conflict and Prospects for Reconciliation in Bosnia, Croatia, and Yugoslavia," *Journal of International Affairs* 50.1 (Summer 1996), pp. 221–252.

10. Radovan Karadzic, personal interview. In *Pogledi,* 12 November 1993, in *FBIS-EEU-93–228,* 30 November 1993, p. 41. Quoted in Norman Cigar,

Genocide in Bosnia: The Policy of "Ethnic Cleansing" in Eastern Europe (College Station: Texas A&M University Press, 1995), p. 101.

11. Mitja Velikonja, "Liberation Mythology: The Role of Mythology in Fanning War in the Balkans," in Paul Mojzes, ed., *Religion and the War in Bosnia* (Atlanta: Scholars Press, 1998), p. 38.

12. Zimmermann, p. 25.

13. Richard Holbrooke, *To End a War* (New York: Random House, 1998), p. 24.

14. Christopher Bennett, *Yugoslavia's Bloody Collapse: Causes, Course, and Consequences* (New York: New York University, 1995), p. 63.

15. Bennett, p. 63.

16. Ramet, "Nationalism," p. 77.

17. Cf. Serbian Academy of Arts and Sciences and the Writer's Union. As Ramet reports, many Serbian intellectuals "[longed] for a return to village life as the only authentic life." *Vreme* (1 March 1993), trans. In Foreign Broadcast Information Service, *Daily Report* (Eastern Europe), 24 March 1993: p. 57. Quoted in Ramet, "Nationalism," p. 77.

18. Sabrina Petra Ramet, "Nationalism and the Idiocy of the Countryside: The Case of Serbia," *Ethnic and Racial Studies* 19:1 (January 1996), p. 71.

19. Lenard Cohen, *Broken Bonds: The Disintegration of Yugoslavia* (Boulder: Westview Press, 1993), pp. 156–157.

20. Sells, p. 73.

21. Eastvold, p. 29.

22. See Robert Kaplan, *Balkan Ghosts: A Journey Through History* (New York: St. Martin's Press, 1993) and Dame Rebecca West, *Black Lamb and Grey Falcon: A Journey Through Yugoslavia* (New York: The Viking Press, 1941).

23. Sarajevo is one of the few places in Europe over the past 800 years where Jews have never been evicted.

24. Darko Tanasković, "Why Is Islamic Radicalization in the Balkans Being Covered Up?" *Eurobalkans* 15 (Summer 1994), p. 35. Quoted in Cohen, p. 60.

25. Pešić and Mostov, p. 38.

26. Velikonja, p. 33.

27. Francine Friedman, "The Bosnian Muslim National Question," in Paul Mojzes, ed., *Religion and the War in Bosnia* (Atlanta: Scholars Press, 1998), p. 2.

28. Lev Kreft, *Estetika in Poslanstvo* [Esthetics and Mission] (Ljubljana: Znanstveno in publicisticno sredisce, 1994), pp. 144–146.

29. Cohen, p. 49. See also Esad Ćimić, *Socijalističko društvo I religija* (Sarajevo: "Svjetlost," 1966), pp. 167–169.

30. Orthodox Serbia, with its connections to Russia, uses the Cyrillic alphabet; Catholic Croatia and Slovenia, on the other hand, use the Roman alphabet employed throughout Western and Central Europe.

31. Cohen, p. 59.

32. Esad Ćimić, "Okrugli stol-'Što je vjerski rat," in Ivan Grubišć, ed., *Konfesije i rat*, p. 294.

33. Dean G. Pruitt and Jeffrey Z. Rubin, *Social Conflict: Escalation, Stalemate, and Settlement* (New York: Random House, 1986), p. 94.

34. As Misha Glenny recounts his conversation with a Serb policeman outside Sarajevo,

> He was not a man of evil. On the contrary, he explained how he found it very difficult to shoot at the other side of his village, because he knew everybody who lived there. But the war had somehow arrived and he had to defend his home. The man was confused and upset by the events, but he now perceived the [Muslim] Green Berets and the [Croat] Ustashas to be a real threat to his family.
> "We cannot let them form an Islamic state here," he said with genuine passion. "Are you sure they want to?" I asked him. "Of course they want to. I don't understand why you people outside don't realize that we are fighting for Europe against a foreign religion."

Misha Glenny, *The Fall of Yugoslavia: The Third Balkan War* (London: Penguin, 1992), p. 170.

35. Zimmermann, p. 210.

36. In light of the complexity of the issues, this chapter will focus on religion's role in Serbian nationalism, with incidental attention to other ethnoreligious groups as they help to illuminate the major focus.

37. Paul Mojzes, *Yugoslavian Inferno* (New York: Continuum, 1994), pp. 125–127.

38. Justinian, *Novella* 6 Praefatio. *Corpus iuris civilis* 3.35–36, ed. Theodor Mommsen, Paul Krüger, Rudolf Schoell, and Wilhelm Kroll. 3 vols. (Berlin: Repr. Hildesheim, 1993). Quoted in Lester Field, Jr., *Liberty, Dominion, and the Two Swords: On the Origins of Western Political Theology (180–398)* (Notre Dame: University of Notre Dame Press, 1998), p. 255.

39. Ibid.

40. Justinian, Novella, CXXXVII, translated by S. P. Scott in *The Civil Law* (Cincinnati, Ohio: 1932), Vol. XVII, pp. 152–156. Reprinted in Leon Bernard and Theodore B. Hodges, eds., *Readings in European History* (New York: Macmillan, 1958), pp. 57–58. http://www.fordham.edu/halsall/source/justinian-nov137.html.

41. *Popis stanovnistva 1953, Knjiga I, vitalna I etni?a obele^zja* (Belgrade: Savezni zavod za statistiku, 1959), pp. 278–279. Cited in. Cohen, pp. 45–46.

42. Tone Bringa, *Being Muslim the Bosnian Way: Identity, Religion [?], and Community in a Central Bosnian Village* (Princeton: Princeton University Press, 1995), p. 21.

43. The original religious affiliation of the Slavic Muslims is a question of considerable political delicacy. According to the Serbs, the Muslims were originally Orthodox Serbs; according to the Croats, they were originally Catholic Croats; in addition, they have been identified with the Bogumils, adherents to an offshoot of Christianity denounced as a heresy by both East and West.

44. In the wake of the war between NATO and Serbia over Kosovo, the story has been retold enough that it does not need to be repeated here. For further information see Tim Judah, *The Serbs: History, Myth, and the Destruction of Yugoslavia* (New Haven: Yale University Press, 1997), esp. pp. 29–47.

45. At that time, Western Europeans characterized as "Greeks" all of the Christian peoples of the Balkans.

46. Sells 38.

47. In fact, cavalry under the command of Stephen Lazarevich, a son of Prince Lazar, was instrumental in helping the Turks defeat a crusader army commanded by King Sigismund of Hungary. Rather than self-sacrificially contributing to the defense of "Christian Europe," Serbs actively assisted the aggressors. While, given the political realities of life under Ottoman occupation, this is not necessarily a stain on the character of the Serbian nation, it does deal a decisive blow to Serbian nationalists' laments of unappreciated martyrdom.

48. "Appeal by the Clergy" in Gordana Filipović, *Kosovo: Past and Present* (Belgrade: Review of International Affairs, 1989), pp. 355–360. Quoted in Michael Sells, "Serbian Religious Nationalism, Christoslavism, and the Genocide in Bosnia, 1992–1995," in Paul Mojzes, ed., *Religion and the War in Bosnia* (Atlanta: Scholars Press, 1998), pp. 201–202.

49. Cohen, p. 56.

50. Ibid.

51. Cohen, pp. 71–72.

52. Cohen, p. 71.

53. Paul Hockenos, "Church Is among Few Allies of Bosnian Serbs," *National Catholic Reporter* 31.32 (16 June 1995), p. 11.

54. Ed Vulliamy, *Seasons in Hell: Understanding Bosnia's War* (New York: St. Martin's Press, 1994), p. 65.

55. Cohen, p. 69.

56. Cohen, p. 70.

57. Foreign Broadcast Information Service-Eastern Europe-95-032 (16 February 1995), pp. 29–30.

58. Hiermonk Sava, "There is place for all in Kosovo but we depend on extremists" [Radio Free Europe interview] (http://www.rferl.org/bd/ss/iview/jersava.html), 9 December 1998.

59. Ramet "Nationalism," pp. 78–79.

60. James L. Cairns, "Interrupted Dialogue," *The Christian Century* (21–28 April 1999), p. 440.

61. Sveti arhijerejski sabor SPC [Holy Synod of the SOC], *Politika* (5 November 1994).

62. One example of this approach is provided by Marko Oršolić in his description of the Sarajevo-based "International Center for Promoting Interreligious Dialogue, Justice, and Peace, 'Zayedno' [Together]," which brings religious leaders from the main traditions together to explicitly "counter the religious separation of people based on an erroneous notion of God, who undoubtedly in Judaism, Christianity (Orthodox, Catholic, and Protestant) and Islam is one and the same" (263). To this end, he calls for the use of "an objective contextual hermeneutics which is more important than the continuous affirmations of religious hierarchies about things that belong to the essence of all religions" (264). Marko Oršolić, "Multireligious and Intercultural Center 'Zayedno,'" in Paul Mojzes, ed., *Religion and the War in Bosnia* (Atlanta: Scholars Press, 1998).

63. Ramet, pp. 78–79.

64. Pešć and Mostov, p. 39.

65. Quoted in Zimmermann, p. 212.

66. For examples of existing work, see Kenneth McRae, ed., *Consociational Democracy: Political Accommodation in Segmented Societies* (Toronto: McClelland and Stewart, 1974) or Arend Lijphart, *Democracy in Plural Societies: A Comparative Perspective* (New Haven: Yale University Press, 1977).

67. Cf. S. J. Tambiah, "Ethnic Conflict in the World Today," *American Ethnologist* 16:2, p. 343. Cited in Larry A. Dunn, "The Roles of Religion in Conflicts in the Former Yugoslavia," http://cis.georgefox.edu/ree/html_articles/DUNN.YUG.html.

68. Gerard F. Powers, "Religion, Conflict, and Prospects for Peace in Bosnia, Croatia, and Yugoslavia," in Mojzes, *Religion and the War in Bosnia*, p. 240.

69. As the day on which Christ's victory over death is celebrated, Easter is considered by Orthodox Serbs to be the climax of the Church year.

70. Greg Gaut, "NATO Was Blind to Religion's Role in Balkans," *National Catholic Reporter* 35.33 (2 July 1999), p. 20.

71. William Jefferson Clinton, "Address to the Nation," 16 December 1998. http://www.pub.whitehouse.gov/uri-res/I2R?urn:pdi://oma.eop.gov.us/1998/12/16/12.text.2.

72. Powers, p. 245.

73. In this regard, although it was intended for domestic application—specifically relating to the constitutionality of state-sponsored salary increases for teachers in nonpublic schools—the tripartite test set forth by the Supreme Court in *Lemon v. Kurtzman* in 1971 provides useful guidance for religious monitoring overseas:

1. A policy or action must have a secular purpose as its primary motivation.

2. "Its principal or primary effect must be one that neither advances nor inhibits religion."

3. It must not "foster 'an excessive . . . entanglement with religion'" on the part of the U.S. government.

In cases when it looks questionable as to whether such a test can be met, consideration should be given to handling the situation through the influential NGO sector rather than the traditional "track one" channels.

12

Truth and Reconciliation

The South Africa Case

H. RUSSEL BOTMAN

One of the recent developments in peacebuilding and conflict resolution is the introduction of the phenomenon of "reconciliation," prompted primarily by the nature of ethnoreligious conflict. Such conflicts occur between enemies living geographically close to each other, and they are no longer simply a matter of the "guts and blood" of professional soldiers. Millions are displaced and orphaned. Ethnoreligious encounters are frequently based in issues of identity, often manifested in terms of stereotypes, fear, hatred, and more often expressed as conflicts of irreconcilable causes or interests.

Diplomacy and large-scale peacekeeping are no longer enough. The quest for reconciliation has become an indispensable part of peacebuilding. Commissions for Reconciliation have recently mushroomed all over the globe and more specifically in Latin America[1] and Africa. Among the countries that have resorted to reconciliation are the following: Chile (1978), Brazil (1979), Uruguay (1986), Argentina (1983, 1986, 1987, 1989), Guatemala (1986), Honduras (1987), El Salvador (1987, 1983), Peru (1995), and now also South Africa. The Truth and Reconciliation Commission of South Africa has captured the attention of peacebuilders and scholars in many places.[2]

This chapter critically examines the role of religion in the apartheid conflict and in the subsequent reconciliation process in South Africa. Subsequently, I examine particular conceptual questions related to the peacebuilding capacity of reconciliation. I then discuss specific implications of the South African case study for peacebuilding.

RELIGIOUS AND POLITICAL ROOTS OF APARTHEID

The truth and reconciliation process is rooted in the deep-seated conflicts of South Africa's apartheid history.[3] This history has both religious and political aspects.

Richard Elphick points out that some of the most intimate matters of white and black culture, politics, and sociality have been debated at length and with passion in religious communities.[4] These debates were conducted largely in Christian terms. The issues of integration and segregation were first debated in churches and, more specifically, in the white Dutch Reformed Church before they actually emerged in political institutions. The celebration of communion, a sacred ritual in Christianity where celebrants share bread and wine in a symbolic form of table communion, was instrumental in establishing the conflict. The sacraments, specifically communion, formed part of the inner core of white ethnic identity over and against other identities. While whites were allowed in communion, Khoisan converts (converts from the first peoples of South Africa) were not included in communion until the nineteenth century. Allowing Khoisan people to communion led to the beginning of formal church apartheid in the Dutch Reformed Church (DRC) in the nineteenth century.

In 1831, a DRC congregation was founded among the Khoi-Khoi people near Grahamstown. White people, who have moved into the area, were invited by the Khoi-Khoi people to join the church. Very soon, some white congregants petitioned the local church council asking for the separate celebration of Holy Communion. The matter was referred to the supervisory body, the Synod of the Dutch Reformed Church. The Synod of 1857 addressed this issue and formally adopted the following resolution:

> The Synod considers it desirable and according to the Holy Scripture that our heathen members be accepted and initiated into our congregations wherever it is possible; but where this measure, as a result of the weakness of some, would stand in the way of promoting the work of Christ among the heathen people, then congregations set up among the heathen or still to be set up, should enjoy their Christian privileges in a separate building or institution.[5]

With this decision the DRC first affirms the desirable way of unity expressed in the Bible. Indeed, they seem to say, according to the bible, the unity of races in one religious institution was more in line with the Christian scriptures. However, this position would no longer serve as the ultimate orientation of the Dutch Reformed Church because of the "weaknesses of some." The reference to the "weakness of some" refers to the racism of the white members who have petitioned Synod. The word "heathen" refers to people of color.

The apartheid policy of separate development was essentially forged in the DRC's mission policy (1935). However, the historical roots of the mission policy go back to the nineteenth century. The missionary policy environment within DRC circles emerged in the growing conflict of the South African Missionary Association (established in 1799) with the DRC. A contentious issue was the place of Christians from the indigenous population within the church. Discussion in the synods of 1824, 1826, 1829, 1834, and 1837 focused significantly on the question of missions and the institutional place of indigenous Christians.

It is my proposition that these embryonic missionary discourses came to a head at the ninth synod of the DRC, where the famous desirability choice was made in 1857. Although the formal missionary policy of the DRC came into being in 1935, the resolution of 1857 established the institutional framework and the official pattern by which the social features of racial separation and the policy of separate development would unfold in the church. It is generally accepted that the white Dutch Reformed Church (DRC) played a very formative role in the making of apartheid.[6] Therefore, the official mouthpiece of the DRC could proclaim proudly in 1948: "As a church, we have always worked purposefully for the separation of the races."[7]

The National Party also won the election in 1948 and soon established the political framework of the apartheid regime. Since then the DRC was sometimes stereotyped as the National Party in prayer. However, the historical evidence and the nature of political lobbying indicates that the National Party was much rather the DRC in power. In 1950, the apartheid regime introduced the Group Areas Act whereby people could live, go to school, and be buried only in geographical areas designated for the racial group of their legal classification. The DRC actively lobbied government for these and other oppressive legislation. Controls were established to monitor the movement of black people, manipulate their education, restrict their access to work and opportunities, alienate them from their land, and prohibit marriages across the color line. The most important measure of control was the "pass laws" whereby black people received an identity-book. This book had to be signed by every employer and every individual providing them with accommodation in an area not designated for their race classification.

People were classified in racial groups promulgated by law. Such racial classification would determine one's political and economic opportunities. It also determined one's mortality rate since access to social security and welfare were selectively allocated according to racial categories.

The repression increased during the 1960s. On 2 March 1960, a group of people marched in Sharpeville to pile up and burn their passes. The police opened fire and created the horrifying event known as the Sharpeville massacre. The Truth and Reconciliation Commission would later be established with 1 March 1960 as its first day for investigation. In 1976, the student uprising erupted as the first students were shot in Soweto. The resistance intensified as the repression became more brutal.

In 1980, the United Democratic Front was launched. This front united religious organizations, civic bodies, nongovernmental, and political organizations in their anti-apartheid activism. This was also the time in which religious leaders such as Allan Boesak and Desmond Tutu became household names in many parts of the world. Religious organizations such as the South African Council of Churches, the Call of Islam, and individual leaders of the Jewish community in Cape Town played prominent roles in the United Democratic Front. The front became the united "voice of the voiceless." Facing this measure of political and religious activity as well as international diplomatic pressure, the United Nations declared apartheid a crime against humanity on 13 December 1984.

P. W. Botha, then president of the apartheid regime, responded with the decree of the first state of emergency in 1985. In terms of the act, any person in state uniform could arrest anybody and imprison him or her for 14 days without charge or trial if they had reason to believe that such a person was a threat to the state. They were not required to reveal their reasons, allowing a situation in which many arrests could take place on the basis of "belief" rather than "reason." The human dignity and human rights of people were trampled on under the state of emergency.

F. W. de Klerk, the last president of the apartheid regime, was eventually obliged by the economic and political conditions in the country to release Nelson Mandela from a lifelong sentence in 1990. This opened the way for a negotiated settlement as the country faced vast economic and military weaknesses.

RELIGION AND RECONCILIATION

South Africa is by far an example of a place where religious themes mark the oppression of and conflict related to apartheid. Apartheid was started first as a religious phenomenon and initially institutionalized in the church. Some perpetrators referred to the fact that they have tortured people believing that the revolutionary forces represented a threat, not only to the state, but also their religion. They were simply protecting their faith against the atheists and communists. They have acted in obedience to a government that claimed to rule the country in the "name of almighty God," meaning the Christian God.

Dr. Wolfram Kistner was among the first in South Africa to raise the question regarding the role of faith communities in relation to perpetrators in the apartheid history:

> The society and the religious or ideological community or cultural group which has contributed towards shaping the mind of the offender shares in the responsibility of the offence and is in need of repentance on its part and forgiveness on the part of God and the victims with the view to facilitating a process of healing and taking precautions against a repetition of the offence.[8]

The religious community, among others, have contributed toward shaping the mind of the offender. The "church hearings" held by the Truth and Reconciliation Commission (TRC) were in a sense also meant to help the religious communities see their own complicity in the gross human rights violations of the apartheid era. At these hearings many churches made submissions regarding their own culpability.

Although violators must indeed be held politically and individually responsible for their dastardly acts, the faith communities that formed the perpetrators' mind must also come to terms with the reality of their part in the offenses. Kistner correctly suggests that the religious community and their institutions must take responsibility for their part in fostering ethnoreligious conflicts.

How did the DRC relate to the TRC? Except for the brief statement of Rev. Freek Swanepoel, then moderator of the DRC, at the church hearings of the TRC, the church has not gone any further with the process of truth-telling than the content of "The Story of the Dutch Reformed Church's journey with Apartheid, 1960–1994." This statement of "confession and witness" begins with the event of the Cottesloe meeting of the World Council of Churches. The church has rejected the Cottesloe resolutions in light of its criticism of apartheid. In its statement the DRC acknowledges "past mistakes" (1.1.1), that apartheid was "church policy" (2.4.5), that the church "pushed hard" to get the National Party regime to enact laws against mixed marriages (2.5.1), to establish group areas (2.5.2), Bantu education (2.5.3), and that the DRC received secret funding from the apartheid government for propaganda purposes (4.6). The DRC even acknowledges that it has provided a theological and biblical justification for apartheid in the 1974 "Race, Peoples and Nations in the Light of Scripture."[9]

Since 1986, the statement further emphasizes, the church has been moving away from the vestiges of apartheid. It then regarded the biblical justification of apartheid as an error to be rejected. The journey with apartheid is, therefore, the statement maintains, a matter of the past.[10]

THE JUSTICE CONNECTION IN RECONCILIATION

One of the most burning questions in reconciliation processes is the nature and place of justice. Difficult debates ensue about the primacy of justice for the true resolution of past conflicts. However, the central question in reconciliation is not whether justice must be done, but how. This crucial question leads to four main proposals: justice as revenge, justice as retribution, justice as redistribution, and justice as restoration.

First is the idea of justice as revenge. Individuals or organizations may feel that the legal and political system of a society has been eroded or are not adequately representative to deliver justice to the victims or those who were dependent on them. Then people take the course of justice into their own hands. Street courts and other ways of dealing with justice in society arise. Examples of such actions were reported in Rwanda and the former Yugoslavia. The revenge option can condemn a society to a deadly spiral of retaliation.

Second, there is the option to handle justice in the form of the predominantly Western legal system. Where the criminal justice system is regarded, historically and socially, as the most adequate instrument to deliver justice to society, the option of retribution is enacted. The Western criminal justice systems are viewed as fairly advanced forms of dealing with justice in democratic societies; they are seen as instruments that strengthen human rights in society and promote the rule of law. Germany's Nuremberg option is an example of this form of justice. Perpetrators are charged for offenses before a court of law in which psychologists, religious leaders, and other social service professionals have a meager role to play in the decision-making process. This option depends on the existing criminal justice system in each country.

The criminal justice system focuses on guilt and blame and seeks criminal motive, incriminating evidence, an objective measure of truth, witnesses of broadly defined integrity, and, preferably, a confession by the perpetrator. South Africans who argued strongly for retributive justice include the family of Steve Biko, the activist and leader killed by apartheid agents while in police custody. Willa Boesak argues for justice as retribution in his book *God's Wrathful Children* (1995). He finds religious justification in the idea that the Christian scriptures claim that "Vengeance belongs to God" (Rom. 12:19) and that God appoints civil authorities as rightful administrator of punishment to the evildoer (Rom. 13:14).[11] The focus on crime in retributive justice tends to become an industry[12] and depends on the very issue that sometimes leads to torture, namely, interrogations that extract a confession. It further separates justice from social healing in a way that tends to marginalize victims and their continued suffering. The offender and the crime take central stage, while the victim and the pain dissolve in the notion that the state takes the case as its own against the offender.

The third option, distributive justice, calls on government to take a primary legislative position not only in the criminal justice system, but also in the civil justice system. In the civil justice system victims or their representatives become part of the process after retribution has been achieved and compensation can be sought. Distributive justice seeks legislation to redistribute the wealth of a nation to include the victims of its ethnoreligious conflict that goes beyond the ordinary social security responsibility of the state. The focus is placed on the material loss of the victims or their immediate descendants. Instead of the term "victims," people then prefer the designation "survivor." The latter moves the debate beyond the need for aid to the claim for redistribution. The benefits that resulted from the conflict should be redistributed justly to include recognition of the resultant disadvantage suffered by the survivor. Two theologians, Tinyiko Maluleke and Molefe Tsele, argued strongly for distributive justice. Molefe Tsele points to a direct connection between reconciliation and the biblical notion of the jubilee (Leviticus 25:9–10).[13] The process should not end with reconciliation, but should also return survivors to a better social and economic status and thus restore their human dignity. Maluleke criticizes the reparations proposals of the TRC. The proposal calls largely for symbolic and community-based reparations. The symbols want to remember victims and the other reparations focus on rebuilding local communities after the atrocities. Maluleke accuses the TRC of "dealing lightly with the wounds of my people."[14] The focal point of reconciliation is the survivor and not the nation or community structures.

Restorative justice is the most critical form of justice in the structuring of reconciliation processes. Restorative justice returns the voice of the victim, whether alive or dead, from the periphery to the center. When the victim is alive, the person's own voice is heard. When the victim is deceased, the voice is represented by family. The crime was not directed at the state, as legal procedure often argues. The crime was personal, familial, and relational. It connects the perpetrator and the victim eternally. Lawyers do not replace the perpetrator or the survivor, although they may have such representatives as advisors. The survivor receives every right to question the perpetrator, over and against normal legal procedures. The perpetrator, similarly, can confess to the truth without fearing the aggressive legalese of lawyers representing the survivor. Restorative justice is a meeting of human beings who are hurt, degraded, and angry but willing to reach out to an element of mercy and grace in the human spirit. Dialogue, memory, and embrace form the rituals of restorative justice. It takes its point of departure in the assumption that healing of memory, restoration of human dignity, and the reconstruction of devastated communities are achievable in post-conflict situations. It assumes that embrace is more beneficial to society than any form of exclusion of people based on grounds of racial, gender, ethnic, religious, class, or cultural entities. While other forms of justice base themselves on evaluations of the past, restorative justice is orientated to the future. The question is not "how combatants *have* lived" but "how the next generation *is going to* live." This future orientation calls on predecessors of future generations to accept the humiliation of dealing with the past in order to leave a conciliatory heritage to their children. Restorative justice is based on the dual meaning of the word *remember*. On the one hand, it means to remember cognitively, to call to mind or recall events of the past. It is thus directly related to memory and to the symbolism of memorials. On the other hand, it means incorporating, remembering, returning to membership, and restoring community. Both meanings are captured and expressed in restorative justice. Restorative justice is thus community seeking. Although the notion of restorative justice is not captured in Western legal systems, its has undisputed origins in the cultures of Africans, the Maori, and the first peoples of North America[15] where notions of community have always been more important than mere individualism.

Restorative justice relates directly to the biblical understanding of reconciliation. Christianity has always been concerned about memory, confession, guilt, and forgiveness in the interest of reconciliation. These themes have been constituted through the Christian tradition as public events and rituals.[16] In the same way, national processes of reconciliation express the public nature and political meaning of these Christian themes. Restorative justice focuses on the two meanings of freedom, namely, *freedom from* and *freedom for*. It invites people into a certain memory of the past that also frees them from it. Simultaneously, it frees people *for* the future, for each other, and for God. Restorative justice is, therefore, embedded in the Christian narrative, memory, and identity.

Restorative justice includes the need for confession but removes it, as in Christianity, from the realm of retributive justice, placing it in the context of a common search for reconciliation.

Restorative justice does not call for cheap reconciliation. It does not fly in the face of a victim's pain and continued suffering, ignoring the dehumanization caused by conflicts. In Christianity a distinction is drawn between *cheap* and *costly* grace. Therefore, concrete reparation and restitution are not excluded. The perpetrator has a responsibility in this regard and so does the state.

Restorative justice belongs to the ambit of negotiated settlements. It therefore takes on a political rather than a mere religious meaning. Parties in conflict may get to a point where their research and common sense show that the continuing destruction of infrastructure and life outweighs the opportunities and benefits of continuing the struggles. They then may decide on the adoption of "a sunset clause" in which the parties accept the principle that none of them will leave the conflict as the only winner. In the "sunset clause" they simply agree to let the sun set on the conflict and engage each other in negotiation for a settlement. Reconciliation becomes thus a public political reality.

THE SPECTER OF AMNESTY

Two additional questions normally arises during the negotiation of political settlements:

1. Shall the *truth* be told about the conflict, the political motivations, and the human rights abuses?
2. Should perpetrators and their officers be *sanctioned?*

Negotiated settlements have thus been plagued by the issue of amnesty. The word "amnesty," which has often been connected to reconciliation, evolved from the root *amnesia,* a medical term meaning "loss of memory" or "forgetting." However, in the negotiation phase of post-apartheid South Africa, amnesty was elevated to a constitutional principle. The negotiators included amnesty as a principle in the transitional constitution of the country. The principles established in the transitional constitution became binding on the nature and form by which the constituent assembly could draft the proposed constitution for the country in the structural reform phase.

The inclusion of the amnesty clause in the reconciliation process of South Africa caused an almost unnatural cohabitation of retributive justice with restorative justice. However, the amnesty clause was adopted on the basis that society should be willing to redeem a perpetrator who willingly incriminates him- or herself. Second, since evidence may be destroyed, the testimony of perpetrators is crucial to establishing the truth. Amnesty was given where the truth was fully disclosed. The act must have been of a political nature, as opposed to a criminal act and must have occurred between 1 March 1960 and 5 December 1993. The amnesty committee followed firm judicial procedures and was thus modeled on court hearings. The amnesty committee consisted of lawyers. They applied their minds to the following issues:

- The motive of the person who committed the act.
- The context in which the act was committed, whether it was part of a political uprising or disturbance.
- The legal and factual nature of the act, including its gravity.
- The object against whom the act was directed and the objective of the act.
- Whether the act was carried out by order or approval of a political body, institution, or individual.
- The relationship between the act, the political objective, and the proportionality of the abuse.

Ironically, the amnesty process enacted by the Promotion of National Unity and Reconciliation Act of South Africa did not require contrition on the part of the perpetrator. A person could state that they would repeat the acts under the same circumstances and still receive amnesty.

THE RISK OF IMPUNITY

The war in Bosnia-Herzegovina, the genocide in Rwanda, and the poststructural quest in Chile illustrate the dramatic consequences of impunity. The Bosnian-Serb leaders openly defy arrest and trial. The international tribunal of the United Nation's Security Council in Arusha was crippled by lack of resources and uncertainty of purpose that create the conditions for impunity in Rwanda.

Impunity is the means by which people accused of human rights abuses and crimes against humanity escape arrest, trial, and official sanction. Impunity can be achieved through amnesty laws passed or decreed by governments to provide for blanket amnesty. The perpetrator walks away without having made any disclosure of the atrocities. It can result from presidential pardons given to convicted perpetrators. Impunity can also occur by default through omission or silence. Impunity occurs, therefore, when governments lack the political will, sufficient power to impose the rule of law, or sufficient pressure from society.

The legalization of impunity or the omission of sanction after a conflict is an obstacle to national unity and reconciliation.[17]

PROBLEMS WITH THE RECONCILIATION PROCESS

The idea of reconciliation should be approached with great caution and a fair measure of hermeneutical suspicion. Within the North American context, the process is mostly used to write about forgiveness. Certain, less critical scholars even go so far as to defend the idea of "forgiving and forgetting." In this case reconciliation takes the form of the psychological need of the individual to continue with life after serious trauma. There are people who see reconciliation as nothing more than another word for tolerance. With this entry point, unbearable pressure is placed on the victim to forgive. Such forgiveness does not necessarily lead to reconciliation. Reconciliation is a quest for national unity and concrete embrace of enemies for the sake of future generations. As such, its exceeds the outcomes sought by mere tolerance.

In the same way, South Africans have also voiced their concerns with the process. We had voices claiming that the process was "too religious," "too male," "too cheap," and " too bad on history."

TOO RELIGIOUS

The commission was seen as portraying itself too much as a Christian initiative. This occurred at the beginning of the human rights' abuses hearings with the sometimes-inappropriate comments of an exclusive Christian nature by some of the commissioners. "The commission's brief was to be inclusive and respectful of all who appear in its hearings, no matter their personal, religious or political beliefs."[18] This accusation has surfaced often with reference to the role and clerical robe of Desmond Tutu as well as the frequent references to forgiveness[19] as understood by Christians.

It is my contention that much of this form of critique is a matter of perception rather than an historically justifiable position. Only naivete would make one think that you can unearth a Judeo-Christian metaphor, applying it as if it has mere secular roots. Separating the strategy from the ethics of responsibility and freedom that precede it in the Judeo-Christian philosophy and theology of reconciliation is a recipe for destruction rather than reconstruction.

Too Male

The truth commission was well in progress when the first woman appeared before it. The women were also more often mothers making enquiries about the fate of their children, husbands, and brothers. Women remain the silent victims of many conflicts, wars, and horrible torture. The commission functioned initially with a "gender-neutral truth."[20] Gender is a key aspect of political conflicts. The apartheid regime impinged on the human dignity of women daily and specifically in torture chambers. Their rights to security, family, movement, legal equality, equity, and decency were systematically violated by the apartheid regime. How will future commission secure that truth will be seen also in terms of its gender basis? Will the voices of women for women be heard in future reconciliation processes? Future generations deserve to know the truth of gendered violence as well.

Too Cheap

Molefe Tsele, a South African theologian, has said already in 1996 that reconciliation without the jubilee of the poor is meaningless in South Africa.[21] Tinyiko Maluleke accused the Truth and Reconciliation Commission of "dealing lightly with the wounds of my people."[22] Both Tsele and Maluleke are of the opinion that reconciliation has a material implication, and rightly so. To date, the South African government has not been able to find an adequate strategy to deal with the need for reparation and restitution. I have argued that a fundamental learning process for perpetrators is the lesson of restitution.[23] However, the amnesty clause prevents victims from laying claims against perpetrators, provided they have proof that the perpetrator did not "fully" disclosure the matter.

Too Bad on History

The past receives special attention in the life of a Truth and Reconciliation Commission. This can easily lead to the idea that such a commission is actually busy with the historian's profession. Its recorded works represent a particular view of the history of gross human rights violations in South Africa. Historians have recently accused the commission of treating historical data inadequately. They regard the following piece of legislation as proof that the commission was responsible for writing "its report as history":

> Establishing as complete a picture as possible of the nature, causes and extent of the gross human rights violations which were committed between 1 March 1960 to 5 December 1993, including the antecedents, circumstances, factors and contexts of such violations, as well as he perspectives of the victims and the motives and perspectives of the persons responsible for the commission of the violations.[24]

The commission failed, they claim, to meet its epistemological and methodological responsibility to history.[25] The chief researcher of the commission, correctly, replied that the critics take it for granted that there are no limitations to academic history and that it therefore should have been rigorously applied to systematize the traumatic stories of victims.[26] It will be tragic if historians will not see that they have a separate role to that of the commission, a role that goes, methodically and epistemologically, beyond that of a juridical commission.

THE NECESSITY OF A RECONCILIATION FOR PEACEBUILDING

The Truth and Reconciliation process was, for all its weaknesses, also strongly defended. I identify three main categories of defense. Critics were accused of "unreasonable expectations," "firing at a ship sailing uncharted waters," and "not fully understanding its contribution to the building of a human rights culture internationally."

Right at the beginning of the process academics and faith community were requested to outline their thoughts on the possible outcomes of this process. Theologians at the University of the Western Cape warned against overrated expectations and indicated that the commission is a legal instrument with a limited function. At most its work could become a national symbol for the separate and continuing role of religious communities to further the cause of reconciliation.[27]

Indeed, the Truth and Reconciliation process was an attempt to do what has not been done before. Confronted with the Nuremberg option of the post-Nazi period, on the one hand, and that of the Chilean "blanket amnesty" model, on the other, South Africa has opted for a process of restorative justice driven by the narratives of the victims.[28] "Certainly," says Gardner, "the TRC is in uncharted waters. A fair number of countries have attempted, through commissions of one sort or another, to investigate events and deeds that have taken place in times of political injustice and strife; but none of these commissions has had quite the same terms of reference, both for seeking and hearing evidence and for granting amnesty, as our TRC. The TRC has, then, no precise precedents to fall back on: it finds itself engaged in a continuous legal, social and moral experiment."[29]

I have argued that the Truth and Reconciliation process is a necessary element of modern peacebuilding because it focuses on the root issue of ethnoreligious conflicts. Such conflicts are no longer the frightful encounter of professional soldiers on secluded operational fields. They occur on the streets of innocent communities and in the schoolyards of primary school children. These conflicts uproot innocent and defenseless civilians, trample on their human dignity, and strip them of their inalienable human rights. Seen against this background, the real task of reconciliation commissions is not merely to establish truth for its own sake, to listen to victims as a juridical novelty, to interrogate perpetrators of torture as an outcry against violence, or even to come to terms with the past as if one can ever close the book on it. Fundamentally, truth and reconciliation processes are limited, but necessary instruments to fight the scourge of human rights abuses that are at the heart of the continuing hatred between former enemies, painful trauma suffered by women and children, and the brewing anger of seeing torturers walking the streets unaccountable to their victims who continue to suffer the consequences.

Critics forget too easily that the legislation determined that the Truth and Reconciliation Commission's task was to investigate gross violations of *human rights*.[30] Having said that, one should also consider the possibility of saying that human rights is geographically indivisible. Is it conceivable that local truth is, so far as human rights violations are concerned, also global truth? Can we build a human rights culture through the achievable strategy of reconciliation if only local peoples and local ethnic groups must mirror themselves in the pain of past conflicts? Is it, perhaps, not needed that the nations of the world, the politicians of every sovereign country, and that the religions of the world gaze into the mirrors of the stories of victims in Africa and Latin America seeking an understanding of their own roles and complicity in local conflicts and human rights violations? Denise Ackermann, a prominent feminist theologian of South Africa, makes a strong argument for the world needing to "lament" in the face of the conflicts and wars of our times, especially in the light of South Africa's reconciliation process.[31]

CONCLUSION

Reconciliation belongs to modern peacebuilding as human rights abuses belong to ethnoreligious conflicts. They are by nature connected. The South African case is one of the most important contributions to the building of a human rights culture and consciousness, which is the crux of peacebuilding in modern times.

On the last day of the legal life of the commission, it announced that the doors would be kept open until midnight for any late submission of amnesty applications. Minutes before midnight a most extraordinary drama unfolded. A small group of young people, in their twenties and all of them black, arrived at the desk for amnesty applications with their form fully completed. Their application states:

> (1) That we as individuals can and should be held accountable by history for our lack of action in times of crisis; (2) that none of us did what we could have done to make a difference in the anti-apartheid struggle; (3) that in exercising apathy rather than commitment, we allowed others to sacrifice their lives for the sake of our freedom and an increase in our standard of living; (4) that apathy is a real and powerful phenomenon and perhaps the most destructive one in our society; (5) that society takes a leap forward when individuals hold themselves accountable for their action commensurate with change that needs to be made.[32]

These young people understood, perhaps better than many of us, that apathy in the face of conflict as well as in the structural reform phase remains crucial to the making and unmaking of the future.

Ordinary people everywhere could bring an end to human rights violations if their apathy can be turned to action. This should be attempted so that people may leave their comfort zones where personal, familial, tribal, ethnic, national, and professional survival rank higher than acting in the interest of a human rights culture and consciousness.

In this, South Africa and Chile are in agreement: the main intention of reconciliation is for a nation to say "Never and Never again" to human rights abuses.

NOTES

1. Charles Harper, ed., *Impunity: An Ethical Perspective. Six Case Studies from Latin America* (Geneva: World Council of Churches, 1996).

2. Roswith Gerloff, "Truth, A New Society and Reconciliation: The Truth and Reconciliation Commission in South Africa from a German perspective,"

Missionalia, 26:1 (1998): pp. 17–53; Leo J Koffeman, "Waarheid, Verzoening en Vergeving in Zuid-Afrika," *Ruimte Voor Vergeving* (Kampen:Kok, 1998), pp. 133–146; Geiko Muller-Fahrenholz, *The Art of Forgiveness: Theological Reflections on Healing and Reconciliation* (Geneva:WCC, 1997); Dwayne E Williams, "Liberating the Past from the Future, Liberating the Future from the Past: Race and Reconciliation in the United States and the New South Africa" (unpublished).

3. One should actually take into account that Dutch and English colonialism bear concomitant responsibility for the legacy of South Africa's economic and cultural problems and conflicts. However, the direct political conflicts arose from the apartheid policies of the National Party.

4. Ralph Elphinck and R. Davenport, *Christianity in South Africa: A Political, Social and Cultural History* (Cape Town: David Philip, 1997), p. 1.

5. Chris Loff, "The History of a Heresy," in John De Gruchy and Charles Villa-Vicencio, eds., *Apartheid Is a Heresy* (Cape Town: Philip, 1983), pp. 17–19.

6. H. Russel Botman, "A Critical Testimony on The Document Church and Society," in Páraic Réamonn, ed., *Farewell to Apartheid? Church Relations in South Africa. Studies from the World Alliance of Reformed Churches*, No 25 (Geneva: WARC, 1994); H. Russel Botman, "'Dutch' and Reformed and 'Black' and Reformed in South Africa: A Tale of Two Traditions on the Move to Unity and Responsibility"; Ronald A Wells, ed., *Keeping Faith: Embracing the Tensions in Christian Higher Education* (Grand Rapids: Eerdmans, 1996); John de Gruchy, *Bonhoeffer and South Africa* (Grand Rapids: Eerdmans, 1984); John de Gruchy, *Liberating Reformed Theology: A South African Contribution to an Ecumenical Debate* (Grand Rapids: Eerdmans, 1991); Z. Mbali, *The Churches and Racism: A Black South African Perspective* (London: SCM, 1987); Dirk J Smit, "Reformed Theology in South Africa—A Story of Many Stories," *Acta Theologia*, 12/1(1992): pp. 88–110; P. J. Strauss, "Abraham Kuyper, Apartheid and Reformed Churches in South Africa in their Support of Apartheid," *Theological Forum*, 23/ 1 (1995): pp. 4–27.

7. *Kerkbode*, 22 September 1948, pp. 664–665.

8. Wolfram Kistner, *The Legacy of the Past in the New South Africa* (unpublished paper, 1994), p. 16.

9. For a more comprehensive description of the relationship between the DRC and the TRC, see H. Russel Botman, "The Offender and the Church," in James Cochrane, John De Gruchy, and Stephen Martin, eds., *Facing the Truth: South African Faith Communities and the Truth & Reconciliation Commission* (Cape Town: David Philip, 1999), pp. 126–131.

10. See ibid. for a critique of this position.

11.Willa Boesak, *God's Wrathful Children* (Grand Rapids, Grand Rapids: Eerdmans, 1995).

12. See Nils Christie, *Crime Control as Industry: Towards Gulags, Western Style* (New York: Routledge, 1994).

13. Molefe Tsele, "Kairos and Jubilee," in H. Russel Botman and Robin M Petersen, eds., *To Remember and to Heal: Theological and Psychological Reflections on Truth and Reconciliation* (Cape Town: Human and Rousseau, 1996), pp. 70–78.

14. Tinyiko S. Maluleke, "Dealing Lightly with the Wounds of My People?: The TRC process in Theological Perspective," *Missionalia,* 25.3 (1997), pp. 324–343.

15. Interesting studies have been conducted about these questions by people such as Howard Zehr, "Restoring Justice," in Lisa Barnes Lampman, ed., *God and the Victim: Theological Reflections on Evil, Victimization, Justice and Forgiveness* (Grand Rapids: Eerdmans, 1999), pp. 131–159.

16. See the article by Dirkie J Smit, "Confession-Guilt-Truth-and-Forgiveness in the Christian Tradition," in Botman and Petersen, eds., *To Remember,* pp. 96–117.

17. Charles Harper, *Impunity,* pp. viii–xvi.

18. Mark Hay Ukubuyisana: *Reconciliation in South Africa* (Pietermaritzburg: Cluster Publications, 1998).

19. Tutu's latest book argues as he has done throughout the process that there is no future without forgiveness. Desmond Tutu, *No Future without Forgiveness* (London: Rider, 1999).

20. See B. Goldblatt and S. Meintjies, "Dealing with the Aftermath of Sexual Violence and the Truth and Reconciliation Commission," *Agenda,* 36 (1997); Annelet van Schalkwyk, "At a Gendered Truth: Women's Testimonies, the TRC and Reconciliation," *Journal of Constructive Theology,* 5:1 (1999); I. Olckers, "Gender-neutral Truth: A Reality Shamefully Distorted," *Agenda,* 31 (1996).

21. Molefe Tsele, "Kairos and Jubilee," in Botman and Petersen, *To Remember,* pp. 70–78.

22. Tinyiko S. Maluleke, "Dealing Lightly with the Wounds of my People: The TRC Process in Theological Perspective," *Missionalia,* 25:3 (November 1997), pp. 324–343.

23. H. Russel Botman, "Justice that Restores: How Reparation Must be Done," *Track Two* (Cape Town: University of Cape Town, December 1997), pp. 17 and 48. The ethical dimensions of reparations have been explored in an Afrikaans paper written by H. Russel Botman, "Die bevryding van Kain? Etiese nadenke oor die dader in die versoeningsproses," *Scriptura: International Journal of Bible, Religion and Theology in Southern Africa,* 69:1 (1999), pp. 111–124.

24. Truth and Reconciliation Commission, *Truth and Reconciliation Commission of South Africa Report*, 5 vols., Vol. 1, Chapter 4 (Cape Town: Human and Rousseau, 1998), para. 31 (a).

25. Anthea Jeffery, *The Truth about the Truth Commission* (Johannesburg: South African Institute of Race Relations, 1999); Deborah Posel, *The TRC Report: What Kind of History? What Kind of Truth?* (unpublished paper at conference: Commissioning the Past, 1999); Colin Bundy, *The Beast of the Past: History and the TRC* (unpublished conference paper, 1999).

26. Charles Villa-Vicencio, *On the Limitations of Academic History: The Quest for Truth demands both More and Less* (unpublished paper, 2000).

27. This argument has been pursued at length in H. Russel Botman, "Towards the Embrace of Political Reconciliation," *The Way: Contemporary Christian Spirituality*, 39:4 (1999), pp. 338–340.

28. The uniqueness of the South African process has been described, e.g., by Dullah Omar (Minister of Justice), "Introduction to the Truth and Reconciliation Commission," in Botman and Petersen, *To Remember*, pp. 24–26.

29. C. Gardner, "Under Fire in Uncharted Waters," in *Natal Witness*, 22/08/1997.

30. H. Russel Botman, "Die bevryding van Kain? Etiese nadenke oor die dader in die versoeningsproses," *Scriptura: International Journal of Bible, Religion and Theology in Southern Africa*, 69:1 (1999), pp. 111–124.

31. Denise Ackermnann, "On Hearing and Lamenting: Faith and Truth-Telling," in Botman and Petersen, *To Remember*, pp. 47–56. She refers to Dom Helder Camara's cry in Dorothy Solle's *Suffering* (transl. E. R. Kalin; Philadelphia: Fortress): "How much longer will anti-communism have to serve as a pretext for the support of injustices that cry to heaven? How much longer, under the pretext of fighting the terrorist, will there be a use of terrorism by the police and military authorities?" (p. 56). She proceeds by telling the story of a certain Bernie drafted into the South African army as promising teenager. She explains how his life changed after being deployed in the operational area of Angola, about his two divorces, his insomnia, his nightmares, and eventually his suicide. She concludes: "I mourn for Bernie. He was my son-in-law" (p. 56).

32. Quoted from Public Lecture of Michael Lapsley, *Confronting the Past and Creating the Future: The Road to Truth, Healing and Forgiveness* (unpublished, 4 May 1998).

13

Northern Ireland

Religion and the Peace Process

PATRICK GRANT

The best-known description of the Northern Ireland Troubles of the past thirty years is that Protestants and Catholics are so at odds with one another that violence, massive destruction to property, and widespread civil unrest have resulted. The media by and large have promoted this view and have popularized the use of religious labels to describe the opposed factions. Consequently, Northern Ireland can often seem a curious backwater in which people are taken up by an archaic religious squabble, pitiably out of date in modern Europe.

In June 1970—approximately a year after the first serious outbreaks of violence—leaders of Northern Ireland's four main churches (Roman Catholic, Presbyterian, Church of Ireland, Methodist) issued a statement proclaiming that whatever else was causing the rapid increase in civil unrest, religion was not to blame.[1] Understandably, the churches felt embarrassed and threatened by the idea that a religious war was in the offing, and, in solidarity, they delivered a disclaimer intended no doubt to be preemptive. But the churches' reassurance that religion was not the culprit made little impression on the more widely broadcast rhetoric of the news media, for whom the main antagonists seemed all too clearly Protestants and Catholics.

Eventually, the main church groups revised their opinion about the part played by religion in the conflict, and although the media generally have stuck to the religious labels, they usually point out also that the Troubles have a political dimension, and that Protestants want Northern Ireland to remain part of Britain, whereas Catholics want Britain to leave Ireland so that the North and South (which became a Republic in 1949) can be united.

Surprisingly—at least at first view—the church leaders' statement of 1970 is widely shared among certain liberal, secular academics who are likewise convinced that it is misleading to describe the Troubles as religious. For these commentators, religion is a red herring, and they argue that it serves Britain's interests to present Northern Ireland as a sectarian feud among warring Irish factions, with Britain as the hapless mediator attempting to preserve law and order and to bring the situation "back to normal," as the Northern Ireland Information Service once liked to say.[2] In short, from a left-liberal point of view, the religious dimension enables Britain to conceal its colonial history in Ireland and avoid acknowledging its responsibilities in having done much to produce the disastrous situation there. It is easy to predict how this kind of analysis would then go on to argue that sectarian differences are used by the ruling class to divide people in Northern Ireland—especially its workers—by leading them to believe that their religious heritage needs protecting above all else. Meanwhile, ruling class hegemony remains undisturbed.

But although they arrive at similar conclusions, the left-liberal analysts and the 1970 church leaders clearly do so for different reasons. Whereas the churches want to claim that religion should not be used to justify or explain political violence because religion is too important, the secular commentators (certainly in more extreme cases) want to say that religion is merely a mode of false consciousness distracting us from the real political issues. Nonetheless, one thing that emerges even from these differences is that religion remains an issue. Whether you are a believer or an unbeliever, a devoted Christian or a devoted Marxist, a liberal commentator or a journalist, when you deal with Northern Ireland you will find yourself facing the religious question. Why is this so? Let us look briefly at the broader history.[3]

With some justification, England for hundreds of years feared that Ireland could be a staging post for invasion; consequently, the best way to ensure England's safety was to control Ireland. Certainly, from the time of the Spanish Armada to the second world war, there was a clear strategic advantage for England to maintain a presence in Ireland. Even Karl Marx thought that the revolution would get to England through

Ireland, and there was further speculation along these lines by the Soviets until quite recent times.[4] Indeed, the notion that modern Ireland might turn out to be England's Cuba has found its way into commentary on modern Northern Ireland in various contexts, despite the fact that by the late twentieth century the strategic and economic advantage of Northern Ireland for Britain had much declined.

The period of the Renaissance-Reformation marks a crucial juncture in England's strategy in dealing with the Irish question, not only because England's fear of invasion was inflamed at that time by the Spanish Armada (1588), but also because, uniquely among European nations during the Reformation, the majority of the Irish population did not adopt the ruling monarch's religion. That is, when the English became Protestant under Henry VIII, Ireland remained Catholic. Consequently, in 1536, Henry VIII reacted by declaring himself and his heirs heads of the church in Ireland, thereby establishing a Church of Ireland within the Anglican communion, even though at that time Anglicans constituted only some 10 percent of the population.

As is well known, armed resistance to English rule has been a common thread in Irish history, and during the Renaissance-Reformation period the most rebellious part of Ireland was the North. By way of putting down uprisings led by Ulster gaelic chieftains, James I in the early seventeenth century transplanted Scottish and northern English Protestant settlers into the Province of Ulster, which at that time comprised nine counties rather than today's six that are a consequence of the partition of Ireland in 1920. These planters were given lands confiscated from gaelic natives, and in return remained loyal to the crown, helping to secure English, Protestant interests in this especially recalcitrant part of the country.

The seventeenth-century planters are of course the ancestors of today's Ulster Protestants, who still feel threatened by the descendants of the gaelic natives whose land their forebears took. Today's Ulster Protestants continue to remain overwhelmingly loyal to Britain, though they are also apprehensive that they will be deserted, there being no strategic British interest today in Northern Ireland, which, indeed, has become a considerable drain on the British exchequer. Not surprisingly, loyalty ranks high among the virtues admired by Ulster Protestant Unionists, who feel, for instance, that their sacrifices on behalf of Britain in two world wars—especially at the battle of the Somme in 1916—deserve to be honored by Britain's continued support.

It is easy to see, even from these summary remarks, how, from the seventeenth century, English rule in Ireland was directly associated with the Reformed religion. For instance, when Protestant settlers were slaughtered in a rebellion in 1641, the English response was also ferocious, and in 1649 Oliver Cromwell made no bones about justifying the mass killing and deportation of native Catholic Irish on religious grounds, believing himself to be attacking the treacheries and barbarism of popery. As is well known, the most important day in Ulster Protestant folk history is the anniversary of the Battle of the Boyne, which occurred in 1690 when the Protestant William of Orange defeated the English Catholic monarch James II. William's victory is commemorated annually in Northern Ireland with parades and carnivalesque activities that, among other things, celebrate the securing of the English monarchy for Protestantism. The so-called "marching season" in today's Northern Ireland remains highly contentious, mainly because it seems triumphalist to the non-Protestant minority, most of whom are Catholic and whose political sympathies are by and large nationalist.

After William ascended to the English throne, heavily repressive measures were taken against the native Irish. Draconian penal laws were drawn up by the Irish Parliament and directed specifically against Catholics, though Presbyterians were also affected, especially through the Test Act of 1704, requiring attendance at the eucharist of the established church by all office holders under the crown. For our purposes, it is sufficient to note that the penal laws, which were extremely harsh, confirmed the association between the reformed religion and English occupation. At the start of the eighteenth century, the native Catholic Irish constituted over 75 percent of the population, while owning just 14 percent of the land.

Given these facts, it is hardly surprising that when Daniel O'Connell championed a campaign for Catholic emancipation in the early nineteenth century, religion and nationalism should be closely linked. Emancipation for the native Irish would mean relief from the penal laws, but because these laws were specifically anti-Catholic, it was impossible to disconnect political emancipation from religion. Here the die was cast for much that has followed until the present day.

As the nineteenth century progressed, a highly authoritarian form of Catholicism increasingly found common cause with Irish nationalism, which in turn was energized by a revival of ancient Celtic mythology and culture. In the mid-nineteenth century, Cardinal Paul Cullen introduced church reforms reflecting his own pro-Vatican, anti-English, and anti-Protestant views. And as pressure mounted for Home Rule, the combination of heroic, Gaelic romanticism and an authoritarian Catholic church helped to produce a distinctive brand of cultural nationalism that remains very much a force to be reckoned with today, though its influence is now waning.

The cross currents within this state of affairs are many and complex, but I have highlighted some core issues without which modern Northern Ireland cannot be well understood. With these in mind, it is easy to see how, when the twenty-six counties of what is now the Republic of Ireland became a Free State after partition in 1920, its constitution would likely reflect Irish national values, which were also religious. The architect of the 1937 Constitution was Eamon de Valera, whose chief adviser was the Rev. John Charles McQuaid, later Archbishop of Dublin. Neither doubted the importance of religion to Irish national identity, and in this regard the 1937 Constitution made two very significant claims: first, in the new Irish state the Catholic Church would be accorded special authority; second, the six counties of Northern Ireland by right belonged within a united Ireland, and, consequently, the Free State (and, later, the Republic) laid claim to them.

These contentious Articles have since been amended—the first in 1972, and the second in 1998 as a result of the Good Friday Agreement, the landmark document with which the peace process culminated, enabling the establishment of a power-sharing Executive that, at the time of writing, is still in operation, however much under duress. But if, in 1937, you were an Ulster Protestant living in a divided Ireland, the new Constitution would be deeply threatening. Partition had occurred in 1920, after an armed rebellion in Dublin in 1916, which was followed by a treaty allowing the British to continue governing the six counties in the north. A brief civil war followed in the South, in which anti-treaty and pro-treaty forces fought about their differences over partition. The pro-treaty forces won, and the anti-treaty faction became the modern Irish Republican Army (IRA), which holds itself to be the legitimate government of Ireland. In the North, partition was welcomed by Protestant Unionists, who had threatened violence if their desire to remain British was not honored. For their part, the British were able to maintain Atlantic-facing ports in Ireland and to reap the benefits of the Belfast shipbuilding industry, which was at that time the world's finest (where else could the *Titanic* have been built?).

British self-interest and Ulster Unionism therefore worked together to secure the six counties of Northern Ireland—modern Ulster—as British. But not all the inhabitants of Northern Ireland were Protestant Unionists, and a minority of Catholics, whose sympathies were for the most part nationalist, found themselves living under British jurisdiction and governed by a Northern Ireland Parliament devolved to Stormont (just outside Belfast) and securely in the hands of Ulster Unionists. Between 1921 and 1972 (when Britain reassumed direct rule from Westminster), Northern Ireland was governed by a single party, overwhelmingly Protestant and loyal to the crown, and which treated the Catholic minority population badly, through systemic discrimination and political gerrymandering. Although there is debate about the extent of anti-Catholic discrimination, there is an overwhelming consensus that it occurred, and that Northern Ireland's Catholic minority had a just grievance.[5]

In the 1950s and 1960s, Catholics made up roughly one-third of Northern Ireland's one-and-a half million population. But things slowly shifted, and according to analysts of the 1991 census (which is problematic because of noncooperation in filling out the forms), Catholics now number about 42 percent. In short, the Catholic minority is large, and since partition it is readily seen by Protestants as the vanguard for a takeover by nationalists bent on a united Ireland. As we see, in 1937— and for some time after—a united Ireland would have accorded a special place to the Catholic Church, which in turn would restrict civil liberties—especially on matters such as divorce, contraception, and censorship—in a way that Protestants feared and resented. Consequently, at the outbreak of the Troubles in 1969, if Catholics had a just grievance, so also Protestants had just cause for apprehension.

With all this in mind, it is easy to see why commentators on Northern Ireland should be drawn to the labels "Catholic" and "Protestant" as the most effective shorthand for describing the situation. But just as the media have not been entirely wrong to latch on to these labels, so also the left-liberal analysts who point to England's colonial interests in Ireland have not been entirely wrong to insist that it is misleading to present the current conflict in the North as mainly about religion. As we see, history conspired to produce a situation where a complex "double minority" problem has emerged, with two main opposed political groups defined by their religious identities. On the one hand, Northern Ireland's Protestants would be a minority in a united Ireland, and they fear the hegemony of the Catholic Church; on the other, Northern Ireland's Catholics are a minority in Northern Ireland, and they have resented being treated as second-class citizens and potential traitors. The highly uncomfortable, mirror-imaged interplay of anxieties and antagonisms between these two groups has been modified in recent years by the diminishing power of the Catholic Church, especially in the Republic,[6] and by the relinquishment of the Republic's constitutional claims to the North.[7] Also, anti-discrimination legislation has been vigorously pursued within Northern Ireland.[8] Still, old resentments have died hard, and sectarianism is alive and well in Northern Ireland today, often frighteningly intensified by the violence that has occurred during the past thirty years.

After their message of 1970, the churches developed a more measured response to the complexities of the situation, and in 1976 a much praised report entitled *Violence in Ireland* was submitted by a working party appointed by the Irish Council of Churches and the Roman Catholic Church Joint Group on Social Questions. Among other things, the report deplores sectarianism, and accuses the churches in general of not adequately facing up to the widespread bitterness and ignorance that have helped to produce it. The report also acknowledges that religion has indeed played a part in the conflict, though the authors are not prepared to describe this role precisely, because the issues are complex.[9]

In 1993, a further interchurch working party produced a monograph entitled *Sectarianism. A Discussion Document.*[10] This interesting study provides a careful analysis of how sectarianism depends on stereotypes and the maintenance of vicious cycles of reciprocal violence and recrimination. It also acknowledges that sectarianism is often transmitted unconsciously, and suggests that blame for its continuance must be widely shared. Finally, it calls for increased ecumenical effort to assist in mutual understanding and in the difficult work of reconciliation.

These three reports show a developing self-understanding and sophistication on the part of the participating church representatives who are concerned with assessing the problem of violence in Northern Ireland, and, in that light, describing the duties and responsibilities of the main religious groups. As Ian Ellis points out, the Troubles have done much to bring the main churches together, especially at the leadership level, even as communities at the grass roots often have become increasingly polarized under the influence of an ever-luxuriating sectarianism, especially fomented by violence.[11] Certainly, the degree to which church leaders are capable of good sense and charitable Christian intelligence is evident in a trio of books published in the 1990s by Catholic, Church of Ireland, and Presbyterian leaders.

Catholic Archbishop Cahal B. Daly's *The Price of Peace* (1991), Church of Ireland Archbishop Robin Eames's *Chains to be Broken. A Personal Reflection on Northern Ireland and its People* (1992) and Presbyterian Moderator John Dunlop's *A Precarious Belonging. Presbyterians and the Conflict in Ireland* (1995)[12] are well informed, conscientious, and reassuring. All three authors explore the implications of their own positions in relation to the conflict, and each maintains an integrity that does not prevent—and indeed would welcome—ecumenical cooperation in bringing to bear the basic Christian principles of forgiveness and reconciliation to ease the suffering and bigotry that all three deplore. In each case, a personal view becomes transparent both to the claims of denominational allegiance and also to the overarching good that is not served by making denominational differences an insuperable sticking point. In short, were it left to the Dunlops, Eamses, and Dalys of Northern Ireland, Christians there would likely get along well enough, and certainly without violence.

It is difficult to list briefly the extensive ecumenical initiatives and cross-community Christian agencies that have worked and continue to work in the spirit these three books describe. Ian Ellis provides a useful summary in *Vision and Reality. A Survey of Twentieth Century Irish Inter-Church Relations* (1992), and the recent publication by the Churches Advisory Group of the Community Relations Council, *A Directory of Cross Community Church Groups and Projects in Northern Ireland, 1999*[13] likewise lists a wide range of initiatives at all levels of church organization. These include broad-based resource agencies such as the Irish Council of Churches, the Irish School of Ecumenics, and the Mediation Network for Northern Ireland Churches Programme. There are also denominational resource groups, such as the Presbyterian Church in Ireland Peace and Peace-making Committee, and the Forum for Catholic Women, among others. There are ecumenical communities, such as the Corrymeela Community and the Columbanus Community of Reconciliation, as well as numerous local clergy groups, interchurch groups including clergy and laypeople, and "twinned churches" that have entered into partnership across the denominational divide.

Individual efforts by clergy and religiously motivated laypeople create a further complex web of mediations both among the paramilitary factions and between the paramilitaries and government. For instance, in 1987, Fr. Alex Reid and Fr. Gerry Reynolds helped to secure a truce between the INLA (Irish National Liberation Army) and the IPLO (Irish People's Liberation Organization); in 1994, Rev. Roy Magee was a key figure in bringing about the CLMC (Combined Loyalist Military Command) ceasefire; and the Feakle Talks between Protestant church representatives and the IRA helped to bring about the IRA ceasefire of 1974. Interventions of this kind are plentiful and immensely varied, partly because involvement of religious people, however well intentioned, is not always free of bias, and there are many shades and half lights that call for particular discernment rather than homogenizing generalization. Nonetheless, clearly there is much good will among many Christians in Northern Ireland, and the widespread practice of Christian patience, forbearance, and forgiveness has quite possibly been a major contributing factor in preventing the conflict from escalating into all-out civil war. Still, this might leave us even more perplexed as to why the violence has in fact continued for so long, and why the wisdom of many church leaders has made insufficient inroads into the culture of sectarianism among the population at large.

One answer, as I have intimated, is that not all clergy are equally ecumenical and there are varying degrees of willingness to participate in ecumenical ventures, which often are conducted in relatively safe, non-inflammatory ways that avoid dealing with the main divisive issues. Morrow and colleagues find that a good deal of anti-Catholic sentiment persists among Protestant clergy—especially Presbyterians—and only 34.1 percent of the Protestant clergy surveyed were actively working with Catholic clergy.[14] The best example of outright hostility to ecumenism is the Free Presbyterian Church, founded in 1951 by the Rev. Ian Paisley, who has become notorious for the extremity of his opinions. He is exactly the kind of figure the media love to hate, so lurid and ferocious is his anti-Catholicism and so blatant and powerfully expressed are his opinions. On the one hand, Paisley confirms the British public relations view of Northern Ireland as pitiably archaic; on the other, he feeds nationalist suspicions that many Ulster Protestants are bigots. Consequently, for different reasons Paisley's enemies delight in him, but he is also a force to be reckoned with, not least because of his personal presence and rhetorical abilities.

Paisley is remarkable also in having founded a church of his own—a new denomination—as well as, in 1971, the Democratic Unionist Party (DUP). Moreover, Northern Ireland has three representatives at the European Parliament, and Paisley is routinely returned as Northern Ireland's first choice candidate. He is also routinely returned as MP to Westminster. At the same time, many of his opinions are crackpot. For instance, in 1984 he published a pamphlet, *The Woman Rides the Beast,*[15] devoted to the exegesis of a recently issued postage stamp commemorating the European Parliament, and which he interprets through the Book of Revelation. The iconography of the stamp is taken as a sign that the promises of Revelation are coming to pass, and the conclusion is that the Pope, who is Antichrist, is behind the development of the European Common Market, which is Babylon, and therefore part of a massive plot to destroy Protestantism, fomented by Jesuits.

Just as fantastical, but more directly pertinent to the Northern Ireland Troubles is the following statement by a DUP councillor at an annual Party Conference in 1991, at which he refers to the B Specials (a part-time, notoriously sectarian special constabulary disbanded by the British government in 1969) and to the UDR (the Ulster Defense Regiment, an army unit formed to replace the B Specials as part of the offensive against the IRA. The UDR was stood down in 1991[16] as a result of collusion among some of its members and loyalist paramilitaries). Here are the councillor's reported words: "Rome's aim is to destroy Protestantism, our children, our children's children, our way of life and the

Bible. Popery in Rome, with the aid of Romish priests, ensured the demise of the B Specials, of which I was a member. The UDR attempted to defend Ulster from Romanism, but it too has fallen."[17] To claim that the disbanding of the B Specials and the UDR is a Romish plot, and that Ulster is a last redoubt of Protestant integrity has a good deal in common with Paisley's view of the Common Market, and certainly the cliché that Ulster Protestants tend to see themselves as a besieged community is evident here in an extreme form. But, still, what is going on? How could so many people repeatedly vote Paisley into both the European Parliament and Westminster?

One clue is provided by John Whyte's excellent book, *Interpreting Northern Ireland,*[18] in which he points to studies showing how Northern Irish people often hold more hard-line opinions than they declare openly; that is, many people who talk liberally vote conservatively. For this reason, it is often difficult to gauge how deeply embedded sectarian animosities actually are, and this is true even among some people who might find themselves involved in ecumenical ventures, but who might harbor less generous feelings than their public actions suggest. One of Paisley's main appeals is that he declares openly what many people feel secretly, and more people are relieved by this than are willing to say so. Generally, in the public view, Paisley is regarded (his dedicated followers aside) with a mixture of embarrassment, fascinated horror, and some amusement. Such reactions are often no doubt genuinely felt, and the majority of Ulster Protestants would vigorously dissociate themselves from Paisley and from Free Presbyterianism in general. Indeed, Duncan Morrow and colleagues have determined that more Protestant clergy from outside the Free Presbyterian Church would prefer to enter into ecumenical relations with Roman Catholics than with Free Presbyterians.[19] Still, Paisley's personal success is as unsettling as it is palpable, and one way to explain it is in terms of the privately harbored anxieties I have mentioned. It seems that the people who send Paisley (his opinions about the Euro-stamp notwithstanding) to the European Parliament do so partly because they know that, in a crisis, he would be less likely to sell out Ulster than more conciliatory unionists who might well concede too much to nationalism and find themselves on a slippery slope toward a united Ireland. Certainly, the Ulster shibboleth "Not an inch" is unflinchingly maintained by Paisley, and a considerable number of voters apparently find that they don't want this principle to slip entirely from the public view. Here it is worth remembering that although the landmark Good Friday Agreement (1998) was affirmed by 71.1 percent of the electorate, approximately 50 percent (the exact figure is disputed) of Unionist voters rejected it.

Paisley makes much of this, and wants to wreck the Agreement. He does so, basically, in the name of Protestantism.

No figure representing Catholic and nationalist interests quite compares to Paisley, and the different ways in which religion plays into unionism and nationalism are interesting, but too complex to consider in detail here. Suffice it to say that the old, well-established compact between Catholicism and nationalism remains still alive and well despite frequent nationalist assertions that religion plays no part in political aspirations to a united Ireland. The fact is that the overwhelming majority of the Catholic population are nationalist, and cultural nationalism often bears a distinctly Catholic ethos of which Protestants are all too well aware, even though many nationalists resist admitting this. Significantly, as McElroy shows, 91.4 percent of Catholic priests favor Irish unity, and 87.9 percent say they would vote for the moderate nationalist Social Democratic and Labour Party (SDLP).[20] McElroy says there is probably a significant level of "hidden support" among Catholic priests for Sinn Fein (the political wing of the IRA), and no respondent in his survey supported unionism. Certainly, in times of crisis the Catholic dimensions of nationalism are likely to emerge unmistakably, as, for instance, at IRA funerals or during the hunger strikes of 1980 and 1981. Yet the fact that nationalist sectarianism is often unacknowledged by those who transmit it contributes to its virulence, as the complex *pas de deux* continues to engage both sides of the "community divide," as it is often called.

The difference between liberal principles and underlying hard-line attitudes is reproduced in various ways throughout Northern Irish life and culture. It is reflected, for instance, in the fact that clergy can easily find themselves having to rein in liberal aspirations that are opposed by their congregations.[21] In such a situation, anxieties and prejudices harbored at the grass roots can quickly rebuke church leaders who might be judged too idealistic in their approach to the gospel's radical teachings about forgiveness and reconciliation.

In this context, it is worth noticing that the two main props sustaining sectarianism in Northern Ireland are an all-but-universal endogamy, enforced by powerful taboos against marrying out of one's community into a so-called "mixed marriage," and an equally strongly segregated education system. There are some indications that the rate of mixed marriages is increasing, and the integrated schools movement has also been making headway. Still, in the late 1990s, only perhaps 9 percent of couples were in mixed marriages, and schools remained obdurately segregated along religious lines, especially at the primary level, though there is some significant, recent cross-community enrolment at the secondary level.[22] What remains overwhelmingly clear is that a rigorously enforced endogamy and segregated education enable the "two communities" to perpetuate their separate identities. And here we move to a key difference—fundamentally important for understanding the role of religion in the Northern Ireland conflict—between those who aspire to live by religious principles and those for whom religion is mainly a mark of group identity.

Analysts of Northern Ireland have in recent years increasingly come round to the idea that the conflict can best be described as ethnic. That is, each of the two communities is shaped by a shared history, mythology, culture, and sense of destiny, which provide a strong sense of cultural cohesion. It so happens also that in Northern Ireland each of the two main opposed ethnic identities is shaped by a negative image of the other, so interinvolved are their histories. In short, each community is what it is by not being like the other, and, as a result, both are locked into a symbiotic but mutually destructive set of negative interrelationships. Moreover, the key marker of these opposed identities is religion. Here it does not matter if you are an atheist or otherwise uninterested in religious questions or issues; what matters is the community into which you were born, which is either "Catholic" or "Protestant." For that alone you might be shot (or worse), regardless of your heartfelt imprecations against all churches whatsoever, and all religions under the sun.

In their analysis of the 1991 census, Doherty and Poole conclude that the term "religion" was interpreted by respondents in two main ways.[23] The first had to do with faith, church attendance, spirituality, and the like; the second with allegiance to one's birth community. But, as Brian Lambkin has shown in detail, these two senses are often confused when people actually talk about religion.[24] Thus, when the churches in 1970 said that the conflict was not religious, they were right insofar as they referred to religion in the first sense; their revised opinion then came to acknowledge the complexities attendant on the second. In practice, the slippage between the two senses gives rise to a kaleidoscopic variety of nuanced meanings, but for our purposes it is important to understand that insofar as religion in Northern Ireland is a marker of ethnic identity, it is deeply resistant to the kinds of freedom in and through the Spirit by which Christians hope to find themselves liberated from the impersonal demands and mechanisms of a tribal or herd morality.

This brings me to a brief consideration of the paramilitary factions, by means of which I can also return the argument to its starting point. At the outset, I noticed that one main emphasis in left-liberal academic analyses of Northern Ireland is that the real issues are political and economic, and religion has been used for political ends, mainly to divide working people at the expense of their class interests. Another kind of analysis insists with equal conviction that because the conflict is between the Catholic and Protestant communities, religion is obviously central to it. Interestingly, this division of opinion is reproduced among the paramilitary groups on both sides, and has considerable implications for the peace process.

In commenting on Northern Ireland, it is usual to oppose the terms "nationalist" and "unionist" to describe the different political aspirations of people committed to advancing their cause by constitutional means. The main constitutional nationalist party is the Social Democratic and Labour Party (SDLP) and its main opponent is the Ulster Unionist Party (UUP). By contrast, the opposed terms "Republican" and "Loyalist" describe those who believe that their ends can be attained by physical force. The main Republican organization is the Provisional Irish Republican Army (PIRA) (often referred to simply as the IRA or the Provos, or sometimes the Provies); the main Loyalist groups are the Ulster Defense Association (UDA) and the Ulster Volunteer Force (UVF).

The Provisional IRA took its name following a split in the IRA in 1970, when the Provos split off from the parent body led by Cahal Goulding. The split occurred partly because Goulding wanted to take the IRA in a Marxist direction, and to rid Republicanism of its religious baggage. But traditionalists within the IRA resisted the prospect of a godless communism and insisted on maintaining the values of 1916, especially as represented by the mythology of blood sacrifice for Catholic Ireland. In the North, when the Provos emerged to defend the Catholic communities against Protestant attacks, they did so because, from his headquarters in Dublin, Goulding did not want to support what he saw as a sectarian war and he refused IRA assistance to beleaguered Northern Catholics. After the split, the Goulding faction became known as the Official IRA, which—after some intervention in Northern Ireland and some feuding with the Provos—eventually faded away as a paramilitary group and became the Workers Party.

The appeal to Republicans of leaders such as Gerry Adams and Martin McGuinness depends partly on the fact that they are devout Catholics (and therefore traditionalists) and also that they deploy a progressive rhetoric of Republican, anti-colonial socialism (less vigorously when they visit the United States). Though Adams argues that Republicanism is not concerned about religion, on closer examination it is clear that his party (Sinn Fein, the political wing of the IRA), together with the people who vote for it, often maintain the old alliance of religion and nationalist politics in much the same manner as Adams does himself.

IRA funerals, and especially the iconography surrounding the hunger strikes of 1980 and 1981,[25] clearly show how embedded in Catholicism is Provo culture. Jail journals and interviews with Republican prisoners also readily confirm the point.[26] In short, there is a distinct religious element in Republicanism, which often bears, in turn, a considerable freight of latent sectarianism that Republicans have not been keen (or able) to acknowledge.

For various reasons, the sectarianism of Loyalist paramilitaries is plainer. First, they inherit the broadly disseminated sense among many Ulster Protestants that the Northern Catholic community is by and large nationalist and ready to lead Ulster into a united Ireland. Second, unlike the security forces (excluding undercover operatives), the Provos, who are the self-appointed defenders of the Catholic community, do not wear uniforms and therefore are hard to identify. A grievous but all-too predictable conclusion then presents itself—because all Catholics are suspect, and because Catholics don't turn over to the law their elusive Provo defenders with whom they are therefore to be regarded as tacitly in collusion, any Catholic at all is a legitimate target. Besides, the most effective way to show the Provos that they aren't really up to defending the Catholic community is to kill Catholics and thereby terrorize the terrorists, as one Loyalist explained to the journalist Peter Taylor.[27] The naked sectarianism of many Loyalist killings is one of the most horrendous aspects of the Troubles, and it is also one of the least well reported.

Nonetheless, some Loyalists have increasingly entered into a socialist analysis of their situation, partly as a consequence of becoming more educated about such matters while in jail. The UVF folk-hero, Gusty Spence, has been at the heart of this political development among Loyalist prisoners, and one result was the emergence in 1979 of the Progressive Unionist Party (PUP) as the political wing of the UVF, roughly analogous to the relationship between Sinn Fein and the IRA. The present leader of the PUP is David Ervine, an ex-UVF prisoner and an able politician. But Ervine's life has been threatened by other Loyalists who feel that PUP socialism is a betrayal of the root principles of Loyalism, which are religious, and that the PUP's analysis will lead to a dangerous rapprochement with the socialist elements of Republicanism. Just as it has been difficult for the Provos to remove the Catholic ethos from Republicanism, so also, Loyalism at the grass roots wants to protect what is often called in Northern Ireland "the Protestant way of life" and in both cases "religion" (again mainly as a marker of ethnic identity) has a bearing on how and why violence is conducted.

As I have pointed out, the churches have done much to counteract violence and promote peace and reconciliation, especially in local communities. On the political front, officials at the highest level in London and Dublin have worked with increasing cooperation to find ways to force unionists and nationalists to compromise on the constitutional issues, and, as is well known, the United States played a significant part in the peace process that led to the Good Friday Agreement of 1998. President Clinton's posting of Senator George Mitchell as independent chair of the talks leading to the agreement was especially significant, and Mitchell has written about his experiences in a judicious and often moving book, *Making Peace*.[28] The economic policies of the European Community and judgments on Northern Irish events by the European Court of Human Rights have also helped with what has become an immensely complex set of political and economic negotiations, a dazzlingly intricate example of the local-global nexus in operation. Such negotiations have occurred, by and large, independently of initiatives taken by people whose main concern is with religion. Of course, there are many cross currents—for instance, Ian Paisley is a pastor and an MP; Father Des Wilson is an outspoken proponent of liberation theology, whose views complicate any simple distinction between religion and politics. And it would be difficult to assess, for instance, the degree to which religion has played a part in the politics of John Hume and David Trimble, the 1998 Nobel Peace Prize winners.

There is much to be learned from the Northern Ireland Troubles not least because no comparable conflict is so closely documented, as scholars are increasingly coming to realize. As a laboratory for discovering the mechanisms by which violence is induced, justified, or concealed, and how insidiously violence can contaminate civil life and politics, Northern Ireland offers unparalleled opportunities for research. Given the sectarian elements of the conflict, students interested in relationships between religion and society can also come to understand how immensely varied are the processes by which religious values and language might be annexed to practices that offend against the best principles of the religion in question. In this context, one might also come to understand how profound is the grip of history on the political consciousness of many religious people, and how profoundly the feeling-structures of individuals can be shaped by narratives that build the idea of a religious inheritance into a history of oppression, colonial settlement, and so on. The elusive and often dangerous interplay among the senses of the word "religion," and how often these senses are misunderstood, might also provide a salutary lesson in the pressing need for critical vigilance and discrimination in matters pertaining to the uses and abuses of religion in general, as with any other social institution. Finally, one might learn to appreciate the enduring efficacy of a spiritual critique of moral behavior based on the depersonalising imperatives of group solidarity alone, and within which individuals are seen merely as representatives, governed by stereotypes and confined by necessities that prevent the freedom that Christianity teaches is a consequence of living in the Spirit. Such things of course can be learned in many places besides Northern Ireland, and it seems they need to be learned perennially. Yet the fact remains that one main legacy of these troubled years in Northern Irish history is likely to be the sheer richness and density of the documentation now available, which, among other things, provides such a complex view of how religion is involved both in the making of violence and the making of peace.

NOTES

1. For a summary of the churches' statement and the left-liberal debate, see Oliver P. Rafferty, *Catholicism in Ulster 1603–1983. An Interpretative History* (London: Hurst, 1994), p. 270.

2. See David Miller, "The Northern Ireland Information Service and the Media: Aims, Strategy, Tactics," edited by Bill Rolston and David Miller, *War and Words. The Northern Ireland Media Reader* (Belfast: Beyond the Pale Publications, 1996), pp. 208 ff., and especially p. 211.

3. The following account draws on standard sources among an extensive literature. See, for instance, R. F. Foster, *Modern Ireland, 1600–1972* (Harmondsworth: Penguin, 1988); Oliver MacDonagh, *States of Mind: A Study of Anglo-Irish Conflict 1760–1980* (London: Allen and Unwin, 1983); Patrick Buckland, *A History of Northern Ireland* (Dublin: Gill and Macmillan, 1981).

4. See D. R. O'Connor Lysaght, ed., *The Communists and the Irish Revolution*, Part 1, "The Russian Revolutionaries on the Irish National Question, 1899–1924" (Dublin: Litereire, 1993).

5. See John Whyte, *Interpreting Northern Ireland* (Oxford: Clarendon, 1991; first published, 1990), pp. 61–64.

6. See Mary Kenny, *Goodbye to Catholic Ireland* (London: Sinclair-Stevenson, 1997).

7. Referenda on both sides of the border in 1998 resulted in—among other things—an overwhelming support by voters in the Republic for relinquishing Articles 2 and 3 of the 1937 constitution, laying claim to Northern Ireland.

8. This has taken place on many fronts, through a series of Fair Employment Acts and the work of the Fair Employment Commission. See Sydney Elliott and W. D. Flackes, *Northern Ireland. A Political Directory, 1968–1999* (Belfast: Blackstaff, 1999).

9. *Violence in Ireland. A Report to the Churches* (Belfast: Christian Journals, 1976), pp. 76, 20.

10 *Sectarianism. A Discussion Document* (Belfast: Department of Social Issues of the Irish Inter-Church Meeting, 1993). The Working Party members are listed on p. 159.

11. Ian Ellis, *Vision and Reality. A Survey of Twentieth Century Irish Inter-Church Relations* (Belfast: Institute of Irish Studies, 1992), pp. 125 ff.

12. Archbishop Cahal B. Daly, *The Price of Peace* (Belfast: Blackstaff, 1991); Archbishop Robin Eames, *Chains to be Broken. A Personal Reflection on Northern Ireland and its People* (Belfast: Blackstaff, 1992); John Dunlop, *A Precarious Belonging. Presbyterians and Conflict in Ireland* (Belfast: Blackstaff, 1995).

13. For Ellis, see note 12. *A Directory of Cross Community Church Groups and Projects in Northern Ireland, 1999* (Belfast: Community Relations Council, 1999).

14. Duncan Morrow, John Greer, and Terry O'Keeffe, *The Churches and Inter Community Relationships* (Coleraine: Centre for the Study of Conflict, 1994; first published, 1991), p. 39.

15. The tile page reads: *The Woman Rides the Beast. A Remarkable Prophetic Fulfilment. The EEC Prophetically Considered* by Ian R. K. Paisley, M. P., Northern Ireland's First Elected European M.P. (1984). (No further publication data are printed.)

16. In 1992, the UDR merged with the Royal Irish Rangers to form the Royal Irish Regiment.

17. See *Sectarianism. A Discussion Document*, p. 20, cited from *The Irish Times*, 21 December 1991.

18. John Whyte, *Interpreting Northern Ireland*, pp. 4 ff.

19. Duncan Morrow, John Greer, and Terry O'Keeffe, *The Churches and Inter Community Relationships*, pp. 34–35.

20. Gerald McElroy, *The Catholic Church and the Northern Ireland Crisis 1968–86* (Dublin: Gill and Macmillan, 1991), pp. 66 ff.

21. Duncan Morrow et al., *The Churches and Inter Community Relationships*, pp. 84 ff.; 243 ff.

22. I deal with these issues in detail in *Breaking Enmities. Religion, Literature and Culture in Northern Ireland, 1967–97* (London: Macmillan, 1999), pp. 72 ff.

23. Paul Doherty and Michael A. Poole, *Ethnic Residential Segregation in Belfast* (Coleraine: Centre for the Study of Conflict, 1995), p. 95.

24. Brian Lambkin, *Opposite Religions Still?* (Aldershot: Avebury, 1996), pp. 39 ff.

25. The first hunger strike in 1980 was called off before any of the strikers died. In the second strike of 1981, ten men died, having entered the strike at intervals of approximately ten days. This was probably the most significant political event in the history of Republicanism since 1916, and it enabled the emergence of Sinn Fein as the political party representing IRA interests in Northern Ireland.

26. See, for instance, Brian Campbell, Laurence McKeown, and Felim O'Hagan, *Nor Meekly Serve My Time. The H-Block Struggle 1976–1981* (Belfast: Beyond the Pale, 1994).

27. See Peter Taylor, *Loyalists* (London: Bloomsbury, 1999), p. 97.

28. George J. Mitchell, *Making Peace* (New York: Alfred A. Knopf, 1999).

14

Religious Peacebuilding

From Potential to Action

JUDY CARTER AND GORDON S. SMITH

From the crusades, inquisitions, and holy wars of the past to the jihads and so-called religious conflicts of the present day, religion has a long history of implication in violence and war.[1] Over the past three millennia, millions have been killed in the name of somebody's God—notwithstanding the strict proscriptions against killing affirmed by the world's great religions. Even today, as Little and Appleby note in their introduction, religion is seen as a leading contributor to the "intolerance, human rights violations and violent extremism" afflicting the world at the start of the twenty-first century.

Understandably, therefore, suggestions that religion might play a role in conflict prevention, mitigation, and resolution, or in peacemaking and post-conflict peacebuilding, often meet with a certain skepticism—if not outright opposition. In truth, the dissonance between the teachings of the world's religions and the violence of some of their adherents has engendered not only criticism but cynicism.

Yet the evidence and argument of the foregoing chapters are compelling: The world's religious traditions, each in their own way, offer a rich abundance of insight and guidance for the promotion of peace. The challenge (especially for the secularized Western world) is to bring religious beliefs to the political agenda for constructive and practical effect.

The challenge, in fact, is twofold. The first challenge is to clearly understand the religious content in specific episodes of conflict and its connection to other causal factors of violent conflict, most notably desires to effect structural, economic, political, and social change. As the September 11, 2001, attack on New York's World Trade Center illustrated, twenty-first-century conflicts are increasingly complex, ubiquitous in their impact, and in dire need of new, effective prevention and management tools. The second challenge is to integrate the wisdom, spirit, and techniques of the world's religious traditions into the politics and practice of contemporary conflict management, resolution, and prevention. The argument here is that the failure to recognize the place of religion in the dynamics of conflict and peacemaking has too often resulted in misunderstandings, inappropriate and sometime disastrous policies and actions, and most important, missed opportunities. To reduce the risks of those mistakes, a small but growing number of scholars and practitioners[2] are making the case for reintegrating religion into society and politics, specifically for its peace-promoting potential.

To realize that potential and make positive change, however, will require, first, understanding and, second, carefully thought-through action. Responsibility for discerning and developing appropriate and effective roles for religion and religious actors belongs jointly to political, religious, and nongovernmental organizations and their leaders. What we aim to offer now is an array of practical recommendations that political, religious, and nongovernmental leaders can readily adopt, modify, and put to work in the interests of peace.

As earlier chapters have demonstrated, the space for religion in international and intrastate conflict prevention, management, and resolution, in diplomacy and in peacebuilding, is theoretically expansive yet hardly explored. The object surely must be to turn theory into practice. The world's religions, as we will show in this concluding chapter, offer much wise counsel on how to prevent, mitigate, and resolve conflict, and how to nurture peacebuilding efforts. We will explore their teachings, and from them draw general principles and specific recommendations for measures that political, religious, and nongovernmental actors can use to better promote peace. Working from the premise that religion can make a positive contribution to peacebuilding, our goal is to make our own contribution, however modest, to the development of a global "culture of prevention."[3]

LESSONS OFFERED

Although experience with the use of religion in conflict remediation is still too limited to offer conclusive "lessons learned," there is enough practical experience and ample age-old wisdom in the world's religious traditions to compile "lessons offered" by them.

Reflecting on the teachings of the world's major religions, what is striking is the similarity of their ethical foundations and underlying principles. Equally remarkable is the way in which the principles of these religions parallel the findings of theoreticians and practitioners working in the field of peace and conflict studies. The world's religions all preach peace. They all advocate a social code resembling the golden rule: Do unto others as you would have them do unto you. They all regard as virtues kindness, charity, compassion, honesty, fairness, justice, equality, tolerance, respect, nonviolence, humility, forbearance, self-discipline, moderation, and forgiveness. That the world's religions profess so much in common is an optimistic fact. Common ground and shared goals, conflict theorists agree, are precursors to peace. And while most of the prescriptions from the world's religions were originally directed to co-religionists to settle their own differences peacefully, the same principles are available to be applied to conflicts between members of different faiths. That is a crucial point. Expanding the community to which religious principles and virtues are applied is critical to the achievement of world peace.

To date, the field of peace and conflict studies has offered many *secular* theories, approaches, and techniques for conflict prevention, management, and resolution and peacebuilding. Yet violence and war recur, and peace remains frustratingly elusive. Too often missing, suggest contributors to this volume and others, are *spiritually inspired* approaches and methods.[4] As we will see, the world's religious traditions offer many, as well as diverse lessons for preventing and ending violent conflict, and for building lasting peace.

JUDAISM

The oldest of the Abrahamic faiths, Judaism offers detailed advice on the promotion of peace. For a start, Judaism advocates preventing conflict and its escalation. Early intervention and resolution are easier and less costly, especially in human costs, than trying to make peace after a long, bitter dispute. As well, there is an important injunction against the dangerous politicization of religion.

Judaism is noteworthy in that it recognizes that identity, and fear of its destruction, can be critical issues in conflict, and it acknowledges the connections between identity, belonging, and place. Judasim teaches that respect, honor, and understanding are central to conflict prevention, management, and resolution and peacebuilding. To reduce and resolve conflict, Judaism encourages parties to "find grace" in each other, and courage and humility within themselves. Disputants should sit and listen empathetically to each other's stories. They should let go of their need to be right and lose a little face, for the sake of peace.

If disputing parties cannot settle their differences, Judaism recommends that a community member offer to intercede. The Judaic conception of intercession suggests the impartial intervention diplomats, negotiators, and mediators practice nowadays should be reevaluated. Instead of the impartiality and neutrality that much of the current literature recommends, Judaism intimates that engaged, compassionate concern may be more constructive.

Lessons about interceding can be drawn from the story of Aaron. Intervenors and disputants alike are urged to look at all the parties involved, see their anguish and rage, and truly understand their suffering. Second, parties should endeavor to ease each others' burdens. Intervenors should commit to staying with disputes, with no deadlines, until peace is made. They should not jet in and out; instead, intervenors should make long-term commitments to peacebuilding and be willing to undertake repeated overtures aimed at building peace.

Judaism offers important insights for peacemaking and peacebuilding in its treatment of the key themes of mourning and forgiveness. For peace to endure, disputants must mourn and recover from the losses they have suffered during the conflict. Otherwise, lingering resentments may spark future conflicts. These themes run through the five-stage healing process advocated by Judaism and comprised of acknowledgment, *aveilus* or mourning, forgiveness, *teshuva* or repentance, and construction of a shared future. The losses each party has suffered must be acknowledged. Disputants should grieve, ideally together. They should forgive each other. They should apologize and make amends. Finally, they should focus on building a new future together.

The Judaic concept of *teshuva* requires a repentance that is sincere, substantial, and continuing. Remorse and restitution must be linked. Judaism suggests that if peace is to endure, parties must transform themselves—their thinking, their actions, and their relationships. This is especially true of conflicts that have endured for several generations, where the parties feel the conflict is deeply connected to their own identity.

The other notable insight of Judaism is its recognition that disputants are interdependent, both in war and peace. Judaism urges disputants to assume responsibility for each other's healing, and offers a range of *mitzvahs* that can help build and preserve peace, such as limiting consumption of shared resources. This broad sense of social responsibility contrasts with the emphasis on individual rights and freedoms found in many other Western cultures. It also serves to remind us how intimately connected personal security has become to the well-being of strangers who may be at war halfway around the world.

CHRISTIANITY

From Christianity, the second youngest of the three Abrahamic faiths, come a variety of rules aimed at the promotion of peace. The Sixth Commandment, for example, expressly declares: "Thou shalt not kill." Scriptures elsewhere instruct Christians to love one another and their enemies. And there is the familiar passage (from Mathew 5:9), "Blessed are the peacemakers."

From the history of Christianity itself comes the useful typology distinguishing different kinds of peace: *eirene,* a brief moment between repeating conflicts; *pax,* the absence of war due to an imbalance of military power; and *shalom,* the presence of peace by choice and design. The first concept implies that conflict is a Hobbesian inevitability, and war, with all its attendant suffering, is humankind's permanent condition. Under the second category, peace is maintained through oppression backed by the threat of force. Only within the third concept is peace seen as a conscious, holistic, community-wide choice aimed at maximizing citizens' well-being. It is the latter that Christianity advocates.

Christianity offers provocative arguments both for and against the use of force. Some Christians hold that force is never justifiable. Others hold that it is, sometimes, for example, when conditions are unbearably oppressive. Two related lessons from this debate are worth noting: War may be justifiable to achieve some higher end—but, if so, the force used must be limited and certain "just war" standards must be upheld

There is an essential link, in Christian teaching, between peace and justice. There is also the recognition that violence is often perpetrated under the guise of preserving political stability. Historically, of course, there are many instances of Christianity being co-opted for political purposes, often with the effect of inciting conflict.

Northern Ireland is a case in point. So is South Africa. Its long, oppressive history of apartheid and painful attempts to facilitate truth and reconciliation illustrate the consequences of the misuse of religion. Bosnia imposes a recent brutal reminder of what can happen when disputes over religion, politics, ethnicity, and land become completely entangled, often as a deliberate leadership strategy. Outsiders failing to see the complexity of these interactions will neither understand the conflict nor, perhaps, have much to offer much in the way of resolution.

Lessons to be drawn from these examples underscore the importance of guarding against the co-option or politicization of religion.
Other pitfalls to avoid are intolerance, hypocrisy, and forced conversion.
Despite its past, Christianity's recent history illustrates how religion can
help promote peace. Interventions mounted by Christian groups and
individuals in the twentieth century, among them Quakers, Mennonites,
and Roman Catholics, have helped mitigate conflicts throughout Africa
and Central and South America.[5] Increasingly, moreover, Christians are
working with non-Christians. Christian intervenors have been especially
successful in situations involving political instability and transition.

From these Christian experiences there are practical lessons to be
drawn for peacemaking and peacebuilding. And, once again, these
lessons resonate with recommendations from the conflict theorists. High
on the list of attributes helpful when intervening in others' conflicts are
firsthand familiarity with local customs, language, and culture, access to
information, established relationships with disputants, communication
and political skills, and vision. Presence on the ground among the parties, understanding cultural differences and sensitivities, working at the
grassroots level, attempting to address social inequities, and a long-term
commitment are all thought to be important. Confession, apology, forgiveness, reconciliation, and restitution also figure prominently in the
advice Christianity offers to disputants seeking peace.[6] Nonviolent resistance, as exemplified by Martin Luther King Jr., is offered as an effective
and just alternative to violent conflict.

ISLAM

From Islam, the youngest of the Abrahamic faiths, come many classic
teachings pertinent to peacebuilding. Especially relevant is Islam's concept of *umma,* which demonstrates how a broad definition of community and cooperation can help overcome conflict—and how religion can
be used to transcend differences and disputes. In contrast to the individualistic cultures that dominate the developed Western world, the collec-
tivist culture of Islam and many other developing societies illustrates the
power of inclusivity, superordinate goals, and communal responsibility.
Careful stewardship of joint resources is an aspect of communal responsibility of obvious significance.

Despite the stereotypes attached to Islam by the violence of some
fundamentalists, it is a pacifist religion in its original incarnation. In
addition to advancing harmonious relations among fellow Muslims,
Islam advocates tolerance of other faiths and provides for peaceable

relations with non-Muslims. That Muslims have made many peaceful agreements with their neighbors is evidenced by history.

Another lesson offered by Islam goes to the relationship between private beliefs and public affairs. In contrast to contemporary Judaism and Christianity, which call for a separation between church and state, Islam advocates the intertwining of religion and governance. Westerners tend to eschew Islam's integration of faith and state, partly because of the extreme consequences associated with the imposition of sharia law. Nevertheless, it should be recognized that Islam does offer an alternative to secular society and its social ills.

On the other hand, the Islamic experience offers sobering reminders of what can happen if religion is co-opted by extremists or if religion constitutes a group's dominant and defining identity—especially when that identity is threatened or perceived to be threatened. Some Muslims consider secular Western culture to be the epitome of evil and amorality. They fear that the West's current economic agenda of globalization will bring with it Western decadence, depravity, and godlessness. In this antagonism lies the potential for conflict. In understanding and address-ing these concerns lies the potential of prevention and peace.

Islam offers many lessons for conflict prevention, mitigation, and resolution as well as peacebuilding. The way in which Islam permeates all aspects of Muslim life encourages intervenors to take a comprehen-sive, multifaceted approach to the conflicts they seek to ameliorate. It encourages intervenors to look broadly at the history out of which the conflict arose and the context in which it persists. It reminds intervenors to "seek first to understand" before making recommendations as to what should or should not be done.

Recent history speaks to the necessity of careful conflict analysis, to disentangle religion from political, structural, economic, or other causal factors. It suggests that intervenors should ensure that violent fundamen-talism and terrorism are not rooted in unmet basic needs, oppression, injus-tice, a desire for autonomy, or fears for identity. An examination of funda-mentalism suggests the importance of guarding against the manipulation, selective interpretation, and, in some cases, outright distortion of religious teachings. At the same time it underscores the responsibility of onlookers to bear in mind that small but vocal groups rarely represent the majority.

In addition to these many cautions, Islam offers insight into the potential power of religion, if directed toward peaceful ends. Islam sug-gests that parties seeking to broker peace can do so by appealing to reli-gious beliefs to raise discussions to a new, spiritual level. They can appeal to superordinate values and goals. And they can inspire dis-putants to make agreements they would not otherwise make.

With regard to conflict resolution, Islam advocates mercy and forgiveness. From Dar al-Sulh, the house of peacemaking, invented to provide a third realm midway between Dar al-Islam, the Abode of Submission, and Dar al-Harb, the Abode of Warfare, can be drawn a lesson on the importance of creating neutral zones in which disputants can find safety and meet to discuss their differences peacefully. The invention of Dar al-Suhl illustrates the importance of devising creative solutions to difficult problems.

In contrast to the Abrahamic faiths, religious traditions originating in Asia tend, in their teachings, to be more inclusive and tolerant. Confucianism, Hinduism, and Buddhism offer lessons on how religion and governance can be juxtaposed and how beliefs can inform policy and action. Confucianism, Hinduism, and Buddhism contrast with the Abrahamic faiths in that they tend to encourage an inward focus and discourage proselytization. Instead of trying to persuade others to their beliefs and win new converts, adherents to Eastern faiths tend to focus on making themselves and their fellow believers better people. Another theme evident in Confucianism, Hinduism, and Buddhism concerns the interconnectedness of human beings with one another and with the environment. All three discourage the acquisition and excess consumption of material possessions and worldly goods. From this approach flow insights about the need to conserve and steward the planet's finite resources responsibly and fairly. All three draw attention to the inextricability of peace and sustainability, and to the choices and changes this interdependence implies.

HINDUISM

Perhaps the most useful lessons Hinduism has to offer spring from its long-standing pluralism. Unlike other world religions, which recognize a single dominant deity, incarnate prophet, and single sacred text, Hinduism comprises many sects with many beliefs and traditions. Hinduism's capacity to accommodate others' beliefs is exemplary. Unlike the adherents of other faiths who insist that theirs is the one true religion, Hinduism allows that there are many different but equally acceptable paths. Pluralism and its more modern cousin, syncretism (the blending of diverse religious beliefs), suggests an inviting path to peace.

The other lesson for which Hinduism is celebrated is *ahimsa,* or nonviolence. Best exemplified by Mahatma Gandhi, nonviolent opposition or peaceful resistance offers an alternative means of pursuing one's needs or effecting change. From Gandhi come lessons, similar to those of Judaism, on the virtue of changing one's own perceptions. Equally important is *kshama,* or forgiveness. Hinduism offers ideas on how reframing and reinterpreting events and letting go of anger and hurt can help disputants find peace, within and between themselves. From the story of Khandikya and Kesidhwaja comes a reminder that disputants are often interdependent, in both their conflict and its resolution. They need each other's help to end their dispute.

On issues of territory, by contrast, Hinduism is instructive in that its own history shows the lengths to which people will go in disputes over land. For some Hindus, religion, identity, and territory are deeply interrelated. If one of these values is threatened or actually lost, conflict can be expected. On the topic of peacebuilding, Hinduism offers counsel on forgiveness and taking a long-term view. Finally, as a solution to the misuse of religious texts, Hinduism explicitly proposes a return to original teachings.

BUDDHISM

Born out of frustration over irreconcilable religious differences, Buddhism provides lessons on pacifism, nonviolent opposition, tolerance, moderation, and holism. Buddhism has much to offer regarding conflict and violence prevention. Buddhism's allowance for multiple interpretations of Buddha's teachings, and its acceptance of other religions and simultaneous adherence to them, are a model of open-mindedness from which much can be learned. Furthermore, Buddhism's focus on humility and self-improvement present correctives to the self-righteousness that tends to cause and exacerbate conflict.

Buddhism's emphasis on empathy and compassion suggests useful approaches to the management and deescalation of conflict. Also worth noting is the role ritual can play, and the potential for interfaith and grassroots peacebuilding, provided such initiatives are culturally inclusive and appropriate. Buddhist teachings expressly condemn retaliation, revenge, and violence. Recommended alternative strategies for dealing with conflict range from complete disengagement to active nonviolence to engaged neutrality.

Another preventive lesson offered by Buddhism concerns the value of education in the inculcation of peaceful minds. With its vision of peace radiating outwards, like ripples on a pond, from the individual to the family to the community, Buddhism consciously addresses the systemic, potentially contagious nature of conflict and offers wise advice on humanity's interdependence and the need for peace to be cultivated holistically and globally. It suggests an alternative metaphor to conflict's tendency to a downward spiral—namely, its mirror image, an up-trending helix of peace.

With its emphasis on asceticism, Buddhism offers an alternative to the materialism and consumerism dominating secular society. It holds that self-indulgence and worldly wants may more wisely and satisfyingly be substituted by spiritual riches and transcendence. In this Buddhism offers advice on global sustainability.

A final lesson to be gleaned from Buddhism concerns governance. The integration of beliefs, politics, and actions in traditional Buddhist cultures contrasts with the segregation that characterizes developed, secular societies. Traditional Buddhism places religious actors in constructive roles in education, community problem solving and decision making, local politics and civic life, by way of providing political advice and spiritual counsel and helping to resolve conflicts. It illustrates how decisions can be made by consensus at the community level, with ample opportunity for citizen participation. Buddhism's religiously respectful system of participatory governance offers an alternative to prevailing hierarchical models of governance.

At the same time, Buddhism warns against the dangerous severing of religion from civic affairs.[7] Cambodia's history provides a poignant lesson on what can happen if religious actors become complacent, apathetic, disengaged, or powerless. It underscores the need for religious actors to play an active, constructive role in civic affairs.

CONFUCIANISM

Additional lessons regarding governance and leadership can be derived from Confucianism. Instead of heavy-handed governance characterized by strict laws backed by the threat of military force, Confucius advocated a bottom-up approach. Leaders and governments, he suggested, must *earn* the respect, trust, esteem, and loyalty of those they wish to represent by setting fair, virtuous examples that citizens want to follow.

With regard to conflict, Confucianism offers lessons on prevention and resolution. Harmony is at the heart of Confucianism. In contrast to other religions, Confucianism sees peace as humanity's natural condition and conflict as the aberration. When conflict erupts, the solution, according to Confucianism, is to restore harmony. To do this, listening and respecting differences are essential. So is education. Indeed, Confucianism claims that education is central to conflict prevention and resolution, and to peacebuilding. First, education can be used to develop attitudes and skills directed at preventing conflict. Second, if conflict occurs, education can be used to help disputing parties better understand each other and their conflict, and then to resolve their differences.

Like other collectivistic cultures, Confucian societies hold that an individual exists only in relationships with others. Thus, fulfilling familial duties and social obligations is paramount and ritual can be used to help maintain harmonious relationships.

From Confucianism comes a further belief that peace cannot be achieved merely by diplomacy, political compromise, or legal agreements. Rather, it must be achieved by people—individuals who desire peaceful relations. Peace, according to Confucians, is not a legal issue; it is a moral issue. It must be built step by step, one person at a time. Confucianism therefore suggests that peacebuilding should be a permanent, continuous process.

Confucianism offers timely lessons on leadership. Leaders can nurture peace, but they cannot force it. They should listen carefully to their constituents and seek to achieve harmony among their voices.

One final lesson from Confucianism concerns individual responsibility and change. Restoring and preserving harmony requires the transformation of one's self, attitudes, and relationships. Confucianism encourages critical reflection, and places responsibility for change on individuals. In this important sense, Confucianism points to the potency of grassroots actors in peacemaking and peacebuilding.

AMERICAN INDIAN

One last spiritual tradition, just now beginning to be studied for lessons in conflict analysis, is that of North American Indians. Especially illuminating are North American Indian views regarding holism and interdependence. In most American Indian spiritual traditions, relationships and reverence are central. They radiate outwards in concentric circles, from family to clan to tribe to the environment and its elements and inhabitants, to the sky and stars.

One lesson to be drawn from the American Indians' holistic worldview and respect for all creation concerns global sustainability. All humans depend on the earth's resources for their sustenance. The inability to meet basic needs, along with uneven resource allocation, are seen as primary causes of conflict. American Indian spirituality therefore reinforces the belief that peace and sustainability are inextricably intertwined.

American Indians' emphasis on harmony and balance, as exemplified in the Navajo concept of *hozho,* offers lessons on the curative and preventive power of restorative justice. Unlike punitive justice, which dominates most of the world's legal systems, making amends acknowledges the wrong committed, the harm others have suffered, and the contrition required. More important, restitution restores harmonious relationships and diminishes the risk of revenge and future conflict. Once again, the importance of addressing root causes and effecting change looms large.

American Indian spiritual traditions offer several provocative lessons on politics, governance, and leadership. First, participatory decision-making and consensus leadership are seen as integral elements of democracy and conflict prevention. Second, history shows that the white path, in which leaders and governance focus on peace, and a red path, where the focus is on conflict, often coexist. Third, American Indian tradition suggests that war and peace should be separated, so that one administration handles the affairs of war while another promotes peace. Related is the suggestion that peace should be promoted ceaselessly, even during war. Fourth, it suggests that commitment, vigilance, and persistence are required to preserve peace. Finally, it suggests that, during war, sanctuaries should be provided in which people, including aggressors, can find refuge.

Another lesson we can take from some of these aboriginal religions concerns the power of language. According to the Navajo, "language does not describe the world, it determines how the world will be."[8] Words can have either a destructive or constructive effect. The moral for those living in today's "argument culture"[9] is to speak softly and carefully. On the positive side, storytelling has great explanatory and curative powers, lessons that can be applied to conflict resolution and peacebuilding initiatives. Similarly, ritual, prayer, and ceremony can be used to reduce negative or hostile feelings and encourage amity and peace.

A last lesson we can take from North American Indians concerns their sense of community, time, and responsibility to future generations. American Indians are directed to take into consideration the interests of children who will be born *seven generations* hence. Taking a long view is important to preventing, alleviating, and resolving conflict and peacebuilding.

INTERFAITH

Still another area in which religion offers promise is in interfaith initiatives. From intervenors' point of view, interfaith activities offer opportunities to collaborate, share the work of building peace, and learn from each other. Teaming up with other religious and nonreligious actors also models the behaviors required to promote peace. From disputants' point of view, on the other hand, interfaith initiatives offer an opportunity to get beyond political posturing and the pieces of paper on which peace agreements are written. They give disputants, especially at the grassroots level, a chance to move from the intellectual and political realm to the emotional and practical realms of peacebuilding.

Interfaith activities give disputants a chance to sit and listen to each other, to learn about each other's hopes, dreams, fears, needs, and anxieties. They provide opportunities to acknowledge and share each other's pain, mourn losses, forgive, and begin healing. They can facilitate the discussion of mutual concerns, invention of creative solutions, and development of a shared vision for the future. Interfaith initiatives also offer opportunities for the personal and interpersonal transformation required to build peace. Because they can represent a microcosm of the society in which they occur, successful interfaith initiatives have the potential to demonstrate progress and inspire others to attempt similar collaborative projects. Examples mentioned in this volume illustrate the potential of interfaith initiatives to encourage understanding and transform relationships.

RECOMMENDATIONS

Two conclusions of telling and practical significance emerge from the preceding chapters. First, the analysis, prevention, and resolution of conflict all demand consideration of religion's place in the dynamics of violent conflict and peacebuilding. Second, the teachings and practices of religions themselves can contribute to the prevention, management, and resolution of conflict—and promotion of peace.

What is often less obvious, however, is how to apply the lessons offered by the world's religions to specific cases. To secure maximum utility from the many rich and promising lessons offered by the world's religions, leaders require a more systematic and compact array of propositions and recommendations for ready modification and application. To that end, and by way of summary, we advance the following points— first to government and political leaders, then to religious leaders, and finally to leaders of nongovernmental organizations and others interested in civil society.

The salience of each proposition or recommendation will vary with circumstances, of course. But they are all aimed at fostering, locally and globally, a stronger and healthier culture of prevention.

Building a culture of prevention can be conceived as a repeating three-step process, which keeps expanding and escalating, like a mirror image of conflict's down spiral.[10] The first step is to prevent violent conflict from occurring. The second is to keep conflicts that have broken out from growing more violent or spreading. Managing existing conflicts involves containing them, mitigating their impact, and deescalating violent or potentially violent disputes. The third step is actually to resolve the conflict. To do this, parties must envision a new future, rebuild relationships, and address the underlying structural causes of conflict.

In attempting to prevent conflict and promote peace, political, religious, and nongovernmental leaders may find themselves in one of two different situations. They may be parties to a conflict involving the organization they represent, or they may be intervening in someone else's conflict. In either case, the specific strategies and actions advisable for those wishing to promote peace will vary, depending on the particulars. But the following recommendations, or at least many of them, can be applied both to conflicts where religion has been identified as a major factor and those where it has not. The steps that political, religious, and nongovernmental leaders can take are detailed separately here, but many of these recommendations are not mutually exclusive and could be employed by any category of actor. [11]

Political Leaders

For political leaders who seek to take initiatives to promote peace, the first resort is to prevent conflict from erupting. As the Carnegie Commission on Preventing Deadly Conflict points out, there are structural and operational means of doing this. Other steps political leaders can take are as follows:

1. With regard to conflict generally, and so-called religious conflicts specifically, political leaders and their advisors should take religion more fully into account. This advice applies most urgently to leaders in the secularized West, where religion is too often misunderstood or neglected in policy calculations. Political leaders need to understand better the central role that religion plays in many people's lives—not only in other regions of the world but in their own countries. They need to understand how religion permeates belief and behavior, especially in non-Western politics, and factor religion into their thinking, policies, and actions.

2. Within their own countries, political leaders should give careful thought to integrating religion as a force for peace into political and civic life, and then try to develop constructive roles for religion and its adherents in making and executing policy.

3. Leaders must recognize that threats to others—real and perceived—range far beyond the familiar and obvious concerns about military or economic encroachment. Moral and religious values may also be at stake. In short, we can easily be surprised by what others consider threatening. Western moral standards (or the apparent lack thereof), for example, are considered a menace by adherents of some religious traditions. Likewise, economic development and globalization are seen as threats by some—not least because they can lead to the exploitation of human and natural resources and jeopardize the environment. Political leaders must take care to ensure that they are not contributing to conflict, even inadvertently.

4. At the same time they are trying to prevent conflict, political leaders must take care not to suppress it or prevent change.[12] Conflict, per se, is not always bad.[13] It can help advance reform, remedy wrongs, and establish a new social equilibrium. The evil to be prevented and stopped is the use of violence to force or block change. It is the essence of good governance to manage change peacefully. Political leaders can help channel disputants' passions and energies toward peaceful change and away from violence. Appeals to religious values can encourage pacifism, in both domestic and foreign conflicts.

5. Political leaders need to watch carefully for early warning signs of violence, both within their own and in other communities. Tell-tale indicators of violence include the co-option of religion for political ends, a rise in religious extremism, increasing intolerance and oppression, human rights abuses, media rhetoric or manipulation, social instability, and the build-up of weapons.[14] To monitor emerging conflicts, political leaders may find it helpful to work cooperatively with religious and nongovernmental actors, who can bring intimate knowledge of the issues and parties and superior local intelligence to bear on activities of timely prevention.

6. When (or, better, before) violence appears imminent, political leaders should act decisively. Early intervention and prevention are ultimately much less costly than struggling to manage and resolve conflict after it has turned violent. Many early intervention strategies are available, ranging from conventional political and economic sanctions to the threat of military force. Alternative strategies include, for example, Judaism's prescriptions for intercession.

7. When intervening in others' conflicts, political leaders should take a holistic, long-term view like that found in Buddhism, Confucianism, and American Indian religious traditions. In many so-called religious conflicts, religion is only one of several causal factors. What is

truly at issue can be basic survival or security, justice or fairness, to more complex issues such as the need for recognition, respect, autonomy, and self-determination. Equally often, fear can play an incendiary role and precipitate violence.

8. Political leaders and their envoys should be willing to spend as much time as it takes for disputants to articulate and explain their concerns. They should invest the same time, patience, empathy, and compassion as Aaron, Judaism's peacemaker, and contemporary Christian peacemakers. Quick fixes are unlikely to last. Political actors should analyze conflicts carefully, do thorough research, not presume to know what is best, and employ multi-track intervention approaches.[15]

9. As a general rule, political leaders should not try to settle others' conflicts for them. Rather, they should try to empower disputants with the means and the knowledge to find their own solutions. Peace crafted by disputants is far more likely to be implemented and endure. In addition, encouraging disputants to find their own solutions contributes to their self-sufficiency and builds their problem-solving and community-building capacities.

10. To help resolve and prevent conflict, political leaders should endeavor to help address the underlying structural causes of violent conflict. Only when people can meet their basic needs for food, shelter, water, and safety, and fulfill higher order aspirations for justice, fairness, freedom, autonomy, self-determination, and a decent quality of life is peace likely to achieved and sustained.

Religious Leaders

There are many actions religious leaders and actors can take to promote conflict prevention, management and resolution, and post-conflict peace building.

1. Religious leaders, whether parties to a dispute or acting as external intermediaries, serve peace best by first recalling and emphasizing the principles and virtues professed by all the world's major religions—particularly the values of tolerance and nonviolence. Religious leaders can and should help prevent and resolve violent conflicts by reminding their own co-believers of their duty to peace.

2. To help prevent violent conflict from igniting, religious leaders must respond effectively to the excesses of their co-religionists. They must ensure that their faith is never used to justify aggression or violence.

If others of their faith are promoting intolerance, enmity, or violence, leaders should hold them accountable, declare their error, and act to prevent the harm they do.

3. Similarly, religious leaders should guard against the co-option of their faith and its teachings for political mischief. If religious leaders find that the teachings of their faith have been exploited or distorted, they should encourage their followers to "go back to basics" and promulgate anew their faith's original pacific teachings.

4. To help prevent religious conflicts, religious leaders and their followers should respect others' beliefs. Proselytization and conversion should never be coercive.

5. To promote peace, religious leaders can undertake to learn about others' beliefs and endeavor to understand why others believe and behave as they do. Leaders can encourage their own followers and other religious and secular leaders and actors to do the same. They can offer to teach members of their faith the tenets of others, and support interfaith initiatives.

6. Religious leaders can play a uniquely informed and influential role in the detection of early warning signs of violence. To contribute to prevention, they can help uphold and promote basic human rights norms and the rule of law. They can speak out when they discover human rights being violated. If international laws or norms are being broken, they can bring these violations to the attention of agencies such as the United Nations or the media. They can help victims find refuge and protection.

7. One of the most valuable contributions religious leaders can make to the prevention of conflict is to set a good example. They can be models of tolerance and inclusivity. They can challenge and try to counteract discrimination and stereotyping when they find it. They can advocate the use of nonviolent resistance as an effective alternative to violent confrontation. When confronted with extremism, they can look beyond people's behavior to see what causal factors or unmet needs may be driving them, and then help them take their concerns forward in a peaceful, constructive manner.

8. While there is much that religious leaders can do to help prevent violent conflict, their greatest contribution may lie in helping to manage and resolve it. After all, whether or not religion is a direct cause of strife, it is often important in the lives of victims on both sides of the conflict. It is often central to their identity, faith, and hope. For that very reason, religion can play a pivotal role in restoring and strengthening peace.

9. Religious leaders and actors sometimes enjoy certain advantages that enable them to go where they wish and to do things secular actors cannot. In general, religious leaders have a reputation for honesty, integrity, impartiality, fairness, and compassion—even outside their own community of believers. They may be associated with large or well-funded international organizations, which they can call upon for assistance. This can allow religious leaders to act and direct resources faster than either governmental or non-governmental actors. Religious actors often possess firsthand knowledge of local issues, can gain local residents' cooperation easily, and often enjoy a high degree of political immunity. When religious actors possess such attributes, they should put them to good use.

10. When undertaking to help manage or resolve a conflict, religious leaders should volunteer to intervene early and make a long-term commitment to helping disputants. Throughout, they can discourage violence and encourage dialogue. They can shuttle messages back and forth between adversaries, and provide sanctuaries where disputants can safely meet and talk. They can promote resolution by reminding disputants that virtues such as compassion, fairness, justice, respect, and humility are precursors to peace, if not prerequisites. When helping disputants negotiate, religious leaders can help them judge when to give in and compromise. They can help disputants save face—or, if appropriate, lose it. Such appeals can facilitate accommodation by leaders who fear loss of support among their own constituents, giving leaders a safe, acceptable way to make concessions and end hostilities without risking mutiny—or even their lives.

11. In contributing to post-conflict peacebuilding, religious leaders can shepherd the mourning, apology, repentance, and forgiveness processes that must occur before true resolution and peace are possible. Religious actors can ensure that the losses and sufferings of each side are acknowledged. They can encourage disputants to grieve together and help create the shared ceremonies, rituals, and monuments that will help heal disputants' hurts. Religious leaders can encourage disputing parties to apologize to each other and offer atonement that is sincere, substantial, and consistent. If religious institutions themselves are at fault, their leaders can admit the wrongs committed, apologize, and make amends.

12. Religious and other leaders can help ensure that grieving is complete to diminish the risk of renewed violence. Because peace and justice

are linked, religious leaders can support the use of truth and reconciliation commissions, and promote the restorative justice advocated by many American Indian religious traditions.

13. Religious leaders can encourage disputants to turn their attention to the future, to the society and to relationships that must be rebuilt. They can help disputants change their thinking, their actions, and their relationships to facilitate genuine transformations. When helping disputants to craft and begin working toward a new vision for the future, religious leaders can help them explore and choose options that are mutually acceptable and beneficial. At this stage, praying together for guidance to make wise decisions may be appropriate. Religious leaders can encourage disputants to be creative, and learn to collaborate with each other and outside agencies.

14. Most important of all, and more than anyone else, religious leaders can knowledgeably appeal to disputants on the basis of their spiritual beliefs and shared values. In conflicts involving religious differences, religious leaders can speak directly and authoritatively to disputants' beliefs. In conflicts that are not overtly about religion, religious leaders may appeal to common moral standards and values, to spirituality, or to the superordinate goals of peace and justice. By interjecting a spiritual dimension into negotiations, religious leaders can elevate them to a higher level. By appealing to values, they can help inspire disputants to move beyond their own positions and look more broadly at their responsibility to end their dispute and the suffering it inflicts.

Nongovernmental Leaders

Although nongovernmental leaders and actors sometimes find themselves in the middle of violent conflicts, most of their work occurs after a conflict or disaster has occurred. Their special strengths and potential are realized in post-conflict situations when relationships must be restored and civil society rebuilt.

1. Nongovernmental leaders can publicize conflicts and bring them to world attention, appeal to the public and other agencies for aid, and cooperate in relief operations. They can call for a cessation of hostilities and encourage reconciliation. When the conflict is very violent, nongovernmental along with political and religious leaders can help ensure, at minimum, respect for "just war" norms. In some situations, they can offer to mediate or take other measures of conflict resolution.

2. Once a peace arrangement has been brokered, nongovernmental leaders can help to restore relationships and rebuild community. To help repair relationships, nongovernmental actors can promote interfaith communication and collaboration. They can facilitate discussions that will restore trust, social capital, and, consequently, civic capacity. Intervenors can help cultivate and nurture participatory governance and consensus decision-making, as advocated by Buddhism, Confucianism, and American Indian religious traditions. They can help ensure that civil society is revitalized and vibrant, so that peace will endure.

3. Nongovernmental leaders can help former disputants design an agreed-upon vision for the future, and work toward its achievement. In this work, they can encourage a broad definition of community. They can take an inclusive, holistic global view—acknowledging, for example, the Muslim concept of *umma* and North American Aboriginal concepts of unity and cosmic interconnectedness. In some situations they may be able to use prayer, ritual, and shared ceremony to inspire deliberations, strengthen relationships, and celebrate successes.

4. To help rebuild civil society, nongovernmental leaders can work in concert with disputants as well as religious and political leaders to create institutions, agencies, and associations that promote communication, mutual education, collaboration, and peacebuilding. These can range from formal initiatives aimed at promoting democratic electoral and legal reform to informal groups and community clubs devoted to enriching civic life. Here again, NGOs can exploit their own nonsectarian character as sympathetic intermediaries.

5. Nongovernmental as well as others leaders can pay special attention to the needs and interests of grassroots citizens to help ensure that peace agreements are implemented and refined and built on over time. They can encourage the transformation that is required and help disputants put provisions in place to deal with future conflicts.

6. Nongovernmental agents can promote peace through education. Education can exert considerable influence in conflict prevention, reduction, and cessation. Intervenors can use education to heighten people's awareness of and sensitivity to conflict, and the issues causing it. They can use education to expand and alter disputants' understanding of one another, the root causes of their conflict, and available measures to resolve it. Intervenors can explain through education different religious traditions, thereby countering intolerance and discrimination. Through education they can provide people with training in conflict prevention, management, and resolution and the skills of peacebuilding.

7. Nongovernmental leaders can draw on religious teachings to promote the deeper social and spiritual meanings of peace. They can use religious concepts such as balance, harmony, and *hozho* to emphasize the importance of relationships and reciprocal obligation. They can encourage parties mourning the past to shift their focus to the future. They can emphasize hope and forgiveness. Using the theme of transcendence, they can encourage disputants to focus on building a society in which peace endures.

In sum, political, religious, and nongovernmental leaders and actors all need to take similar steps to promote peace—listen, learn, understand, and respect. They need to take maximum advantage of the lessons offered by the world's religious traditions. To promote prevention and peace, they need to think broadly and inclusively, endeavor to empower disputants, and make addressing the structural causes of conflict one of their top priorities.

CONCLUSION

Making peace constitutes one of the greatest leadership challenges of the new millennium. As we have seen, the world's religions have the potential to make a unique and substantial contribution to that great goal. They all advocate peace. They all set out the moral justifications and practical courses of action that can inform conflict prevention, peacemaking, and peacebuilding. They affirm the imperatives of cooperation and a peaceful human society. And they enjoin us all to respect each other and our communities, even as we pursue our own aspirations.

The teachings of the world's religions offer wise counsel, healing solace, and enduring hope. By seizing on the wisdom of those traditions, we are given the opportunity to transform conflict's fearful downward spiral into an ascending spiral of peace.

NOTES

1. Thanks to John Hay who reviewed and edited the chapter.

2. An excellent overview of the issues, theory, and implications can be found in chapters contributed by Edward Luttwak, Barry Rubin, and Stanton Burnett in the book edited by Douglas Johnston and Cynthia Sampson, *Religion, The Missing Dimension of Statecraft* (New York: Oxford University Press, 1994). A good introductory discussion on religion, conflict, and politics is pro-

vided by George Moyser in "Politics and Religion in the Modern World: An Overview" in the volume he edited entitled _Politics and Religion in the Modern World_ (London: Routledge, 1991). Mark Juergensmeyer's book _Terror in the Mind of God: The Global Rise of Religious Violence_ (Berkeley: University of California Press, 2000) provides a chilling insight into religiously motivated terrorism and violence.

3. The notion that a culture of prevention is required was first put forward by former secretary general of the United Nations Boutros Boutros-Ghali, in _An Agenda for Peace_ (New York: United Nations, 1995) and further developed by the _Carnegie Commission on Preventing Deadly Conflict_ (Final Report) (Washington, DC: Carnegie Corporation of New York, 1997).

4. The need to add spirituality to political decision making is discussed in Johnston and Sampson, 1994, and Johnston and Eastvold (in this volume). An argument can also be made for the wisdom of expanding the discussion about the role of faith in conflict and peacebuilding beyond the strict confines of organized religion to include the vast array of other traditional and new "spiritual" beliefs, which are rising in both number and popularity.

5. For an overview of Christian peacebuilding efforts see Cynthia Sampson, "Religion and Peacebuilding," in William Zartman and Lewis Rasmussen, eds., _Peacemaking in International Conflicts: Methods and Techniques_ (Washington, DC: United States Institute of Peace Press, 1997).

6. These points are discussed in this volume by H. Russel Botman.

7. Catherine Morris and Eva Neumaier document the effects of disengagement in this volume.

8. Michelene Pesantubbee, this volume.

9. Deborah Tannen offers informative insights on the "argument culture" and impact of language in _The Argument Culture: Stopping America's War of Words_ (New York: Ballantine, 1999) and _The Argument Culture: Moving from Debate to Dialogue_ (Toronto: Random House, 1998).

10. Suggestions that peace be seen as an upward spiral can be found in the recommendations made by the Carnegie Commission on Preventing Violent Conflict, p. xviii; Joyce L. Hocker and William W. Wilmot, _Interpersonal Conflict_, p. 35; and the Glaford Continuous Improvement Model. The nested paradigm Jean Paul Lederach presents in _Building Peace: Sustainable Reconciliation in Divided Societies_ (Washington, DC: United States Institute of Peace, 1999), p. 56, and the emphasis Harold Saunders places on sustained dialogue in _A Public Peace Process: Sustained Dialogue to Transform Racial and Ethnic Conflicts_ (New York: St. Martin's Press, 1999) both reinforce the notion that peace must be built step-by-step in ever-expanding circles over time.

11. William Zartman and Lewis Rasmussen discuss the nature of conflict in the twenty-first century and what steps might be taken to end it in "Toward the Resolution of International Conflicts" and "Peacemaking in the Twenty-First

Century: New Rules, New Roles, New Actors," in *Peacemaking in International Conflicts: Methods and Techniques,* pp. 3–29 and 23–50, respectively.

12. It is possible that conflict suppression during the Cold War contributed to the rash of intrastate conflicts currently plaguing the globe.

13. Mary Parker Follett, *Constructive Conflict* (1925; Reprinted in 1995 by Harvard Business School Press) and others since have noted that conflict has positive attributes.

14. The Carnegie Commission discusses early indicators, p. xxi.

15. Traditional diplomatic approaches are not effective for dealing with complex intrastate conflicts explains Andrew S. Natsois in "An NGO Perspective" in *Peacemaking in International Conflicts: Methods and Techniques,* pp. 337–361.

CONTRIBUTORS

Scott Appleby is Professor of History and the John M. Regan, Jr. Director of the Joan B. Kroc Institute for International Peace Studies at the University of Notre Dame. He received his Ph.D. in the history of Christianity from the University of Chicago in 1985. Appleby is the author, editor or co-editor of ten books on religious modernisms and fundamentalisms in the nineteenth and twentieth centuries. His most recent book, "The Ambivalence of the Sacred: Religion, Violence and Reconciliation" (Rowman & Littlefield, 2000), was commissioned by the Carnegie Commission on Preventing Deadly Violence.

Andrea Bartoli is the Director of the International Conflict Resolution Program at Columbia University's School of International and Public Affairs and Chair of the Columbia University Conflict Resolution Network. As a member of the Community of St. Egidio, Dr. Bartoli has been actively involved in conflict resolution since the early 1980s focusing on Mozambique, Algeria, Burundi, Kosovo and the Democratic Republic of the Congo (DRC); ICRP initiatives are currently focused in Colombia, East Timor, Myanmar (Burma) and northern Iraq. Dr. Bartoli is a graduate of the University of Rome, Italy. He completed his doctoral studies at the University of Milan, Italy. His most recent publications include "'Mediating Peace in Mozambique'" in *Herding Cats: Multiparty Mediation in a Complex World* (edited by Chester A. Crocker, Fen O. Hampson, Pamela Aall, USIP, Washington: 2000) and *Somalia, Rwanda and Beyond* co-edited with Edward Giradet and Jeffrey Carmel (Crosslines, Cambridge, 1995).

Judith A. Berling is Professor of Chinese and Comparative Religions at the Graduate Theological Union in Berkeley, CA. She received her Ph.D. from Columbia University in 1976. She taught Chinese religions for 12 years at Indiana University, and has been a visiting professor at Stanford,

University of Chicago Divinity School, and Vanderbilt University Divinity School. Her two major books are *The Syncretic Religion of Lin Chaoen* (1980) and *A Pilgrim in Chinese Culture: Negotiating Religious Diversity* (1997). She has lectured extensively and written numerous articles and chapters on topics relating to Chinese religion. She is a past president of the American Academy of Religion, a founding co-editor of *Teaching Theology and Religion,* and a member of the United Board for Christian Higher Education in Asia.

H. Russel Botman is Professor and Dean Alternate of the Faculty of Theology at the Stellenbosch University, South Africa. He received his Ph.D. from the University of the Western Cape where he also served as Dean of the Faculty of Religion and Theology. He works primarily in questions related to Christianity and Society (Public Theology). He is the author of a significant number of publications and co-edited the book *To Remember and To Heal: Theological and Psychological Reflections on Truth and Reconciliation* published by Human and Rousseau, Cape Town. He is a consultant to the World Alliance of Reformed Churches on economic globalization.

Judy Carter is completing her Master's degree in Conflict Analysis and Management at Royal Roads University. She has over 20 years experience as a journalist and runs her own communication and media relations consulting business. She works with private and public sector clients throughout North America. Areas of interest include rural land use, environmental conflict, and conflict prevention. Her most recent book is *Farming with Neighbours: A Guide for Canadian Farmers on Preventing and Resolving Community Conflicts over Farming Practices.*

Harold Coward is a Professor of History and is the Director of the Centre for Studies in Religion and Society at the University of Victoria. He received his Ph.D. from McMaster University. With a teaching focus on India, comparative religion, and ecology, he has supervised numerous students for their M.A. and Ph.D. degrees both at the University of Victoria and at the University of Calgary. He is a Fellow of the Royal Society of Canada. He has been the recipient of numerous research grants from SSHRC and the Ford Foundation. He has been a Visiting Fellow at Banaras Hindu University and the Institute for Advanced Studies in the Humanities, Edinburgh University. He has written sixty-two articles and is author/editor of thirty-two books, including: *Hindu Ethics* (1988); *The Philosophy of the Grammarians* (1990); *Derrida and Indian Philosophy* (1990); *Mantra: Hearing the Divine in India* (1991); *Population, Consumption, and the Environment* (1995).

Diane D'Souza is currently the Associate Director (Praxis) of the Henry Martyn Institute in Hyderabad (India), where she has lived since 1985. She is actively involved with local grassroots programmes aimed at building bridges of relationship across religious boundaries. She is also engaged in conflict resolution training and mediation at community, NGO, police and government levels. Her scholarly research and teaching have focused mainly on Muslim women and their issues, with a more recent emphasis on the devotional activities of Shiah women in Hyderabad. She sees her role as mother of three and wife of one as critically shaping her perspectives as scholar and activist.

Frederick M. Denny, who was born and reared in Vermont, is Professor of Islamic Studies and the History of Religions and Chair of the Department of Religious Studies at the University of Colorado at Boulder. He received his Ph.D. from the University of Chicago in 1974 and held academic positions at Yale University and the University of Virginia before moving to Colorado in 1978. He is the author of the widely used college textbook *An Introduction to Islam* (2nd edition, 1994), as well as articles on various aspects of Islam and Muslim life based on field work in Egypt and Indonesia. He is founder and general editor of the scholarly book series "Studies in Comparative Religion" at the University of South Carolina Press and member of the editorial boards of *The Muslim World, Studies in Contemporary Islam, The Journal of Ritual Studies,* and *Teaching Theology and Religion.* His most recent research has been on Muslim communities in North America and Islam and human rights.

Jonathan Eastvold is a graduate student in the Department of Politics at Princeton University. Prior to Princeton, he served as Special Assistant to the President of the International Center for Religion & Diplomacy and as a Fellow at the National Center for Leadership.

Rajmohan Gandhi is an author, occasional visiting professor, and cofounder of the Centre for Dialogue and Reconciliation, New Delhi and Mumbai. He was a Member of the Indian Parliament, 1990–92, and Research Professor with the Centre for Policy Research, New Delhi, 1992–2000. He has taught South Asia's history and politics at the University of Illinois at Urbana-Champaign and at Emory University, Atlanta. His books include *Revenge and Reconciliation: Understanding South Asian History* (New Delhi: Penguin, 1999); *The Good Boatman: A Portrait of Gandhi* (New Delhi: Viking, 1995); *Patel: A Life* (Ahmedabad: Navajivan, 1990); and *Eight Lives: A Study of the Hindu-Muslim Encounter* (Albany, NY: SUNY, 1987).

Patrick Grant is Professor of English at the University of Victoria, British Columbia, Canada. He was educated at the Queen's University of Belfast and at Sussex University. In 1990 he was elected Fellow of the Royal Society of Canada. He is the author of numerous books, including a trilogy on literature and the idea of the person. Other titles deal with the New Testament as literature, Western mysticism, literary Modernism, the scientific revolution, and the literature and culture of the English Renaissance. He has written two books on modern Northern Ireland: *Breaking Enmities. Religion, Literature and Culture in Northern Ireland, 1967–97* (1999), and *Hardened to Death. Rhetoric and Violence in Northern Ireland, 1968–98* (forthcoming).

Marc Gopin is the author of *Between Eden and Armageddon: The Future of World Religions, Violence and Peacemaking* (New York and London: Oxford University Press, 2000), as well as, *Holy War, Holy Peace: Moving Religious Traditions Toward Peace in the Palestinian/Israeli Conflict* (New York and London: Oxford University Press, forthcoming). Gopin works in the Middle East on conflict resolution, has trained over 600 students in conflict resolution practice in the context of global religious traditions, and is an adjunct professor of diplomacy at the Fletcher School for Law and Diplomacy, Tufts University. Gopin received his Ph.D. from Brandeis University, and is currently serving part-time as rabbi of Temple Beth Shalom in Cambridge, Massachusetts.

Douglas M. Johnston is president and founder of the International Center for Religion and Diplomacy. He is a distinguished graduate of the U.S. Naval Academy and holds a Masters Degree in Public Administration and a Ph.D. in Political Science from Harvard University. He has served in senior positions in government, business, the military, and academia, including six years at Harvard where he taught international affairs and was founder and director of the University's Executive Program in National and International Security. His most recent assignment was as Executive Vice President and COO of the Center for Strategic and International Studies. He is the principal author and editor of *Religion, the Missing Dimension of Statecraft* (Oxford University Press, 1994) and *Foreign Policy into the 21st Century: the U.S. Leadership Challenge* (CSIS, 1996).

David Little is the T.J. Dermot Dunphy Professor of the Practice in Religion, Ethnicity, and International Conflict at Harvard Divinity School, and an Associate at the Weatherhead Center for International Affairs at Harvard University. He received his Ph.D. from Harvard. He was Senior

Scholar in Religion, Ethics and Human Rights at the United States Institute of Peace in Washington, DC, where earlier he was a Distinguished Fellow. He was a member of the U.S. State Department Advisory Committee on Religious Freedom Abroad from 1996 to 1998. He has held positions as Professor of Religious Studies at the University of Virginia, stinguished Visiting Professor in Humanities at the University of Colorado, and the Henry R. Luce Professorship in Ethics at Amherst College and Haverford College. He has written in the areas of moral philosophy, moral theology, history of ethics, and the sociology of religion, with a special interest in comparative ethics, human rights, religious liberty, and ethics and international affairs. Little is co-author with Scott W. Hibbard of the USIP publication, *Islamic Activism and U.S. Foreign Policy* (1997) and author of two of the volumes in the USIP series on religion, nationalism, and intolerance (RNI), *Ukraine: The Legacy of Intolerance* (1991), and *Sri Lanka: The Invention of Enmity* (1994). Little's recently published articles include: "Rethinking Human Rights: Review Essay on Religion, Relativism, and Other Matters," in the *Journal of Religious Ethics* (Fall, 1998), "A Different Kind of Justice: Dealing with Human Rights Violations in Transitional Societies," in *Ethics and International Affairs* (1999).

Catherine Morris is the managing director of Peacemakers Trust, a Canadian non-profit organization for research, education and consultation in conflict resolution and peacebuilding. She is the former Executive Director of the Institute for Dispute Resolution at the University of Victoria. She holds degrees in literature and law from the University of Alberta and is a current member of the Law Society of British Columbia. Since 1983, she has been involved in leadership roles with numerous local, provincial, national and international conflict resolution organizations including several initiatives in Thailand and Cambodia since 1994. She has practiced and taught arbitration, mediation and facilitation in a range of civil society, public and academic settings. She is a director of the British Columbia Mediator Roster Society and a member of the Ethics Appeal Board of the Society of Professionals in Dispute Resolution. Her publications include works on mediator ethics and qualifications, conflict and culture, community conflict resolution, and dispute resolution education.

Eva K. Neumaier is Professor and Chair of East Asian Studies at the University of Alberta. She received her Dr. phil. and Dr. phil. habil. from the University of Munich (1966, 1976) in Tibetan and Indian Studies. Her work is primarily in Tibetan Buddhism with a focus on rDzogs chen literature, the integration of Buddhist elements with local religious beliefs, and in Ladakh Studies. She is author of several books, the latest one *The Sovereing All-Creating Mind: the Motherly Buddha,* 1992 and numerous articles and book chapters on issues of Buddhism and Tibetan religions.

Michelene E. Pesantubbee is Assistant Professor in the Department of Religious Studies at the University of Colorado at Boulder. She received her Ph.D. from the University of California at Santa Barbara in 1994. She specializes in American Indian religious traditions with a primary emphasis on Southeastern American Indian religious traditions and religious movements. She is the author of "From Vision to Violence: The Wounded Knee Massacre," in *Millennialism, Persecution, & Violence* (2000) and "Beyond Domesticity: Choctaw Women Negotiating the Tension Between Choctaw Culture and Protestantism," *Journal of the American Academy of Religion* (1999). She is a member of the Society for the Study of Native American Religious Traditions and is currently Chair of the Native Traditions in the Americas Group, American Academy of Religion.

Gordon S. Smith is Executive Director of the Centre for Global Studies at the University of Victoria. He also holds appointments as Senior Fellow at the Liu Centre for the Study of Global Issues at the University of British Columbia and Visiting Professor at the Diplomatic Academy of the University of Westminster. He chairs the board of the International Development Research Centre and has recently authored *Altered States: Globalization, Governance and Sovereignty.* Dr. Smith has been Canadian Ambassador to NATO, Deputy Minister of Foreign Affairs and the Prime Minister's Personal Representative for the G7/8 Summits.

INDEX